Getting the Most Out of
Clinical Training
and Supervision

To Nancy,
a pleasure working with you!

Carol Falender PhD
4-12-13

Getting the Most Out of
Clinical Training
and Supervision

A GUIDE FOR PRACTICUM
STUDENTS AND INTERNS

Carol A. Falender and Edward P. Shafranske

American Psychological Association • *Washington, DC*

Published by
American Psychological Association
750 First Street, NE
Washington, DC 20002
www.apa.org

To order
APA Order Department
P.O. Box 92984
Washington, DC 20090-2984
Tel: (800) 374-2721; Direct: (202) 336-5510
Fax: (202) 336-5502; TDD/TTY: (202) 336-6123
Online: www.apa.org/pubs/books
E-mail: order@apa.org

In the U.K., Europe, Africa, and the Middle East, copies may be ordered from
American Psychological Association
3 Henrietta Street
Covent Garden, London
WC2E 8LU England

Typeset in Goudy by Circle Graphics, Inc., Columbia, MD

Printer: Maple-Vail Book Manufacturing Group, York, PA
Cover Designer: Naylor Design, Washington, DC

The opinions and statements published are the responsibility of the authors, and such opinions and statements do not necessarily represent the policies of the American Psychological Association.

Library of Congress Cataloging-in-Publication Data

Falender, Carol A.
 Getting the most out of clinical training and supervision : a guide for practicum students and intern / Carol A. Falender and Edward P. Shafranske. — 1st ed.
    p. cm.
 Includes bibliographical references and index.
 ISBN-13: 978-1-4338-1049-7 (alk. paper)
 ISBN-10: 1-4338-1049-2 (alk. paper)
 1. Interns (Medicine) 2. Clinical clerkship. 3. Medical students. I. Shafranske, Edward P. II. Title.

 RA972.F35 2012
 610.76—dc23
                              2011026358

British Library Cataloguing-in-Publication Data

A CIP record is available from the British Library.

Printed in the United States of America
First Edition

DOI: 10.1037/13487-000

CONTENTS

Preface .... *vii*

I. Becoming a Competent Supervisee 1

Chapter 1. Beginning Clinical Practice Under Supervision 3

Chapter 2. Entering Competency-Based Supervision 17

Chapter 3. Expectations and the Path to Good Supervision 35

II. Developing Clinical Competence Through Supervision 53

Chapter 4. Developing Competence to Practice
in a Diverse World 55

Chapter 5. Developing the Therapeutic Alliance
and Managing Strains and Ruptures 81

Chapter 6. The Use of the Self in Psychotherapy 107

v

Chapter 7.   Case Conceptualization: The Practice
               of Clinical Understanding... 135

Chapter 8.   Practicing Ethically 159

III. Advancing Reflective Practice in Supervision............................. **189**

Chapter 9.   Transforming Supervision to Be More Successful........ 191

Chapter 10.   Becoming a Reflective Clinician................................. 211

Appendix A: Competency Benchmarks.. 217

Appendix B: The Practicum Competencies Outline:
              Report on Practicum Competencies 249

Appendix C: Practices and Beliefs Questionnaire................................ 263

References 269

Index 293

About the Authors 303

PREFACE

Entry into practicum, internship, or any other supervised professional experience can be both exciting and daunting. Although clinical training and supervision have always been considered essential to the professional development of a counseling or clinical psychologist, it is only recently that attention has been focused on the factors that lead to their effectiveness. Understanding those factors and entering into clinical supervision with such preparation will place you at a significant advantage in both your clinical work and your own eventual work as a supervisor.

Our goal in writing this book was to provide an easily accessible resource to jump-start your process of being a supervisee. It will serve as a platform to prepare you to thrive and succeed in practicum, internship, or other supervision contexts based on an understanding of the state-of-the-art practice of supervision, of your developing clinical skills, and of yourself as a supervisee. While useful as a text in practicum or internship settings and as a reference guide, it will be an important resource to guide both you and your supervisors to structure more optimal training opportunities and experiences.

Supervision is the major means of transmission of the foundations of the psychology profession to students, trainees, and supervisees in development. Supervision provides an opportunity for you to reflect on and process the psychotherapy you are conducting and obtain an integrated sense of the practice of psychotherapy, theory, and your personal contributions to the process. You will learn how to maximally utilize these, building on your strengths and competencies, so you can effectively perform psychotherapy with integrity, manage emotionally reactive responses to clients, and comply with ethical and legal considerations. You will be integrating multicultural considerations and reflecting on the lens through which the client and supervision are constructed. Whether supervision is conducted one on one or in a group, face to face or from a distance by means of technology, you will flourish in a relationship with a supervisor that is marked by a sense of safety, support, and an appropriate level of challenge. This book provides you with tools—both conceptual and practical—to get the most out of clinical supervision and to develop competencies required for professional practice as a psychologist.

Throughout this book you will read a great deal about competence. The competencies movement represents a major shift in clinical supervision. Understanding its background and context will be a significant strength for you. In our previous volumes, *Clinical Supervision: A Competency-Based Approach* (Falender & Shafranske, 2004) and *Casebook for Clinical Supervision: A Competency-Based Approach* (Falender & Shafranske, 2008), we laid the groundwork for a competency-based approach to clinical supervision. Our approach explicitly identifies knowledge, skills, and values assembled to form clinical competencies so you and your supervisor may develop and use transparent evaluation strategies to meet criterion-referenced standards in the context of evidence-based treatments and the local context (Falender & Shafranske, 2007). That means you can develop goals around specific areas you and your supervisor agree are in development and identify tasks to help you work on these, and your progress will be systematically tracked in the context of other supervisees at your level of training.

A significant part of your preparation for supervision is self-assessment: considering the various competencies agreed on for the profession and scaling your level of competence, including both areas of strength and those in development. The two measures included in this book are Hatcher and Lassiter's (2007) *Practicum Competencies Outline: Report on Practicum Competencies*, which artfully tracks the development of competencies in the formative first years of graduate school through practicum training (see Appendix B), and Fouad et al.'s (2009) *Competency Benchmarks: Foundational Competencies*, which identifies competencies from entry into graduate school through licensure (see Appendix A). These documents orient all clinical training and will guide you in the process of enhancing development and accurate self-assessment. You can enhance the accuracy through self-assessing small "bits" of your behavior and then receiving feedback from your supervisor to provide perspective and guide your clinical practice.

Another central aspect of your development and supervision is your process of *reflection*, the nonjudgmental attending to physical and mental processes (Epstein, 1999). As a supervisee, you will progress from reflecting on the clinical work you have previously conducted (called *reflection-on-action*) to internalizing the reflective process and *reflecting-in-action* as you conduct therapy. Schön (1983) described a reflective practitioner as someone who "reflects on the phenomena before him and on the prior understandings which have been implicit in his behavior." (p. 69). In this book, we include many Reflection Activities to provide frames for you to consider various situations and possible responses. We encourage you to engage in these activities, because you will not only learn more about the competencies under discussion but also gain experience in reflective practice.

The book is organized to provide a structure for you to systematically embrace and enhance the experience of supervision. In addition, it provides practical approaches to help you deal with many of the issues you will encounter in conducting psychotherapy and its supervision. This book will be your guide through practicum, internship, and other supervised experience, ensuring that you play an active role in gaining the competencies of the profession of psychology and being a most effective supervisee.

OVERVIEW OF THE ORGANIZATION OF THE BOOK

This book is organized into three major parts: (a) Part I: Becoming a Competent Supervisee; (b) Part II: Developing Clinical Competence Through Supervision; and (c) Part III: Advancing Reflective Practice in Supervision. The chapters in Part I provide an overview of the supervisory process, emphasizing the competencies that you need to develop and the processes that will be used to support your development. In Part II, we present chapters that introduce core areas of clinical practice, including multicultural competence and diversity, the therapeutic alliance, uses of the self in psychotherapy, case conceptualization, and professional ethics. These chapters focus on enhancing your understanding and competence as a clinician and highlight the unique ways in which clinical supervision advances competence. This section therefore is a bit of a hybrid, addressing both clinical and supervisory competencies. The two chapters in Part III amplify two themes that run throughout the book: (a) the importance of reflective practice and (b) the collaborative nature of the supervisory process. This book addresses the kinds of challenges and problems that can occur in supervision and provides practical suggestions to help you improve your supervision experience through the use of reflective practice and collaborative engagement. We conclude the book with a discussion of reflective practice as integral to professionalism, competence development, and self-care, and we present approaches to enhance these career-sustaining competencies. We have found that understanding the competency-based goals of supervision and the means by which supervision intends to achieve those goals provides a road map to embark on a journey that will be both professionally and personally rewarding.

A NOTE TO SUPERVISORS AND PRACTICUM INSTRUCTORS

Clinical supervision plays the central role in the training and professional development of a clinical or counseling psychologist. It is the setting in which the knowledge and skills learned in graduate studies are applied in the real world of clinical practice, and it is the setting in which students become clinicians and competence is developed. Supervision is now recognized as a unique competence, and a burgeoning literature is now articulating its unique features as well as investigating the factors that influence its effectiveness.

In *Clinical Supervision: A Competency-Based Approach* (Falender & Shafranske, 2004) and subsequent work, we presented a model of supervision oriented to the development of specific clinical competencies. We advocate in this approach the explicit identification of knowledge, skills and values or attitudes that are assembled to form competencies, and we recommend that both evaluation and training be directed to the individual components that make up the competence, as well as their integration into a functioning competency. This approach has been well received within the clinical training community and is in step with the competencies movement in professional psychology. While many resources exist to support the supervisor's professional development and practice, few resources are currently available to assist practicum students and interns in becoming competent supervisees. Thus, we wrote this text to provide a resource that would complement our model of competency-based supervision and prepare students to get the most of clinical training and supervision. It was our view that if practicum students and interns became better informed about their roles as supervisees, the competencies that they were expected to develop, and the ways in which supervision was intended to support their professional development, they would be better prepared to meet the challenges and expectations inherent in training. We also wanted to provide them with a clear understanding of the responsibilities that are involved in being a supervisee as well as a sense of the perspectives that supervisors use when conducting supervision. Throughout the text, we emphasize the collaborative nature of the supervisory relationship, the importance of identifying and evaluating competencies, multicultural competence, reflective practice, and other core aspects, and we encourage supervisees to approach participation in supervision as a professional competence. And while we address the text to supervisees specifically, given the collaborative nature of this endeavor, supervisors should find the book a useful guide to the supervision process from their perspective as well.

I

BECOMING A
COMPETENT SUPERVISEE

1

BEGINNING CLINICAL PRACTICE
UNDER SUPERVISION

Becoming a successful supervisee represents a milestone in your psychology training. Entering your practicum and internship each marks the beginning of a new chapter of learning in clinical practice, with challenges and opportunities unlike those in your previous education. In addition to honing your clinical skills, you will be sharing your work with your supervisor. Supervision requires a transition from classroom learning to developing clinical competencies with clients supported by a collaborative supervisory relationship. As you feel empowered, you will be expected to actively participate in guiding the course of supervision, ever mindful that the supervisor has ultimate responsibility for your client as well as for your evaluation and for *gatekeeping,* that is, screening your suitability for entry into the psychology profession.

Your professional identity developed during clinical training will be the foundation of your psychological practice and your career. Psychologists looking back on their careers attributed formal supervision (and experiences gained as a supervisee) as a major influence on their development as professionals (Orlinsky & Ronnestad, 2005). So, whether you are embarking on your first training rotation, an internship, or a fellowship, supervision is critically important for your development as a psychologist.

Reflection Activity. As you begin your clinical and supervision experience, imagine you are just about to see a client. Think about the setting; your feelings; and the client's behavior, presentation of problems, and reaction to you. Imagine your response, your helping behaviors, the impact the client has on you. Stop for a minute and reflect on that experience. Then imagine going to your first supervision session to discuss your client. What thoughts and feelings come up? What would you imagine would be most helpful for you? Spend a few minutes thinking about people who have supervised or directed you in the past. Which people have been most effective, and which have been most influential in your development to date? If you have not had prior supervision, think about individuals who have been most influential in helping you get where you are today. What did they do that was effective and/or influential?

This exercise may elicit a range of feelings and images. It may help you to begin to think about some of the unknowns of clinical practice and your supervision—and your own feelings. Now let's proceed to think about some of the important things that will make your supervision experience most beneficial.

Supervised practice is the cornerstone of your education and training as a psychologist (Falender & Shafranske, 2004, p. 3). Supervision provides a means to ensure client welfare and facilitate your development of competence. You will transform from a *student* of psychology to a *practitioner* of psychology. It is no small task to go from studying treatment to actually conducting treatment; it is somewhat like the difference between watching someone ski and actually skiing yourself. Although not as physically perilous, learning to conduct psychotherapy does require a certain kind of psychological dexterity and a willingness to "hit the slopes" and to learn to apply feedback with each new "run." Fortunately, supervisors are generally well acquainted with the clinical terrain and know how to help you develop your skills, as well as to provide support and guidance. Competence is developed through repeated cycles of practice informed by self-reflection, mutual problem solving, supervisor feedback, and then more practice. The first step in getting the most out of clinical training is developing your understanding of supervision.

Ironically, while substantial attention has been directed to the process of clinical supervision (Falender & Shafranske, 2004, 2008), the role of the supervisee has been sorely neglected. Supervisees are eager for such information and training (Lyon, Heppler, Leavitt, & Fisher, 2008). The complexity of supervision is that, while you are refining your clinical practice relationships and skills, you will most likely feel vulnerable revealing your developing clinical work to your supervisor. You will find such disclosure is the heart of supervision.

Unlimited opportunities are available through clinical supervision, including in-depth reviews of your clinical work, the experience of the supervisory relationship, and a greater understanding of clients as you use yourself as a valuable tool in the therapy and supervisory process. Working with a variety of models, theories, and populations, you will hone skills and achieve greater insight so that you can develop and excel. Never before will you have encountered a situation requiring self-awareness and openness to discuss your personal beliefs, perspectives, and worldview—in the context of each client and supervisor. Supervisors and supervisees may have overlapping or different theoretical orientations, approaches, and worldviews. Attitude, receptivity, and preparation will be paramount to get the most out of supervision and training.

Part of the training and supervision process involves risk: taking on challenges and taking chances. Instead of simply remaining in your comfort zone or narrow area of experience, performing familiar interventions or seeing clients of only a particular age or diagnostic category, you can grow exponentially (and become more comfortable) working with a wide range of clients and clinical problems. An important strength that will be tested and enhanced in clinical training is your openness to a wide range of experiences. Your stress may increase in the short term, but the result will be increased skills and confidence in the long term. The time you spend being supervised is an opportunity to gain increased competencies across multiple dimensions. It is a time to grow and develop under the watchful eye of your supervisor.

Whether you approach the training site with great excitement, energy, and anticipation, or with some trepidation about the expectations and your ability to fulfill them, you will be entering an environment that is very different from the classroom and other educational settings. For one thing, the A+ grades you may have received in your academic career will not be given in your practicum or internship. You are expected to *not* be fully competent; development will occur with support and guidance from your supervisor. Supervisors admire supervisees who wish to work on enhancing *metacompetence*—that is, knowledge of what you do *not* know! And knowing what one does not know is difficult. A supervisor will value a supervisee who works on increasing accuracy of self-appraisal, identifying areas of relative weakness along with strengths and integrating feedback, over one who self-assesses as highly competent in all assessed areas.

As you enter supervision, think of your own experience to this point. Has anyone ever described in depth the role that you are assuming as a supervisee or intern, or what will be expected of you? That is our task in this book.

WHAT IS CLINICAL SUPERVISION?

Definitions of *supervision* are abundant and varied, but the general consensus is that clinical supervision constitutes a distinct professional practice (Falender et al., 2004; Kaslow et al., 2004), an area of competency requiring specific training, and the major mechanism for transmission of competence to future generations of the profession as well as a means of monitoring and ensuring quality and protecting both clients and the profession. J. M. Bernard and Goodyear (2009) defined supervision as "an intervention provided by a more senior member of a profession to a more junior member or members of that same profession . . . is evaluative and hierarchical, extends over time, has the simultaneous purposes of . . . monitoring the quality of professional services . . . and serving as a gatekeeper" (p. 7). Approaching supervision from a competency framework, Falender and Shafranske (2004) have defined *clinical supervision* as

> A distinct professional activity in which education and training aimed at developing science-informed practice are facilitated through a collaborative interpersonal process. It involves observation, evaluation, feedback, facilitation of supervisee self-assessment, and acquisition of knowledge and skills by instruction, modeling, and mutual problem-solving. Building on the recognition of the strengths and talents of the supervisee, supervision encourages self-efficacy. [Supervision] ensures it is conducted in a competent manner in which ethical standards, legal prescriptions, and professional practices are used to promote and protect the welfare of the client, the profession, and society at large. (p. 3)

This understanding of supervision contains has a number of implications for you and provides guidance as to what is required as well as how to get the most out of supervision.

Supervision is a *collaborative* process: You are expected to actively participate. Unlike in academic education, where the learning objectives and activities are usually predetermined by the professor, supervisors want you to take stock of your training needs and collaborate with them throughout the process. At the beginning of supervision, depending on your level of previous experience, it is likely that the supervisor will be more active and provide significant direction, structure, and support. As you develop your clinical skills and experience, the process becomes increasingly collaborative, with you contributing more, reflecting, and assuming greater responsibility while still being responsive to and respectful of supervisor's input and direction. Even as supervision becomes increasingly collaborative and you gain in self-confidence and efficacy, collaboration occurs in the context of the *power differential*. This term refers to the supervisor's power, through evaluative and gatekeeping functions, to maintain client safety and the standards of the profession of psychology.

You will find that supervisors approach the power differential with varying degrees of discussion. Some supervisors will engage you in discussions of the differential and promise immediate feedback and transparency in sharing with you their impressions of your progress.

You can gain a great deal from supervision by being open and responsive to feedback and by actively collaborating in evaluation through self-assessment and participating in the variety of ways that your supervisor may use to impart knowledge and facilitate development. You will be working with your supervisor to ensure the application of ethical standards, legal proscriptions, and professional practices to protect the welfare of the clients.

CONTRIBUTING TO THE FOUNDATION OF EFFECTIVE SUPERVISORY PRACTICE

The process of supervision can also be broken down into a set of processes and a set of attitudes, what we have termed the *pillars* and *superordinate values*. You contribute to the effectiveness of supervision and the supervisory alliance by understanding and actively participating in these processes and affirming these values.

Supervision is supported by three interrelated pillars (Falender & Shafranske, 2004): (a) the *supervisory relationship*, (b) *inquiry*, and (c) *educational praxis*. Your *supervisory relationship* is the true foundation of all supervision; your relationship with your supervisor will be of utmost importance. The two of you will develop goals and specific tasks that each of you will complete to attain said goals.

> *Reflection Activity.* Think about a particular goal you have for your supervision. Then think about what you could do to work to attain this goal and what your supervisor could do to assist in this.

Working collaboratively with your supervisor, you will use data from your self-assessment of competence to target areas of your strength and those in development. You can facilitate this process by reflecting on and sharing learning activities that have been effective for you in the past.

Inquiry relates to understanding your professional training, who you are as a person, and your personal contributions to the therapeutic process. Inquiry also extends to the idea that the supervisor does not hold all of the answers: You, the supervisee, are a vital part of the supervision process and will learn to pose questions, form hypotheses, pursue answers, and then reflect on these with your supervisor. A commitment to self-reflection, and assessment and preparation to use the supervision session effectively, are essential.

Educational praxis refers to all the learning strategies your supervisor uses. These include instruction, observation, role play, reflection, and modeling, to name a few. Actively participating in learning activities, following through with recommendations, and providing feedback to the supervisor regarding the usefulness of the training approaches contribute to the quality of your development.

> **Reflection Activity.** Consider learning strategies that have been most effective for you. Do you prefer reflective, active, passive, or interactive learning, or a combination?

The following supervisory superordinate, or overarching, values are major components of the foundation of practice (Falender & Shafranske, 2004):

- *integrity in relationship*—honesty, the capacity of being always mindful of the highest ethical principles;
- *ethical values–based practice*—the integration of values and ethics in all aspects of practice;
- *appreciation of all aspects of diversity*—a competency you will develop in training and an ethical prerequisite to practice and supervision that relates to integrating awareness of diversity, status, and context of the client and yourself; and
- *science-informed practice*—the application of clinical reasoning and judgment and to the essential nature of knowledge of evidence bases and outcomes in the evolving science of practice.

You will complement your supervisor in conducting professional activities, while being guided by these superordinate values.

TRAINING SETTINGS

As you enter your supervision site, knowledge of the setting and context will be very helpful. In the following sections, we provide background information on the various clinical training settings and their evolving practices.

Practicum

Practicum provides your first formal opportunity to begin clinical practice. Practicum rotations are usually 1 year long and matched to your level of training and experience. You will complete a number of training rotations during graduate school, often with different clinical populations (e.g., adults, families, children) and involving different professional activities (e.g., psychotherapy, psychological assessment, consultation) and in a variety of settings (e.g., hospitals, community mental health centers, university counseling centers). If you are carrying a full load of academic courses (with pressures to excel), the large complement of practicum experience several days a week may require commuting to a distant site. Coping with all of this can be very stressful.

According to the Council of Chairs of Training Councils Practicum Workgroup (2007), practicum comprises

> all supervised pre-internship training experiences conducted under the auspices of the graduate program in settings providing professional psychological services. The practicum promotes the integration of academic knowledge with practical experience, and prepares the student for future training in professional psychology, particularly for the internship that follows. In practicum, students apply and extend the knowledge, skills and attitudes learned in the program's didactic and classroom-based experiential components to produce increasingly sophisticated levels of understanding and skill. (p. 1).

Internship

Completion of an internship is a requirement of all accredited graduate psychology programs (APA, 2009). Internship hours count toward licensure and are regulated by state and provincial boards.[1] States vary in the number of hours they require; the number ranges from 1,000 to 2,000 (Tracy, Bucchianeri, & Rodofa, 2011). Internship training builds on the practicum and provides a capstone experience, readying you for graduation, postdoctoral training, and entering the profession. After you have completed your coursework, as an intern you may relocate to another part of the country, leaving behind friends and trusted faculty. As an intern, you assume a clinical caseload commensurate with a full-time job, with the associated productivity expectations, including supervision, adjunctive seminars, paperwork, and other program activities. You may be working on your doctoral dissertation as well. Intregrating and applying the multiple parts of training and experience in clinical

---

[1]State and provincial regulations and requirements for licensure as a psychologist are available at the website of the Association of State and Provincial Psychology Boards (http://appic.org/http://www.asppb.org/HandbookPublic/before.aspx). The handbook offered on that site contains critical information for individuals who plan to practice in a particular state or province after licensure, considering that the licensure requirements are highly variable.

work to gain the most from the corresponding clinical supervision is both a challenge and an opportunity.

CLINICAL SUPERVISION TRAINING TODAY: HISTORY AND CONTEXT CULTURE SHIFT

Recognize your training is taking place as a major shift is occurring in how the psychology profession assesses education, training, and professional competence, including the effectiveness of clinical supervision. At all levels of the training process—from practicum through internship and postdoctoral training, and even in postlicensure continuing education—there has been a shift from *input* to *output* (DeMers, Van Horne, & Rodolfa, 2008; Rubin et al., 2007). Instead of solely evaluating curricula content, practicum, or internship experiences—the *input* that goes into the training of a psychologist—the focus has now shifted to the psychologist's demonstration of *output*, that is, competencies (Roe, 2002). Many leaders in psychology training have advocated for a "culture of change" (Roberts, Borden, Christiansen, & Lopez, 2005) reflecting the shift to competencies. The revision represents a significant change in training and is important to understand. Output (i.e., competencies) comprises the measurable knowledge, skills, and values or attitudes consensually agreed on by members of the profession. Assessment of competence includes attention to your performance and evolving competences in the parallel universes of supervision and client intervention. Supervisors evaluate not only clinical competencies but also the abilities and attitudes that you demonstrate in actively and collaboratively working hard in supervision. Success in the process of supervision is a core competency for psychologists. Being an effective supervisee will facilitate your development and consolidation across curricular arenas.

EXPECTATIONS FOR PERFORMANCE IN A PRACTICUM

The landscape of clinical training and supervision during practicum is in flux. Some of the expectations for supervisee performance are spelled out; others are unstated. Historical inconsistencies in practicum training arose because this training sequence has been generally unregulated by state and provincial boards and may not be consistently overseen by graduate programs. There is substantial leeway in structure, supervision, and support (Kaslow, Pate, & Thorn, 2005; Lewis, Hatcher, & Pate, 2005), and the degree of collaboration and communication between the site and the graduate program can vary. Practicum sites often focus primarily on service delivery rather than training, whereas internship sites are designed and structured as training sites (Lewis et al., 2005). Although practicums may have rotations—time-limited clinical experiences with a different supervisor in a specific program or service (e.g., therapeutic preschool, adolescent day treatment, inpatient unit)— you will find such rotations are common in internship and postdoctoral training. In the majority of states, practicum hours do not count toward supervised professional experience or licensure; however, practicum hours need to be carefully tracked for internship application, and are in transformation as an increasing number of states are counting them toward licensure. Those states are following the recommendation of the American Psychological Association (APA; 2010b) that consideration for admission to licensure is based on "the equivalent of two full-time years of sequential, organized, supervised, professional experience prior to obtaining the license. This training may be completed prior or subsequent to the granting of the doctoral degree" (p. 6). Note that 1 of the 2 years must be a predoctoral internship. APA's (2010b) Model Act for State Licensure of Psychologists lays regulatory groundwork so that states may make legislative changes for licensure to occur immediately after internship. Practicum expectations are evolving, as guidelines for practicum training have been proposed by Association of State and Provincial Psychology Boards Task Force on Practicum Guidelines for Licensure (2009) and by the National Council of Schools and Programs in Professional Psychology (2009).

EXPECTATIONS FOR PERFORMANCE IN AN INTERNSHIP

Internships are highly articulated, described on websites and in elaborate materials available during the application process.[2] Some supervisees will be licensed after completion of their internship. Completion of internship is considered a capstone experience, or culmination, which provides integration and consolidation of all training experiences.

STATUS OF SUPERVISION

As the practice of supervision has evolved in the past decade, and continues to do so, work on theory, empirical support, and elaboration have all

[2]The Association of Psychology Postdoctoral and Internship Centers website (http://www.appic.org) contains information about predoctoral internships and postdoctoral fellowships and the Internship Matching Program. Information about accreditation of predoctoral internships and postdoctoral fellowships are available at the website of the APA Commission on Accreditation, Office of Program Consultation and Accreditation (http://www.apa.org/ed/accreditation/).

dramatically increased, as evidenced by increasing numbers of publications on supervision. One of the most important developments in clinical training—which will affect you as a supervisee directly—is the identification of competencies that define the practice of psychology.

The Competencies Conference, initiated by the Association of Psychology Postdoctoral and Internship Centers, occurred in 2002. It had multinational and diverse representation from education, training, practice, public interest, research, credentialing, and regulatory constituency groups (Association of Psychology Postdoctoral and Internship Centers, 2002; Kaslow, 2004; Kaslow et al., 2004). It was cosponsored by the major training councils, APA, credentialing and regulatory bodies, ethnic–minority psychology organizations, and other educational and professional institutions (Kaslow et al., 2004). A product of the conference was the Competencies Cube (see Figure 1.1; Rodolfa, et al., 2005), a three-dimensional model that delineated domains of knowledge, skills, and attitudes that are *foundational* competencies for all psychologists, as well as *functional* competencies that broadly define what psychologists

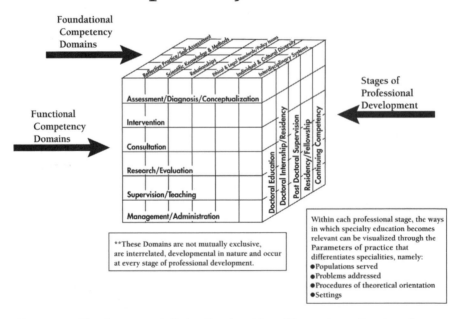

Figure 1.1. The Competency Cube. Reprinted from "Competency Benchmarks: A Model for Understanding and Measuring Competence in Professional Psychology Across Training Levels," by N. A. Fouad, C. L. Grus, R. L. Hatcher, N. J. Kaslow, P. S. Hutchings, M. B. Madson, . . . R. E. Crossman, 2009, *Training and Education in Professional Psychology, 3*(4, Suppl.), p. S7. Copyright 2009 by the American Psychological Association.

do, with stages of professional development spanning doctoral education to specialization postlicensure and continuing competency beyond that.

Another result of the Competencies Conference was The Practicum Competencies Outline (see Appendix B) expanding on work initiated by the Association of Directors of Psychology Training Clinics in 2001 (Hatcher & Lassiter, 2007). The outline defines competencies for practicum training and operationalizes component knowledge, skills, attitudes, and metaknowledge expected by the end of practicum training with behavioral anchors for assessing the development of these competencies from early to advanced practicum training.

In 2003, the APA Board of Educational Affairs convened a task force to measure competencies and needs for competency assessment, which resulted in what are called *Competency Benchmarks*. Building on the Competencies Cube, work groups defined each foundational and functional competency, identifying essential components and behavioral anchors that progress with development. The Competency Benchmarks work group determined that additional components beyond those first articulated in the earlier conference were necessary to reflect the full range of competencies for professional psychologists. The foundational and functional competencies are described in Table 1.1. The Competency Benchmarks (see Appendix A) (Fouad et al., 2009) outlines core foundational and functional competencies in professional psychology across three levels of professional development: (a) readiness for practicum, (b) readiness for internship, and (c) readiness for entry to practice with essential components and behavioral anchors.

The Competencies Outline and Competency Benchmarks provide a scaffolding for professional development from a student's entry into graduate school to licensure and independent practice. An understanding of these benchmarks will provide structure for your graduate school, practicum, and internship experience toward achieving essential competencies. Graduate students surveyed confirmed the course of development of trainee competencies as laid out in benchmarks to be reflective of their experience (Kamen, Veilleux, Bangen, VanderVeen, & Klonoff, 2010). A goal is for you and your supervisor to plan and chart your progress toward increased competence drawing on the Foundational and Functional Competencies presented in the benchmarks.

> **Reflection Activity.** Using the Competency Benchmarks (see Appendix A), select one foundational competence and one functional competency, choosing the behavioral anchors appropriate to your level of training and assess your level of competence at this time. Reflect on some of the ways that you demonstrate the competence as well as consider how you might strengthen that competence, anticipating the next stage of development.

TABLE 1.1
Foundational and Functional Competencies as Defined by the Competency Cube and Competency Benchmarks

Competency	Definition
Foundational competencies	
Professionalism	Professional values and ethics as evidenced in behavior and comportment that reflects the values and ethics of psychology, integrity, and responsibility.
Reflective Practice/ Self-Assessment/ Self-Care	Practice conducted with personal and professional self-awareness and reflection, with awareness of competencies, and with appropriate self-care.
Scientific Knowledge and Methods	Understanding of research, research methodology, techniques of data collection and analysis, biological bases of behavior, cognitive–affective bases of behavior, and development across the life span. Respect for scientifically derived knowledge.
Relationships	Relate effectively and meaningfully with individuals, groups, and/or communities.
Individual and Cultural Diversity	Awareness, sensitivity, and skills in working professionally with diverse individuals, groups, and communities who represent various cultural and personal background and characteristics defined broadly, consistent with American Psychological Association policy.
Ethical Legal Standards and Policy	Application of ethical concepts and awareness of legal issues regarding professional activities with individuals, groups, and organizations.
Interdisciplinary Systems	Knowledge of key issues and concepts in related disciplines. Identification and interaction with professionals in multiple disciplines.
Functional competencies	
Assessment	Assessment and diagnosis of problems, capabilities, and issues associated with individuals, groups, and/or organizations.
Intervention	Interventions designed to alleviate suffering and to promote health and well-being of individuals, groups, and/or organizations.
Consultation	The ability to provide expert guidance or professional assistance in response to a client's needs or goals.
Research/Evaluation	Generating research that contributes to the professional knowledge base and/or evaluates the effectiveness of various professional activities.
Supervision	Supervision and training in the professional knowledge base and of evaluation of the effectiveness of various professional activities.
Teaching	Providing instruction, disseminating knowledge, and evaluating acquisition of knowledge and skill in professional psychology.
Management– Administration	Manage the direct delivery of services and/or the administration of organizations, programs, or agencies.
Advocacy	Actions targeting the impact of social, political, economic, or cultural factors to promote change at the individual (client), institutional, and/or systems level.

Note. Data from Rodolfa et al. (2005) and Fouad et al. (2009).

As you progress through the chapters in this book, think of them as a series of building blocks you can use to assess and expand both your clinical and supervision competence. You will see that clinical and supervision competence are interlocked and build on each other. Self-assessment will serve as the foundation of your development; the specific knowledge, skills, and attitudes of clinical practice and supervision will be the scaffolding as your competence and confidence increase.

To close the chapter, review the following list that represents a sample of the knowledge, skills, and attitudes you will develop during training.

Knowledge

1. Knowledge of the role of practicum and internship in professional development.
2. Knowledge of roles of the supervisor and supervisee.
3. Knowledge of contemporary trends in the assessment of competence, including an understanding of Competency Benchmarks.
4. Knowledge of the principles involved in evidence-based practice in psychology.
5. Knowledge of competency-based clinical supervision.

Skills

1. Ability to actively participate in supervision involving self-reflection, self-disclosure, openness to feedback, exploration of therapeutic process, and mutual problem solving.
2. Ability to apply the principles of evidence-based professional practice and to actively participate in competency-based clinical supervision.

Attitudes

1. Values the importance of professional development.
2. Respects the supervision process and respects the clients and their diversity and worldviews.

2

ENTERING COMPETENCY-BASED SUPERVISION

In clinical supervision, you transform from student to supervisee, from a passive recipient absorbing knowledge imparted by "all-knowing" faculty to an active participant in the therapy process. All the clinical theories and skills you have studied will be at the forefront of your learning as you implement them in practice. At the same time, you will find yourself broadening your view from a more traditional, individualistic approach, to one that incorporates systemic and contextual perspectives. An understanding of the larger social and political contexts shift your analysis from one objective reality to multiple subjectivities that comprise values, attitudes, and contextual perspectives of yourself and your clients (Brabeck & Brown, 1997). You may find yourself introducing your supervisor to innovations in the field or eliciting your supervisor's input by proposing alternative hypotheses, conceptualizations, and/or interventions. Supervision is a collaborative process that ensues even from the onset of supervision as supervisors appreciate and respect supervisees' strengths, competencies, emotions, and background. Such collaboration does not change the nature of the supervisory relationship or require symmetry in power or equivalence in responsibility.

An essential lesson for each supervisee to learn is to be very clear who is the primary supervisor for each case. You may find you have multiple supervisors and levels of supervision at your practicum or internship site and at your graduate school. Your primary supervisor is the individual who holds responsibility and liability for your clinical work with each client. If your various supervisors disagree, be sure to discuss and clarify other input with your primary supervisor. If you are in a practicum seminar at your graduate school, you may find your professor has different perspectives on your clinical work. Your site supervisor is usually your primary supervisor; so bring those ideas and perspectives to your site supervisor to organize your intervention strategy.

COMPETENCY-BASED CLINICAL SUPERVISION

In this era of *competency*-based training and clinical supervision, a major task will be for you to enhance your knowledge, skills, and attitudes/values, the three components of competency. "*Competency-based supervision* is an approach that explicitly identifies the knowledge, skills, and values assembled to form each clinical competency and develop learning strategies and evaluation procedures to meet criterion-referenced competence standards in keeping with evidence-based practices and the requirements of the local clinical setting" (Falender & Shafranske, 2007, p.233). *Criterion-referenced* means you will be compared with a consensually developed standard of competencies that is expected at your current level of functioning. You will have the opportunity to preassess your knowledge, skills, and attitudes, using an appropriate measure (e.g., Competency Benchmarks [see Appendix A] or Practicum Competencies [see Appendix B]) before beginning your practicum or internship. Competencies will help you and your supervisor determine the appropriate knowledge, skills, and values or attitudes as you proceed in your clinical work. Evaluation strategies and feedback will be linked to these competencies. Additional competencies will be site specific, corresponding to the cultural, contextual, and diversity aspects of the local setting. For you, the supervisee, the competency assessment process entails reviewing knowledge and skills, examining personal values and attitudes, understanding the lay of the land of the context you are entering, and in general, getting up to speed very quickly so that you can start applying your didactic training in the real world setting with clients—where it really counts.

You and your supervisor will establish a mutual supervisory alliance and, in the process, an emotional bond. The heart of developing such an alliance, whether in supervisory or clinical relationships, is collaboration—that is, working together constructively to achieve a goal. You and your supervisor will remain mindful of the power differential–advocacy balance; that is, even though there is a supervisory alliance, your supervisor holds the power and responsibility to evaluate, to give feedback to the school and licensure board, and to make the final decision to pass or fail you on your sequence of training.

Your supervisor also has the role of advocate for you in your professional development. A step toward establishing a quality supervisory alliance is discussion of the power inherent in the supervisor role as well as the importance of *transparency* in evaluation and in feedback. In the best of circumstances, supervisors will provide you with ongoing or formative feedback and invite joint discussion of expectations, evaluation procedures, and tools to use the feedback effectively. This is what we mean by transparency.

One of the most important insights that psychologists report concerning their training is the idea that clients can and do function as therapist trainees' teachers (Orlinksy, Botermans, & Rønnestad, 2001). For example, post-internship supervisees have reported learning many things from their clients, including how to conduct therapy while attending to feelings and self-awareness, pace the treatment in accordance with each client's needs, and set boundaries with ease (Stahl et al., 2009). They also learned more about the personal limitation of needing to be liked and how that need influenced the treatment. They reported being struck by how hard it is to change: Behavior is maintained by multiple factors, and clients may replicate relationships in therapy that exist out of therapy (Stahl et al., 2009).

Why is all this important as you begin a practicum or internship? With the terrain of training quickly changing, you are entering a realm with many challenges. Supervisor expectations may not bet clearly articulated, and so you need to be mindful of your training needs and develop skill in communicating these to your supervisor. It is also possible that you may find yourself more highly trained in certain areas than your supervisor—in diversity competence, for example—which could complicate the relationship, especially in regard to the power differential (e.g., Is the supervisor open to learning from the supervisee? How does that work?). Also, you will need to be prepared to face unique challenges that arise from the constantly changing complexion of training, your special role in the growing collaboration with your supervisor, and the differences you will likely experience with varying supervisors.

Attitudinal Shifts: Beginning Supervision

As you begin supervision, you may need to make shifts in your attitudes and behaviors. A significant portion of early supervision is socialization, which helps you establish patterns of supervision interaction with increased comfort, perspective, and humor. As you begin, you may prefer a more didactic format in which you ask questions that the supervisor answers, and you then integrate that information into your treatment interventions. Or you may prefer simply listening to the supervisor present a formulation or treatment intervention. Although a preference for such a process is understandable (because it resembles classroom learning), a shift to a collaborative supervision interaction is desirable for your supervision to be truly effective. The shift from a fairly didactic form of supervision process to one that aims at self-reflection, management of emotional response to client presentation, and understanding relational dynamics, including dynamics influencing the supervisory relationship, are all required because of the challenges of working with clients who are experiencing significant psychological difficulties. Because of the intensity and severity of the clients' cases, and your own developing sophistication and integration, it may be beneficial for you to be receptive to a more complex, developmentally driven, competency-based supervision model. It is important to always remember that you and your supervisor are in this process together, for the benefit of the client. Ideally, you will have the opportunity for live, video, or audio supervision that can complement the self-reflection, self-assessment, and your verbal report of the therapeutic process. Comfort with and skill in the use of live or recorded sessions are essential to maximize gains from the supervisory process.

Supervisee Disclosure

A related attitudinal shift is disclosing to your supervisor. As the supervisory relationship transforms from a didactic one to a more collaborative endeavor, it increasingly encompasses emotional and personal factors with respect to the client. As you begin a practicum or internship, you may prefer to share your emotional reactions with your peers rather than your supervisors; however, disclosure of emotional reactions and other factors allows for a quantum leap in supervision process.

You may fear that disclosures to a supervisor will result in a negative evaluation. How difficult will it be to share personal responses to clients with the supervisor, knowing that he/she is also your evaluator? You may be anxious about disclosing your own feelings, beliefs, attitudes, and emotional responses toward your clients. Concerns about evaluation may have been a significant part of your student role; however, now that you are transitioning to a professional role, the concept of evaluation requires modification.

Both your and your supervisor will remain attentive to the line between psychotherapy and supervision. Supervision self-disclosures always focus primarily on the client, or on the supervision process and its relation to the client. Disclosure does not include elaborate explorations of your childhood, personal relationships, or other information not directly related to the client and psychotherapy; however, it is appropriate for you and your supervisor to discuss and manage your strong emotional responses—for example, countertransference, or client aspects that trigger unusually strong emotional response—that occur in therapy as well as to explore and repair strains and ruptures that arise in the supervisory or client relationship (see Chapters 5 and 6, this volume).

WHAT YOU NEED TO KNOW: SUPERVISION THEORIES

In addition to understanding what supervision is, it is helpful to understand the process of supervision from various theoretical perspectives, starting with developmental. Some supervisees expect mastery too early or criticize themselves for the experiences and challenges they are—or are not—having. In states of doubt, self-criticism, and confusion, it can be hard to get the most out of supervision or to know what to ask for. Theories of development are important to understand and gain insight into stages in the journey toward professional competency.

Although some professionals have questioned the empirical status of developmental theories (Ellis & Ladany, 1997; Inman & Ladany, 2008), Stoltenberg and McNeill (2009) presented some compelling support, and it seems commonsensical that stages of progression would exist. For example, Kaslow and Rice (1985) described the stress of beginning clinical training, a transition from student to professional, a model that resonates with our experiences. Supervisees are typically eager to be professionals, yet they require significant supervisor guidance and support. As you progress developmentally in your internship, you will find yourself entering a sort of professional adolescence, in which you are mastering clinical skills but still facing uncertainty about your professional identity and life postinternship (Kaslow & Deering, 1994).

Remember that the training process is developmental; performance expectations will be tailored to your competency level: A supervisor will play a very different role for a beginner than for a postdoctoral fellow approaching licensure. Supervisors describe multiple differences in performance as a function of development of the supervisee. Clinical errors, fearing silence, interrupting clients, holding somewhat judgmental attitudes, overidentifying with clients, and general skill deficits are all descriptors of beginning supervisees (Weatherford, O'Shaughnessy, Mori, & Kaduvettoor, 2008). Supervisees perceive themselves as gaining greater control over the supervision process as they obtain greater experience in psychotherapy (Quarto, 2002).

Stoltenberg and colleagues described a developmental progression of behavior of the supervisee that they called the *integrative developmental model* (IDM; Stoltenberg, McNeill, & Delworth, 1998; Stoltenberg & McNeill, 2009). According to this model, supervisees progress through four levels, from Level 1, when one is a novice, through Levels 2 and 3; to Level 3i, at which point the indivudal continues to develop and achieve integration of his or her professional development (see Table 2.1). The model states that supervisees

TABLE 2.1
Integrative Developmental Model: A Summary for Supervisee Development

Level	Description
Level 1: Entry-level supervisee	Clinical novice with high motivation, dependent, focused on self and your own performance. High levels of motivation. Supervision: You benefit from structure, direction, and supportive, skill-based supervision, with focus on how to do it; prescriptive interventions with structure, support, and guidance; in addition to a high level of monitoring, ideally through observation, or audio or video review.
Level 2: More advanced supervisee	Significant experience and integration of skills and practice. You may be assigned significantly more difficult cases and clients, feel less adequate, and thus experience a lessening of motivation. A shift occurs from a focus on the self to a focus on the client. Supervision: You will find you are ready for analysis of more complex factors, such as personal reactivity, confrontation regarding discrepancies between behavior and emotions or attitudes, and integration of theory. Supervisors will use varied techniques.
Level 3: Therapist	Engage in less turbulent practice by increasingly engaging in emerging reflection-in-action, considering possible interventions and directions while conducting the therapy. Your increasing skill in self-assessment leads you to realize strengths and areas that need improvement. Your motivation moderates but is never as high as it was at Level 1. Supervision: While on the threshold of significant independence and autonomy, you require a sophisticated level of supervision, and monitoring is still required to ensure client safety and your continuing development.
Level 3i: Advanced Therapist	Ongoing integration and development. Moving towards being considered an expert by colleagues.

Note. Data from Stoltenberg and McNeill (2009).

develop along three primary dimensions: (a) motivation, (b) self–other awareness, and (c) dependence–autonomy. As one develops and progresses through the levels, an appropriate amount of autonomy increases, while anxiety and dependence decrease.

Whereas some have considered anxiety to be characteristic during Level 1 of the IDM, Ellis (2009) suggested that research does not support the existence of anxiety in Level 1 supervisees when they are in a secure supervisory relationship. We believe that at Level 1 you will experience emotional reactivity or countertransference reactions to client presentations even if you have a secure relationship with your supervisor. Therefore, at each level you should talk to your supervisor when a client triggers an unusual personal emotional response.

At Level 2, you will have consolidated significant experience and integration, but you may have moments—for example, when confronting a difficult client—of pondering why you did not simply become a certified public accountant, because at some points in your training numbers seem very appealing and much less problematic than people. Even the most talented (and the most-self-aware) supervisees experience doubts and need support to gain additional skills, knowledge, and confidence With the support of your supervisor and your own advancing clinical acumen, you will develop increased confidence and benefit from a wide range of supervision interventions, including what Stoltenberg and McNeill (2009) referred to as *catalytic interventions*: moments in which supervisors present you with a radically different formulation or view of a situation you have presented. Catalytic interventions can create turbulence, but they also can lead you to integrate and expand your existing repertoire of skills and gain perspective on therapy.

At Level 3, you may be very advanced but Stolenberg and McNeil (2009) caution that you will still require supervision and are still in development. Structure of supervision may be diminished, and you may focus on personalizing your style. When you reach Level 3i, the primary goal is to achieve integration of knowledge and skills, enhance performance consistency, and increase self-awareness (Stoltenberg & McNeil, 2009).

Stoltenberg and colleagues (Stoltenberg & McNeill, 2009; Stoltenberg et al., 1998) point out that there is substantial variation within and between levels such that, for example, you may be functioning at Level 1 in child assessment but at Level 3 in cognitive–behavioral treatment of anxiety in adults. In addition, not all supervisees begin at Level 1, just as not all psychology interns begin their training at a predetermined level. Previous experience, knowledge, skills, and values, and a multitude of other factors may influence the level at which a supervisee is functioning, so no assumptions should be made simply on the basis of an individual's year of graduate training.

Stoltenberg and McNeill (2009) described the importance for all levels of facilitative interventions, warmth, respect, and nurturance. Catalytic interventions, or ones that promote more abrupt change or reformulation, may be useful at any level but are used more regularly at Level 2.

Reflection Activity. After reviewing the aforementioned stages, identify the one you believe yourself to be in at present. Does your self-assessed level correspond to your preferred supervisory interventions?

Although your development may seem more complex and less linear than the levels outlined in the IDM, the model will help you understand some of the unique challenges and experiences you will encounter in clinical training.

Theories assist to understand that some of the difficulties, pain, and stress you will experience as you complete your practicum and internship are completely normative and related to your developmental progression from trainee to licensed therapist. Developmental theory provides a backdrop for understanding the Competency Benchmarks (see Appendix A), the behavioral anchors that provide a metric to evaluate your readiness for practicum, internship, and entry into practice.

PROCESS-BASED SUPERVISION THEORIES AND MODELS

Other theories of supervision include *process-based*, or *social role* models. Several of these (J. M. Bernard & Goodyear, 2009; Holloway, 1995) were developed to provide comprehensive descriptions of the components, roles, tasks, and processes that take place within supervision to help classify these events. J. M. Bernard's (1997) *discrimination model* includes process (or intervention) skills that include all the behaviors that distinguish counseling as a purposeful interpersonal and therapeutic activity. The model comprises *personalization skills*, which include the supervisee's features as an individual that contribute to the therapeutic process, and *conceptualization skills*, which include the supervisee's ability to make sense of clients' information and determine an appropriate and effective response (J. M. Bernard, 1997). Bernard further described three possible roles the supervisor may assume with respect to the supervisee: (a) the *teacher* role, with the supervisor responsible for determining what is required for the supervisee to become competent; (b) the *counselor* role, whereby the supervisor facilitates explorations of the interpersonal or intrapersonal reality of the supervisee; and (c) the *consultant* role, in which the supervisor serves as a resource but encourages supervisee to trust his or her own thoughts, insights, and feelings about the client.

Other supervisors may extrapolate their supervision practice from their preferred psychotherapy model; thus, a cognitive behavioral therapist would conduct parallel cognitive behavioral supervision (Newman, 2010), a psychodynamic therapist would conduct parallel psychodynamic supervision (Sarnat, 2010), and so forth. A possible limitation might be that the supervisor's preferred psychotherapy model does not address such aspects as cultural or legal and ethical considerations in the supervision process (Falender & Shafranske, 2010).

PROFESSIONALISM

As you transition into your practicum or internship, a transformation in your professional identity will occur. This transformation is marked by a developing sense of professionalism that will be different from quasi-friendships or research relationships with clients. Changes in your demeanor will occur as you learn to balance development of the therapeutic relationship with the ethical and legal and reporting requirements of the duty to warn, abuse reporting, and risk assessment.

A part of your transition to psychology professional is learning to think like a psychologist, approaching problem solving through both a psychological and scientific lens. Components of thinking like a psychologist include critical thinking and logical analysis; scientific inquiry integrating professional literature; problem conceptualization; integrating multiple perspectives; and accessing, understanding, integrating, and using evidence, statistics, technology, and multiple other sources of input (Elman, Illfelder-Kaye, & Robiner, 2005), including ethical and legal standards.

Professionalism is defined as "professional values and ethics as evidenced in behavior and comportment that reflects the values and ethics of psychology, integrity, and responsibility" (Fouad at al., 2009, p. S9) Professionalism is demonstrated in multiple ways. It is attitudinal and behavioral, and it requires a knowledge set. Sometimes the transition to being a professional can be challenging. For example, in regard to personal attire, what's perfectly acceptable (or normal) on a college campus is often inappropriate in a professional setting. Supervisors may even feel a bit awkward pointing out inappropriate professional dress, hoping that you will just kind of "get it." This is where self-assessment and professionalism come in.

Professionalism develops through one's career. Professionalism is an openness to improvement, responsivity, and the ability to change (Elman et al., 2005). Elements of professionalism include responsibility, reliability, honesty and integrity, maturity, respect for others, the ability to self-critique, altruism, interpersonal skills, and the absence of chemical or psychological impairments (e.g., substance use, mental illness; Arnold, 2002). These descriptors include relationships with peers as well as clients. Professionalism is a foundational competency of psychology.

Reflection Activity. Review the Section on Professionalism in the Competency Benchmarks (see Appendix A). Self-assess your level of development. Make note of areas in which you would like to focus attention in supervision.

TRANSITION TO EVIDENCE-BASED PRACTICES

Just as there has been a major shift in competence assessment practices in graduate education and clinical training (from input to output), so too there has been a similar change in the way psychologists practice. After years, if not decades, of discussion and debate concerning which forms of treatment should be practiced by psychologists, the American Psychological Association (2006) established a standard for practice called *evidence-based professional practice:* "Evidence-based practice in psychology (EBPP) is the integration of the best available research with clinical expertise in the context of patient characteristics, culture, and preferences" (p. 273).

Although evidence-based professional practice is official American Psychological Association policy, its implementation varies across different academic programs, training institutions, and supervisors. Some supervisees will find that they have more training and experience in evidence-based treatments than do their supervisors or other clinicians at a practicum or internship setting. There is often a substantial delay in transmission of practices to community settings, in some cases estimated to be as long as 17 years! (Balas & Boren, 2000). As supervision research and practice increasingly parallel the evidence-based treatment movement, you may find that supervisors are basing their supervision practices on state-of-the-art competencies research and research specific to component parts of the supervision process. You also may encounter a tension between a perceived imperviousness to empirical evidence and your supervisor's genuine concern about the relevance and utility of existent research and its balance with relationship and experiential factors. Evidentiary support is accruing at an increasing rate for multiple theoretical models beyond cognitive behavior therapy; for example, compelling support has been presented for psychodynamic models (Shedler, 2010), which emphasize the importance of relationship factors, affect, and emotional expression, among other dimensions. Other research has placed emphasis on the working alliance instead of on specific treatment protocols (Wampold, 2010). This debate, which has extended into the mainstream press (Baker, McFall, & Shoham, 2009), includes concern about practicing clinicians' use of the extant scientific literature as well as the controversy between therapists who advocate and use evidence-supported practices and those who factor in relationship and clinical experience. Baker et al. (2008) concluded that psychologists in private practice rely on clinical experience rather than scientific literature and that many are unaware of evidence-based treatment approaches, including treatment manuals and are generally unprepared to adapt to the changing health care system. The intensity of your and your supervisor's beliefs and attitudes toward evidence-based practice and the movement of many large organizations and providers toward evidence-based treatment will be important aspects of your continuing clinical experience. You might find yourself in the middle of this controversy, or in training environments that are transitioning to evidence-based practice or integrated approaches to health and mental health.

Supervisors who integrate evidence-based practices into their clinical work may do so in supervision as well. Some evidence-based models have supervision manuals or protocols that were developed to enhance fidelity to the model and an associated systematic approach. In addition, some supervisors may use systematic assessment of outcomes of both client and supervision process using outcome measures like those developed by Lambert (2010). Some supervisors may use client-reported outcomes of their current manifestations of presenting symptoms or levels of distress to guide training developments and changes in supervision interventions. Your reports of outcomes such as the strength of the supervisor–supervisee alliance and your own satisfaction with supervision can be tools to help the supervisor assess his or her effectiveness.

THE RECOVERY MODEL

Another example of a major change in mental health provision that you as a supervisee need to understand is the *recovery model* in mental health (Amering, Schmolke, & Stastey, 2009). Supervisees enter clinical settings and supervision expecting that the therapist and supervisor will make the treatment decisions and plan and implement therapy. However, in the recovery model the client, referred to as the *consumer,* is empowered to make treatment decisions to determine the course of therapy. The President's New Freedom Commission on Mental Health final report (2003), which brought the recovery model into mainstream mental health treatment, defined *recovery* as follows:

> the process in which people are able to live, work, learn and participate fully in their communities. For some individuals, recovery may be the ability to live a fulfilling and productive life despite their disability. For others, recovery implies the reduction or complete remission of symptoms. Science has shown that having hope plays an integral role in an individual's recovery. (p. 13)

The recovery model is being generally adopted in the field of community mental health and, more broadly, internationally. The model requires a dramatic transformation in the role of the clinician from expert to collaborator, directed by the goals of the consumer. The term *recovery* refers to the subjective experience of optimism about outcome that comes about through consumer empowerment, collaboration, and the consumer finding and taking on meaningful roles in his or her own life. Evidence regarding recovery from schizophrenia and serious mental illness has been compelling (Davidson, Rakfeldt, & Strauss, 2010; Warner, 2010) and includes reports of individuals who previously were incapacitated and unable to work having families and meaningful lives by building on their individual strengths and capabilities. Although clinicians typically focus on symptom reduction, the recovery model embodies the consumer perspective: empowerment to live with one's mental illness with hope, civil rights, and a sense of accomplishment. Consumer self-determination and self-care are hallmarks of the model. Strength-based and proactive, competency-based supervision is highly compatible with recovery approaches and provides a process for both consumers and supervisees to collaborate and coconstruct empowerment. In supervision, you will join the supervisor in respect to consumer collaboration, collaborative treatment planning, and goals formulated through a strength perspective. In the strength-based model, the clinician assists the consumer in identifying personal strengths to enhance in treatment.

RESPONDEAT SUPERIOR

Another attitudinal shift as you enter supervision is gaining full understanding of the concept of *respondeat superior*, or vicarious liability: the fact that the supervisor and the organization or agency for which the supervisor works bear responsibility for your work with clients and will be held liable for your actions. Although you may be well aware of this fact, because it is emphasized at every juncture in training, it is important for you to understand that your supervisor's perspective is shaped by his or her responsibility to keep the best interest of the client as his or her highest priority. In graduate school, and especially in coursework, faculty hold the *student* as their highest priority. The transition to understanding this shift of responsibility in its entirety is a significant part of assuming your supervisee role. There will be times when the supervisor disagrees with your assessment of a client or family case, or when your supervisor requires you to intervene in a particular manner or make a mandated report to fulfill the duty to warn and protect. It may be difficult to understand why the supervisor is invoking his or her power and legal responsibility, especially when the situation seems much less clear than it did in your ethics class back when you were a student in a classroom. In other circumstances, the supervisor will strongly suggest or require you to change interventions or approaches, usually because of a lack of client improvement or some complexity of the case, such as contextual factors (e.g., cultural). These are times of maximal learning and opportunities for you to be open to alternative interpretations.

BALANCING MULTIPLE ROLES IN CLINICAL SUPERVISION

Another shift in thinking that takes place during your training is that you will gain an understanding of the multiple roles supervisors are balancing, which may comprise a combination of administrative, professional, teaching, supervisory, and clinical functions as well as serving on multidisciplinary treatment teams. The multiple relationships a supervisor may be negotiating will include various layers of responsibility and contact. A supervisor's administrative responsibilities in the agency or setting (including, e.g., productivity requirements; client billing; maintaining the site's financial health; accreditation site visit planning; and other contextual factors, including dealing with boards of directors, interdisciplinary teams, etc.) may have to be balanced against your training needs as a supervisee. Sometimes, an event may seem inexplicable, and the supervisor may in fact not be able, for various reasons (e.g., confidentiality) to provide an explanation. Examples of such an event include a supervisor transferring your client to a different clinician, assigning a particular case or cases to one of your peers, joining you in a session, or directing you to conduct an assessment or intervention. There may be legal, ethical, or contextual issues influencing such decisions that the supervisor is not permitted to discuss.

SELF-ASSESSMENT, SELF-DIRECTED ASSESSMENT SEEKING, AND BEGINNING

Having considered the multiple shifts you will need to make during your time as a supervisee, it is now time to translate this knowledge into actual practice. Your attitude toward the process of self-directed assessments is a most important factor. A significant skill is the habit of self-directed assessment seeking and the ability to absorb external feedback into your own developing sense of your strengths and your weaknesses (Eva & Regehr, 2008). A critical step, then, is to approach self-exploration with curiosity and to be thoughtful and reflective regarding the feedback you likely will receive from multiple sources.

Unfortunately, in the process of education to this point you may not have had much experience in self-appraisal, receiving focal feedback from supervisors, or identifying areas where you need to grow or improve or the specifics of what you do not know. Neither may you have had elaborate experience reflecting on feedback and integrating it into your own self-evaluation. Research indicates that self-assessment is difficult and, without practice, is inaccurate (Dunning, Heath, & Suls, 2004). In fact, individuals who assess themselves as being most competent are often those who by other objective means are rated as substantially *less* competent; conversely, those who believe themselves *less* competent are observed in objective work ratings as substantially *more* competent than their own self-ratings (Davis et al., 2006; Dunning et al., 2004). Sometimes you may feel as if you know nothing; those self-assessments tend to be more a reflection of your developmental level as a supervisee, a lack of confidence, and self-criticism than of a true lack of knowledge.

Self-appraisal, reflection, and self-directed assessment seeking (Eva & Regehr, 2008) are first steps in your training, and may be transformational. Instead of simply viewing a list of behaviors (e.g., the behavioral anchors in the Competency Benchmarks in Appendix A or the competencies outlined in the Practicum Competencies Outline in Appendix B), and self-rating without direction, the self-appraisal process requires *critical reflection*, which entails stepping back and thoughtfully analyzing anchors, considering contextual variables, and freeing yourself from prejudgments about what you *should* know at this juncture. Then, after receiving input from supervisors and even fellow trainees, you must thoughtfully integrate feedback into your self-appraisal. The more reflective and thoughtful you are in your self-appraisal, the easier it will be to develop a supervision plan and incorporate feedback into it.

COMPETENCE AND BEGINNING

Competence is an ethical requisite for clinical work and may be confusing to understand at the onset of supervision. *Competence* is defined as a combination of the requisite knowledge, skills, and attitudes or values for effective performance (Falender & Shafranske, 2004). A definition of *competence* from the medical literature is the "habitual and judicious use of communication, knowledge, technical skills, clinical reasoning, emotions, values, and reflection in daily practice for the benefit of the individual and community being served" (Epstein & Hundert, 2002, p. 227). Note that this definition draws together technical skills and clinical reasoning with knowledge, personal factors, and reflection. This definition is the template for many of the self-assessment measures featured in this book.

READINESS FOR PRACTICUM OR INTERNSHIP: STAGES OF CHANGE

Now consider your own attitudes and readiness to begin supervision. The *stages of change model* (J. M. Prochaska, Levesque, Prochaska, Dewart, & Wing, 2001) relates to a theory of how ready an individual is to change (see Chapter 6, this volume, for a discussion of this model). The phrase *stages of change* refers to a circle of readiness for change, in this context, openness to the supervision process, including input and feedback. This framework was derived from clinical work with smoking cessation, and it has subsequently been broadly applied to multiple contexts. You may be familiar with it from your coursework. However, as we apply it here to supervision, we discuss the various stages of change, which range from Precontemplation through Action, and identify how one's readiness influences the supervision process.

In the preliminary stage, *Precontemplation*, the supervisee is not entertaining thoughts of change; that is, the supervisee may not be ready to view client material through a different lens or to integrate new formulations. In *Contemplation*, the next stage, the individual may be beginning to see some areas of exception or ways that different perspectives, theoretical frames, or interventions might be useful. In the *Preparation* and *Action* phases, the supervisee begins to be eager and open to change and to revise, reformat, and see material through a variety of different perspectives and models. Degrees of readiness will be manifest in interactions with the supervisor. The more ready the supervisee is to change—that is, the further along toward the Action phase the supervisee is—the more positive the supervisory relationship will be (Aten, Strain, & Gillespie, 2008).

Consider how each stage of readiness is manifest in a supervisee's behavior toward the supervisor and how the supervisor may perceive that supervisee. For example, a supervisee in the Precontemplation stage might be perceived by a supervisor as less than eager for supervision. Supervisees in the Precontemplation stage might communicate excitement to have the internship experience, and the belief that so much was learned in practicum that there is a need for only a bare minimum of supervision, saving time for both supervisor and supervisee. Or they may express an attitude of "I learn more from my clinical work, so I would prefer to maximize my clinical contact and minimize supervision." These sorts of attitudes, which are characteristic of the Precontemplation stage interfere with supervision. Supervisees with Precontemplation-type attitudes are communicating a meta-message that is ethically and legally untenable. Supervisors likely will prefer to know whether a supervisee is in the Precontemplation stage, so that readiness to change can become a focus of the beginning supervision process.

Supervisees in the Contemplation stage are thinking about some benefits from supervision but are still generally unsure about change. A supervisee in this stage might say, "I feel very prepared for this assignment but am beginning to think about additional areas in which I might develop and grow." The supervisor may assist the supervisee in developing collaborative goals to assist in moving toward the Preparation and then the Action stage.

In the Preparation stage, supervisees begin to articulate ideas for how they should move into the Action stage, as it is considered the ideal state in which to enter the supervision process. Supervisees in the Action stage are actively involved in all aspects of their training, open to viewing clinical material through alternate frames and perspectives, and motivated to change and grow to engage in supervision through meaningful action.

READINESS FOR PRACTICUM OR INTERNSHIP: SPECIFIC COMPETENCIES

After assessing readiness to change, the next step is to assess readiness for a practicum or internship. Hatcher and Lassiter (2007) developed baseline competencies for practicum readiness. The following Reflection Activity provides a useful exercise in self-assessment. It is intended to facilitate individual development and growth and can help you determine your specific areas of relative strength and weakness—and it is desirable to have many areas of development!

> *Reflection Activity.* To practice self-assessment as well as to become acquainted with the competencies supervisors will draw upon in their evaluations, complete the following brief exercise.
> 1. Practicum students should refer to Practicum Competencies Outline (Appendix B) and self-assess your level of development using the competencies described in Section A. Interns should self-assess their competency as described in both the "Readiness for Practicum" and "Readiness for Internship" sections of the Competency Benchmarks in Appendix A.
> 2. Appendix B describes the baseline competencies for entry into practicum. Many of the areas listed are difficult to self-assess. Some data suggest that peers are the best "objective" raters of individual performance, so an additional exercise is to discuss this section with several of your classmates who are also entering practicum so you can compare impressions. To begin, simply consider the following paragraph from Appendix B:
>
>> Before beginning practicum the student should possess and demonstrate a set of basic personal and intellectual skills, attitudes and values, and a core of professional knowledge. This core knowledge and these skills, attitudes and values are baseline competencies of the professional psychologist. We argue that it is inappropriate to undertake formal clinical professional training with students who have not acquired these skills. The work of subsequent clinical training is to shape and refine these baseline skills into professional skills. (Hatcher & Lassiter, 2007, Part I)

3. For each self-assessment section, identify steps to increase competency in each area of proposed development and create a self-study plan.

Reflection, especially focused self-reflection, prepares you in multiple ways for practicum. In addition to the Practicum Competencies Outline in Appendix B, your training setting may have its own competencies documents for self-assessment with areas specific to the population served, services provided, and context. Be sure to study those and complete a comprehensive self-assessment in which you consider the complexity of overlapping categories.

Reflection Activity. Self-assess your previous education and training, including classroom work up to this point. This assessment will provide an analysis of previous work or a plan for prospective development.

Note that the assessment indicates some expected levels for supervisees in their readiness for practicum, readiness for internship, and readiness for entry to practice. Because this is a developmental trajectory, few areas are fully achieved by practicum students. Sometimes supervisees underestimate their previous training and experience.

To help illustrate the process of assembling knowledge, skills, attitudes, and competencies in the clinical task of an intake, consider an example of a supervisee beginning to do an intake with a 5-year-old child and the child's family. The supervisee reported feeling ill prepared to carry out an intake with such a young child. The supervisor collaborated with the supervisee to systematically assess areas of the supervisee's knowledge, including knowledge of child development, developmental milestones, normative behavior for children transitioning from preschool into kindergarten, social and emotional factors, presenting problems and their relative severity in this age cohort, children's responses to clinical interviews, play techniques that are useful in intake, theoretical models, family systems, attachment behavior, communication patterns, child diagnoses, and cultural and diversity factors. The requisite skills include interviewing and building rapport with 5-year-olds and their parents, working with children in the context of a family, using play during the interview, and using specific assessment tools. Attitudes include experience with children and child interviewing; respect for the child and family; respect for the developmental status of the child and how this translates into the interview process; appreciation of the cultural and diversity aspects of the child and family, including other ecological systems in which the child is embedded; and valuing the child's position in the family constellation. Once the supervisee had clarified the core competencies, she realized she actually had had substantial background in life experience, coursework, and research interviewing protocols and that with supervision, was ready for the task.

> *Reflection Activity.* Reflect on your readiness to work with the child described by considering your own knowledge, skills, and experience in the categories described.
>
> Take time to self-assess feelings about becoming a supervisee. Think about beginning to see clients, entering supervision, and learning from experienced clinicians who will be supervisors. Write down any feelings, expectations, and thoughts, and complete all reflection activities, as these reflections will guide you in the following chapters.

CONCLUSION

Self-assessment provides you a preliminary map for the development of skills, knowledge, and attitudes and values, all of which are components of competency. An awareness of your readiness in all of these areas is an important contribution to your interactions with your supervisor. Areas that you identify as in need of improvement or additional work can be a platform for discussions with your supervisor or a faculty member. Although difficult, such disclosures are critical.

Clinical supervision is integral to the professional development of a psychologist; its impacts are felt throughout your career. Through active collaboration, a supervisory alliance forms that provides the means to develop clinical competence as well as skills in self-reflection and self-assessment. In the following chapters, we build on this foundation and present ways to get the most out of clinical supervision and training.

3

EXPECTATIONS AND THE PATH TO GOOD SUPERVISION

Supervisees often are unclear about their supervisors' expectations of them in supervision. This lack of clarity can be a roadblock to good supervision. The purpose of this chapter is to help you set your expectations and then translate those into good supervision practices. In general, you should expect from your supervisor respect, support, and concern for and attention to learning processes and personal factors that influence your worldview and the resulting clinical interventions you use.

Some questions you may be asking yourself at this point are "How does one assume the role of a supervisee?" and "What is effective supervisee behavior?" Although supervisors may indeed have expectations, the psychology literature contains little specific discussion or empirical analysis of behaviors, attitudes, values, and skills supervisors value. Nor is there much information about what supervisees prefer or expect from supervisors.

Reflection Activity. Think about what you expect from clinical supervision. Make a list of components. Compare your list with the following one:

- learning, refining, and perfecting clinical skills;
- expecting a strong supervisory relationship marked by mutual respect;
- integrating theoretical conceptualizations and empirical research into clinical practice;
- experiencing safety in supervision to explore and reflect on clinical work and experience;
- receiving feedback, both positive and constructive, to enhance learning;
- exploring the impact of the self on work with clients;
- exploring the role of diversity of the supervisee, supervisor, and client in the process; and
- expecting that the supervisor will model and exemplify ethical and legal practice.

Now, think about a previous supervision experience you have had or, if you haven't previously been in supervision, reflect on an experience in school, in a job, or any activity in which teaching or training was involved. Consider both positive and negative aspects. What experiences stand out? Do critical incidents—unresolved or exceptional interactions with previous supervisors—readily come to mind? List one or more critical incidents. What did you learn from these? As you consider each critical incident, think about what actually happened in supervision and what ideally could have happened.

Insights from these and other Reflection Activities in this book would be useful to discuss with your current supervisor. Most supervisors will appreciate your input regarding the supervisory styles or behaviors that you found highly effective in the past. Sometimes it is difficult to discuss previous supervision that was problematic, because you may fear your present supervisor will brand you as problematic as well, but in fact supervisory relationships benefit from such disclosures, especially when they are framed in terms of what was learned.

If you do not feel comfortable discussing a past incident with your current supervisor, try discussing it with faculty and/or peers. Unprocessed past negative supervisory experiences could reduce your trust in and openness with your present supervisor, creating distance in the relationship. Previous exemplary supervision may lead to high expectations for the future and could narrow your openness to the range of what constitutes effective supervision. An example of a proactive approach would be stated thus: "I find that I benefit most from feedback targeted to specific behavior as it comes up so I can grow and change."

SUPERVISOR EXPECTATIONS

One way to ensure success in supervision is to understand and meet your supervisor's expectations. Supervisors' assumptions about supervisee performance often go unspoken. This can later produce a strain in the relationship: as supervisees may be disappointed (or confused) by negative evaluations in areas they never considered. Some guidance in identifying supervisor expectations comes from a pilot instrument, the Supervisor Utilization Rating Form (SURF) (see Exhibit 3.1; Vespia, Heckman-Stone, & Delworth, 2002), which was designed to describe and facilitate supervision. This measure provides guidance in balancing what supervisors expect of supervisees with what supervisees expect from supervisors. This process has been referred to as *role induction,* or the process of understanding, with great specificity, a supervisor's expectations of the supervisory relationship, including its component parts such as the individual categories described below. Expectations are developmentally based, with some distinct differences as a function of you and your supervisor's level of competence.

To understand what supervisors and supervisees value in a supervisee and in the supervision process, it will be useful to rate how important each item in Exhibit 3.1 is (or will be) for you as a supervisee. There is no correct or incorrect answer. This is a useful tool that can be used to compare supervisee and supervisor ratings. In preparation for supervision, complete this form first, and ideally share it with your supervisor, who may wish to complete it also and compare his or her responses with yours in an attempt to clarify supervision expectations. Articulation of what is important to the supervisor will be important and should reduce misunderstanding and conflict.

Now, look at Exhibit 3.1 again and think about which items or groups of items represent areas of strength and which represent areas in which you feel you need further development. Do not worry, as because items all developmental and represent a continuum. Finally, place a star next to the items that are most important to you. These starred items may provide a portal through which you can work on to organize your expectations to synchronize with your supervisor's expectations some of which are articulated, and others

EXHIBIT 3.1
Supervisor Utilization Rating Form (SURF)

Rate using a scale from:

0	1	2	3	4	5	6	7	8	9	10

Not at all important   *Extremely important*

Use the stem "How important is it to . . ." and then assign the number corresponding to how strongly you believe this is important for you to do in the supervision process.

Your Attitudes and Preparation
Demonstrate willingness to grow   1 2 3 4 5 6 7 8 9 10
Prepare for supervision sessions   1 2 3 4 5 6 7 8 9 10
Identify important issues to discuss   1 2 3 4 5 6 7 8 9 10
Demonstrate respect and appreciation for   1 2 3 4 5 6 7 8 9 10
  individual differences
Set goals for supervision considered appropriate   1 2 3 4 5 6 7 8 9 10
  by both supervisor and supervisee

Your View of Your Own Supervision Process
Actively participate in supervision sessions   1 2 3 4 5 6 7 8 9 10
Be open in interactions with supervisor and staff   1 2 3 4 5 6 7 8 9 10
Make work available for observation and feedback   1 2 3 4 5 6 7 8 9 10
Ask for help when appropriate   1 2 3 4 5 6 7 8 9 10
Demonstrate awareness of own strengths and   1 2 3 4 5 6 7 8 9 10
  weaknesses
Talk openly about counseling-related difficulties   1 2 3 4 5 6 7 8 9 10
  in supervision
Collaborate with supervisor in directing the flow   1 2 3 4 5 6 7 8 9 10
  of supervision sessions

Your Ability to Admit Mistakes and Difficulties
Discuss issues related to the supervision relationship   1 2 3 4 5 6 7 8 9 10
  when brought up by supervisor
Implement supervisor's directives when client welfare   1 2 3 4 5 6 7 8 9 10
  is of concern to supervisor
Critique own work   1 2 3 4 5 6 7 8 9 10
Listen attentively to supervisor   1 2 3 4 5 6 7 8 9 10

Your Process and Receptivity to Feedback
Invite feedback from supervisor   1 2 3 4 5 6 7 8 9 10
Accept feedback in a nondefensive manner   1 2 3 4 5 6 7 8 9 10
Make effective decisions about whether and   1 2 3 4 5 6 7 8 9 10
  how to incorporate supervisor feedback
Give supervisor feedback regarding needs and wants   1 2 3 4 5 6 7 8 9 10

Your Insight Into Process
Demonstrate understanding of own personal   1 2 3 4 5 6 7 8 9 10
  dynamics as they relate to therapy and supervision
Talk openly about feelings related to supervision and   1 2 3 4 5 6 7 8 9 10
  work with clients

EXHIBIT 3.1
Supervisor Utilization Rating Form (SURF)   *(Continued)*

Your Treatment/Supervision Outcomes

Demonstrate ability to see things from multiple perspectives	1 2 3 4 5 6 7 8 9 10
Take responsibility for consequences of own behavior	1 2 3 4 5 6 7 8 9 10
Implement supervisor's suggestions if agreed upon	1 2 3 4 5 6 7 8 9 10
Comply with agency policies and procedures	1 2 3 4 5 6 7 8 9 10
Be able to discuss the ethical guidelines relevant to the supervisory or counseling relationship	1 2 3 4 5 6 7 8 9 10

Note. Adapted from "Describing and Facilitating Effective Supervision Behavior in Counseling Trainees," by K. M. Vespia, C. Heckman-Stone, and U. Delworth, 2002, *Psychotherapy: Theory, Research, Practice, Training, 39,* p. 60–61. Copyright 2002 by the American Psychological Association.

of which are not formally discussed. Once identified, they can be more easily addressed.

Now consider each group of items and what you can learn from them. The first section, "Your Attitudes and Preparation," contains items that include demonstrate a willingness to grow, to prepare for supervision sessions, to identify important issues to discuss, to demonstrate respect and appreciation for individual differences, and to set goals for supervision that both you and your supervisor consider appropriate. These items represent the attitudinal and behavioral setting dimensions for supervision. They connote an openness and eagerness to learn from the supervision process, an active approach to preparation for each supervision session, and a willingness to both engage in forming a supervisory alliance and in having respectful interactions with your supervisor and clients, attending to individual and cultural differences. Preparation entails thinking about the process of developing a supervisory alliance, reflecting on your reactions to that process, and determining some preliminary goals to help you achieve it. If you are unsure about any of these components (and it is fine to be unsure), then simply be prepared to develop them collaboratively with your supervisor early on.

The next group of items in Exhibit 3.1, in the section titled "Your View of Your Own Supervision Process," represent expectations for active participation and transparency in the supervision relationship, including an openness to make disclosures about work and openness to feedback. There is also the expectation that the supervisee will know to ask for help when he/she is unsure about any aspect of the client, clinical setting, or intervention. A supervisee strength is the ability and willingness to self-assess with openness to exploring both strengths and areas that require additional work and development. Talking with your supervisor about difficulties or areas that are not proceeding well with a client or in the supervision process can be quite challenging for you as a supervisee. Additional items in this section focus on talking openly about counseling-related difficulties in supervision and collaborating with your supervisor in directing the flow of supervision sessions. Supervisors may encourage supervisees to take ownership of and actively participate in the training process.

Items in the "Your Ability to Admit Mistakes and Difficulties" section relate to a core skill in the supervision process: acceptance of one's fallibility. These items include issues related to the supervision relationship when identified by supervisor, implementing supervisory directives when client welfare is of concern to supervisor, critiquing one's own work, and listening attentively to the supervisor. Openness to discuss both what has gone well and what has gone awry is a signature strength in supervision. The self-identification of areas of lesser competence also a benefit of supervisee accurate self-assessment. Some supervisors will model this behavior and provide examples of areas in which they believe they have erred, as well as what can be learned from that experience.

Areas addressed in the "Your Process and Receptivity to Feedback" section of Exhibit 3.1 focus on a related skill: openness to both giving and receiving feedback. It includes incorporating feedback into ongoing supervision and using feedback as a tool to gain what is needed from supervision. With an increasing awareness of *process*—that is, what is underlying what you and your client say and do in session—you will be opening the door to the most effective clinical practice. Although accepting feedback, especially negative feedback, is difficult, with greater self-awareness, it will be easier to integrate into your repertoire. The more practiced you become in respectfully asserting observations and self-knowledge about the processes that are the most beneficial to you in clinical supervision, the easier it will be for you to be respectfully assertive with clients.

The two items under the "Your Insight Into Process" section in Exhibit 3.1 reflect an openness to viewing one's clinical work from the perspective of the self as an active participant and as a shaper of process. The ability to reflect on these factors is a developmental continuum. As you grow and develop your clinical skills, you increase your ability to step back and gain an understanding of the underlying process of your interaction with clients, in your attention to the underlying meaning of the communication and any agendas (e.g., the client's) that may be influencing it, and to initiate *metacommunication*, or reflection on process, described in Chapters 5 and 9.

Items in the last category, "Your Treatment/Supervision Outcomes," relate to an ability to take responsibility for the consequences of one's behavior, to view behavior and conceptualization from multiple perspectives, to follow through on supervisory input and direction, to adhere to agency policy, and to identify and discuss ethical issues that arise. All of these are cardinal components of a supervisee's ethical and legal behavior.

We add to this a core competency of clinical work assessing client outcomes and bringing weekly data from a client report measure into the supervision session. Attention to patterns of behavioral problem ratings obtained through client self-report can be integrated into the supervision session and is associated with enhanced client outcomes (Reese et al., 2009; Worthen & Lambert, 2007).

TRANSLATING EXPECTATIONS INTO PRACTICE

In the following sections, we describe the general factors that contribute to good supervision and its converse: lousy, or even harmful, supervision. We also address the critical aspect of the effect of feedback on your performance and explain ways to deal with all variants of feedback.

Initiating an Effective Supervisory Relationship and Alliance

The supervisory relationship or alliance provides the foundation of your supervision. It is initiated during the first few sessions of supervision and strengthened throughout. You and your supervisor will establish this relationship by identifying and defining goals and particular objectives to achieve those goals during the training sequence. This process will require that you and your supervisor collaboratively identify, within a competency framework, your areas of strength and those that are more rudimentary and in need of development. The supervisory alliance is not formed in one or two sessions; it may take five to seven, or even more. In one study, two thirds of the supervisees sampled described their supervisory alliance as improving or remaining homeostatic over time (Ladany, Walker, Pate-Carolan, & Evans, 2008). For a review of basic clinical skills, including helping skills, reflective listening, and affect attunement, see Chang, Scott, and Decker (2006) and Hill (2009).

Getting Practical: What to Do During the First or Early Supervision Sessions

You can make a big impact on the course of the supervision by your approach to your early supervision meetings. It will be helpful if you spend some time before your first supervision session thinking about your expectations. It is completely normal to be anxious at the onset of clinical work and supervision; your supervisor expects that and will be supportive. Supervisors typically provide increased structure and support in response to supervisees' anxiety, helping to outline interventions and therapy plans. If the supervisor disregards or misunderstands your anxiety, explain to him or her your developmental level, your newness to the situation, the client group and diagnosis with which you have had the most experience, and any specific concerns you have regarding being effective with a particular client.

Openness to New Experience and Feedback

What does openness to new experience and feedback look like in practice? Your supervisor will infer your openness when you are thoughtful, consider his or her input and questions, are nondefensive, and respond to any inquiries the supervisor may have. You may demonstrate openness by taking a positive, open-ended approach with interest, enthusiasm, respect, and curiosity, characteristics that should extend to your considerations of the therapeutic relationship, the supervisory relationship, and the parallel process or isomorphism of the two, or to the relationship between what is happening in the therapy situation and the supervision session. Your personal factors will influence the clinical session and supervision. These include cultural competency factors relating to your own multiple cultural identities and those of the client, as well as legal and ethical considerations. Although these may seem like tall orders, each will become second nature as you progress.

Preparation

In preparation for your clinical work, review any available materials, including case files, relevant literature, or descriptions of clinic/setting procedures. This might include formulating preliminary conceptualizations, intervention ideas, possible theoretical approaches, evidence-supported approaches for the particular characteristics of the case, diversity factors and how they relate to your case conceptualizations, legal and ethical issues, things that do not seem to fit together in the information compiled, and asking direct questions to learn the supervisor's opinion and impression of aspects of a specific case or conceptualization.

Your supervisor most likely will begin by gaining an understanding of your current level of competence from the competency self-assessment for the Practicum Competencies (see Appendix B) or Competency Benchmarks (Appendix A). Although competencies can always be enhanced, it is important to hone strong self-assessment skills that can help you identify specific areas for development as your supervision begins.

Your first supervision session may be devoted primarily to building an alliance with the supervisor, or helping to understand various aspects of the setting and the supervisory expectations, or the supervisor may expect you to plunge directly into the cases. Be prepared to present clinical work to your supervisor. In many cases, a supervisee's verbal report is the supervisor's only information about what is transpiring in the client session. Ideally, your supervisor will encourage you to supplement this input with live observation and/or video or audio review. You and your supervisor's reflection on the session will be helpful; however, do not despair if the session was confusing, or elicited strong feelings in you, or if you are uncertain about how or what to present to the supervisor. These feelings are normative, and it is the supervisor's task to help you clarify observations, identify emotional reactions to clients, and work on case conceptualization and treatment planning.

Once you have reviewed all the case materials available on your assigned cases, and the documents disseminated by the setting, additional preparation might include the following:

- Diagnostic possibilities and how to proceed with a differential diagnosis
- A preliminary case conceptualization that integrates the client's history, onset, presenting problems, developmental status, contextual factors, diversity and cultural factors
- Questions you identify in your review of the available information
- Legal and ethical considerations
- Emotional responses to the client and his or her presenting problems
  - Are there similarities between your client or someone close to you and/or to the client?
  - Does the client remind you of someone?

What to Do

How can you promote a quality supervisee–supervisor relationship? The following strategies are useful to enhance this alliance in the preliminary phases of your development:

- Listen carefully and clarify anything you do not understand.
- Follow through on all supervisory suggestions. If you are unclear about how to do this, express interest in learning more about particular strategies or interventions and ask for more structure as to how to do so. If your supervisor suggests researching particular studies regarding the supervisee's client diagnosis, or identifying evidence-based practices, intervention research, or meta-analyses relevant to the case, bring a list of the references, or the articles, to your next supervision session and prepare a brief summary of conclusions as they pertain to the clinical case.
- Make supervision meetings a top priority; avoid being late or cancelling.
- Identify effective specific and finite supervision strategies, either from previous experience or as the supervisory relationship

develops; for example, "It was very helpful when you told me about your own emotional response to the new client"; "That was interesting to contrast two possible intervention strategies for the same client!"; or "I was appreciative that you told me what to do when my client was expressing suicidal ideation last week. I did not want to process or reflect! I just wanted an answer, so thank you!"

- If a formal supervision agenda is being used, take responsibility for preparation and organization needed with respect to that structure.
- Be open and accessible to discussions of worldview and multiple diversity identity comparisons among the client, your supervisor, and yourself and how these affect your assumptions about, attitudes toward, and interventions with clients.
- Consistently report on areas the supervisor has raised in previous supervision sessions that he or she indicated required follow-up.
- If you disagree with your supervisor, respectfully express your concern or disagreement, along with your rationale, and discuss.
- Inquire about the use of client outcome measures and whether the data they provide might be a valuable tool in supervision (this would include you creating spreadsheets or graphs of client weekly self-report data on symptoms to incorporate into the supervision session; Reese et al., 2009; Worthen & Lambert, 2007).
- Follow through on all supervisory directives when the supervisor invokes imperative such as "You must . . ." or implies imperative. Be sure to clarify which supervisory statements are imperatives, if you are unsure.
- Take responsibility for your professional development and practice by seeking out resources, including reading, self-study, and continuing education programs.
- Before introducing innovations into practice, introduce them in supervision.

What Not to Do

Now consider the converse of successful supervisee and supervisor behavior. What behaviors do supervisors see as problematic? A study provides us with some insights on this (Wilcoxon, Norem, & Magnuson, 2005). High on the list is a lack of willingness to want to grow or change. Such supervisees may appear to have unresolved personal issues that limit their openness to clients or to supervision, are fearful of change, are unwilling or unable to examine the self (in the context of the client being treated), are socially limited, lack sensitivity and respect, are distrustful or defensive, are unwilling or unable to accept feedback, have a limited skill and knowledge base, have a limited motivation for learning, and/or demonstrate an inadequate understanding of the counseling process (Wilcoxon, Norem, & Magnuson, 2005). Supervisors prefer a supervisee who says, "I am unsure how to implement that type of child therapy but would love to learn," to one who says, "I feel like everything I need to know I learned in my last placement."

Group Supervision

Group supervision differs from individual supervision in various ways. Supervisees generally give group supervision high scores, above those for individual supervision (Goodyear & Nelson, 1997). A major difference between individual and group supervision is the potential for group validation, camaraderie, and peer support (Carter, Enyedy, Goodyear, Arcinue, & Puri, 2009). Helpful events in group supervision include self-reflection modeled in the group, which leads to increased self-understanding in an environment of support and safety, along with a high quality of support from peers and the general positive impact of peers (Carter et al., 2009). Enhanced group cohesion results from identification of cultural conflict that arises between group members by the group supervisor (Enyedy et al., 2003). In fact, studies of group supervision have indicated that overall the experience is a positive one but that sometimes hindering multicultural events, or cultural misunderstandings regarding clients or between group members, interfered with growth occurring within the group. Researchers have concluded that it would be better when multicultural events or incidents occur to attend to them within the group supervision context (Kaduvettoor et al., 2009). Vicarious learning through peers was a significant strength and contributed to the group climate (Riva & Cornish, 2008), supporting the idea that you can be a powerful force in the group process and that significant learning can occur between you and the other supervisees.

ENHANCING SUPERVISION EFFECTIVENESS

We suggest that supervision can be continually improved through collaboration, thoughtful reflection, and, most important, your personal commitment. You can demonstrate such a commitment by actively considering how to further contribute to the learning process and providing feedback to your supervisor. The following Reflection Activity provides some guidance as to how you can begin to enhance supervision.

In addition to identifying and initiating the aforementioned positive supervision strategies, you can readily contribute to enhancing the effectiveness of supervision by actively engaging in disclosure and in learning to effectively receive and give feedback.

Disclosure

The strength of the therapeutic alliance you establish with your client influences treatment outcome (Norcross, 2002). If you experience difficulty

EXHIBIT 3.2
Components of the Supervision Process

1. Supervisee observed the supervisor's clinical practice or participated in cotherapy
2. Supervisor observed the supervisee's clinical practice (live, audiotaped, or videotaped).
3. Supervisor used role play to clarify clinical issues or assess supervisee's skills.
4. Supervisee practiced skills in the supervision sessions.
5. Supervisor evaluated supervisee's performance in relation to best practice.
6. Supervisor praised the supervisee's performance.
7. Supervisor gave constructive feedback regarding clinical skills/development.
8. Supervisor provided written feedback of supervisee's performance.
9. Supervisor reviewed supervisee's clinical notes and reports.
10. Supervisor provided guidance and suggestions about clinical skills and methods.
11. Supervisor verbally described a new skill.
12. Supervisor demonstrated a new skill.
13. Audiovisual teaching demonstrations (CD-ROMs, video/ audiotapes, or Web) were used.
14. Supervisor provided suggestions about readings.
15. Supervisor facilitated reflective practice by the supervisee.
16. Supervisor facilitated problem solving by the supervisee.
17. Supervisor discussed supervisee's feelings and concerns and gave emotional support.
18. A written agenda was negotiated and used.
19. Written minutes (supervision documentation) were recorded.
20. Preparation occurred before the supervision session.
21. Content of clinical sessions is discussed in supervision.
22. Plans for future practice (e.g., clinical session plans) are discussed.

Note. From "Outcomes of Training in Supervision: Randomised Controlled Trial," by D. J. Kavanagh, S. Spence, H. Sturk, J. Strong, J. Wilson, L. Worrall, . . . R. Skerrett, 2008, *Australian Psychologist, 43,* p. 99. Copyright 2008 by John Wiley & Sons. Reprinted with permission.

developing an alliance with your client, then it is essential to discuss this difficulty in supervision. The process of exploring such a topic will strengthen the supervisory alliance. Having a strong supervisory alliance is positively associated with more supervisee disclosure (Ladany, Hill, Corbett, & Nutt, 1996), identifying and discussing countertransference (Daniel, 2008), and overall satisfaction with supervision (Ladany, Ellis, & Friedlander, 1999). Supervisees who do not have a strong alliance with their supervisors are less likely to disclose a range of issues.

What types of things do supervisees *not* tell their supervisors? According to one study, 97% of the supervisee respondents did not disclose certain information to their supervisors. Some of these topics included negative reactions to their supervisors (90% of those who failed to disclose), personal issues (60%), clinical mistakes (44%), evaluation concerns (44%), general observations about clients (43%), and negative (i.e., critical, disapproving, or unpleasant) reactions to their clients (36%; Ladany et al., 1996).

Think about each of these topics and identify which would be most important to disclose. Which would be of most concern to supervisors? As supervisors ourselves, we can tell you that it is most important that supervisees disclose all of the things that influence their work with clients, most certainly clinical mistakes and negative or general reactions or observations concerning clients. Although such disclosures may be difficult for you, they are an extremely important part of supervision, and their discussion and resolution will result in your enhanced competence in providing therapy.

Feedback and Evaluation

Feedback is information communicated to you from your supervisor regarding aspects of your clinical work and your competence, including knowledge, skills, attitudes, behavior, and presentation, for the purposes of enhancing your clinical performance as well as the supervisory relationship. Feedback from your supervisor may track your developmental progress in discrete behavioral terms and is an essential part of clinical supervision. Feedback may be positive, praising, or constructive, identifying areas of omission or advising that you reformat one or more aspects of your clinical practice. Feedback may also be corrective, critical, or negative, making it more difficult to receive. You may receive feedback informing you that your behavior or practice is not acceptable. The term *corrective feedback* often refers to discrepancies between expected and actual performance. Supervisors may be fearful of giving such feedback, believing—incorrectly—that constructive performance feedback will place a strain on the supervisory relationship. Supervisors usually find it easier to give a supervisee feedback about his or her clinical skills than about professionalism or other foundational competencies (Hoffman, Hill, Holmes & Freitas, 2005).

Ongoing feedback, a desirable part of supervision, is a type of formative evaluation that functions to adjust and support your course of professional development. *Summative evaluation*, in contrast, refers to a formal appraisal of competency, or progress toward completion of performance criteria, and is given at set time intervals several times per year and at completion of a practicum or internship.

How to Receive Feedback

Receiving feedback in a professional manner is a significant skill. Ways to facilitate feedback—and increase the probability that you will continue to receive feedback—include the following:

- welcoming the feedback and expressing an openness and receptivity to explore and act on it;
- participating actively in self-assessment, so that when you receive feedback it fits into a framework familiar to you;
- conceptualizing feedback as part of a developmental progression;
- engaging in a reflective process with curiosity to consider, understand, weigh, and seek examples for clarification;
- exploring feedback's relationship to other aspects of your performance; and
- expressing appreciation for the feedback and the thought and effort it entailed on the part of your supervisor.

Feedback is harder to accept if it is perceived as negative, inaccurate, or unempathic, and it can even be demotivational. If the negative feedback is incompatible with your self-assessment, and especially if your supervisor has not been providing ongoing feedback about developing concerns or performance issues, you may find it more difficult to accept. However, generally it is easier to accept even critical or harsh feedback if you believe it is accurate and it coincides with your own self-assessment. Research has suggested that accepting negative feedback is easier if you have a strong supervisory relationship (Hoffman et al., 2005), but in fact you still may feel betrayed when you receive corrective or negative feedback from a trusted supervisor.

A key factor is how you use feedback to inform your own practice and self-assessment. Supervisees who are open and receptive to feedback gain extra credence and respect from their supervisors.

Giving Your Supervisor Feedback

The skill of giving feedback will serve you in good stead throughout your professional career. If your supervisor elicits feedback, you may feel more comfortable beginning with areas of his or her strength and then discussing the structure of the supervision hour (e.g., format, amount of time spent on conceptualization, theory, intervention). Although it is advisable not to use what are called "feedback sandwiches" too often, you may find them a desirable technique. The sandwich might begin with praise such as "I value our supervision hour so much" and then adding a corrective "filling," such as "I wish we could spend more time on individual diagnostic issues" and then, finally, the addition of a second cookie: "Overall, supervision is great." A limitation of feedback sandwiches is that the recipients become conditioned to expect that praise or positive feedback will be followed by some negative feedback. The positive feedback becomes a discriminative stimulus or cue that corrective or less positive feedback will follow.

What If Your Supervisor Does Not Give Feedback?

Supervisors do not always give feedback to supervisees. In one study (Ladany & Melincoff, 1999), 98% of supervisors of graduate students withheld some feedback from them, in particular if the supervisor had a negative reaction to the supervisee's professional or counseling performance, a relevant professional issue, or a negative response to the supervisee's performance in supervision. This research was conducted before the Competency Benchmarks (Appendix A) and Practicum Competencies (Appendix B) were available, so we hope that these documents will provide assistance to supervisors in framing and normalizing feedback. Anchoring feedback and appraisals in competencies documents may reduce feelings of subjectivity and enhance a comprehensive review of the supervisee's performance.

Early in supervision, your supervisor may engage in collaborative discussions of alternative strategies instead of correcting perceived errors. Ideally, as you progress, your supervisor will give frequent feedback, both positive and constructive, and will elicit your feedback regarding the process of supervision. If either or both do not occur, you may request it. The request may be as simple as, "It would be so helpful for me to get specific feedback about how you are viewing my development." You also could suggest anchoring feedback in the Practicum Competencies (Appendix B) or Competency Benchmarks (Appendix A) with a review of your self-assessment ratings.

What If You Disagree With Your Supervisor's Feedback?

If you don't understand the rationale for feedback about your behavior, or feel your supervisor has misunderstood some aspect of your work, you may ask your supervisor to discuss it further with you to gain greater clarity. You may respectfully present research or clinical articles that support your analysis or position. Be guided by the premise that feedback is intended for your development and, if integrated into your training nondefensively, can foster your professional growth. However, if you disagree with your supervisor and do not feel heard by him or her, this may introduce a strain in the supervisory relationship. The strain will need to be addressed to ensure that it does not interfere with supervision and, ultimately, client care. If the pattern of feedback continues, with you strongly disagreeing and feeling misunderstood and yet your supervisor not seeming receptive to your concerns, bring the situation to the attention of clinical faculty at your graduate school to gain direction on how to proceed.

As we have stated, getting the most out of clinical supervision requires collaboration. You are responsible for ensuring that the supervisor is aware of your self-assessment and that supervision is conducted at a level that is synchronous with your developmental status. The tools we provide in this chapter, and especially in Chapter 9, provide ways for you to enhance the structure of and to be knowledgeable about supervision practices.

Receiving Difficult Feedback

Supervisors are trained and strongly encouraged to give corrective feedback early, which is in your best interest, because it gives you the opportunity to grow and benefit from that feedback and incorporate necessary changes in behavior. Even so, corrective or even negative feedback is difficult to receive. Supervisees generally have a history of strong academic achievement and success. It can be disheartening to receive corrective feedback, sometimes for the first time in your academic career. Even if you are in agreement with parts or all of the feedback, the reality of the power differential is significant, potentially resulting in you feeling powerless and overwhelmed. The feedback may feel like an injury of sorts, decreasing your feelings of confidence and self-efficacy. Ideally, your supervisor will tie the feedback to a specific performance area, facilitating your understanding of the steps or behavioral markers associated with movement toward competency. Thus, a first step in incorporating feedback into your work is to be sure you understand the feedback and are not simply agreeing to end the session or move on to safer areas. Managing feedback and incorporating it into performance is a significant competency.

What should you do if you feel overwhelmed or incapacitated by negative or corrective feedback? Such feedback may elicit feelings of helplessness or despair, or it may trigger memories of parental or educational settings that were less than positive, bringing on a flood of negative affect. Supervisors giving negative feedback may be stressed and uncomfortable and less able to model reflection; however, a critical component of receiving negative feedback is listening to it and reflecting on it. The supervisor should be helpful in contextualizing the feedback and ensuring that it is comprehensible to you. Supervisors may rush though giving corrective feedback, and you may have to ask him or her to slow down to ensure that you understand everything that he or she is communicating. Taking performance feedback seriously is an essential aspect of being a supervisee. Regard the receipt of feedback as like being at a crossroads: You can choose the pathway toward open acceptance and reflection, with effort to enhance performance, or you can choose a path that might eventually require the supervisor to give greater amounts of negative feedback, including feedback on the way you are dealing with the feedback! Arguing about the feedback, refusing to discuss it, or withdrawing from the feedback meeting all signal a supervisee who is not open or responsive, adding another layer of behavior that does not meet the competence standards. If you feel too overwhelmed to process feedback at that time, express your surprise at or difficulty with the specific feedback and ask for some time to reflect on it. If you believe the feedback is incorrect, then it is good practice to reflect, organize, review the feedback, and present to your supervisor a measured thoughtful response.

Supervisees/Trainees With Competence Problems

What if a supervisee is told he or she is a "Trainee with Competence Performance Problems (TCPP)?" (Elman & Forrest, 2007); that is, what if that supervisee is not meeting the criteria for performance in the training setting? Definitions of TCPPs have varied but may relate to general performance or ethical issues. A large percentage of training settings reported the dismissal of one student every 3 to 5 years. The emotional impact of being so identified is significant: It can elicit pain, anger, or disappointment as well as other emotions even stronger than those elicited simply by constructive or negative feedback. The best approach if you are identified as a TCPP is to listen to the feedback, ask for time to process it, and then gain a greater understanding of it through active discussion. The TCPP designation is generally the culmination of multiple performance feedback indicative of failure to meet competency requirements.

Is TCPP designation a final designation? No. Data indicate that many supervisees address the competency areas in question, grow substantially, and emerge stronger and more effective. In one study, over three quarters of students identified as TCPPs improved significantly during the action plan/remediation process (Elman, Forrest, Gizara, & Vacha-Haase, 1999). Many supervisors suggest that the way a supervisee responds to corrective or negative feedback is a critical part of the process. Openness, nondefensiveness, reflection, and motivation to change are excellent attitudes and behaviors to address correction.

It may be that your training setting does not have formatted procedures in place to assist in the clarity of the process once the TCPP designation has been given (D. S. S. Miller, Forrest, Elman, 2009). After a designation of TCPP status, the ensuing steps include specifically explaining to the supervisee about the particular behavioral anchors that are not meeting the performance criteria and the development of an action plan for remediation, with timelines and/or deadlines for work completion with specific criteria to be met. Arranged check-ins to address the supervisee's progress toward completion of these criteria will be regularly scheduled. The supervisor serves the dual roles of helping develop the strategies for improvement and monitoring and overseeing the process of remediation as well as the steps to follow if the competencies are not successfully accomplished.

Assuming that the supervisee has been reflective and open to the supervisor's extensive feedback, and has made gains in designated areas, the training process should get back on track. Supervisees have reported that supervisors who worked with them through successful remediation plans were among the most important and influential in their careers.

CONCLUSION

Clarity and congruence in expectations are vital ingredients of successful supervision. With the tools we have provided in this chapter, you will be able to enhance clarity and achieve effective communication with your supervisor and effectively take part in the normative processes of feedback and monitoring to strengthen your growth, preparing you for the next steps of professional development.

II

DEVELOPING CLINICAL COMPETENCE THROUGH SUPERVISION

4

DEVELOPING COMPETENCE TO PRACTICE IN A DIVERSE WORLD

With the increasing multicultural diversity of clients, supervisees, and supervisors, multiculturally clinical and supervision practices are more essential than ever to competent practice. Unfortunately, multicultural-diversity competence is commonly misunderstood. Supervisors may seem to be dismissive of clients' diversity; infer incorrect diversity statuses or assumptions; or suggest assessment, interventions, or labels that appear culturally insensitive. Ideally, supervisors model the self-assessment of multicultural competence, addressing knowledge, assumptions, attitudes, perceptions, feelings, and biases early in supervision. However, you may find yourself playing an influential role in leading discussions about and interventions regarding multicultural considerations.

In this chapter, we address the complexities of defining and implementing multicultural competence in supervision, the essential self-knowledge acquired through self-assessment and reflection, and the dynamics of the multicultural supervision interaction. We propose steps and strategies to enhance multiculturally competent supervision. We also offer specific activities to assist you in gaining gain enhanced self-knowledge and preparation for supervision.

Incorporating diverse aspects of your client, your supervisor, and yourself into practice and supervision in a respectful, inclusive way is complex.[1] A difficulty in doing this has been the translation of multiculturalism standards and guidelines into day-to-day practice. The concept of *cultural humility* facilitates reflective process and translation. Cultural humility incorporates a lifelong commitment to self-evaluation and self-critiquing, addressing and redressing power imbalances in the client–therapist–supervisor dynamic, a commitment to developing mutually beneficial and nonpaternalistic clinical and advocacy community partnerships (Tervalon & Murray-Garcia, 1998). By formalizing the essential aspect of self-appraisal in combination with self-critiquing, adding humility to the equation, a transformation occurs. Instead of conceptualizing particular behaviors, humility is a mind-set of openness and awareness. Implementation of cultural humility involves not simply understanding concepts but also integrating them into one's clinical work, worldview, and supervision. This chapter contains the building blocks that will help you enhance your cultural perspective with regard to diverse clients and bring it into the supervision process.

The multiple definitions of *multicultural supervision competence* draw attention to both the supervisor's and the supervisee's examination of cultural issues that influence how to effectively counsel diverse clients (Leong & Wagner, 1994), development of cultural awareness, and exploration of the cultural dynamics of the supervisory relationship. Other definitions address the underlying cultural assumptions of traditional theories (Robinson, Bradley, & Hendricks, 2000) and multicultural competence as an essential aspect of conducting ethical and effective practice with diverse clients (Ancis & Ladany, 2001). We have defined *multicultural supervision* as

> Awareness, knowledge, and appreciation of the interaction among the client's, supervisee-therapist's, and supervisor's assumptions, values, biases, expectations, and worldviews; integration and practice of appropriate, relevant, and sensitive assessment and intervention strategies and skills, and consideration of the larger milieu of history, society and socio-political factors. (Falender & Shafranske, 2004, p. 125)

Worldview, a concept central to multicultural competence, refers to the intersection of traditional (or nontraditional) belief structures, attitudes toward

---

[1]Multiple guidelines and codes shape practice and define multiculturalism. They include the American Psychological Association's (APA's) Ethical Principles of Psychologists and Code of Conduct (APA, 2010a; hereafter Ethics Code); APA's (2003b) Guidelines on Multicultural Education, Training, Research, Practice, and Organizational Change for Psychologists (hereafter Multicultural Guidelines) and the Report of the APA Task Force on the Implementation of the Multicultural Guidelines (APA, 2008); as well as specific guidelines, including Guidelines for Psychological Practice with Girls and Women (APA, 2007); Guidelines for Psychological Practice with Older Adults (APA, 2003a); and Guidelines for Psychotherapy with Lesbian, Gay, and Bisexual Clients (APA, 2011; APA, Division 44/Committee on Lesbian, Gay, & Bisexual Concerns Task Force, 2000).

the importance of the here-and-now (e.g., a present vs. future or past orientation), one's relationship with nature (e.g., an advocate vs. adversarial relationship), and one's general outlook (e.g., optimism vs. pessimism) (Ibrahim & Kahn, 1987). Worldview differences dramatically affect therapy and supervision. For example, the therapist may be very focused on future academic consequences of a child's behavior, whereas the parent of the child who is the client may be concerned with present harmony and relationships within the family. As a result, the treatment will proceed as if the two were speaking different languages!

Reflection Activity. Consider aspects of your own worldview as described above.

KNOWING ONESELF AND OTHERS

How do you begin? Self-knowledge is essential to competence in multicultural supervision, so a preliminary step is self-awareness. Ask yourself, "Who am I as a cultural being?" Psychologists and supervisees have been faulted for a unidimensional approach to diversity, that is, considering only one aspect—typically, ethnicity—and stereotyping by assuming that everyone in that particular category is similar (Falicov, 1998). In contrast to this approach is the concept of *multiple identities* or an *ecological niche* (Falicov, 1998): the intersection of multiple diversity dimensions within each individual.

Reflection Activity. To more fully understand your personal intersection, self-identify on the following dimensions of diversity:

Age _____ _____
Gender _____ _____
Gender identity _____ _____
Race _____ _____
Ethnicity _____ _____
Culture _____ _____
National origin _____ _____
Religion _____ _____
Spirituality _____ _____
Sexual orientation _____ _____
Disability/ableness _____ _____
Language _____ _____
Socioeconomic status _____ _____
Migration status _____ _____

Acculturation	_____	___
Rural/urban	_____	___
Educational level	_____	___
Rural versus urban residence	_____	___
Other relevant attribute	_____	___

Now, consider how each rating relates to privilege. Privilege refers to personal privilege, unearned social rewards received by members of the dominant culture, or the dominant quality of membership in particular groups. Often, privilege connotes invisible ways certain diversity factors are associated with prestige, privilege, and special opportunities not available to others. Think of ways your specific dimensions of diversity have resulted in privilege for you in particular settings or contexts.

Next, consider *oppression:* the experience of powerlessness, or being burdened by unjust circumstances. Oppression may be manifest as racism, sexism, ageism, or homophobia. The more specific term *sociopolitical oppression* refers to being minimized, shamed, devalued, and/or marginalized by others who may be powerful, or intimidating, or both (Miville et al., 2009).

Privilege and oppression translate into cultural power (or lack thereof); therefore, the degree of privilege one receives in society often is based on one's cultural identity (Sue, Arredondo, & McDavis, 1992).

Reflection Activity. Think about the multiple dimensions of diversity in the list in the preceding Reflection Activity. Consider which ones are associated with oppression as well as the contexts or circumstances in which oppression may occur, and note this. How might this knowledge influence your clinical practice and supervision?

Discussions of privilege and oppression are rare in supervision, yet both have significant influence, compounding the power differential between you and your supervisor and potentially leading to misunderstanding and strain.

Reflection Activity. Consider each dimension of diversity with respect to a particular client or family you have encountered (be attentive to the great variations that can exist within a family). Consider how worldviews, and consequently therapy, might be affected by differences or overlaps among the diversity dimensions; for example, within a family, there might be different degrees of acculturation, with the child speaking fluent English and the parents remaining monolingual in their native language. The parents may have a more traditional worldview, adhering to beliefs, traditions, and practices from their country of origin (as may be evidenced, e.g., by strict parenting rules about dress, requiring that the child come straight home after school), whereas the child may be more strongly influenced by culture in the United States, including the popular media and his or her peers.

Your supervisor, client, or you may make inferences about a dimension of diversity of the other(s) on the basis of that person's' appearance, behavior, or practices. These inferences may or may not be correct. Assumptions and attitudes frame the clinical process and can lead to misunderstandings, which may introduce strain or even ruptures in the therapeutic or supervisory process. An example would include assuming, on the basis of a person's name or appearance (e.g., a client, supervisee, or supervisor) that he or she is of a particular ethnicity, with subsequent inferences made based upon the initial erroneous assumption.

Reflection Activity. First, rate yourself in terms of cultural competence. Do you consider yourself extremely culturally competent, moderately culturally competent, or not very culturally competent? Then self-assess with the measure developed by Hansen and colleagues (2006) with items derived from the APA (2003b) Multicultural Guidelines (see Appendix C). After completing the survey, consider your strengths and areas in which you might need further development as a prelude to identifying the various areas of diversity competence in supervision highlighted in this chapter. The survey provides a framework to help you consider your degree of cultural encapsulation, that is, your definition of reality according to one set of cultural assumptions disregarding contrary evidence. Licensed psychologists who completed the survey after indicating their level of cultural competency displayed a gap between their self-assessed competence and their actual multiculturally competent practices (Hansen et al., 2006).

Another dimension of diversity that is often neglected during supervision and treatment planning is the respectful assessment of religion and spirituality beliefs (Russell & Yarhouse, 2006). Respect for clients' various and diverse religious beliefs is generally accepted as reflective of good psychotherapy but does not necessarily actually occur in practice (Frazier & Hansen, 2009); specifically, in one study, although the majority of respondents respected religious beliefs, in practice they did not actively communicate respect for clients' religious/

spiritual beliefs, initiate and explore religious/spiritual differences between themselves and their clients, use religious metaphors in treatment, promote autonomy and self-determination of highly religious clients when the clients' values differ from their own, or self-assess their own competence to counsel clients with strong religious views (Frazier & Hansen, 2009).

> **Reflection Activity.** Consider your training and personal background and how you integrate religion and spirituality into your clinical practice and supervision.

RACIAL/ETHNIC IDENTITY DEVELOPMENT

A person's level of racial/ethnic identity development is an important factor in supervisory relationships (Constantine, Warren, & Miville, 2005; Ladany, Inman, Constantine, & Hofheinz, 1997). Racial identity development for a White person requires acceptance of "Whiteness" and how one's personal behavior may collude with or contribute to racism (Helms, 1995). Unintentional bias, manifest as *aversive racism*—a form of bias in which the individual verbally endorses egalitarian attitudes yet experiences negative emotions when interacting with individuals of various racial/ethnic groups— is subtle and often outside one's conscious awareness (Dovidio, 2001). It may arise in supervisory dyads when one or both is fearful of introducing the topic of prejudices and personal biases and lack skills and competence (Sue, Torino, Capodilupo, Rivera, & Lin, 2009). One manifestation of bias is *microaggressions*, small events that occur in everyday exchanges. Microaggressions may be behavioral, verbal, or environmental, unintentional or intentional, and they send denigrating, invalidating, hostile, or disparaging messages and can have a harmful or unpleasant impact (Sue et al., 2007). Examples include saying to an Asian American supervisee "You speak really good English," or commenting, to anyone, "That is retarded," or calling a young female therapist "Honey."

Your supervisor may engage you in a self-assessment of comparative levels of ethnic identity development. Supervisor–supervisee dyads in which the supervisor is at the same or a more developed level of racial identity development (progressive) than the supervisee have been associated with stronger supervisory alliances (Bhat & Davis, 2007). Conversely, a regressive supervisory relationship results when the supervisee has a more sophisticated racial identity than the supervisor. Race is a powerful factor in supervision regardless of whether there is perceived difference (Constantine et al., 2005) or similarity (Jernigan, Green, Helms, Perez-Gualdron, & Henze, 2010); however, it is often neglected.

RACIAL OR CULTURAL MINORITY IDENTITY DEVELOPMENT

According to Sue and Sue (2007), there are five distinct stages to one's development of racial or cultural minority awareness:

- Stage 1: Conformity (prior to self-reflection).
- Stage 2: Dissonance (self-doubt, questioning one's cultural worth while appreciating one's own racial/cultural group).
- Stage 3: Resistance (total immersion in one's racial/cultural identity, pride and hostility).
- Stage 4: Introspection.
- Stage 5: Integrative awareness (integration of racial/cultural identity with personal identity, and appreciation of differences).

WHITE OR MAJORITY IDENTITY DEVELOPMENT MODEL

Sue and Sue (2007) also delineated five stages of the *White or majority identity development model:*

- Stage 1: Awareness of one's personal identity based on a specific ethnicity with its own cultural context.
- Stage 2: Awareness of the privileges connected with one's ethnic identity as well as one's own stereotypes, prejudicial attitudes, and previous conditioning.
- Stage 3: Awareness of paternalistic and colonial attitudes and their impact on others.
- Stage 4: Awareness of and dealing with one's fear and anger, building a personal cultural ethic, exposing oneself to cross-cultural experiences.
- Stage 5: Integration, claiming "person of white color" as part of one's own conscious identity.

Reflection Activity. Review the stages that Sue and Sue (2007) provided and consider your personal developmental level of ethnic identity.

Dealing With Differences Respectfully and Competently

Dealing with differences respectfully is an essential component of practice, but it also represents a challenge. Respect is manifest in understanding and empathy and is reflected in the Foundational Competencies in the Competency Benchmarks (see the sections titled "Professionalism," "Relationships," "Reflective Practice/Self-Assessment/Self-Care," and "Individual and Cultural Diversity" in Appendix A). Respectful treatment entails consideration of your own self-appraisal of multiple identities in relation to those of the client and his or her family members, in the context of culturally sensitive diagnosis and treatment intervention.

Simple behaviors or verbalizations that reflect a particular therapist's frame of thinking may lead the client or supervisor to inaccurate conclusions. Making assumptions about the particular identity of your supervisor or client, can create a significant rupture in the supervisory or therapy relationship. You may find, too, that supervisors make assumptions about your cultural, ethnic, or other status, for example, assuming that you are bilingual or a member of a particular cultural group.

What should you do if your supervisor does not discuss diversity, multicultural factors, or racial identity? Broaching the subject of diversity and multiple cultural identities will be helpful because it is central to culturally competent treatment (J. M. Bernard & Goodyear, 2009). You could introduce a model of culturally-adapted psychotherapy (e.g., Gallardo, Yeh, Trimble, & Parham, 2012). The complexity of the potential imbalance, given the power differential between you and your supervisor, is great, and it can have a significant impact on the ethical treatment of clients and on a quality supervision experience. Supervisees value the introduction of culture into supervision

(Burkard et al., 2006; Inman & Ladany, 2008), so how could you proceed if your supervisor seems unwilling to address this topic? Simply stating your belief in the importance of culture and diversity is a first step. The power of the Competency Benchmarks as an anchor of self-assessment and competencies in the ongoing supervision process cannot be understated. You could use, for example, the Competency Benchmarks section "Individual and Cultural Diversity" (see Appendix A) to explain how this area influences the three components of competence: (a) attitudes, (b) knowledge, and (c) skills.

Supervision Practices

Ideally, early in supervision, as you and your supervisor are establishing a supervisory alliance, your supervisor may introduce the topic of diversity factors that differ between you and the client as well as among the three parties of supervisee–therapist, supervisor, and clients. These factors and the differing worldviews people hold are central to framing effective interventions with clients and supervisors. As with diversity in general, a stance of cultural neutrality is not perceived as neutral but as dismissive of or lacking respect for or interest in diversity perspectives, an intrinsic part of clinical practice. Your degree of comfort discussing worldviews and diversity may vary depending on both your supervisor's and your own personal history in supervision and with power and oppression and various interpersonal variables, including the degree to which you trust your supervisor, the training setting, and how well the supervisory relationship is developing. The mere fact that the supervisor raises the topic of cultural perspective will be a great strength. Be guided, however, by the caveat that self-disclosure should be done in the interest of the client and, in the training context, in the interest of the developing supervisory relationship so that you can provide optimal services to clients. The supervisor should be guided by the same principles. For example, supervisors may initially address such variables as a client's generation cohort, and age, as well as regional and ethnic differences as they can affect a client's worldview and assumptions about treatment. Verbalizing these topics will help you feel more comfortable reflecting on your own perspectives, and how they are similar to and different from the client's, as well as your assumptions regarding clinical, client, or general case material.

Adding to the complexity of developing multicultural competency is the fact that each individual has worldviews and perspectives specific to his or her ecological niche, life experience, values, and beliefs and perspectives. These worldviews are malleable, influenced by context, attitude, and perspective. The way your clients, your supervisor, and/or you present to others may be significantly influenced by culture and perceived status (e.g., lack of eye contact, deferential, formal). Individual clients may evoke very different and unacknowledged responses from you and your supervisor that could relate, at least in part, to diversity (including generational) variables. Although diversity and the various perspectives that clients, you, and your supervisor may hold are often neglected, they are essential parts of supervision.

How can you incorporate *cultural infusion*—an awareness and appreciation of the various worldviews held by different cultures—into your training and work with clients? Depending on how well developed the supervisory relationship is, you may find it easier or more difficult to infuse culture into your work. Trust is an essential part of cultural infusion. The introduction of personal diversity factors by either party (e.g., you and your supervisor) too early in the supervision process may be awkward because sufficient trust has not yet been established to offset your worry about the power differential and the potential for a negative evaluation. Furthermore, you and your supervisor may have different comfort levels in discussing racial issues (Utsey, Gernat, & Hammar, 2005). As the collaborative supervisory relationship evolves, your supervisor will assess and gain knowledge, skills, and attitudes from you while also imparting them to you. You might find it useful to highlight the importance of culture as a factor in your own and your clients' development. Explicitly introducing diversity factors in therapy and supervision is associated with a stronger supervisory alliance as well as creation of an environment that is more conducive to discussion of diversity variables.

CULTURAL BORDERLINES

Falicov (1995) suggested that both client–therapist and therapist–supervisor dyads share *cultural borderlines* (p. 376), a term derived from anthropology that refers to areas of overlap between individuals. Thus, for example, overlapping occupations, states or countries of origin, religion, or race could be a cultural borderline between you and your supervisor, or you and your client, that strengthens your connectedness.

Once cultural borderlines have been identified, it follows to think about your engagement with the client, areas of understanding or connection, and ways your supervisor can assist you in preventing overgeneralization from personal experiences or making inferences that do not apply to that particular client; all of these practices are in adherence with ethical (APA, 2002) and multicultural guidelines (APA, 2003b).

> *Reflection Activity.* Think of one example in which a supervisee's belief structure could share a cultural borderline, or conflict, with that of a client. An example could be a supervisee belief in the supernatural. Think of another instance and consider the impact of each of the following:

- Supervisee's belief
- Client's belief
- Supervisor's belief
- Cultural borderlines between client and supervisee
- Potential areas of conflict

Consider a biracial supervisee whose parents went through a difficult divorce when she was 10 and who now seems suspicious and impatient toward her client, an African American divorcing father who presented in therapy claiming he wants to negotiate a better relationship with his two young children, for whom he shares visitation.

What are the available options when you identify a strong response in yourself to an aspect of a client's presentation that is specifically related to diversity and personal history? Even incidental disclosures by clients may trigger strong responses. If a client discloses that she has inherited $1 million from a wealthy uncle, you might be hard pressed, as an individual still in training and not yet earning a significant salary, to not have feelings about your own economic situation, or you might erroneously assume that the client must have no worries as a result of her ample money. As with other aspects of client presentation, supervision is the ideal place to discuss such responses and to learn strategies to differentiate yourself from your clients as well as to manage any such responses appropriately to inform the therapeutic process. Supervision is the proper environment in which to examine biases and prejudices and, through education and modeling, your supervisor can help you learn to work effectively with particular clients and ensure a respectful and culturally competent treatment process (Mintz et al., 2009).

Several approaches to supervision describe cultural infusion, which often is specific to a particular diversity status. *Culturally responsive supervision* is defined as showing appreciation of or interest in the client's as well as of your own culture and your multiple identities and their impact on your worldview, and then placing the clinical presentation and conceptualization into a cultural frame (Burkard et al., 2006).

Group-specific models for cultural responsivity are useful in helping to understand the interaction of various diversity categories. These include *affirmative clinical supervision*, which addresses gender identities and sexual orientations (Halpert, Reinhardt, & Toohey, 2007); the *multicultural developmental supervisory model* (e.g., Latinas supervising other Latinas; Field, Chavez-Korell, & Rodriguez, 2010); the *queer people of color resilience model* (Singh & Chun, 2010); and the *intersectional, postcolonial model* (Hernández & McDowell, 2010), which addresses ethnicity, race, and sexual orientation. Each of these models also addresses privilege and oppression.

In contrast to culturally responsive supervision, in culturally *unresponsive* supervision supervisors intentionally dismiss the relevance of culture or engage in intentional and unintentional acts of omission regarding cultural issues. If the client is White, then a discussion of culture and diversity may be left out because it is deemed irrelevant, without regard for the multiple identities encompassed under the vast variations of racial/ethnic Whiteness (e.g., country of origin, socioeconomic status, ethnic and cultural background). It is unsurprising that more frequent discussions with the supervisor about culture predicted greater supervisee satisfaction in general, especially for international supervisees (Mori, Inman, & Caskie, 2009).

Successful Multicultural Supervision

What behaviors do experienced supervisors view as successful multicultural supervision when ethnicity of the supervisor and you differ? Through use of a Delphi method,[2] supervisors at university counseling centers identified behaviors that facilitated supervisee growth and development, personally or professionally, or that helped to bridge ethnic/cultural barriers between the supervisor and supervisee when the two were of different ethnicities (Dressel, Consloi, Kim, & Atkinson, 2007). The focus was on supervision, not providing insight into client issues. The following list includes the top 20 rated items of successful multicultural supervision from the supervisors' perspective (Dressel et al., 2007):

- creating a safe (nonjudgmental, supportive) environment for discussion of multicultural issues, values, and ideas;
- developing my own self-awareness about cultural/ethnic identity, biases, and limitations;
- communicating acceptance of and respect for supervisees' culture and perspectives;
- listening [to] and demonstrating genuine respect [for the] supervisees' ideas about how culture influences the clinical interaction;
- providing openness, genuineness, empathy, warmth, and [a] nonjudgmental stance;
- validating integration of supervisees' professional and racial/ethnic identities and helping to explore potential blocks to this process;
- discussing and supporting multicultural perspectives as they relate to the supervisees' clinical work;
- attending to feelings of discomfort experienced by [supervisees] concerning multicultural issues;

---

[2]The *Delphi method* is a quantitative research technique that comprises a progressive series of sorting tasks in which experts reach a consensus of critical importance regarding the items being sorted.

- supporting supervisees' own racial/ethnic identity development;
- presenting myself nondefensively by tolerating anger, rage, and fear around multicultural issues;
- providing supervisees a multiculturally diverse caseload to ensure breadth of clinical experience;
- attending to racial/ethnic cultural differences reflected in parallel process issues (supervisor/supervisee and supervisee/client);
- discussing realities of racism/oppression and acknowledging that race is always an issue;
- acknowledging, discussing, and respecting racial/ethnic multicultural similarities and differences between myself and supervisees, and exploring feelings concerning these;
- addressing a broad range of differences (e.g., learning styles, interpersonal needs, sexual orientation, religious/spiritual beliefs, race);
- checking out the supervisory expectations with supervisees;
- initiating discussions about the importance of culture;
- acknowledging and discussing power issues in supervision that may be related to racial/ethnic multicultural differences;
- encouraging supervisees to share, within supervision, their personal and professional cultural background and experiences;
- consulting colleagues willingly about my own reactions to racial/ethnic concerns from supervision; and
- acknowledging my own lack of knowledge on racial/ethnic multicultural differences and inviting supervisees to give me feedback and teach me.

The items on this list offer insight into goals to which both you and your supervisor should be attuned. They provide a road map to help you identify areas in which you would benefit from introduction or further exploration in supervision practice. This list also provides the range of supervisee behaviors that supervisors in the study prioritized and thus valued, and it illuminates the importance of your openness to attention and inquiry into diversity on the part of your supervisor. Introducing this list in supervision is another strategy you can use to increase the focus on diversity.

Unsuccessful Multicultural Supervision

Now consider the following list of *unsuccessful* supervision behaviors identified by supervisors (Dressel et al., 2007):

- lacking awareness regarding my own racial/ethnic/cultural biases and stereotyping;
- overlooking and/or failing to discuss cultural issues;

- becoming defensive around racial/ethnic/cultural issues;
- failing to establish a working alliance and safe environment;
- not recognizing the power of the supervisory role;
- making assumptions about supervisees' experiences or beliefs, based on their ethnicity or culture;
- presenting a particular point of view that was rigid and dogmatic;
- ignoring gender issues in relation to [the] cultural/socioeconomic backgrounds of myself and my supervisees;
- not acknowledging or discussing racial/ethnic/cultural differences between myself and my supervisees;
- not exploring together the impact of different cultural, socio-economic, and gender backgrounds on how we conceptualize clients and the therapy process;
- being inattentive and insensitive to supervisees' insecurities in addressing multiculturalism/racism;
- not supporting and encouraging a supervisee's own racial/ethnic identity development;
- not having a diverse caseload for supervisees[,] thus limiting opportunities for discussion of racial/ethnic/cultural issues;
- failing to recognize my own position of racial/ethnic privilege;
- treating supervisees as "spokespersons" for their whole racial/ethnic group;
- invalidating importance of multicultural supervision by not dedicating enough time to it;
- not learning about and considering supervisees' racial/ethnic/cultural background;
- not acknowledging and encouraging supervisees when they use issues of ethnicity in an appropriate and relevant manner in the course of their work with clients;
- assuming supervisees' cultural awareness without justification;
- having poor boundaries that were intended to create openness but instead contributed to dual role conflicts with supervisees;
- insufficient consultation/peer supervision for me to work out my own racial/ethnic/cultural issues; and
- not inviting supervisees to bring [it] to my attention if [they feel] that I have done/said something they see as racist and then discussing it (p. 59).

All of these practices are associated with supervision that is lacking in diversity competence. Omission of discussions of multicultural competence is unethical and/or does not meet generally accepted standards of practice. These two lists of successful and unsuccessful supervision components can serve as valuable tools in the supervision process to help you collaboratively identify with your supervisor strengths and areas in need of development. Both also can be used as developmental tools to guide supervision.

MULTICULTURALISM IN GROUP SUPERVISION

Group supervision is a valued and increasingly popular modality. Incidents may occur in the supervision group that may create a sense of diminished comfort or even strain or rupture. Unfortunately, there is a slight trend toward a decrease in what is known as *process discussion*, or discussion in the here-and-now about what is occurring in the group regarding the cases being presented and isomorphic, or parallel, group dynamics (Riva & Cornish, 2008). Sometimes, group supervision looks like individual supervision in a group, with individuals simply presenting each case to the group supervisor as little or no group interaction takes place. A skilled supervisor will address critical incidents, hurtful or insensitive comments, or disrespectful behavior as it occurs or shortly after such an incident occurs, when the group is less reactive. A relatively new term, *difficult conversations*, refers (in one of multiple meanings) to addressing the critical issue in a timely manner and in a respectful, proactive way (Forrest, Miller, & Elman, 2008). Difficulties with critical issues arise in multiple ways, often a sequence similar to the following:

- An incident occurs.
- The supervisor experiences discomfort or a lack of clarity about raising the issue of the incident, or is concerned about the impact of the incident on one or more supervisees.
- General group safety is compromised in the absence of addressing the incident.
- The supervisor does not bookmark or note the event, such as "Something significant happened, and we need to reflect on how to address it."
- The requisite safety is not felt by the group members.
- The supervisor lacks the necessary knowledge or skills to facilitate discussion and movement toward some resolution.
- The group rules of respect, multicultural sensitivity, confidentiality did not exist or were not adhered to.

Critical incidents may arise from the behavior of the client, one or more supervisees, the supervisor, or an interaction between or among of any of these. Creating a climate of multicultural openness that is instilled throughout all aspects of the supervision process is a critical component of culturally responsive group supervision. Such a climate may result from the integration of multicultural issues throughout the group supervision processing and the active involvement of a supervisor who is multiculturally competent (Kaduvettoor et al., 2009).

What can you do to repair strains in group supervision? Having trusting peer relationships is a central component of effective group supervision. The peer group could request a time to process what happened each week in group supervision, or the group members could identify a critical incident to the supervisor as an educational topic to address and then provide relevant resources, such as articles about the critical issue.

Examples

Now that you have completed some self-assessments and considered several frameworks for culturally responsive supervision, we invite you to consider how the frameworks and multiple diversity and ethical standards influence resolution of the dilemmas posed in the following examples, which relate to both group and individual practice.

Example 1

The supervisee is coleading an adult group in a community mental health center. He was absent from one meeting and heard from another practicum student several weeks later that one of the group members had made a pejorative comment about the supervisee's ethnic group (Arabic). The other coleader of the group had not told him, and the supervisee's peer told him that no response was made to the comment and that apparently none of the clients were aware that the absent coleader was of Arabic descent. The supervisee was very concerned, not so much personally but because he felt it represented a recurrent theme he had observed in the group of disrespect toward multiple cultural identities, including gender, sexual orientation, and race. The supervisee brought up the issue in his group supervision meeting. The supervisor asked him whether he was personally offended and, when the supervisee demurred, instructed that if another slur is made against Arabs, the supervisee should simply disclose to the group that he, a valued group leader, is Arabic, to show the group members how invalid stereotypes are. The supervisee felt very uncomfortable with this plan but was unsure how to address his feelings of discomfort. His peers in the group meeting were silent.

What aspects would be uncomfortable for you if this situation arose? What are possible ways you could approach the issue? Can you think of a way to activate the staff or the client to reflect on the process? Are there possible parallels between what happened in the clinical group and what happened in group supervision?

In a case like this, is supervisee comfort the major guiding factor? If the supervisee could think through with the supervisor and fellow group supervisees what is important in terms of integrity and respect in a treatment group, a different resolution likely would arise. Perhaps the supervisee could respond to the supervisor that the approach the supervisor suggested is interesting but that he wonders whether it will really address the underlying issues. For example, the group leaders could think about how to introduce the incident to process the meaning of pejorative comments on group process. The ensuing discussion could address how mutual respect among group members is a central group value because it enhances trust and safety, and then the coleaders could help the clients identify creative ways to demonstrate respect. What if the group is primarily skill based? Would this intervention still be helpful? The question could lead you to think about the underlying goals and assumptions of the group and the desired outcomes of the group therapy. The behaviors endorsed, whether explicitly or implicitly, in a skills group are a model for behavior outside of group.

Example 2

The supervisee believes that marriage is sacred, a vow that is not to be broken. In his first group supervision case in practicum, the wife of a couple he has seen twice called him and left a message that she just had a one-night fling with a person at work and wants to be sure that the supervisee–therapist is especially sensitive to this issue and does not raise any questions about marriage fidelity or extramarital affairs in the couple's session that night. The supervisee feels torn among his loyalty to the couple, whom he has identified as his client; to the wife who called and left the message; and to his own values, which frame this disclosure as a violation of his own spiritual and personal values. He is concerned why the wife chose to call him to disclose this. He is also concerned about ethical and legal considerations in defining the client and the limits of confidentiality in couples therapy. How important is this to bring up in group supervision? It if is brought up, how could it best be done?

If the supervisor or group members believe in the sanctity of marriage and frame their interventions on the basis of that belief, expressing grave discomfort about extramarital relationships, how would that affect supervision in this case? There are several diversity and ethical considerations and principles to be considered.

First, how could the supervisee address the pertinent areas of cultural consonance and dissonance with respect to his client (i.e., the couple) within the supervision group? Supervision can help the supervisee differentiate his own beliefs and feelings from those of this wife and her husband. The supervisor and the other supervisees in the group can help highlight the supervisee's self-awareness and may suggest a targeted approach to discussion with the couple in areas not previously addressed. It is possible that a discussion of religious and belief structures relating to marriage may reveal fissures between husband and wife. The supervisee's confidence, comfort, and clarity will provide an excellent backdrop to the ensuing couple discussion—and to the group process. What are some ethical principles that will be important?

The first ethical principle that might come to mind is *confidentiality*, which should have been addressed in the original therapy contract (see the APA [2010a] Ethics Code, especially Standard 4.02, "Discussing the Limits of Confidentiality," and Standard 10.02, "Therapy Involving Couples or Families"). The supervisor may also address the supervisee's response to the wife's call, including any concerns or implied meaning, and the feelings elicited by the wife's disclosure of an extramarital dalliance. How would the husband view the disclosure? How will the supervisee proceed to ensure that his own belief structure does not direct the process or resolution? Considering the supervisee's personal values, the supervisor–supervisee dyad also should review relevant sections of the APA's (2003b; see also APA, 2008) *Guidelines on Multicultural Education, Training, Research, Practice, and Organizational Change for Psychologists* (hereinafter *Multicultural Guidelines*).

Guideline 1 encourages psychologists to become more aware of their thoughts, assumptions, and beliefs about other people and to strive to be aware when these are detrimental to others (APA, 2003b). General recommendations for Guideline 1 include increasing self-awareness and knowledge of one's own worldview as well as an understanding of personal and cultural biases (including individualist or collectivist biases) that may influence behavior toward others. To this end, psychologists should be sure to do two things: (a) become aware of personal attitudes and biases and (b) seek increased contact with members of other cultural groups.

Guideline 2 provides guidance for psychologists on becoming knowledgeable about the history, worldviews, and values of members of cultural groups other than their own and on understanding how stigma may affect others' individual psychological processes. General recommendations for Guideline 2 include the acquisition of knowledge about historical forms of oppression and immigration patterns into the United States and about racial identity development models. The following are some actions individual psychologists are encouraged to take:

- Take others' perspectives and encourage empathy for others.
- Actively "decategorize" or "recategorize" individuals into new groups.
- Avoid suppression of attitudes toward others; instead, bring one's attitudes into conscious awareness (e.g., by completing the

Implicit Association Test online; see http://www.understanding
prejudice.org/iat).

- Understand the effects of stigmatizing individuals and groups.
- Increase one's own learning concerning the multicultural bases of psychological and educational theories and practices, including differences between individualist and collectivist societal views.
- Become knowledgeable about how history has been different for the major U.S. cultural groups.
- Become knowledgeable about ethnic and racial identity development.
- Become knowledgeable about acculturation and immigration issues.

These suggestions for implementation of the Multicultural Guidelines (APA, 2003b; 2008) will provide a structure for the supervisee's thinking regarding the husband–wife client and can be extrapolated to the supervisor–supervisee process as well.

These vignettes, and abundant data, illustrate how the attitudes and belief structures of supervisees, supervisors, clients, and one's practicum/internship peers can dramatically influence all aspects of client treatment. Stigmatizing attitudes and beliefs have been implicated in high dropout rates of clients whose ethnicity differs from that of the therapist (e.g., Wang & Kim, 2010). Some culturally mediated errors include overpathologizing cultural differences (Whaley & Davis, 2007); lack of culturally based relationship-building skills and empathic communication (Fuertes et al., 2006); omitting discussions of racial issues (Thompson & Jenal, 1994); a lack of specific diversity knowledge and skills (Burckell & Goldfried, 2006); issues with general expectations based on gender, or other attitudes toward clients (Bowers & Bieschke, 2005); and a lack of culturally competent assessment skills, including attention to oppression and socioeconomic status (Neufeldt et al., 2006).

In the next few examples, we present some client presentations that might affect your supervisor and you very differently.

Example 3

The supervisor is highly punctual and is very dismissive of anyone who is late. He learns that the supervisee has been seeing a male client who is typically 15 to 20 minutes late for each therapy session. The supervisee explains that being punctual is not culturally syntonic for this client (i.e., it is a value not compatible with the client's specific culture) and that, furthermore, the client comes from across the city, and transportation is unreliable. The client has demonstrated many other aspects of growth and progress, so the supervisee has put punctuality on the back burner for the time being. The supervisor tells the supervisee that the client's therapy must be terminated if he does not come 5 minutes early for each of the next sessions. He also chastises the supervisee for not disclosing this issue directly to him. The supervisee apologizes for the non-disclosure and admits she might have been protecting the client because of what she had learned in graduate school about various cultures and their perceptions of time. The supervisee is unsure what other steps she can take, but she begins to collect articles about differences in conceptions of time and the importance of understanding this for culturally competent treatment to bring to supervision. She is elated when the next week the supervisor praises her efforts and commends her for expanding his cultural sensitivity and then revisits and revises the conditions for that particular client's treatment.

Example 4

A 60-year-old woman is depressed because of the death of her spouse. To the 65-year-old supervisor, the client may seem young while at the same time seeming very old to the 26-year-old supervisee–therapist. The supervisor might be reflecting on personal borderlines (i.e., the similarities of the client's deceased spouse to her own husband), whereas the supervisee might be confused as to why the supervisor is suddenly so quiet, introspective, and sad, not performing as she normally does to a vast range of clinical presentations. The supervisee could comment on how different the supervisor's response to that particular client is compared with the reactions she has shown in the past.

Example 5

The supervisee's client, a Japanese graduate student in engineering, is in the United States on a student visa and presents with anxiety over his future, worries that he will not be able to obtain a green card to become an American citizen, and general fears that keep him awake most nights and are interfering with his ability to do his assignments or to stay awake in class. He is fearful of disclosing the full details of his presenting problem because of the impact on his immigration status, but he hints broadly about substance abuse. He has been cheating on exams in several classes with electronic messaging devices to shore up his grades to bolster his green card application.

First, consider your own emotional response to this situation. What personal variables and historical perspectives might assist or constrain you (and your supervisor) in response to this client? How easy would it be to talk to the supervisor about cultural borderlines (e.g., if both you and this client were graduate students) or other areas that might intersect?

The supervisee's responses to this client could range from empathy for his plight to feelings of anger about his cheating—which could be exacerbated by the knowledge that the client is in classes with some of the supervisee's friends, who might be penalized by his cheating's effect on the grading curve. If the supervisee were also studying in the United States on a student visa, then the client's situation might elicit a wide range of connectedness responses (or not).

Next, consider what your degree of comfort would be in discussing the range of reactions with your supervisor and his or her knowledge of and experience with visa and immigration issues. How open is the supervisee to discussing the varying perspectives of what is a very sensitive topic? How confident can the supervisee be that the supervisor will maintain confidentiality and not require the supervisee to disclose this information to immigration authorities?

How could the supervisee address the client's issues in the clinical session? First, it would be much easier, and more productive, if the supervisee shares his feelings with his supervisor before seeing the client again. This is one of the times when supervisee and/or supervisor self-disclosure, targeted and specific to the presenting situation, can be enormously helpful. If the supervisor were to self-disclose that she has worked with many international students and has significant empathy for the complexities of visa and mental health issues—and even describe another instance in which these issues played out—then an entrée to discussion and sharing feelings will occur. Cultural borderlines are an excellent frame for the discussion, because even the most well-intentioned therapists at times find themselves overwhelmed, or saying things that they did not intend, if the cultural borderlines and related issues were not processed and dealt with prior to therapy with the client.

The realities of the limits of confidentiality and disclosure should be carefully considered, with legal consultation as needed, to ensure that neither you nor your supervisor make promises you cannot keep (Koocher, 2009). Disclosures relating to threats of violence against others might be an exception to confidentiality. We discuss this topic further in Chapter 8.

ADDITIONAL ISSUES

In the following sections, we discuss a few specific issues that you should consider as you develop into a multiculturally competent therapist, including religion and spirituality, bilingual supervisees' experience, and the concept of social justice.

Religion and Spirituality

One often-neglected area in which clients and therapists belief structures may differ is religion and spirituality (Russell & Yarhouse, 2006). Many more clients than therapists affirm that religion and spirituality play a major role in their lives (Shafranske, 2005; Shafranske & Malony, 1990). When one considers the requisite parts of competency—knowledge, skills, and values—it becomes clear that without these, psychotherapy with clients who affirm religion and spirituality beliefs as central to their lives may be out of one's area of competence. Now consider an instance in which the supervisee is competent in areas of religion and spirituality that overlap with those of the client. In this instance, the supervisee may have greater competency to understand and proceed with integration of religion and spirituality in therapy, whereas the supervisor does not. In such a case, instead of the supervisor holding the power, the supervisee has the power of knowledge. Cultural borderlines may be effective in enhancing your knowledge and understanding as a therapist, but they need to be carefully monitored to prevent overidentification or overgeneralization.

Barnett and Johnson (2011) proposed a useful eight-step decision-making process to address religious issues and problems in therapy:

1. Respectfully assess the client's religious or spiritual beliefs and preference.
2. Carefully assess any connection between the presenting problem and religious or spiritual beliefs and commitments.
3. Weave the results of this assessment into the informed-consent process.
4. Honestly consider your countertransference to the client's religiousness.
5. Honestly evaluate your competence in this case.
6. Consult with experts in the area of religion and psychotherapy.
7. If appropriate, and clinically indicated, and client gives consent, consult with client's own clergy or other religious professional.
8. Make a decision about treating the client or making a referral.

It is important that you introduce this decision-making process and discuss it with your supervisor before use with your client.

Bilingual Supervisee Experience

Another intersection of ethics and diversity is the language competency of the supervisor with respect to the client's and supervisee's language fluency. In Verdinelli and Biever's (2009) study, supervisees reported the burden and stress that resulted from the extra responsibilities of being the only English–Spanish bilingual staff member. Some of the tasks added to the supervisees' clinical load included translating, interpreting, and educating. These responsibilities led to feelings of exploitation, isolation, and rejection, as well as concern about the quality of services the clients received. This concern led to an increased advocacy role on the part of the supervisees for the monolingual Spanish clients to try to change or streamline access to mental health services. Supervisees found few, if any, supervisors who were fluent in Spanish, leading to a power imbalance in supervision and, ultimately, conflict. Multiple-relationship issues arise when the supervisee is functioning as a translator, advocate, therapist, and cultural specialist, so the situation is transformed into an ethical dilemma (see the APA Ethics Code, 2010a, Standard 3.05, "Multiple Relationships").

Multiple ethical issues arise when a supervisor is practicing in an area of lesser competence (Campbell, Vasquez, Behnke, & Kinscherff, 2009). Although Verdinelli and Biever's (2009) study had a small sample size, in our experience a bilingual supervisee working with a monolingual supervisor is a common scenario. There are lessons to be learned. A starting point during development of supervision goals and tasks would be to determine what the supervisor can provide and what other resources are available to the supervisee and client. Transparency (e.g., disclosure) and mutuality would be well served by a frank discussion between supervisor and supervisee of realities of supervisor competence, the training setting, and their impact on the supervisory relationship. The result could be an enhanced supervisory relationship.

Social Justice

The theme of commitment to social justice, and the role of practicum and internship in its promotion and achievement, underlies respectful practice and attention to diversity in supervision and practice. Lewis (2010) provided this definition of *social justice:*

> The ultimate objective of social justice involves the fair and equitable distribution of rights, opportunities, and resources between individuals and between groups of individuals within a given society, and the establishment of relations within the society such that all individuals are treated with an equal degree of respect and dignity. (p. 146)

Most attention has been focused on skill in advocacy and intervention to promote social change as a critical component of the training process.

We believe that the requisite value of social justice, and the underlying premises of justice, human rights, and respect, are neglected components of supervision and training (Falender, 2010). In addition to counseling psychology's strong focus, the National Council of Schools and Programs of Professional Psychology adopted a motion in 2004: "Advocacy as a professional value and attitude promotes the knowledge and skills of the professional psychologist toward promoting the interests of individual clients, systems of care, public health and welfare issues, and/or professional psychology itself" (p. 1).

Advocacy is a functional competency in the Competency Benchmarks (see Appendix A). As Lewis (2010) stated, "We cannot lose sight of the fact that a true appreciation of social justice has to include a commitment to changing the social structures and conditions that are the root causes of social injustice" (p. 150). Recommendations for practicum placements include articulation in program descriptions of a commitment to social justice, provision of a working definition of *social justice*, and specific competencies to be achieved during practicum and internship. These competencies might include knowledge of the political process and setting legislative agendas—like the APA advocacy training when psychologists go to Congress to lobby—or skills for work on a particular cause coupled with reflection on that cause through the lens of social justice (Lewis, 2010). At the internship level, social justice projects could be developed with implemented strategies specific to the training site. An additional facilitating process would be reduction of *silos*, or the general tendency that neglects interdisciplinary team training; that is, enhancing collaborative interdisciplinary training that is more reflective of the work environments most graduates will be entering. Obstacles to social justice include an individualistic approach to problems and treatments as well as the desire for a value-free science (Hage, 2005).

Below is a suggested list of competencies for social justice.

- Knowledge
  - Relationship between oppressive experiences and mental illness for disenfranchised groups
  - Discrimination, violence, poverty, and oppression faced by members of minority groups and its impact on coping and heightened risk of mental health and physical health
  - Racial discrepancies in access to health and mental health care
  - Access to mental health care limited by socioeconomic status and language
- Skills
  - Engagement skills with diverse clients
  - Worldview of clients, supervisee, and supervisor and its relevance as a treatment tool
  - Consideration of components of behaviors that exemplify culturally competent treatment
- Attitudes
  - Social justice and advocacy as supervisor and supervisee roles—implicit and explicit values and attitudes
  - Relationship of therapist attitudes, communication, and worldviews and client engagement or non-engagement—and on supervisee engagement in supervision
  - Social justice as focus in supervision

PUTTING THIS ALL TO WORK

The translation of guidelines into practice is a difficult part of the supervisee's continuing development. In general, the tools and frameworks we have provided in this chapter are intended to help you integrate multicultural and diversity competence in all aspects of your practice and supervision. Multicultural and diversity competence are essential components of practice and are associated with enhanced supervisory process and satisfaction. From the outset, in your self-assessment and development of a supervisory alliance, attention to diversity factors, and reflection in general, will pave the way for this integration. As you fully understand the ethical components of doing no harm, respecting client values, and reflecting on one's personal contribution, you will be prepared to address multicultural issues. According to the Competency Benchmarks (Appendix A), individual and cultural diversity comprises "awareness, sensitivity and skills in working professionally with diverse individuals, groups and communities who represent various cultural and personal background and characteristics defined broadly and consistent with APA policy." (Fouad et al., 2009, p. S13).

5

DEVELOPING THE THERAPEUTIC ALLIANCE AND MANAGING STRAINS AND RUPTURES

How do therapists go about creating and cultivating psychotherapy relationships that work? What can they do to form a *therapeutic alliance*—a high-quality working relationship characterized by mutual trust and respect—with their clients, and how does alliance affect supervisory relationships? These are crucial questions, given the importance of the therapeutic alliance and the therapist–client relationship on treatment outcome (Norcross, 2010; Wampold, 2010), as well as the instrumental role these factors play in clinical supervision.

In this chapter, we provide an introduction to what we know about the therapeutic alliance, propose alliance-facilitating behaviors that you as a trainee should use when learning to conduct psychological treatment, identify clinical issues that affect the alliance, offer a model to resolve alliance ruptures, and discuss how supervision can help you develop the skills to build and sustain therapeutic alliances. We also address the role of alliance in the supervisee–supervisor relationship.

Where is the best place to begin? One can find some of the answers to the aforementioned questions by reflecting about the persons and relationships that have contributed positively to your life. Such relationships were likely ones that encouraged you to become the person you are, with people who had faith in the possibilities you sought to achieve; who understood your struggles, doubts, and fears; offered a realistic sense of hope; who challenged you to think differently or to try new behaviors; and, throughout these experiences, who demonstrated respect, warmth, compassion, and integrity. Similarly, these are the kinds of relational experiences therapists offer to clients that contribute in part to the effectiveness of therapy. Although there is much more to psychological treatment than a good relationship, such a relationship provides the foundation for the process of change, and although the development of an empathic, supportive relationship is neither the end-point nor sufficient in itself to bring about change, it is necessary to get the treatment underway and to sustain the therapeutic process.

A quality therapeutic alliance has consistently been found to be associated with improved client outcome (Horvath & Bedi, 2002; Horvath & Symonds, 1991; Martin, Garske, & Davis, 2000), regardless of the kind of therapy conducted or whether outcome is assessed from the perspective of the therapist, the client, or an observer (Horvath, 2001), although slightly higher correlations have been found when clients conducted the assessment and appraised the alliance strength (Martin et al., 2000).

The concept of the working alliance was introduced over 70 years ago (Sterba, 1934); however, it was Bordin (1979) who amplified its importance. He proposed that the therapeutic alliance was an ongoing creation of the client and the clinician, which concerned three interrelated features: (a) change goals and tasks, (b) bonding, and (c) strain. In his view, alliance forms through the client and the therapist as they work together to identify goals, the tasks to achieve those goals, and an emotional bond that

> grows out of their experience of association in a shared activity [and] is likely to be expressed and felt in terms of liking, trusting, respect for each other, and a sense of common commitment and shared understanding in the activity. (Bordin, 1994, p. 16)

Bordin further suggested that strain will commonly occur within the therapeutic partnership, for example, when the client's commitment to the therapy tasks significantly declines or a misunderstanding between the therapist and client occurs. Although such experiences do indeed strain the therapeutic alliance, successfully addressing strains provides opportunities for growth and may actually strengthen it. Although one might assume that relationship variables, such as empathy, likability, warmth, perceived helpfulness, would be the primary factors that influence outcome, Bordin considered the development of the therapeutic alliance to be the essential feature. The following example may help us to better understand the quintessential importance of this alliance. Many of us have had teachers or coaches or piano instructors or therapists whom we really liked, but they may not have been effective in helping us learn, develop an athletic skill, play the piano, or help us to change. What matters in therapy is that the therapist and the client (as well as the supervisor and supervisee) become engaged in a joint effort to address the client's problems (Hatcher & Barends, 2006, p. 293).

This discussion is not just academic: In our view, it is extremely practical, especially when one considers that "the amount of change attributable to the alliance is five to seven times greater than that of specific models or techniques" (Hubble, Duncan, Miller & Wampold, 2010, p. 37). In light of its importance, the clinician should pay close attention to developing the therapeutic alliance and incorporating the practices that facilitate it. Bordin's (1979) model provides both novice therapists and experienced clinicians a framework for conducting therapy, regardless of the theoretical approach chosen. We turn now to a practical discussion of how supervision can assist you as a trainee in applying this model.

GETTING STARTED: FACILITATING THE DEVELOPMENT OF THE THERAPEUTIC ALLIANCE

One of the most important aspects of this model is the emphasis it places on collaboration between the client and the therapist—not just collaboration in theory but as the basis for the therapeutic work itself. Psychotherapy is about the client and therapist actively collaborating to find solutions to the client's problems, not simply treatment a therapist administers to the client, like a medical procedure or a pill. Instead, it is about two people (or more, as in the case of a therapist working with a couple or family) working together. Edward P. Shafranske recalls the following story:

> My first psychotherapy client taught me a lot about collaboration. The community mental health agency where I was beginning my clinical training was located in a busy downtown location. It was early September, the weather was sweltering, and the building was without air conditioning. My first appointment was at 1:00 p.m. With a bit of nervousness, I greeted my client (I'll call her "Betty") and escorted her back to the office that I had been assigned to use, which was at the corner of the building. Just as I started to speak, a deafening noise rattled the walls, startling both of us: A city worker was jackhammering the sidewalk right outside the office. With no other office available (I had excused myself to check), Betty and I were faced with the struggle of talking between blasts of the jackhammer; it verged on the comical. I'd start to say something, she'd start to say something—you get the idea. We could barely complete phrases, much less whole sentences, yet we decided to continue as best we could during

that first session. Somehow we got through that session with a semblance of understanding and our wits about us. Unbeknownst to either of us at the time, that earnest effort to be heard amidst the noise, the commitment to persevere under trying circumstances, was our first act of mutual collaboration and empathic engagement, which set the stage for a fruitful course of treatment.

We aren't recommending the use of a jackhammer as a therapeutic adjunct, but we do think this story illustrates a valuable lesson about collaboration. It points to an approach that novice therapists can take in learning to conduct psychotherapy, or interns who are honing their therapeutic skills, to engage no matter the circumstance (after all, what do you have to lose?) and provide opportunities for collaboration.

The first task in the treatment process is to identify the problems that motivated the client to seek treatment. It is important to think of this not as simply an assignment to be checked off a list but rather as a process of collaborative discovery. With interest and concern, initiate psychological contact with the client by empathically listening and providing an opportunity for collaboration to be initiated. Although a list of symptoms or complaints can be readily obtained by reviewing the client's intake form, it is more valuable—essential, even—to listen to the client's story and encourage the development of the therapeutic alliance by working with the client to understand and to identify his or her goals. In our capacity as supervisors we have noticed that sometimes trainees are so anxious about getting all the information they need to complete the initial intake report that they turn the session into a fact-finding mission. In so doing, they sometimes lose contact with the individual sitting right in front of them. Don't lose the client: Stay engaged and responsive and encourage a collaboration that is aimed at what is most important to him or her; this will get the alliance off to a good start. One study indicated that clients appreciate being given "space" to collaborate or to tell their stories, and many consider these experiences critical incidents in enhancing the alliance (Fitzpatrick, Janzen, Chamodraka, & Park, 2006). Furthermore, the findings of a recent meta-analysis (Tryon & Winograd, 2011) indicated that better outcomes can be expected when the client and therapist agree on therapeutic goals. Therefore, you should begin work on client problems only after you and the client agree on treatment goals and be mindful to not push your own agenda (Tryon & Winograd, 2011).

Drawing in part on the work of Crits-Cristoph and colleagues (Crits-Cristoph, Crits-Cristoph, & Gibbons, 2010), we present in Table 5.1 a summary of therapist behaviors that, in our experience (and many are backed by empirical research as well), help teach supervisees how to foster an effective therapeutic alliance.

TABLE 5.1
Alliance-Fostering Behaviors

Domain	Behaviors
Empathic engagement	Physical presence (appropriate proximity to client; eye contact; smiling at client's greeting; looking at client, rather than at one's notes, during the session; relaxed but engaged posture)
	Psychological presence (listening, understanding, reflecting, emoting, empathizing, responding by clarifying and asking questions reflecting interest, at times "going to the heart of the matter"—circumventing client avoidance)
Agreement on goals	Socialize client to the process of therapy in early sessions
	Explain that goals may change during treatment and therefore check in frequently with the client about their continued commitment to the goals initially agreed upon at the beginning of treatment
	Link the client's beliefs, attitudes, and experiences disclosed in the session to the goals of treatment
	Regularly review goals
Personal role involvement	Examine client's the motivation to change
	Clarify, in a noncritical or nonpejorative way, the stage of change in which the client's commitment and motivation is situated
Interactive coordination	Maintain an empathic stance
	Use "we" statements
	Remind client of the "work together" that is being accomplished
Communicative contact	Use a conversational style (i.e., a back-and-forth discussion but avoiding being chatty and unfocused)
	Repeatedly acknowledge that the client is being heard
	Engage in accurate, empathic responding, using simple reflective clarifications with relatively high frequency
Bond	Maintain the following: ■ Personal role involvement ■ Interactive coordination ■ Communicative contact ■ Mutual affect

After the client's goals have been identified, it is important to reach a consensus with the client about the means to achieve the goals, that is, what the tasks of therapy will be. This step can be challenging for novice clinicians because they have not had much experience and may be uncertain as to which approach would be most helpful. Also, clients vary in terms of their self-understanding and their knowledge of therapy. Some clients have no idea about how therapy works or how to approach solving their problems and are counting on the therapist's expertise to make that determination; others come in expecting (or demanding) a particular form of therapy. It is always useful to inquire about the client's past therapy experiences (positive and negative) and about ways in which the client has successfully faced challenges in the past, as well as how he or she is coping in the present.

> *Reflection Activity.* Select one of your clients and reflect on the process by which you identified therapy goals with that individual. How did you facilitate collaboration? If this is a client you have seen for a long period of time, did the goals change? If so, how did that come about?

> *Reflection Activity.* Recall an instance when you sought assistance, perhaps as a client yourself in therapy, or from a coach, professor, or teacher. Did you feel that your goals were understood? Did you discover that your goals changed over time?

You should develop the appropriate treatment approach for a particular client on the basis of the principles of evidence-based professional practice, which include the integration of the best available research with clinical expertise in the context of the client's characteristics, culture, and preferences (APA, Presidential Task Force on Evidence-Based Practice, 2006). Supervision will provide an immediate resource to help you determine appropriate treatment options as well as to learn from your supervisor how to actually use the principles of evidence-based practice. One initial step you should take is to conduct an initial review of the psychotherapy literature that relates to the client's presenting problems. Although some researchers argue that meta-analyses have demonstrated equivalence between treatments (e.g., Duncan, Miller, Wampold, & Hubble, 2010; Wampold, 2010), others counter that there is insufficient evidence to make differential assessments of the relative efficacy of certain treatments (see the website of the Society of Clinical Psychology, http://www.div12.org). Even if treatments have been found to be equivalent, you should choose a therapy approach that reflects both your and your supervisor's expertise and considers the client's values and preferences.

You and your supervisor will work together to assess your current experience and skills and match the client's treatment to your skill set. The supervisor will expect that some treatments will be outside your level of competence. He or she will take into consideration the client's values (e.g., does the client prefer a more directive, solution-focused approach vs. a more explorative, dynamic approach?), the client's preferred form of collaboration, and the client's readiness to engage in processes of change. The key is to engage in a collaborative process that considers all of these factors and creates the best fit among the client's values, psychological capabilities, and motivation; the expertise of you and your supervisor; and the scientific literature, as applied to the client's goals. When an opportunity presents itself after that first session, you should explicitly check in with the client about his or her goals and introduce the recommended treatment approach. The presentation of the therapeutic approach incorporates what Wampold (2007) considered to be the essential aspect of psychotherapy: "that a new more adaptive explanation is acquired by the patient" (p. 862). Presenting a coherent plan can offer a sense of hope to the client and is therapeutic in itself. In keeping with Wampold's emphasis, the new understanding must be acquired by the client, not just presented by the therapist and summarily enacted. Also, Tryon and Winograd (2011) found that better outcomes can be expected when clients and therapists agree on the processes that will be used to achieve the client's goals; therefore, both you and the client should make an effort to work collaboratively to identify the therapeutic tasks and to routinely obtain feedback about the effectiveness of the processes.

> *Reflection Activity.* Recall a particular client: How did you go about determining the tasks to achieve this client's goals? Did you use the principles of evidence-based practice? How did you elicit the client's collaboration in identifying the tasks to achieve the goals?

Readiness to Engage in the Tasks of Therapy

Treatment motivation is an extremely important issue to consider in the selection of treatment as well as in the timing of interventions. Misjudging a client's readiness to engage in processes of change can lead to frustration, misattunement, and alliance strain for both the client and the therapist. Drieschner, Lammers, and van der Staak (2004) identified six factors that influence treatment that are useful to consider when assessing motivation. They are defined below along with questions to reflect on when assessing your client's motivation:

1. *Level of suffering* is a pivotal determinant of motivation; however, certain forms of psychiatric illness (e.g., major depression) can significantly impair a client's ability to use suffering as a motivator. *Have you considered the level of the client's suffering and*

whether this will serve to support the treatment or be an obstacle, leading to frustration?

2. *Outcome expectancy* logically plays a role in motivation and can be enhanced by self-efficacy. If clients strongly believe that the means to achieve their goals will result in success, and they have a strong sense of personal efficacy, then their motivation will be strong. *Have you clearly communicated to the client the goals that can be realistically achieved if the client commits to the tasks of therapy? Have you addressed all of the client's concerns?*

3. *Problem recognition* involves clients' perception that they are responsible for their behavior and their ensuing problems. Clients who externalize their difficulties and blame others are rarely motivated to change and do not engage in change processes, because, after all, "It's not my fault." *Has the client fully accepted the responsibility for his or her role in the difficulties he or she has been experiencing? Does he or she really understand that progress will primarily be based on his or her efforts?*

4. *Perceived suitability of the treatment* is influenced by satisfaction with the method and rationale of the treatment, agreement on the goals, and perception of the therapeutic relationship. Here is another way to put it: Does the client believe that this is the right treatment, focused on the right goals, delivered in the right relationship? *Have these questions surfaced and, if so, have they been adequately and collaboratively addressed?*

5. *Perceived costs of the treatment* concern not only weighing the anticipated outcomes and financial costs but also the psychological costs resulting from exposure to unpleasant emotions encountered in therapy. *Does the client believe that the benefits will be worth his or her efforts?*

6. *Perceived external pressure* concerns clients' perceptions of the pressures they might be under to commit to processes of change— or, rather, the necessity to earnestly participate in treatment. Psychologists often are referred clients who are coming to therapy only because someone is mandating their participation (e.g., courts, partners, parents, employer, school). *Has the client taken the important step of personal commitment to the therapeutic process, if even marginally? Even a commitment to a "trial run" may be sufficient to get the therapy underway. Investment is what is needed, but sometimes minimal involvement is all that is available.*

These factors are not only useful to consider when assessing a client's readiness to work in therapy, but they also can alert you to issues that will likely affect the client's motivation throughout treatment. If you fail to take into account the client's motivation, you may prematurely engage the client in processes to which he or she is not prepared or motivated to commit, leading to mutual frustration and a strained therapeutic alliance.

The *transtheoretical model of change* (J. O. Prochaska & DiClemente, 1982, 1984; J. O. Prochaska & Norcross, 2010) presents the most sophisticated and widely applied model of temporal factors in change dynamics. Originating in behavioral medicine, the transtheoretical model of change comprises a logical sequence of *stages* of change as well as *processes* of change that provide a useful guide for the process of psychotherapy. Developed on the basis of work with clients,

> the stages represent constellations of attitudes, intentions, and behaviors related to an individual's readiness in the cycle of change . . . although the time an individual spends in each stage varies, the tasks to be accomplished are assumed to be invariant. (J. O. Prochaska & Norcross, 2010, p. 492)

For our purposes in this chapter, these stages can highlight areas of potential misalignment between the therapist's objectives and interventions and the stage of change in which the client is located. The following descriptions of the stages are modified excerpts drawn from J. O. Prochaska and Norcross (2010, pp. 493–496):

- *Precontemplation*. In this stage, there is no intention to change behavior in the foreseeable future. Many individuals in the Precontemplation stage are unaware or only slightly aware of their problems.
- *Contemplation*. In this stage, people are aware that a problem exists and are seriously thinking about overcoming it but have yet made a commitment to take action. Serious consideration of problem resolution is the central element of Contemplation.
- *Preparation*. The Preparation stage combines intention and behavioral criteria. Individuals in this stage are intending to take action immediately and report some small behavioral changes. Like anyone on the verge of momentous actions, individuals in the Preparation stage need to set goals and priorities. In addition, they need to dedicate themselves to an action plan if they so choose.
- *Action*. In this stage, individuals modify their behavior, experiences, and/or environment in order to overcome their problems. Action involves the most overt behavioral changes and requires considerable commitment of time and energy. Modifications of

a problem made in the Action stage tend to be most visible and receive the greatest external recognition. People in this stage must have the skills to use the key action-oriented change processes, such as counterconditioning, stimulus control, and contingency management, to interrupt habitual patterns of behavior and adopt more productive patterns.

- *Maintenance.* In this stage, people work to prevent relapse and consolidate the gains attained during the Action stage. Stabilizing behavior change and avoiding relapse are the hallmarks of the Maintenance stage.
- *Recycling.* As is well known, most people taking action to change their behavior do not successfully maintain their gains on their first attempt. Relapse and recycling through the stages occur quite frequently.
- *Termination.* Termination of a problem occurs when a person no longer experiences any temptation to return to troubled behaviors and no longer has to make any efforts to keep from relapsing.

Although this model reflects its emphasis on explicit behavioral objectives, it can be readily applied to any form of treatment, even approaches that are primarily insight oriented because, in essence, actual behavior change (even of cognitions, which are a type of behavior) is required to solve most, if not all, problems. The importance of this model for our discussion of the therapeutic alliance is that it orients the clinician so that he or she can intervene or focus at the level of change that is appropriate. A mindful clinician is less likely to put pressure on a client or encourage behaviors on the part of the client that are poorly timed and thus avoid placing strain on the therapeutic alliance. It is not uncommon for beginning therapists, in their enthusiasm to facilitate growth (and desire to be successful), to misread the client's *desire* for change as a *readiness* to change—two completely different positions. Some thought patterns characteristic of some of the stages might be as follows: I love to eat, my pants are stretched beyond the limit, and I was just diagnosed with prediabetes (Precontemplation); I am thinking that losing weight might be an option, and I know it's my responsibility (Contemplation); but that doesn't mean I'm ready to plan (Preparation) or to change my exercise or dietary habits (Action), so don't offer me a salad—I'm just contemplating. Therapists need to be observant of where the client is at and use that knowledge to frame interventions directed at the therapeutic issue appropriate to the stage. Highly motivated graduate students who are skilled at setting goals and accomplishing them may have difficulty understanding and empathizing with clients who come in week after week, complaining about the circumstances of their lives but unwilling to make any attempts at change. We also have found that sometimes clients enter therapy with the implicit intent of not making any changes but instead prefer *thinking* about change as a pretense for actually *making* a behavior change. This can put a strain on the therapist that, if not understood and successfully managed, can result in unbridled reactivity on the therapist's part, leading to a strain or rupture in the therapeutic alliance.

In our own work, we have found that a frank conversation with clients about the stages of change, including a description of the model, can be quite helpful in normalizing clients' approaches to their problems. It is particularly useful in encouraging them to honestly see where they are in the change process. Through collaborative exploration, a therapist and client can identify the most appropriate stage of readiness in which to begin the therapy tasks. This allows the therapist to clarify what can likely be accomplished at this stage, consolidating the therapeutic alliance and averting potential alliance strain by, for example, asking the client to do more than he or she is prepared (and willing) to do. If the client does not really understand or "buy into" the framework that will direct the therapeutic process, or if the therapist's interventions are not congruent with the client's level of motivation, then alliance strains will likely occur. As we discussed in Chapter 1, it is not simply the client's readiness to change, but also the supervisee–therapist's readiness to learn, grow, and develop as a professional, that influences effective therapy outcomes.

> ***Reflection Activity.*** Reflect on a personal or professional behavior that you would like to change. Assess your motivation and the stage of change you are in with regard to that desire to change. If you were to seek help to achieve that change, what would you want your therapist, coach, instructor, or someone else, to focus on at this point in your change process?

> ***Reflection Activity.*** Recall both successful and difficult psychotherapy cases you have had. In retrospect, how did the clients' readiness to change, and your desire for them to work to achieve that change, affect the therapeutic alliance?

THE THERAPEUTIC ALLIANCE AND THE PROCESS OF THERAPY

After the therapist and client reach a consensus on the goals and the tasks the client needs to complete to achieve those goals, tailored to the appropriate stage of change, they continue their work together, striving to make gradual gains in understanding and behavior change. With the support, feedback, and guidance of your supervisor, you will learn how to tailor and apply interventions with greater and greater skill. This collaboration will facilitate the development of an emotional bond that will sustain your professional relationship with the client (and supervisor) and build the therapeutic (and supervisory) alliance. The supervisor will provide useful feedback on the pacing of the treatment and help you monitor the impacts of the interventions you are implementing and the quality of the therapeutic alliance. As we all know, however, growth is not without its challenges. As you might anticipate, some clients' motivation may wane, they may become frustrated with the slow pace of change, and/or they may give up on behaviors in which they once had faith. These may lead to feelings of disappointment in the process and in the therapist, which can cause a strain in the therapeutic alliance and may threaten the therapist–client relationship. Although there is nothing you as the therapist can do to make the climb up the mountain any less steep, there are steps that will help you anticipate the challenges along the way.

The solution can once again be found in maintaining a focus on collaboration, consistent with an understanding of the therapeutic alliance. Also, the collaborative work that is done to resolve strains and to build the alliance is often as important as achieving the original treatment goals themselves. The therapist can actively support such a process by encouraging the client to reflect on and engage in open discussions regarding the therapeutic process itself, for example, by revisiting on a routine basis the client's commitment to the therapeutic goals and eliciting feedback from the client about how the therapy is going, the therapeutic alliance, and whether the therapeutic tasks are helpful. Obtaining feedback is essential not only to encourage growth in human negotiation but also to make necessary adjustments to treatment, foster ongoing collaboration, reflect mutual responsibility for treatment outcome, and to head off strains to the therapeutic alliance.

Although we believe that soliciting feedback from clients is essential, it may not be sufficient in every case to accurately gauge the effectiveness of the therapy. Lambert (2010), an expert in outcomes management, opined that clinicians, even when provided with feedback, "do not improve in their ability to detect the important signs of a negative outcome and thereby detect who is at risk for a negative outcome" (p. 261). He advocated the use of outcome management systems on a regular basis, instruments such as the Outcome Questionnaire–45, which can provide the clinician with reliable data to assess the progress of the treatment (Lambert et al., 2004; Lambert & Shimokawa, 2011). You may have the opportunity to use these or similar instruments during clinical training. Information gained from these tools can usefully inform the ongoing dialogue with clients regarding their experience of the therapeutic process and relationship. Making use of such services also demonstrates the therapist's openness to feedback and commitment to achieving the client's goals.

Although most clinicians make concerted efforts to ensure that the therapeutic alliance is maintained, strains to the alliance will inevitably occur, and you as a trainee need to be prepared with understanding and skills to effectively address such strains. Supervision provides the primary means by which to recognize and identify signs of a strained therapeutic alliance, consider its sources, and intervene effectively. We turn now to a discussion of the causes of strains and then to a process model developed to address strains and ruptures.

ADDRESSING STRAINS AND RUPTURES IN THE THERAPEUTIC ALLIANCE

Everything the therapist does (or does not do) affects the client, influences the therapeutic alliance, and either promotes or impedes therapeutic progress. These impacts may be slight and, in the course of treatment, appear negligible, or they may shake the foundation of the treatment relationship and shut down any meaningful collaborative work. Therapist behaviors can also lead to dramatic turning points for clients, resulting in remarkable improvement. The intent of these remarks is not to ramp up your already-considerable (and understandable) anxiety but instead to normalize what in fact is actually going on. Conducting psychotherapy is challenging, and in most instances client and therapist accept that not every empathic reflection perfectly captures the richness of the client's subjective experience; neither does each intervention or homework assignment produce the desired results. In the best of circumstances, the client and therapist arrive at a consensus about the treatment goals and the means to achieve those goals and work collaboratively to obtain therapeutic results; however, strains are inevitable. Although we believe that disparities between a client's readiness to change and the treatment goals and tasks are a primary culprit in alliance strain, other differences between the client and therapist (e.g., attitudes, values, interpersonal styles) may also be at play.

Alliance Strains for Clients

Earlier in this chapter, we emphasized the potential for a weak or nonexistent therapeutic alliance due to the therapist's misjudgment of the client's readiness to participate in the tasks of the treatment. Another source of strain occurs when the therapist ignores or inadvertently devalues matters of importance to the client or is insensitive to culturally anchored experiences, traditions, moral perspectives, and beliefs. Many other situations also can create discomfort or frustration in the client, leading to a strained therapeutic alliance, including the inherent psychological pressure that is involved in psychotherapy—pressure to think, to feel, to relate, to remember, to understand, to try new behaviors—as well as the many moments when empathy doesn't capture the client's experience or interventions may be not quite apt, well timed, or effective. The client may want more or less from the therapist: more direction, less direction, and so forth. He or she may feel controlled, when engaged in a highly directive form of treatment, or may question the usefulness of purely experiential or explorative approaches. It's easy to be out of sync. A lot of toes get stepped on during this therapeutic dance.

Although our discussion to this point has focused on challenges the client may feel, we must point out that strains in the therapeutic alliance are not caused by a one-directional process: Strains can be triggered in therapists by clients just as readily as in clients by therapists. For example, we cannot imagine that a trainee or an experienced clinician would not be affected by a client who consistently rejects, corrects, criticizes, and belittles every attempt by the therapist to be responsive and therapeutic. Both parties in the therapeutic relationship are under pressure, and the dynamics in the relationship may lead to strains in the therapeutic alliance.

Alliance Strain for Trainees

Clinicians as well as clients feel pressure when conducting psychotherapy. This is due to the inherent challenges in developing an alliance out of thin air, so to speak, relating empathically with someone you have just met, coming up with therapy goals and a plan to achieve those goals, working through obstacles to change, managing your own personal reactions to the client, and so on. Also, as a supervisee, you will be doing all this while being evaluated. That's a tall order. Supervisors understand, and they empathize with the legion of demands and pressures that are on their trainees; after all, they faced the same challenges and likely experienced many of the same personal anxieties, doubts, and frustrations (as well as, of course, the satisfaction that comes from helping clients work through suffering and change the course of their lives) when they were trainees themselves. Supervision can not only provide oversight to ensure the best care of the client, it also can normalize a trainee's experience, provide support as well as provide training and feedback to advance the therapeutic process.

Therapists feel strain when clients disengage from the therapeutic tasks and present their complaints as problems that the therapy (and the therapist) is not solving. Frustration with the lack of gains in treatment, client resistance to actively participate in the tasks, interventions that fall short, and so on, can all strain the therapeutic alliance between the clinician and the client. When faced with a therapeutic impasse, therapists often become reactive, less sensitive, and act in ways that potentially may injure the alliance. Frustrated trainees may resort to name-calling (e.g., "that 'borderline' patient"), or subtly distance themselves from the relationship and the treatment process. Although this withdrawal is an understandable reaction, it is exactly the wrong thing to do. Both in supervision and therapy sessions, one needs to engage with even more commitment and reinitiate processes that strengthen the therapeutic alliance. Careful attention to reactivity (or countertransference), including processing one's personal reactions with a supervisor, can diffuse the situation and preempt a rupturing of the therapeutic alliance. Supervisors can also help supervisees identify and address the causes of the impasse.

Some clients present with serious psychological difficulties and deficits in their ability to relate to others. Although we recognize that these personality-based interpersonal difficulties are the very reasons that are bringing them into treatment, their modes of relating will nevertheless trigger reactions in most clinicians and pose significant challenges in forming a therapeutic alliance. For example, clients with hostile–dominant personalities have been found to be less likely to form positive therapeutic alliances, and those with a personality disorder that included histrionic, narcissistic, antisocial, and paranoid features had difficulty in forming and maintaining alliances (Betan, Heim, Conkin, & Westen, 2005). It is challenging for clinicians, regardless of their years of experience, to facilitate the development of an adequate and intact therapeutic alliance with such clients, especially those diagnosed on the borderline–narcissistic spectrum.

Novice therapists may be particularly vulnerable to the provocative behaviors these clients often display. Conducting treatment with such clients, with whom the therapeutic alliance is at best precarious, may lead to feelings of anxiety, fear, helplessness, incompetence, self-criticism, and so on. The therapist, in an attempt to regain a sense of stability, may disengage from the client or try to control the therapeutic interaction, which often escalates the volatility in the relationship. The therapist may begin to feel the very same "out of control" state of mind of the client. It is hard, as Rudyard Kipling once wrote, "to have your wits about you while all others are losing theirs and blaming it on you." The barely formed (or forming) alliance is at most risk in these situations.

Among the most important things therapists can do is to keep their wits about them, paying attention to and working on managing their reactivity. This can be accomplished several ways: by taking a stance of curiosity, reminding oneself that this is a great "training case" (one for the textbooks), and decentering (e.g., taking a step back from reacting, to interrupt the cycle of misattunement, which often escalates client behavior). It is important that, when working with clients who are prone to emotional and behavioral instability, you work closely and openly with your supervisor to process your experiences, ensure your own safety, and learn how to manage rather than act out your reactions. One certainly must monitor risks to the self and others. Although being prone to reacting to provocation is understandable, it is important to adequately contain your emotions and respond to the client appropriately. This will lessen the possibility of a ruptured therapeutic alliance and precipitous termination of treatment.

Thus far, our discussion has touched on situations, both commonplace and rare, that often result in strains in the therapeutic alliance for both client and therapist. Regardless of the root cause, it is crucial to address the strain with the client. Supervision provides the means to help you develop skill in understanding and resolving alliance strains and ruptures, a skill that will be used throughout your clinical career. This includes the supervisor helping you identify signs of strain by reviewing videotapes of therapy sessions, encouraging self-reflection activities, normalizing and accepting the experiences of strain, and giving examples and practicing intervention strategies in role plays to address strains. It is useful to always keep in mind that treatment not only proceeds on the foundation of a strong alliance but is also advanced through the successful resolution of alliance strains.

> *Reflection Activity.* Recall a challenging clinical case and reflect on the nature of the strains for the client and for you. What were the essential causes of the strains? How did you recognize the strains?

ADDRESSING STRAINS/RUPTURES IN
THE THERAPEUTIC ALLIANCE

We begin this section by reaffirming the premise that alliance strains are natural phenomena within the treatment process. Given the demands of the therapeutic process, it is not surprising that both parties at times feel strain. In fact, isn't that the case with most close relationships, whether professional or personal? Strains and crises in therapeutic relationships inevitably evoke a host of personal responses in novice clinicians, who may be at a loss as to what to do and uncertain of how to effectively address negative reactions and impasses. Safran and Muran (2000a, 2000b) and others (Aspland, Llewelyn, Hardy, Barkham, & Stiles, 2008; Katzow & Safran, 2007) have provided clinical models that inform our present discussion regarding the means to resolve alliance strains and ruptures. Safran (2009) offered a number of cogent clinical pointers:

- Therapists should be aware that patients often have negative feelings about the therapy or the therapeutic relationship that they are reluctant to broach for fear of the therapist's reactions. It is thus important for therapists to be attuned to subtle indications of ruptures in the alliance and to take the initiative in exploring what is transpiring in the therapeutic relationship when they suspect that a rupture has occurred.
- It appears to be important for patients to have the experience of expressing negative feelings about the therapy to the therapist, should they emerge, or to assert their perspective on what is going on when it differs from the therapist's.
- When this takes place, it is important for therapists to attempt to respond in an open or nondefensive fashion and to accept responsibility for their contribution to the interaction.
- There is some evidence to suggest that the process of exploring patient fears and expectations that make it difficult for [therapists] to assert their negative feelings about the treatment may contribute to the process of resolving the alliance rupture. (p. 2)

Hill and Knox (2009) found in their review of the literature that having a good relationship before the event that produced the strain makes it easier to resolve the strain: "Furthermore, several client actions seem to facilitate successful resolution, most notably exploring feelings about the relationship. In contrast, client hostility, pathology, and defensiveness hinder resolution" (p. 21). Safran, Muran, Stevens, and Rothman (2008) suggested three types of skills required for the therapist to be able to constructively negotiate alliance ruptures: "a basic capacity for self-acceptance (or at least an ability to work toward it), a willingness to engage in an ongoing process of self-exploration, and a capacity to engage in genuine dialogue with the client" (p. 137).

It is important to also consider that clients and therapists may not always experience interactions in identical ways, so alliance strains can easily be missed or misconstrued. That said, over time a therapist can begin to grasp the client's unique vulnerabilities and the therapeutic partnership can be strengthened by addressing and resolving strains. Also, resolving strains and ruptures not only repairs and revitalizes the alliance but also helps "clients develop a fuller understanding of how they construe events and how that construal effects their interaction with others, and to provide them with a new experience of relating" (Safran et al., 2008, p. 138).

How Supervision Can Help

Values, rather than knowledge or skill, play the elemental role in the therapist's ability to effectively address strains and ruptures in the therapeutic alliance. First, a therapist must value the client and be committed to the client's well-being. This establishes the foundation for the therapist to be fully open to understanding the client's experience from the client's perspective, without defensiveness. This may sound easy, but it actually is not. We can comfortably hear our clients' complaints about others in their lives, but it isn't quite as easy to hear about their doubts in the treatment we are providing, their questioning of our abilities, moments of misattunement, misunderstandings, and so on. It takes real openness to explore with the client what is and is not working in the relationship.

Edward P. Shafranske recalls successfully working through a strained therapeutic alliance:

> [The client said,] "I know you're bright and well trained and everything, but sometimes I think you really don't get it. It's like you care, but only because you are supposed to, that's your job. Sometimes I feel like you aren't really emotionally there; maybe that's an inadequacy you have. But when I feel that, I don't want to be here." It was hard not to react, to defend myself, to assert my care and to cite evidence for my emotional attunement. But that would have been taking care of myself and not the client. It took values and signature strengths (as well as good training) to respond empathically and to share that I understood how hard it must be when she experienced me in those ways. With genuine curiosity (and care), I asked if we could look together at moments when she experienced me as "emotionally not there." She described a point in a session when she felt I was dismissive and nonresponsive, and although that wasn't my own experience, I listened earnestly (as best I could), tried to resonate with her experience, and reflected. We spent a number of sessions on this subject and gradually worked through the strain. The alliance strengthened, and it gave us further opportunity to work constructively together.

Undoubtedly, knowledge, clinical skill, and experience have important roles in effective psychotherapy, but values set the stage for a respectful, open discussion of the client's experience to take place. You as a trainee show your values when you bring into supervision the challenges you are facing. Supervisors know personally the challenges of psychotherapy and will not be surprised to learn of therapeutic impasses, strains, difficulties, and so on: They would be surprised (and, frankly, concerned), if a trainee never reported such experiences.

Your supervisor can initially help you by normalizing the experience of the strain, offering empathic understanding, and guiding and supporting you in the process of resolving the alliance strain or rupture. Supervisors can be helpful in three important ways: by (a) collaborating with you to identify the initial sources and nature of the strain; (b) empathizing with and processing your reactivity, which may have contributed to the rupture; and (c) providing support and clinical direction to initiate resolution. An initial aim is to help you shift from a *reactive* state to one of *responsiveness* so that you can begin the task of understanding the events and dynamics creating the strain. Although therapist reactivity or countertransference may have played a role in the strain, we believe it is more useful for you, as a supervisee, to focus first on the relational dimensions of the clinical interaction. This is because you need to quickly gain an understanding of the interpersonal transactions taking place in order to stop the negative interaction and begin to attempt to repair the therapeutic alliance. This is best done by maintaining attention on the here-and-now interactions in the session rather than by speculating on the role previous relationships may have played in priming the client to experience the therapist in a particular way.

Supervision also provides training in a systematic approach to address the alliance strain with the client and provides oversight and guidance throughout the process. The resolution of strains and ruptures to the therapeutic alliance is based on the therapist's use of *metacommunication*, which involves explorations of the interpersonal experience taking place in the therapy relationship and requires the therapist to "step outside of the relational cycle that is currently being enacted" (Safran & Muran, 2000a, p. 108). In other words, metacommunication is a process by which the therapeutic process itself, including the therapist's behaviors as experienced by the client, is explored. It does not initially aim at correcting misperception, misunderstanding, and clarifying intent; it first encourages disclosure about the impact of the therapist and the therapy on the client and how that is influencing the therapeutic alliance.

RESOLVING ALLIANCE STRAINS AND RUPTURES: A PRACTICAL GUIDE

In this section we present a model that draws on the work of Safran and Muran and their colleagues (Safran & Muran, 1996, 2000a; Safran, Muran, Samstag, & Stevens, 2001; Safran et al., 2008), and a theoretical model advanced by Aspland et al. (2008). We draw liberally from Aspland et al.'s *rational model*, as it is called, and construct a version that retains each element but collapses Aspland et al.'s steps into three major stages. The model we describe next intends to provide a user-friendly, practical guide that you can use to better understand and resolve alliance strains and ruptures (see Figure 5.1). We also incorporate into our discussion the contributions from Safran et al. (2008),

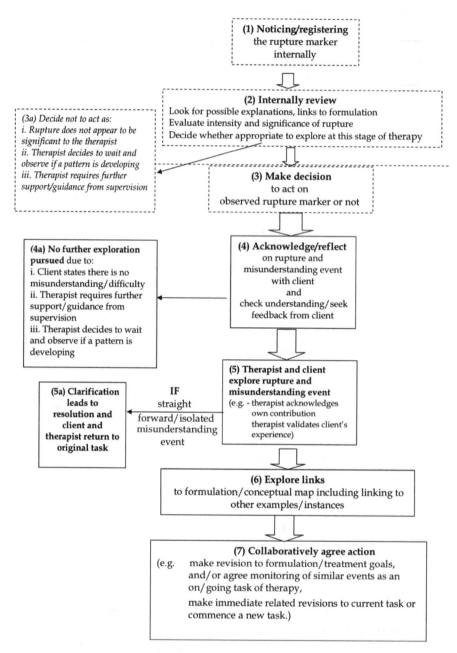

Figure 5.1. The rational model. From "Alliance Ruptures and Rupture Resolution in Cognitive Behavior Therapy: A Preliminary Task Analysis, by H. Aspland, S. Llewelyn, G. E. Hardy, M. Barkham, and W. Stiles, 2008, *Psychotherapy Research, 18*, p. 704. Copyright 2008 by Taylor & Francis. Reprinted with permission.

which place particular emphasis on relationship dynamics. Although we present the stages sequentially, in practice the process is more dynamic, with the focus going back and forth on the basis of the unique unfolding of the therapeutic process.

Stage 1: Identifying the Strain/Rupture Marker

The process of resolution begins with the therapist noticing the strain in the alliance, which may manifest as subtle changes in the client's level of engagement or dramatic signs of deterioration in the therapeutic relationship. Strain/rupture markers include emotional withdrawal, lessening the frequency or depth of disclosures, missing sessions, minimal compliance with the agreed-on tasks of therapy, and so on. The therapist should draw on his or her skills in self-awareness (attention to internal states), affect regulation (tolerating negative emotions), and interpersonal sensitivity (empathy with the client's experience) when recognizing signs of alliance strain and then begin the process of metacommunication (Muran, Safran, & Eubanks-Carter, 2010).

The therapist then internally reviews these changes, evaluates the intensity of the strain or rupture, and looks for possible explanations. There are many reasons why strains occur. Safran et al.'s (2008) orientation emphasizes the interactions in the relationship that result in the client's perception that the therapist's behavior confirms "his or her dysfunctional or pathogenic expectations about relationships" (p. 139). We have found in our own work that strains/ruptures can occur because of frustrations encountered by clients when attempting to change their perspectives or behaviors or when the client experiences interventions as unhelpful.

The therapist then considers whether it is appropriate, at this stage in the therapy, to explore the marker. He or she then decides whether to direct the client's attention to the strain/rupture marker and commence metacommunication. The first stage in the process primarily involves the therapist's observations, self-awareness, and reflection. Although therapists might reflect and make a decision at this time, we find that it usually is more helpful for the trainee to first bring his or her observations of the strain/rupture marker into discussion with his or her supervisor. Through the collaboration within supervision, possible explanations for what's going on can be examined and a decision can be made about the appropriateness of focusing the therapeutic process on the strain. Supervisors must take into consideration not only the ability of the client to engage in metacommunication but also the supervisee's ability to do so. Sometimes it is best to not address the marker directly but to have the supervisee self-correct (with the supervisor's help) any behaviors that might have contributed to the strain/rupture.

Stage 2: Mutually Explore the Strain/Rupture

After deciding to bring the strain/rupture marker into the focus of therapy, the therapist should draw attention when strain reappears in the relationship, or initiate a discussion with the client, sharing his or her obser-vations of what seemed to be changes in the client's behavior or emotional engagement. It is crucial in drawing attention to the rupture marker to do so in a way that does not criticize the client; instead, the therapist should offer observations tentatively and with the intent of understanding the client's experience. As Safran and Muran (2000a) observed, clients may at first deny that any strain or rupture has occurred. Initiating metacommunication requires at least a modicum of an alliance, and the therapist may need to encourage the client to disclose moments when a misalliance is perceived as well as empathically share what he or she (i.e., the therapist) considers might have led to the strain. Therapists must be prepared to acknowledge their own contribution to any strain and to validate the client's experience. In some instances, they will discover that they have in fact made a mistake (e.g., incorrectly noted the time of an appointment, been insensitive to a client's experience or impatient with the client). Hill (2010) provided help-ful suggestions, based on her review of the literature, to therapists addressing negative therapeutic events with their clients:

- If therapists make a mistake, they can apologize, accept respon-sibility for the mistake, and change the offending behavior.
- If therapists are working with clients who express hostility, they can try to empathize and connect with these clients, help the clients talk about their anger, provide an explanation for their behavior to help clients understand it better, and attribute problems to relationship issues rather than to personality prob-lems on the part of the clients.
- If clients do not overtly express anger but therapists suspect that the clients are angry, therapists can help clients explore the possible anger and relate the anger to other situations. (p. 70)

After both the therapist and client understand and have clarified the strain, they can either return to the therapeutic tasks or further examine the alliance strain/rupture within the context of other relationship experiences. In the spirit of alliance building, it is important that the therapist follow the client's lead, that is, keep in mind what the client's goals and tasks are at the present time. Therapists should not impose their interest in examining how the strain/rupture parallels past similar relationship difficulties but should listen for the client's desired solution so that together they can begin to reestablish or strengthen the therapeutic alliance. There will be time to explore these relationship schemas later in therapy, but only if the client remains in treatment. Again, the therapist should follow the client's lead as to how to reestablish an empathic connection and a viable therapeutic alliance.

Safran et al. (2008) offered a useful perspective for understanding what often causes alliance strains and ruptures. According to their view, in cases of strain and/or rupture the therapist has become embedded in a relational cycle with the client, which is compromising the therapeutic alliance. The client is now experiencing the therapist (and the treatment) in a more rigid and negative light. Also, in the context of Bordin's (1979, 1994) theory, the client may divest from the therapy tasks, feeling frustrated with the rate of progress and disillusioned that he or she can actually change or that his or her life situation can change. The therapist may also get caught up in the frustration, leading to a lack of optimism and confidence that the client's goals can be achieved. Through reflection and the help of a supervisor, the therapist can begin to recognize the pattern in which he or she and the client have become entangled. There is no doubt that a client's preexisting interpersonal schemas can play a role in his or her interpretation of the therapist's behavior, but directing attention initially on this material may be experienced as avoidance on the therapist's part or an attack, further exacerbating the strain. The focus should first be directed to the interpersonal events from the client's point of view that contributed to the strain.

It is important to always keep in mind that the client (as well as the therapist) is likely to feel increased vulnerability and exposure when engaging in metacommunication. After a strain/rupture, clients often use forms of withdrawal, which removes them from a subjective sense of danger; others may become confrontational. In both instances there is disengagement from the therapeutic process and relationship. The therapist's invitation to participate in metacommunication asks the client to reengage, to have enough trust to work with the therapist to understand and resolve strains in the relationship. The process also demands of the therapist the ability to be genuinely open to hear the client's experience and to respond instead of react. This requires both parties to tolerate feelings of vulnerability. Supervisors can help supervisees to stay engaged and to be prepared to empathically respond to the client's experience.

If the client is willing and able to explore the links between the strained/ruptured therapeutic alliance and past interpersonal events, then client and therapist gain a bit of distance from the embedded interactional cycle that is causing to strain. In the best of circumstances, they can see how they were both trapped in a negative process, which neither intended. With insight and the benefits of successfully collaborating in the process of metacommunication, the therapeutic alliance can be reinvigorated, the goals and the tasks of the treatment can be reaffirmed, and thus the work can continue.

Stage 3: Reestablishment of the Goals, Tasks, and Therapeutic Alliance

The last stage in the resolution model involves either a recommitment to or a revision of the therapy goals and a discussion of the means to achieve the goals. Both parties having benefited from the experience of having worked through (to the extent possible at the time) a strain/rupture; now they can renew their collaboration and get back to work on the tasks of therapy. They also have a better sense of the kinds of experiences that can derail treatment and, in the best of circumstances, they can use their experience of the strain constructively. As you can see, this approach is deeply rooted in Bordin's (1979) original theory and, from a relational perspective, the therapist's acceptance of and openness to the client's experience can lead to enhanced trust as well as facilitate growth in the client's relational capabilities.

ALLIANCES AND THE SUPERVISORY RELATIONSHIP

Alliances also play a central role in clinical supervision. The same general principles apply: The alliance will form through the process of mutually identifying training goals and the means to achieve the goals. With this in mind, it is important that supervisees and supervisors work collaboratively and not assume that they are in agreement about expectations or needs when they in fact may not be. This requires both the supervisor and supervisee to engage in open and honest discussion about the supervision process. This is probably a bit easier for the supervisor, because she or he is not being evaluated. Supervisees can contribute by actively discussing their training needs and learning preferences and sharing feedback, when asked, about the supervision process (i.e., what is working well and what is not). Most supervisors are highly committed to supervision, enjoy working with supervisees, and desire to form a working alliance. Supervisors want to be successful and to be in positive supervisory relationships, just as much (and sometimes more) than their supervisees. In Chapter 3, we presented numerous examples of the practical things you can do to build a good alliance with your supervisor.

Just as in therapeutic and other relationships, misalliances and strains can occur in clinical supervision. There is great complexity in the roles and responsibilities supervisors have, and this can lead to strains. Just as it is important for supervisors to appreciate the demands and challenges the supervisee is facing, so too is it helpful that you remember that supervisors are juggling multiple responsibilities: to the client (their primary responsibility), to the supervisee, to the academic program, to the profession, and so on. The challenges, frustrations, and worries in case management, especially when therapy is not going well or there are particular risks (e.g., a client's potential danger to self and/or others) all exacerbate the pressure under which supervisors function. Also, strains occur when expectations are not met or individuals' interpersonal or learning styles are out of sync.

For supervisees, just learning to conduct therapy places them in situations of pressure. Misalliances in the supervision can readily occur, for example, if the supervisee perceives the supervisor as not being supportive, engaged, and/or competent; not giving the supervisee what he or she needs; and so on. Challenges in case management directly affect the supervisee, and strains can emerge quite easily when supervisor and supervisee are struggling to address client safety or therapy impasses.

Also, conflicts that the client brings to therapy can be activated in both the therapeutic and supervisory relationships. Although the mechanisms are not completely understood, parallel processes can occur in which the maladaptive ways in which the client relates to significant others in his or her life are repeated in the therapy relationship and then emerge in the supervision relationship. For example, the frustration and powerlessness a client might feel in a relationship in which he or she has limited influence is repeated in the therapy relationship, with the therapist feeling just as ineffectual as the client. This relationship schema then gets repeated in supervision, with the supervisor feeling ineffectual and frustrated with the supervisee. Such dynamics obviously create strain in the alliance. The antidote is for both supervisor and supervisee to metacommunicate their experience, to obtain a bit of distance so they can view the dynamics within the context of the supervisee's relationship with the client. Although not every misalliance is caused by parallel processes, this theory can provide a way of looking at patterns in the supervisory relationship.

CONCLUSION

Psychotherapists are in the business of human relationships, and the foundation for their work rests to a great extent on their ability to facilitate the development of and maintain an effective therapy relationship. In this chapter, we have emphasized the role of the therapeutic alliance, as well as supervisor–supervisee alliances, and described the processes by which such alliances are formed, the common strains and ruptures that can imperil the therapeutic relationship, and approaches to repair such strains. In our view, the ability to foster and sustain therapeutic alliances rests on interpersonal competencies, but in itself it is a clinical competence that can be developed and practiced.

6

THE USE OF THE SELF
IN PSYCHOTHERAPY

The carpenter has a hammer, the surgeon has a scalpel, the therapist
has the self.

—Jeffrey A. Hayes and Charles J. Gelso (2001)

An essential aspect of learning how to function as a psychotherapist
is developing competence in the appropriate use of the self. Unlike the carpenter or the surgeon, who develop mastery of the tools of their trades in a fairly
technical, perhaps even unemotional fashion, developing proficiency in psychotherapy involves learning how to apply one's psychological capacities when
conducting treatment. This is because psychotherapy is fundamentally an interpersonal process. Therapists must learn not only how to identify appropriate
interventions but also how to tailor these interventions to their clients' present
emotional states, motivation, and psychological capabilities, all while keeping
in mind the possible impact they are having on the therapeutic relationship and
alliance. This requires various specific skills. Fortunately, these skills can be
learned and developed through good clinical training. In this chapter, we examine two of the most interesting and important aspects of psychotherapy and
clinical training: (a) how personal factors influence psychological treatment
and (b) how supervision can help the student or intern learn the appropriate
use of the self when functioning as a clinician.

Many years ago, Carl Rogers (1957) proposed six "necessary and sufficient conditions" to achieve therapeutic personality change, and at the top
of his list was the requirement that "two persons are in psychological contact"

(p. 95). Subsequent research, particularly more recently, has pointed to the wisdom of Rogers's early observations about the importance of the relationship for the effectiveness and outcome of psychological treatment (Lambert & Barley, 2001; Norcross, 2010; Norcross & Lambert, 2005; Orlinsky, 2010). One of the central features of an effective therapeutic relationship is the ability of the client and therapist to form and maintain a therapeutic alliance (Horvath & Bedi, 2002; see also Chapter 5, this volume). This is certainly a collaborative enterprise; however, the clinician bears the professional responsibility to do what he or she can to ensure the development and health of the relationship. This is where personal factors come in. Developing a quality therapeutic relationship (or, for that matter, any relationship) requires a host of interpersonal skills, among which the capacity to understand another's experience, to empathize, to emotionally connect, to communicate effectively, and to be self-aware all figure prominently. Each of these capacities is used in conjunction with the technical clinical skills that psychologists develop. In addition, therapists must develop self-awareness of the unique personal factors that influence their understanding of and relating to the client as well as their ability to effectively use clinical interventions.

MAKING CONTACT AND EMPATHIC UNDERSTANDING

Regardless of whether one is practicing cognitive behavioral therapy, psychodynamic treatment, or strategic family therapy, the clinician must establish *psychological contact* with the client and develop a therapeutic alliance. This alliance has long been considered essential to therapeutic progress across all therapies, including cognitive behavioral therapy (Castonguay, Constantino, McAleavey, & Goldfried, 2010). Developing a therapeutic alliance can be challenging because many clients are seeking help because they have conflicts or deficits in relating with others or have suffered in ways that make trust and transparency exceedingly difficult. Also, therapists' own conflicts or personal reactions may interfere with their ability to maintain psychological engagement. The abilities to form a therapeutic relationship and to empathize draw primarily on the clinician's *interpersonal* and *intrapersonal* competencies instead of on clinical technique. Although clinical training informs the ways in which therapists formally structure the therapeutic interaction, the ability to empathically engage clients is based on personal competencies, which we suggest are affected by many past and present personal factors. These factors may serve as a source of identification with the client, leading to empathy, or they may get in the way of understanding the client from the client's point of view. Therapists may become *reactive* to the client, that is, having thoughts and feelings that lead to forms of subtle disengagement that may become so activated (in what has been referred to as *external countertransference*) that their conflicts or internal disquiet leads to inappropriate action. The salient point is that the process of psychotherapy is always affected in some way by the uniqueness of the therapist as a person. We turn now to a brief discussion of how personal factors influence the nature of a therapist's approach to understanding and relating to his or her client.

When clinicians conduct psychotherapy, they use a number of interrelated interpersonal skills: They listen attentively, track emotions, pay attention to nonverbal behavior, and reflexively respond to feelings stimulated in them by the clinical interaction. They also monitor the quality of the therapeutic relationship and intervene in ways to make clients (and themselves) feel more comfortable, to facilitate psychological exploration, and to establish an alliance. These skills become more refined over time through clinical training and practice. They also use simultaneously a number of intrapersonal competencies, although these psychological operations are usually outside of an individual's conscious awareness. Therapists make meaningful the complex stimuli that the client is presenting, including his or her words, gestures, mannerisms, facial expressions, and emotional tone, as well as their own emotional reactions and associations to these stimuli. They organize this information almost instantly (neuroscientists would estimate in a matter of milliseconds) and construct a mental representation of the person who is sitting before them. Emotional reactions of therapists are communicated through their facial expressions before they are even conscious of their feelings. In the course of clinical training, therapists get better at processing the wide range of information generated within the clinical setting as well as become more adept at managing the emotional arousal that is an inevitable part of a therapist's experience. Each therapist possesses a distinct array of interpersonal and intrapersonal competencies that he or she uses when relating with others and in his or her work as a psychotherapist.

These interpersonal and intrapersonal competencies develop out of the distinctive features of therapists' personal lives as they have been shaped by genetics, one's unique individual constitution, environment, culture, and history. Countless interpersonal experiences set the stage for how therapists engage with clients. The internal working models of what constitutes a relationship, which people develop early in life, will likely affect how therapists relate to their clients as well as how they organize their perceptions of clients' behavior in therapy. Other factors rooted in personal and cultural experience, such as beliefs and values, also will contribute to a therapist's ability to effectively be attuned to his or her clients' subjective experiences. Clinical training builds on these psychological capacities and helps supervisees learn how to best use and further develop their relational skills as well how to manage personal reactions to clients.

In our own work, we have found that in therapeutic relationships, as in our personal lives, there are some people with whom we relate well and others with whom we struggle to make a connection. Some relationships seem to bring out the best in our ability to relate, whereas with other clients we may scratch our heads and wonder whether we (or they) possess any interpersonal competence at all. We do not relate to each client equally well or in the same way. We also have found that there are certain issues or situations that may affect our ability to stay in psychological contact with the client in a given moment in treatment. For example, therapists may become overwhelmed by the emotional content when hearing clients' stories of trauma and thus reflexively disengage, either by overidentifying or by withdrawing. If therapists' evaluate the situation carefully, they often find that although their inter- and intrapersonal abilities may seem to be fairly stable traits, personal factors (which are often outside of one's awareness) influence their ability to maintain psychological contact and to empathically understand their clients. Similarly, a therapist's ability to effectively work with a client, to use clinical interventions, and even to understand or reflect on a case or discuss it in supervision, may be influenced by personal factors. As the saying goes, we all have issues, and those issues can and will affect a therapist's ability, for the better or worse, to empathically engage with certain clients around certain issues. This is an inevitable reality in the clinical practice of psychology.

We have found that many kinds of personal factors influence our own professional behavior, because one cannot leave one's personal self outside the consulting room. Fortunately, clinical supervision provides a means of identifying these influences, of becoming familiar with their effects, and of using this awareness to enhance the supervisee's ability to meaningfully and therapeutically engage with the client.

In the following section we provide an overview of the nature and common effects of personal factors on the therapeutic process; introduce a contemporary, transtheoretical approach to countertransference; and present the practical ways in which supervision can help the supervisee to identify and manage potentially harmful personal reactions in both therapeutic and supervisory relationships. We also provide Reflection Activities throughout to enhance self-awareness.

THE INTERFACE OF PERSONAL AND PROFESSIONAL FACTORS

It is commonly acknowledged that personal as well as professional factors influence the conduct of psychotherapy and the development and maintenance of the therapeutic alliance (see Chapter 5, this volume). The term *professional factors* refers to knowledge, skills, and attitudes/values obtained through graduate education, clinical supervision, consultation, and so on—in essence, all of the influences from exposure to the field of psychology. Personal factors, as we just discussed, are integral to the ways in which therapists understand and relate to their clients. One solution to defining *personal factors* would be to simply state that any factors that are not explicitly professional are personal. Although this statement is not incorrect, further explication is needed. Personal factors involve the fundamental ways in which people relate to themselves and to others. This includes how we experience and process emotions; the predominant schemas we use to organize interpersonal relations; and the *worldview*, or global life meaning, that informs our beliefs, values, and assumptions and establishes our goals, which in turn shape motivation and personal satisfaction. Although genetics and one's unique individual constitution certainly play a role in one's individual psychology, for the purposes of this discussion we place particular emphasis on the role of the environment, emphasizing nurture over nature. A rich panoply of contextual influences inform individual development and produce lasting impressions that affect how a person relates, empathizes, thinks, understands, emotes—every aspect involved in human relating. One should never underestimate the enduring role of family, culture, and society on one's personal and professional lives. On this point we wrote the following:

> Each of us, well before we ever entered graduate school or met our first client, formed fundamental ways of relating to others. We assimilated family and culture-bound styles of interpersonal relating, internalized attitudes and beliefs about human nature, and absorbed the worldviews and mores of the ethnic, social, political, cultural, intellectual, gendered, economic, and spiritual communities in which we inhabited. These inescapable frameworks of identify, forged out of interaction with the surround, establish fundamental assumptions about self and others, ethical values, and instill a feeling-sense of being at home in the world . . . Our personal identities reflect dynamic, emergent sources of meaning and motivation . . . we may question (and even reject) the original constituents of our multicultural identities; however, the imprint of these seminal influences remains. (Shafranske & Falender, 2008, p. 98)

How therapists sit with their clients, the emotions that get stirred up in them, the thoughts that are conjured up, the prejudices that reveal themselves, the heartbreaks they have denied, the fantasies that trouble or delight them, how they listen, how they care: All of these are shaped by all of the aforementioned factors as well as by education and clinical training. What can one take from this perspective?

All Understanding Is Perspectival

One practical implication of this perspective is that therapists must pay close attention to the impressions they form about their clients, including the assumptions they as clinicians make, as well as be mindful of potential differences in modes of relating, values, and lifestyle between their clients and themselves. For example, a doctoral student who prizes independence and views personal responsibility, autonomy, and individual accomplishment as hallmarks of maturity may misjudge and potentially pathologize a client from a collectivist culture who makes decisions that are based primarily on the value of interdependence and in consideration of what is good for the family, instead of striving for individual achievement. Another way of putting this is that therapists need to keep in mind that their understanding is always *perspectival* and bears the "inescapable influence of [their own] personal interests, commitments and the cultures out of which [their own] personal meaning is constructed" (Falender & Shafranske, 2004, p. 83). They need to be careful to not implicitly (or explicitly) hold the notion that their own values are universal or intrinsically superior to those of another culture. Sometimes therapists give lip service to this but have not truly examined their biases. This perspective is offered not simply as an interesting (or, for some, a controversial) point of view; instead, it is intended to actually inform practice—to be applied. For example, in the Competency Benchmarks (see Appendix A, this volume), one criterion for readiness for practicum is "Respects and shows interest in others' cultures, experiences, values, points of view, goals and desires, fears, etc." (p. 224). Therefore, it is important in clinical training to actively consider the personal factors that influence one's own understanding and worldview and to cultivate interest in and respect for (although not necessarily agreement with) other worldviews. It is an expectation in clinical supervision that supervisees will demonstrate an openness to considering these issues and will actively reflect on the ways in which contextual factors influence the client's (and therapist's) perceptions of the client's difficulties as well as consider the implications for a course of treatment that is sensitive to the values of the client.

> *Reflection Activity.* Reflect for a moment on your own values and motivations. What motivates you? What do you believe makes for a good life? What role do the following play in regard to your personal goals and satisfaction: relationships, family, achievement, financial success, religious faith? How did you come by the values you hold? Can you think of anyone who holds different values? How do you react when someone you know hold values completely different from your own?

> *Reflection Activity.* Think of examples of clinical situations in which you observed or realized later that your own worldview was different from that of a client and had influenced assumptions you made. How did that realization influence your future work with the client?

Emotional Responsiveness and Relationship Schemas

We turn briefly in this section to consider what science can teach us about personal factors that influence basic psychological functioning, specifically, their role in emotional responsiveness and interpersonal relating, two aspects of critical importance for the applied psychologist. Consider the following example:

> Mr. M is a 57-year-old Pacific Islander, originally from Guam, and a Navy veteran. He reports that his doctor referred him to the outpatient clinic because he has difficulty sleeping: He either sleeps all day, too tired to get up and about, or he can't sleep at all. Beth, a 23-year-old Latina graduate student in counseling psychology, asks about recent events in his life, and Mr. M begins quietly talking about the death of his wife 2 years ago and how he feels confused about whether he should now return home to Guam or remain here in the United States. She listens quietly as Mr. M begins to tell his story, and she notices herself almost becoming tearful, but she remains calm, and when he shifts the discussion to how easily he could buy a large house in Guam, she gently challenges him to stay with his emotions.

Now, imagine the same opening but with a different therapist:

> John, also 23, a Caucasian graduate student in the same program as Beth, is immediately concerned when he hears that Mr. M is having difficulty sleeping, and he initiates a series of questions intended to clarify whether Mr. M is suffering from major depression. When Mr. M begins to talk briefly about his wife's death John listens quietly but does not ask about his affect; after Mr. M mentions the opportunity to buy a big house in Guam, John listens and initiates a discussion on the reasons why Mr. M might consider such a move and how he feels when he imagines being back home. He thought in the moment that it was good that Mr. M was thinking about a forward-looking plan and wanted to reinforce such thinking. Mr. M appeared initially a bit more animated, but then his mood dropped, and he said he couldn't imagine how he would ever be able to make such a big move, let alone clean out his house. John isn't certain in the moment as to what to say or do; like Mr. M, he feels stuck.

These vignettes involve one client, two therapists, and two different beginnings of treatment. Both students are sincere, thoughtful, genuinely caring, and equally well trained. What could lead to such radically different therapeutic processes in the first 15 minutes? Of course, there are many possibilities, especially because this is a hypothetical illustration: There could be differences in the supervisees' treatment orientation, supervisor, and so on. We return to this material in a moment to illustrate a point.

It is a truism that experiences in childhood have a significant impact on later psychological development and functioning (although the nature of the impacts and sorting out the multiple factors that produce such effects are complex topics, subject to ongoing debate and scientific investigation). The interpersonal and intrapersonal capacities that we discussed earlier in this chapter bear the influences of early experience and socialization. For example, there is strong empirical evidence that cultural and familial factors play significant roles in how a person will come to both appraise and express emotion. Scientists have found that although there is strong evidence for the universality of emotion, cultures vary in both judgments about emotion as well as rules for the display of emotional expression. For example, some cultures calibrate the emotional expression of anger to facilitate regularity and order. Collectivist cultures foster displays of emotion to ingroup members that facilitate harmony and relatively less expression of anger (Matsumoto, Yoo, & Chung, 2010). Researchers also have found that family dynamics influence the development of emotional regulation and socialize the nature of emotional expression based on the gender of the child (Morris, Silk, Steinberg, Myers & Robinson, 2007). Consider the socialization experiences Beth and John likely had and the role family and culture may have played in shaping their emotional sensitivity and display tendencies that led them to quite different responses to Mr. M. For example, in the description of John's behavior, it appeared that he moved away from affective experience and quickly jumped to explore Mr. M's ideas about actions to take instead of stopping and exploring Mr. M's feelings related to the loss of his wife. This focus on adaptive cognitions could have been a matter of professional judgment; then again, John might have been more comfortable focusing on that material rather than the affect-laden cognitions related to the death of Mr. M's wife. There are, of course, many other factors that influence one's ability to experience, accurately judge, and express the complete array of emotions, including, in this example, professional factors related to what each of the students believed at the moment to be the proper therapeutic direction.

Recall that in the illustration Beth (unlike John) experienced a wave of powerful emotions after Mr. M's disclosure of his wife's death. Imagine for a moment that Beth was just getting over a breakup of an intimate relationship when she had her session with Mr. M. Might her own experience of loss have played a role in her experience of empathy, and was her emotional reactivity exclusively based on concern for Mr. M? If that were indeed the case, it illustrates the highly personal nature of therapist empathy that sensitizes clinicians in a very real way to relate emotionally to their clients.

Experimental research has found that close emotional relationships influence people's experience of present relationships (Chen, Fitzsimons & Andersen, 2007). Furthermore, people appear to be prone to selectively attend to features in the present relationship that they expect, on the basis of past relationships. For example, if a client had just been involved in an angry confrontation with a loved one in which they were criticized, he or she may be primed to interpret a therapist's inquiry about a missed session as a hostile criticism from the clinician. This transfer of knowledge from past significant-other relationships to help one make sense of current interpersonal experience is common in everyday life (Berk & Anderson, 2000). We suggest that the intensity of the therapeutic interaction provides an environment that is particularly well suited to the activation of emotion-laden schemas. A relationship schema of personal loss may have been activated in Beth and influenced her organization of her experience of Mr. M. Her affective reactivity might have been much different toward Mr. M if she had not recently suffered a loss herself. Experimental research has helped professionals better understand the nature of therapists' personal reactions to clients, which some label *countertransference*. This is consistent with the perspective found in schema-focused therapy: therapists' cognitive, affective, and behavioral responses are likely influenced by their own schemas (Young, 1999). Clinicians need to gain as much awareness as possible about the situations or client behaviors that will likely activate (or have triggered in the past) relational schemas that evoke strong personal reactivity. Such awareness does not prevent activation, but it does provide some context to understand the reactions the therapist is having.

This brief discussion was intended to illustrate how personal factors—in this instance, those based on cultural and gender-based family dynamics related to emotion and the activation of relational schemas—affect clinicians' interpersonal and intrapersonal functioning and thus influence their empathic relation to and psychological contact with their clients. These dynamics do not suggest signs of psychopathology in the clinician but instead reflect normative psychological processes. In training, supervisees have the opportunity to gain awareness of their interpersonal and emotional dispositions, particularly through reviewing videotapes, eliciting the observations and feedback of their supervisors, and self-reflection.

> *Reflection Activity.* Reflect for a moment on your interpersonal relationships, recalling any situations that appeared to have triggered automatic responses on your part. Which situations provoked the strongest emotional reactivity in you? Now think of any clients who triggered such reactions in you. How did you address this with your supervisor or manage the situation in session? If you have not yet begun to see clients, consider job situations or relationships with friends or acquaintances in which you experienced strong emotional reactions. How did you understand and address these reactions?

Values and Signature Strengths

In our view, too often the values and strengths of graduate students and interns are overlooked or given short shrift, yet these personal factors play an immeasurable role in the development and career of a psychologist. The values that inform an individual's decision to enter this profession are important, and important to consider.

The American Psychological Association (2010a) places at the beginning of its "Ethical Principles of Psychologists and Code of Conduct" a set of five General Principles that reflect the values of the profession and to which all psychologists should aspire: (a) Beneficence and Nonmaleficence, (b) Fidelity and Responsibility, (c) Integrity, (d) Justice, and (e) Respect for People's Rights and Dignity. There are, of course, many other values and aspects of character that invigorate and give personal meaning to those who enter this profession. We believe it is important for graduate students and intern supervisees, as well as practicing clinicians, to reflect on the values that inform their commitment to the profession and its ideals. Such deliberate reflection can remind one of the values that gave rise to those commitments and can bolster one's motivation when things get tough. We also believe it is useful for supervisees to reflect on their strengths (some of which include values), because the ability to self-assess is an important professional competence and because identifying such positive qualities will strengthen them.

> *Reflection Activity.* Albert Schweitzer (1935), physician and philosopher, once wrote, "I don't know what your destiny will be, but one thing I do know: The only ones among you who will really be happy are those who have sought and found how to serve"(p. 235). These words are meaningful to us, the authors.
>
> Reflect for a moment on the values that informed your decision to become a psychologist. What are the sources that inspire you, and who are the psychologists or persons who exemplify these values?
>
> In Exhibit 6.1 we present the list of Signature Strengths identified by psychologist Martin E. P. Seligman (2002). We invite you to review the list and identify your Signature Strengths.

We have asserted that personal factors play a significant and inevitable role in psychotherapy. We turn now to a discussion of the potential impacts of such factors and introduce distinctions between effects that may support and enhance the therapeutic process and reactions that may strain the therapeutic alliance and jeopardize treatment.

EXHIBIT 6.1
Signature Strengths

Wisdom and Knowledge
1. Curiosity/Interest in the World
2. Love of Learning
3. Judgment/Critical Thinking/Open-Mindedness
4. Ingenuity/Originality/Practical Intelligence/Street Smarts
5. Social Intelligence/Personal Intelligence/Emotional Intelligence
6. Perspective

Courage
7. Valor and Bravery
8. Perseverance/Industry/Diligence
9. Integrity/Genuineness/Honesty

Humanity and Love
10. Kindness and Generosity
11. Loving and Allowing Oneself to be Loved

Justice
12. Citizenship/Duty/Teamwork/Loyalty
13. Fairness and Equity
14. Leadership

Temperance
15. Self-Control
16. Prudence/Discretion/Caution
17. Humility and Modesty

Transcendence
18. Appreciation of Beauty and Excellence
19. Gratitude
20. Hope/Optimism/Future-Mindedness
21. Spirituality/Sense of Purpose/Faith/Religiousness
22. Forgiveness and Mercy
23. Playfulness and Humor
24. Zest/Passion/Enthusiasm

Note. Data from Seligman (2002).

RESPONSIVENESS, REACTIVITY, AND COUNTERTRANSFERENCE

As we have discussed, personal factors have their greatest impact on a therapist's ability to empathically engage with a client. When a client tearfully speaks of a personal loss, a trauma, an achievement, and so on, an attuned therapist will respond not by offering a "textbook" answer but by communicating empathy, drawing on his or her own personal understanding of the situation and as informed by appropriate clinical technique (perhaps like Beth in the fictitious illustration presented earlier). It is the clinician's ability to be emotionally engaged and to use both personal and professional competencies that facilitates understanding and contributes to the client's sense of being understood. Empathic understanding of the client is similarly required when using manualized treatment protocols to ensure that interventions are well timed and appropriate to the capabilities of the client at the given moment. In sum, personal factors are integral to the therapeutic process and contribute to the appropriate responsiveness of the therapist.

However, there are situations in which a therapist responds in a *reactive* rather than a *responsive* manner. One such instance might occur when the therapist becomes overly emotionally aroused with a particular client or by experiences that the client is describing or reliving, which often can occur in treatments that focus on trauma and abuse. In such a state of reactivity clinicians lose their therapeutic bearings and, instead of using their emotional arousal in the service of empathic responsiveness, act in a manner to reduce that arousal. Such maneuvers result in the loss of psychological contact with the client that in turn forestalls empathic engagement and may compromise the treatment. We suggest that what has happened in such an instance reflects momentary suboptimal intrapersonal functioning. A therapist in a heightened state of arousal is unable to sufficiently contain or process the emotional input, becomes overwhelmed and, in an attempt to reestablish emotional and psychological equilibrium, moves away from the source of the arousal. All of this occurs rapidly and without conscious mediation or intention. Wilson and Lindy (1994) suggested that becoming overwhelmed might be a normal initial reaction, and it is thus understandable for therapists to withdraw or to have difficulty maintaining empathy when processing traumatic events with clients, especially therapists who have a history of personal trauma.

To illustrate further, in a small study of university doctoral students in Texas (Adams & Riggs, 2008), about one third had experienced personal trauma. One quarter of the students were working with trauma clients but had no previous specialized training for working with that population. The students in the study showed a predominance of healthy coping strategies. An adaptive defense style (which involves the use of humor, sublimation, and suppression) was associated with the lowest levels of vicarious trauma symptoms, regardless of a student's own trauma history, whereas a self-sacrificing defense style (a need to maintain an image of the self as kind, helpful, and never angry) was associated with higher vicarious trauma (Adams & Riggs, 2008). Recommendations for supervisees include ensuring adequate training in trauma interventions before treating clients, self-assessing prior trauma history as a potential factor in one's emotional reactivity to clients' presentation of trauma, and introducing the reactivity as a personal factor in supervision as it relates to specific client work.

From this description you might imagine a dramatic interpersonal scene in therapy, but this is rarely the case. Although the internal psychological dynamics are dramatic, the behavioral manifestations may be as commonplace as changing the subject, momentarily suspending attention, becoming distracted, or shifting the focus from emotional processing to intellectualization. Nevertheless, such shifts away from affective resonance break the psychological contact with the client. Again, we intend this not as an admonition, because such reactions are outside of one's volition, but rather as a reminder to prepare yourself to be sensitive to and mindful of these dynamics.

Another situation that may prompt high therapist reactivity is one in which a relational schema in the therapist is activated within the therapeutic relationship. Once again, research on implicit social cognition (Chen et al., 2007) indicates that past experiences can readily activate a relational schema. This can result in the therapist misperceiving the client's intentions, leading to heightened emotional arousal or threat, which activates, within the context of the schema, the therapist's defenses. Therapists who are identified as high in rejection sensitivity may be particularly prone to automatic self-protective reactions. In this case, it is primarily the activation of a relational schema, instead of emotional overarousal, that produces therapist reactivity.

The aforementioned discussion of reactivity is directly related to a construct we briefly mentioned earlier, commonly referred to as *countertransference*. These two terms (i.e., *reactivity* and *countertransference*) describe a fundamental equivalence in the phenomena being described. The distinction primarily is found in the theoretical assumptions, derived from psychoanalytic clinical theory, that are closely tied to the construct of countertransference and for the most part are absent in our use of the term *reactivity*. In our view, reactivity focuses on what is experienced by the therapist, whereas countertransference involves speculation about unconscious conflicts, motivations, and defenses in the intrapsychic life of the therapist. Some clinicians and supervisors find countertransference a bit off-putting because of its historical connection to psychoanalysis. Furthermore, it has been our experience that supervisees are often confused by the many perspectives presented within psychoanalytic theory and end up misapplying the concept, for example, believing that any feelings at all about a client constitute countertransference. We think it is best for supervisees to focus on what differentiates countertransference from other personal reactions or, in our language, what differentiates *reactivity* from *responsiveness*.

Kiesler (2001) identified countertransference as "distinctly different, unusual or idiosyncratic acts or patterns of therapist experience and/or actions toward a client [that constitute] deviations from baselines" in the therapist's usual practice (pp.1061–1062). Countertransference heightens emotional reactivity in the therapist, resulting in nonreflective, and at times unintended, actions, which, in the extreme, threaten the therapeutic alliance and imperil the treatment (Shafranske & Falender, 2008).

When one observes countertransference in oneself, two questions logically emerge: (a) What's going on? and (b) Where are these reactions coming from? Psychoanalysts have dedicated considerable effort attempting to arrive at definitive answers to these (See Table 6.1 for a summary of the various perspectives on these questions; see also Gabbard, 2001, and Shafranske & Falender, 2008). In brief, the therapist's reactions may originate in his or her unresolved conflicts or reflect basic ways of relating to significant others, which may or may not be stimulated by the client's transference or reflect reactions to pressure that is placed on the therapist to respond to a particular role. These positions are considered examples of *subjective countertransference*. Alternatively, countertransference has been viewed as either the creation of the client, who, through the use of *projective identification*, projects mental contents onto the therapist or, in a somewhat similar vein, as attempts by the client to evoke feelings in the therapist that the client cannot tolerate. One perspective that has particular clinical relevance is *objective countertransference*, in which the therapist's reactions are seen to be responses to "the actual personality and behavior of the patient based on objective observation" (Winnicott, 1949, p. 45) and reflect reactions generally elicited in others by the client's maladaptive behavior. Research has found that clients with personality disorders do invoke similar reactions in those with whom they interact, giving some support to this notion (Betan, Heim, Conkin, & Westen, 2005); however, it is difficult to imagine that the dynamics of the therapist are not somehow involved. Finally, perspectives drawn from social constructivism subsume countertransference within a larger framework of *intersubjectivity*, whereby client and therapist and the dynamic interaction that is created mutually construct psychic experience and thus no single origin of countertransference can be specified (Hoffman, 1992). From outside of psychoanalytic theory, Gelso and Hayes (2007) used an interactional model to point out how client actions can trigger emotional and behavioral reactions as areas of therapist conflict are activated; Young (1999) applied a schema-based approach in which maladaptive emotional schemas are stimulated by client behavior; and Bandura, Lipsher, and Miller (1960), demonstrated that when clients display emotions that are anxiety inducing for the therapist, therapists use avoidance, which is then reinforced. Personal factors influence the therapeutic process through their impact on therapist responsiveness and reactivity or countertransference. Regardless of the specific interpretative stance or language chosen to describe these effects, it is crucial for all clinicians to commit to a process of self-discovery to better understand the intertwining of personal factors and professional training in the conduct of psychotherapy.

TABLE 6.1
Historical and Contemporary Perspectives of Countertransference (CT)

Perspective	Description	Historical background
CT as transference to the client's transference	Involves the psychotherapist's emotional response to the client's transference, which is an obstacle to clinician objectivity and interferes with treatment.	Freud's original viewpoint, commonly referred to as the *narrow* perspective. CT originates in the psychotherapist's unresolved issues.
CT as the total emotional responsiveness to the client	Involves the psychotherapist's total responsiveness to the client, seen as primarily originating in the client and a useful source of information to help understand the client.	First proposed by Heimann (1950), who highlighted the usefulness of the clinician paying attention to his or her emotional reactions to help provide insight into the client's dynamics; this is commonly referred to as the *broad* or *totalist* perspective. CT originates in the client.
CT as projective identification	This is an intrapsychic process, involving fantasy, in which the client's mental contents are projected onto the psychotherapist, evoking emotional reactions in the clinician.	Klein coined the term *projective identification*, in which the client projects intolerable aspects of self experience onto the psychotherapist (Klein, 1946). Later theorists suggested that interpersonal pressure applied by the client influences the psychotherapist to further identify with the client's projections (Sandler, 1976). CT originates in the client.
CT as objective CT	Emerges as an emotional response on the part of the psychotherapist to the client that is similar to that of other persons in the client's life.	Identified by Winnicott, *objective CT* reflects the characteristic responses of others when relating to the client that provide important information about the ways in which the client affects others and the nature of the relationships that the client forms (Winnicott, 1949).
CT as enactment	When the psychotherapist acts with the client in a complementary manner that actualizes the client's transference and the psychotherapist's CT responses.	Interpersonal and intrapsychic pressure originating in both the client and the psychotherapist results in the enactment of a role. Both the client and the psychotherapist contribute to CT enactment.

(continues)

TABLE 6.1
Historical and Contemporary Perspectives of Countertransference (CT)   (Continued)

Perspective	Description	Historical background
CT as an expression of intersubjectivity	The psychotherapist's total responsiveness to the client is influenced by the psychotherapist's subjectivity, the client's subjectivity, and the unique relationship and interaction that develops between them.	This postmodern perspective places emphasis on the conscious and unconscious coconstruction of meaning by client and psychotherapist, including multicultural factors and individual differences and similarities, which influence the therapeutic relationship at all times.
CT as schemas derived from a therapist's personal history	Schemas shape therapists' cognitive appraisals and response tendencies about the self, others, and situations.	*Schemas* are cognitive representations of one's past experiences or situations that influence information processing, emotional responses, and behavior. Therapist schemas may lead to cognitive distortions, selective attention, and maladaptive interpersonal and emotional functioning. Emphasis on conscious cognitive processes is found in the related notion of *therapeutic belief systems* (Rudd & Joiner, 1997).
CT as a schematic mismatch and over-match	The schemas that the therapist contributes to the therapeutic relationship may inadvertently corroborate and reinforce the client's maladaptive schemas.	*Schematic mismatch* and *over-match* refer to conditions in which the therapist's schemas about therapy and relationships either confirm the client's negative personal schemas and conditions in which similarities in schemas produce complementary interpersonal reactions. Emphasis is placed on the interaction of the schemas, somewhat similar to the psychoanalytic conception of role responsiveness.

CT as an interference	Personal reactions may interfere with the therapist's ability to be fully present to the actual experience of being with the client.	Although value is placed on the the therapist's authenticity, CT can draw the therapist away from contact with the client or may interfere with the development of unconditional positive regard.
CT as a consequence of therapist interface within the family system	Personal reactions are evoked as the therapist is drawn into the family's dysfunctional pattern of relating.	This perspective subsumes concepts of transference and CT and highlights the multiple forces (e.g., partial identifications, family-of-origin issues, power dynamics) that influence the therapeutic interaction and the nature of the clinician's responses.
CT as the therapist's internal or external reactions originating primarily in the therapist	Involves subjective experiences and emotional responses that originate from unresolved conflicts and psychological vulnerabilities stemming from past and current relationships and experiences.	This transtheoretical perspective places emphasis on the role of the effects of unresolved conflicts and vulnerability that are triggered in the therapeutic relationship and are manifested by forms of avoidant behavior by the therapist.
CT as idiosyncratic acts or patterns of therapist experience	Comprises distinctly different or unusual experiences and responses that differ from the usual baseline of therapist behavior.	This transtheoretical perspective that places emphasis on the phenomenology of CT.

OPPORTUNITIES, EXPECTATIONS, AND CHALLENGES

Clinical supervision provides the setting in which supervisees develop a greater understanding of the ubiquitous influence of personal factors within professional practice; to identify particularly salient attitudes, beliefs, and relational experiences that shape a therapist's response tendencies; and to learn to manage reactivity or countertransference, which may pose threats to the therapeutic alliance. Although not intending to in any way be a form of, or substitute for, personal therapy, supervision does offer an opportunity for supervisees to deepen their understanding of the response tendencies that emerge in professional consultation.

Supervision also fulfills its obligation to monitor the quality of client care by carefully attending to a supervisee–therapist's responsiveness and reactivity, which, as we have discussed, play a critical role in treatment outcome, as mediated through the therapeutic alliance (see Chapter 5, this volume). Similarly, supervisors bear the responsibility to help the supervisees develop competence in "awareness of inner emotional experience" as noted in the Competency Benchmarks (see Appendix A). Every supervisor has his or her own approach to personal factors or countertransference. This is determined by the supervisor's chosen theoretical orientation, personal experiences in training, and the degree of focus the supervisor places on understanding the client and performing case management or in placing emphasis on the supervisee's reactions to the client and on training in general. Therefore, supervisees should not be surprised when they encounter variability in their training; however, it still is their responsibility to develop competence in this dimension of professional practice regardless of your supervisor's predilections.

The following points may usefully inform the supervision of personal factors and the management of therapist reactivity or countertransference (Shafranske & Falender, 2008). Many supervisors hold these perspectives, which will be useful for you as a supervisee to consider:

- It is expected that supervisees, similar to experienced clinicians, will experience countertransference reactions and that such experiences are not uncommon in psychotherapy.
- Personal reactivity or countertransference is not viewed as a failure on the part of the supervisee but instead provides an opportunity to learn about the interaction between the client and supervisee as well as therapist personal factors, which may affect other therapeutic relationships.
- Personal reactivity or countertransference is an informer of the therapeutic process and can provide important insight into the client's relational world, the therapist's relational world, and the relational schemas or internal object relations affecting the

therapeutic relationship. Countertransference has been viewed as having a sort of double helix shape (Epstein & Feiner, 1979): Even when therapist reactivity can potentially damage the therapeutic relationship, it can provide an opportunity to enhance understanding and for the client and therapist to develop increased interpersonal competence in resolving any potential misalliance.

- Reactions, which differ from responsiveness, may elicit positive and/or negative responses in the therapist and take the form of distinctly different, unusual, or idiosyncratic acts or patterns of therapist behavior and/or actions toward a client. It is useful to emphasize the behavioral and interactional dimensions instead of automatically applying theory-based, experience-distant explanations.

- Therapist reactivity may be manifested in actions of the therapist that could negatively affect the client and jeopardize the therapeutic alliance. In light of the responsibility to ensure client welfare, supervisors may intervene to ensure appropriate care.

- How supervisees address and manage countertransference reactions is more important than the fact that they occur.

- Any exploration of supervisee personal factors and therapist reactivity must be specifically related to the conduct of the treatment provided by the supervisee. The boundary between supervision and psychotherapy must be maintained when addressing countertransference reactions.

- Collaborative review of audiotapes and videotapes as well as live supervision provide important means of assisting the supervisee in identifying the influence of personal factors and reactivity.

- Clinical competence includes an awareness of personal factors that influence the therapeutic process as well as skills in effectively bringing countertransference reactions into the service of the treatment. The supervisee is expected to demonstrate a commitment to further develop self-awareness within the supervisory process.

To encourage the examination of personal factors and reactivity in supervision, supervisors may model awareness of personal factors through self-disclosure, inquiring about your personal reactions to clients when discussing cases or reviewing audio or videotapes, and/or explicitly including attention to personal factors and countertransference as a performance requirement in the supervisory contract and perhaps as an area that will be evaluated.

IDENTIFYING AND MANAGING REACTIVITY

We suggest that the ability to identify and manage reactivity is a developmental process that requires commitment and trust on the supervisee's part, sufficient self-awareness, and the provision of a safe and supportive environment by the supervisor. There needs to be a consensus between the supervisor and the supervisee that one of the goals of supervision will be to develop greater awareness of the influence of personal factors and the management of countertransference. It is also useful to consider and discuss the practices of the supervisor and supervisee that will constitute the means to achieve the goal, for example, reviewing videotapes and self-reflection activities. The linchpin in the process will be how the supervisor and supervisee collaboratively work together and maintain an environment of safety and trust while observing and exploring reactions, which may at times be uncomfortable. Rest assured that most supervisees, when reviewing videotapes with their supervisors, initially feel uncomfortable (as did their supervisors when they were in training), but in time one acclimates to the process, and in our own work as supervisors the majority report later that such experiences were some of the most valuable in their training. Personally, we experience a great deal of respect for our supervisees when they really dive into the process of exploration, because we know such a willingness and commitment to self-reflectivity will lead them to become excellent clinicians.

In addition to reviewing tapes and the collaborative work done in the supervision sessions, you can begin to develop habits aimed at increasing self-awareness by committing to a process of reflection immediately after each session with a client. We are not talking about writing up case notes—we mean taking an opportunity to quietly reflect on moments in the session when you experienced a particular affect state, felt uncomfortable, acted in ways that were different from your usual style of practice, and so on. We find it helpful to recall a specific moment as clearly and viscerally as possible while resisting the temptation to quickly and intellectually figure it out. In doing this reflection, allow that moment to once again become vivid in your mind, and just allow thoughts and feelings to emerge with curiosity and acceptance rather than judgment (somewhat similar to mindfulness practice). It can then be helpful to jot down notes to yourself (not case notes) and then consider clinical theories you have learned to facilitate a more complete understanding on your part. With practice, you can begin to identify the personal factors that are most salient to your relating with clients. The following Reflection Activity provides stimulus questions that may be activated at times during your clinical work.

Reflection Activity. In Exhibit 6.2 we present a number of questions and statements intended to elicit personal reactions and associations to help you enhance your self-awareness of issues that may trigger reactivity. If you choose to review these questions, be aware that you may experience moments of discomfort as well as insight. The questions touch on subjects that clinicians often deal with as reflected in the literature and are drawn from our experiences as clinicians and supervisors.

In Table 6.2 we present cognitive schemas that may be evoked when working with clients. Identify the schemas that are most likely to be activated in your own clinical work.

EXHIBIT 6.2
Self-Reflection Activity on Personal Reactions

1. Recall any out-of-the-ordinary reactions to clients (e.g., anger, frustration, boredom, excitement).
2. Recall experiences that, when spoken about by clients, or witnessed by clients, aroused out-of-the-ordinary reactions in you.
3. Recall any clinical situations in which you behaved in a manner different than usual (e.g., ended the session late, disclosed personal information).
4. Reflect on personal factors of which you are quite proud and enjoy having others know about you.
5. Recall personal factors that you find difficult to think about or to reveal.
6. Reflect on your reactions to the following issues or clinical situations:
   - The kinds of people you were attracted to as a child, adolescent or adult.
   - The kinds of people whom you couldn't stand as a child or adolescent or can't stand as an adult.
   - Collecting fees.
   - Setting a boundary, such as refusing a person's or a client's request.
   - Feelings of sexual attraction toward a client or feelings of sexual attraction directed towards you.
7. To whom do you find yourself more or less attracted to in terms of gender, sexual orientation, race, culture, religion, and/or politics?
8. Recall a time when you felt embarrassed.
9. How do you feel when you witness or are told about family violence, trauma, or a sexual attack?
10. How do you feel when you are in a situation of competition? Is it OK to lose, to be wrong, or to win?
11. Which of your clients would you like to have a personal relationship with, and why?
12. Which situations move you to tears? Arouse you to anger? Bore you?
13. Are you relieved when a particular client cancels? From what internal experience are you being relieved?

TABLE 6.2
Therapist's Schema Questionnaire: Guide

Schema	Assumptions
Demanding standards	I have to cure all my patients. I must always meet the highest standards. My patients should do an excellent job. We should never waste time.
Special, superior person	I am entitled to be successful. My patients should appreciate all that I do for them. I shouldn't feel bored when doing therapy. Patients try to humiliate me.
Rejection-sensitive	Conflicts are upsetting. I should not raise issues that will bother the patient.
Abandonment	If my patient is bothered with therapy, he or she might leave. It's upsetting when patients terminate. I might end up with no patients.
Autonomy	I feel controlled by the patient. My movements, feelings, or what I say are limited. I should be able to do and say what I wish. Sometimes I wonder if I will lose myself in the relationship.
Control	I have to control my surroundings or the people around me.
Judgmental	Some people are basically bad people. People should be punished if they do things wrong.
Persecution	I often feel provoked. The patient is trying to get to me. I have to guard against being taken advantage of or hurt. You usually can't trust people.
Need for approval	I want to be liked by the patient. If the patient isn't happy with me, then it means I'm doing something wrong.
Need to like others	It's important that I like the patient. It bothers me if I don't like a patient. We should get along—almost like friends.
Withholding	I want to withhold thoughts and feelings from my patients. I don't want to give them what they want. I feel that I'm withdrawing emotionally during sessions.
Helplessness	I feel I don't know what to do. I fear I'll make mistakes. I wonder if I'm really competent. Sometimes I feel like giving up.
Goal inhibition	The patient is blocking me from achieving my goals. I feel like I'm wasting time. I should be able to achieve my goals in sessions without the patient's interference.
Excessive self-sacrifice	I should meet my patients' needs. I should make them feel better. Patients' needs often take precedence over my needs. I sometimes believe that I would do almost anything to meet their needs.
Emotional inhibition	I feel frustrated when I'm with this patient because I can't express the way I really feel. I find it hard to suppress my feelings. I can't be myself.

Note. From *Overcoming Resistance in Cognitive Therapy* (p. 256), by R. L. Leahy, 2001, New York, NY: Guilford Press. Copyright 2001 by Guilford Press. Reprinted with permission.

Therapist Disclosure

One area for special consideration related to personal factors concerns therapist disclosure to clients. Think for a moment about your opinions about therapist disclosure. Do you think that disclosure is helpful? Can a therapist ever *not* disclose? What would you feel comfortable disclosing to a client, and what would you not feel comfortable disclosing? The answers to these questions more than likely reflect your theoretical commitments, experiences as a client and as a therapist, and your supervisor's guidance. A recent qualitative review of the literature (Henretty & Levitt, 2010) reported that over 90% of therapists self-disclose to their clients, and although there are arguments for the potentially positive impact of disclosure, the extant empirical research is quite divergent, limiting definitive recommendations for practice. Great complexity exists regarding the context of disclosure, unique factors that contribute to decisions to disclose, cultural factors, and so on, including potential negative effects of refusing requests for disclosure. Peterson (2002), in writing about the ethics of self-disclosure, noted that therapists must carefully take into consideration the possible impacts and realize that the self-disclosure may not have the desired effects. Spontaneous, nondeliberative self-disclosure suggests therapist reactivity. As in any situation in which reactivity manifests itself in behavior, the therapist should pay careful attention to the nature of the reaction and the dynamics within the therapy relationship. Referring back to the metaphor of the double helix, although such events pose a potential risk to the therapeutic alliance, processing the factors and experiences associated with the unintended self-disclosure in supervision can yield an understanding of heretofore-unrecognized dynamics.

A Model for Processing Countertransference

Learning to manage personal reactivity or countertransference is an extremely important competence developed in supervision. Lack of awareness of countertransference reactions can lead to unwitting misattunement as well as to actions on the therapist's part that may damage the client and compromise the treatment. Because countertransference reactions can be subtle and fly under the radar screen of one's consciousness, collaboration (i.e., with the supervisor) is often required in addition to committed self-reflection to initiate a process in which reactivity can be identified, understood, and appropriately managed. Again, the goal is not to eliminate a clinician's spontaneity or empathy but to become mindful of one's reactions and to learn to discriminate between *responsiveness*, which is usually done in the service of the treatment, and *reactivity*, which often comprises a form of disengagement from the client. In supervision, you will have the opportunity to learn how to recognize countertransference, to understand the contexts in which therapist conflicts or sensitivities may be activated, and to better manage such tendencies in the future. Sometimes, supervisees become aware in the moment that a reaction has been activated, and they can bring the episode to supervision to gain a better understanding of it; however, most of the time it is in supervision that you begin to recognize the signs of reactivity. When reviewing a recording of a session, you and your supervisor will have the opportunity to observe and reflect on both verbal and nonverbal behaviors, emotional reactivity or withdrawal, and conflicted interactions or disengagements by either party that point to countertransference. In the following sections we outline a process to help supervisees manage reactivity. It is drawn from a number of sources (including Bouchard, Normandin, & Séguin, 1995; Ladany, Friedlander, Nelson, 2005; and Shafranske & Falender, 2008) and can be usefully applied in supervision.

State 1: Responsiveness and Engagement

State 1, responsiveness and engagement, refers to the normal and usual course of treatment in which psychological contact with the client is occurring and empathic engagement is facilitating the therapeutic process, regardless of how it is theoretically conceived. The therapist is emotionally involved, may be experiencing a host of reactions throughout the session, and is empathically responsive to the client. This responsiveness not only helps to communicate to the client that he or she is understood but also leads to the appropriate, well-timed identification and use of interventions that are tailored to the needs of the client in the moment. Bouchard et al. (1995) referred to this as an *objective-rational state*, because the therapist may have the subjective impression of engaging with the client from a position of objectivity, as if personal factors were not influencing the interaction.

State 2: Reactive

In State 2, the therapist *reacts* rather than empathically *responds*. As discussed earlier, this state may be triggered by emotional overarousal (e.g., when hearing emotion-laden material, as in the case of child and sexual abuse or trauma), by a therapeutic interaction in which unresolved conflicts in or vulnerabilities of the therapist are activated in the therapist (Gelso & Hayes, 2007), by strains and conflicts aroused in the therapist by role-responsiveness demands of the client (Sandler, 1976), or by the emergence of maladaptive relational schemas in the therapist (Young, 1999). In State 2, the therapist disengages from actual psychological contact with the client through emotional withdrawal or overidentification with the client's experience. Again, such disengagement can be quite subtle, as the therapist directs attention away from experiences with the client that are overarousing or causing conflict.

State 3: Identifying the Marker and Being Reflective

State 3 is initiated by the development of an awareness that something has gone awry: The supervisee–therapist grasps, with the help of the supervisor, that he or she was acting in a "distinctly different, unusual or idiosyncratic" (Keisler, 2001, pp. 1061) manner or experiencing emotional reactions that were unusual or out of place (e.g., confusion, anger, boredom) that interfered with maintaining empathic engagement. Gelso and Hayes (2007) framed countertransference phenomena simply (and nicely) as: "too much, too little, too positive or too negative" (p. 37). *Too much* can take the form of overinvolvement, including loss of perspective, and/or overidentification; *too little* can comprise emotional withdrawal, disinterest, distraction, and/or disengagement; *too positive* could involve a motivation to be overly supportive, a loss of perspective, denial of conflict, and/or negative reactions; and examples of *too negative* include a low level of identification with and empathy for the client and becoming critical and/or frustrated. Each of these reactions compromises genuine attunement with the client and is a form of disengagement in which psychological contact is broken. This awareness leads to the identification of such behavior or experience as a *marker* of therapist reactivity or countertransference. The ability to recognize such markers is a very important achievement for novice clinicians: It requires not only self-awareness and psychological sophistication but also a willingness to examine one's reactions openly and nondefensively.

After identifying the marker, the supervisor will facilitate a process of reflection in which contextual and personal factors that may have influenced the supervisee–therapist's reactivity are explored. The point of such collaborative reflection is not to engage in a psychological analysis of the supervisee–therapist, and certainly not to conduct therapy with the supervisee–therapist, but instead to help him or her identify how certain personal factors (e.g., unresolved conflicts, maladaptive relational schemes, cultural countertransference) affect his or her ability to perform the necessary professional clinical responsibilities. All exploration must be directed toward the supervisee–therapist's conduct in the treatment of the client, not the way the supervisee lives his or her personal life.

Such a process of reflection may include the supervisor eliciting associations from the supervisee–therapist about thoughts, feelings, and reactions in regard to the marker: what had been talked about, emotions the supervisee was feeling, pressures he or she felt, any associations that are coming to mind now, and so on. In addition to such open-ended reflection, the supervisor may introduce psychological theories, examples from his or her own clinical experience, or scientific knowledge to help the supervisee better understand his or her experience as well as encourage the integration of all that the discipline of psychology has to offer to in regard to understanding human experience.

Such a process is not a critique per se but is aimed at developing the skills of reflection and self-awareness that are necessary not only for the supervisee to effectively help the present case but also to begin to develop clinical habits that are necessary for ethical practice.

State 4: Planning

The last state, planning, draws together what has been learned through the process of identifying the marker and the contextual, relational, and personal factors (including client factors) that contributed to the therapist's reactivity and considers the implications for future work with the client. The first step in planning is to consider how the episode of therapist reactivity has influenced the client. Often, this cannot be assessed immediately; it may take subsequent clinical sessions to assess the impact on the client and on the therapeutic relationship and alliance. Sometimes the impact appears to be quite subtle, or seemingly negligible, and it is enough that the therapist, now with greater awareness, simply continues in therapy with the client. In other circumstances, the therapist reactivity clearly has negatively affected the therapeutic alliance and the supervisor must help the supervisee–therapist address the alliance strain or rupture (see Chapter 7, this volume). In either circumstance, it is important that the supervisor and supervisee use the information that has been gleaned through processing the countertransference episode.

Developing Competence in Managing Reactivity and Countertransference

As we have discussed throughout this chapter, personal factors play a significant role in the conduct of psychotherapy, particularly in the way they affect the clinician's ability to empathically engage in therapy. We have suggested that important distinctions need to be made between therapist *responsiveness*, which is necessary for empathic engagement and appropriate application of psychological interventions, and *reactivity*, which results in forms of disengagement and other actions that can potentially harm the client and the therapeutic alliance. We also presented a process model that your supervisors may use in clinical supervision. Although it is certainly true that self-awareness plays a central role in the management of countertransference, other skills and qualities contribute to that competency as well. Gelso and Hayes (2002) proposed a theory of countertransference management that draws on the available empirical literature and experience. In Exhibit 6.3 we present the five factors of their theory and make recommendations (in italics) regarding their application in training.

EXHIBIT 6.3
Five Factors of Countertransference Management

Self-insight	The extent to which the therapist is aware of his or her own feelings, including countertransference feelings, and understands their basis. *It is crucial during graduate school and clinical training that supervisees make a personal commitment to enhance their self-awareness, including developing habits of the mind, such as self-reflectivity and metacompetence (i.e., knowing what one knows and does not know).*
Self-integration	The therapist's possession of an intact, basically healthy character structure. In the therapy interaction, such self-integration manifests itself as a recognition of ego boundaries or an ability to differentiate self from other. *Supervisees should strive (as we all should) to become the healthiest that they can; this involves a commitment to growth, often including psychotherapy.*
Anxiety management	Refers to therapists allowing themselves to experience anxiety and but also possessing the internal skill to control and to understand anxiety so that it does not bleed over into their responses to patients. *This quality reflects the distinction between responsiveness and reactivity. Developing skill in mindfulness, that is, allowing oneself to experience emotional arousal without attaching to the arousal or reacting in addition to gaining insight into conflicts or relational patterns that can trigger reactivity, are essential in managing anxiety and other reactions.*
Empathy	The ability to partially identify with and put oneself into the other person's shoes that permits the therapist to focus on the client's needs despite the difficulties the therapist may experience in the work. Also, empathic ability may be part of sensitivity to one's own feelings, including countertransference feelings, which in turn ought to preventing acting out of countertransference. *Again, the ability to respond rather than to react prepares the therapist to use his or her emotional reactions to the benefit of treatment. In our experience, there are countless opportunities to practice such skills in all one's relationships.*
Conceptualizing ability	The therapist's ability to draw on theory in the work and grasp theoretically the patient's dynamics in terms of the therapeutic relationship. *Graduate students and supervisees should fully commit to learning as much as they can about the therapeutic process, drawing on the scientific literature.*

Note. Italics indicate possible application of factors described. Data from Gelso and Hayes (2002). Adapted from *Casebook for Clinical Supervision: A Competency-Based Approach* (p.106), by C. A. Falender and E. P. Shafranske, 2008, Washington, DC: American Psychological Association. Copyright 2008 by the American Psychological Association.

CONCLUSION

Adrian van Kaam (1966) wrote, "The appeal of a whole person can be answered only by the presence of a whole person" (p. 22). In this chapter, we have sought to clarify how the presence of the therapist can best be applied in psychotherapy. The abilities to make psychological contact with the client and to empathically engage are necessary contributions of the therapist to the therapeutic process. Developing an awareness of the role of personal factors and skill in managing personal reactivity are essential competencies that are initially learned during clinical training and enhanced throughout one's career.

7

CASE CONCEPTUALIZATION: THE PRACTICE OF CLINICAL UNDERSTANDING

If we are facing in the right direction, all we have to do is keep on walking.
—Buddhist proverb

In the most pragmatic sense, case conceptualization gets us facing in the right direction. It provides us with a provisional and ever-evolving conceptual map that orients our clinical understanding and shapes the course of treatment. The centerpiece of the conceptualization provides an explanation that accounts for the client's symptoms and problems, including descriptions of precipitating stressors and predisposing events and conditions (Kendjelic & Eells, 2007, p. 68). Case conceptualization complements the diagnosis and contributes to the development of therapy goals, identifies specific targets for intervention, and "serves as a blueprint guiding treatment as a marker of change" (Eells, 2007, p. 4).

Case conceptualization also contributes to evidence-based professional practice (American Psychological Association, 2006) by integrating theory and knowledge, drawing on the relevant theoretical and empirical literature, as part of the therapist's effort to understand the client. An expanded view of case conceptualization includes the client's values and strengths, the therapeutic alliance, and the client's readiness for change as well as considers the therapist's expertise in developing an understanding not only of the client but also of the case in its entirety.

One of the primary tasks in clinical training and supervision is developing competence in formulating a clear understanding of a case and critically examining the means by which the conceptualization was derived and the assumptions that informed its creation. In other words, during training the issue is not just the accuracy or utility of the case conceptualization but also consideration of your skill in synthesizing information and theory in a logical and internally consistent manner. We cannot imagine any supervision session that does not involve in some way case conceptualization: its development, revision, or application. Supervision aims not only to arrive at a correct (or rather, useful) understanding of the client but also to facilitate competence in case conceptualization. As we discuss further, this requires assembling a host of skills.

WHO IS CASE CONCEPTUALIZATION FOR?

Case conceptualization serves the interrelated interests of the client, you, and your supervisor by providing a coherent understanding of the client's complaints and symptoms; the context and background of his or her problems; and a theory about cure—or, from a nonmedical perspective, the means to obtain a solution to the client's difficulties. Clinical formulation first serves the client. By the time they seek psychotherapy, clients are usually quite demoralized: They feel powerless, unable to meet their goals or to fulfill their expectations and those of others, and they often see themselves as mired in predicaments for which there is no solution (Frank & Frank, 1991, p. 35). They cannot see a way out of their problems or their debilitating state of mind, such as anxiety, depression, conflict, and confusion. There is a vacuum in their capacity for hope. Case formulation addresses this void by providing an understanding that contains within it the seeds of change. It provides "a rationale, conceptual scheme, or myth that provides a plausible explanation for the patient's symptoms and prescribes a ritual or procedure for resolving them" (Frank & Frank, 1991, p. 42). Such language may seem odd in this day of evidence-based practice and empirically supported treatments; however, it captures two essential features found in all psychotherapeutic treatments: (a) It makes the problems the client is facing meaningful and understandable, and (b) it provides the means to work toward a solution. Making sense of one's difficulties can in itself be therapeutic. Also, when client and therapist work collaboratively to construct the case conceptualization, the client's efficacy and engagement are enhanced and his or her strengths are exercised. Experiences that may have been seen as overwhelming are normalized, and complex problems are broken down into more manageable ones (Kuyken, Padesky, & Dudley, 2009). As the therapist collaborates with the client to develop clinical understanding, the two will reach a consensus regarding goals and therapy tasks, which, as we have seen, is integral to the development of the alliance. Consider the following example:

> Johnna is a freshman at a prestigious southern California university. Although initially excited about getting into her first-choice college and meeting new friends, she finds herself depressed and feeling somewhat anxious—not her usual outgoing, friendly self. She made an appointment to see a counselor on the recommendation of her resident advisor, who expressed concern after a conversation with Johnna's roommate, who was worried because Johnna seemed sad and depressed and was sleeping much of the day. In her first counseling session, Lisa, a counseling psychology intern, listened carefully as Johnna talked about how sad and lonely she was; she voiced her upset that she might have made a poor choice of schools and claimed that she couldn't bear the thought of either going home or staying at college. After Johnna tearfully recounted the events of her first three weeks away from home, Lisa described how natural it was to feel anxious and for many students to feel lonely at times on a big campus, without the friends and the support groups they had left at home. Referring to the incidents that Johnna had described, Lisa normalized, without minimizing, Johnna's condition and explained that when people feel anxious they often withdraw, which leads to a feeling of being ineffective, which thus increases one's anxiety and depression. "Of course you feel this way," Lisa concluded. Johnna sighed, and said she knew that what Lisa said was true, but she didn't know what to do, and started again to cry. With only a few minutes left in the session, Lisa empathically comforted Johnna and shared that in their next session, which was arranged for later that week, they could talk more about what to do, but it would be important for Johnna to consider some things she could do to get out of bed during the day, to be active, and to not withdraw—which, Lisa reminded her, was actually increasing Johnna's depressive symptoms— while acknowledging that she understood that staying in her room was momentarily reducing Johnna's feelings of anxiety.

Lisa's way of describing the situation resonated with Johnna, and although Johnna did not leave with a bounce in her step, she did feel understood and now had a way of thinking about her difficulties in a slightly more hopeful (and realistic) way. Even sharing the most tentative and elementary conceptualization with a client can be therapeutic because it can encourage the client to engage in self-understanding, provide hope, and offer the possibility of change.

Case conceptualization also serves the supervisee in that it provides the understanding necessary to formulate and conduct treatment tailored to the client's specific clinical needs. Speaking more broadly, in terms of professional development, performing case conceptualizations challenges you to integrate a voluminous amount of data into a coherent whole, to test assumptions, to apply (and at times question) your preferred clinical theories, to bring to bear what psychology as a science has to offer and to consider the role of culture and context, as well as consider alternative perspectives. Case conceptualization extends beyond a singular case; it contributes to the development of a number of associated competencies. For example, during training, supervisors will not just aim to help you develop your best understanding of your cases; they also will challenge you to consider how you think, access and use data, manage and correct personal biases, and apply both the scientific literature and your knowledge of multicultural factors and client values.

Case conceptualization involves the application of a number of clinical skills, including observation, data gathering, problem identification, diagnosis, hypothesis testing, goal setting, and treatment planning. You will gain experience in the practice of maintaining empathic contact with the client while gathering information and making decisions in the moment about ways to proceed in a session. We have found that most supervisees initially find it challenging to keep all their balls in the air at the same time. In the preceding example, Lisa had to evaluate the seriousness of Johnna's depression, consider risk factors, take into account Johnna's history and culture, and consider precipitants and maintaining factors, while empathically engaging with Johnna and initiating the formation of a therapeutic alliance. That's a lot to be mindful of.

Case conceptualization is also of paramount importance to the supervisor. Because they bear clinical responsibility for many cases, supervisors must quickly develop a clear understanding of each client, including an assessment of risk factors. Although a supervisor may challenge you to consider alternative interventions and to question assumptions, in essence he or she needs to know the case as accurately as possible to be able to provide case management and to ensure client welfare (see Chapter 8, this volume). Concise, well-articulated case conceptualizations will help the supervisor track multiple cases over time, identifying clients who require particular attention and determining, with you, the focus of training.

STRUCTURE OF CASE CONCEPTUALIZATION

Case conceptualization consists of a set of interrelated tasks: data gathering, problem definition and diagnosis, individual diversity and multicultural context, client strengths and protective factors, clinical formulation, therapy goals, the treatment plan, and markers of progress. There is no universal standard for the number of stages or phases or categories; the categories we present next lend themselves for use across different theoretical orientations and are usefully descriptive. In the following section we describe the tasks and provide recommendations for useful practices to develop.

Data Gathering

Data gathering consists of client self-report and collateral reports (from family members and significant others), written information supplied on intake forms, data obtained from standardized psychological instruments (e.g., the Beck Depression Inventory—II [BDI–II]; Beck, Steer, & Brown, 1996) and formal psychological assessment reports, chart review (if available from previous treatment of the client), and clinician observations. This information consists of *descriptive* data.

Practice Considerations

It is important to chart and communicate these data as accurately as possible, without adding inferences, interpretations, or explanations. Your supervisor is interested in unvarnished data or facts (because you are, in effect, his or her eyes and ears). It is important that you make distinctions among what you actually observed, the client's self-report, and theory.

Illustration

Lisa reported to her supervisor that her client was severely depressed. Her supervisor would likely inquire, "Was this conclusion based on client self-report, or did you observe symptoms of major depression?"

Problem Definition and Diagnosis

Problem definition and diagnosis incorporates the client's self-reported presenting problems and those that the therapist observes or learns about from the client, including behaviors or issues that the client may not consider to be problems (e.g., substance abuse) but that contribute to his or her complaints as well as other background difficulties. This descriptive data (based on observations and client self-reports) leads to the articulation of the provisional diagnosis. Factors that maintain the problems and reinforce negative coping strategies should also be reported, as should information obtained from a review of the theoretical and research literature. This information consists primarily of descriptive information; however, theory- and research-informed clinical hypotheses or inferences may be included and presented as such.

Practice Considerations

It is not unusual in the course of treatment, as trust builds and the therapeutic alliance develops, for additional data to be disclosed and other problems that appear to contribute to the presenting problems come to light.

Illustration

In her third session with Lisa, Johnna mentions that one of the reasons why she chose this university was to get far away from her high school friends, especially one in particular: a boy with whom she had, in her words, unfortunately "hooked up with" when she was very intoxicated at a party at her girlfriend's house. She felt embarrassed because her friends found her passed out. She says that she's over what happened to her and that it was her fault because she had been drinking but that she just doesn't like to be reminded about the incident. Lisa presented to her supervisor the multiple problems that appeared to play roles in Johnna's difficulties, placing particular emphasis on problems that were directly associated with her symptoms and that Johnna herself had identified.

Individual Diversity and Multicultural Context

As discussed in Chapter 4, understanding and accommodating in a respectful and inclusive way the multiple aspects of diversity that influence therapeutic and supervisory relationships is a challenge, and doing so in the case conceptualization process is equally complicated. To understand a client fully, the therapist must take into consideration the multicultural context in which symptoms and the client's subjective experience and meaning of his or her difficulties emerged. The clinician must also assess the impact of culture on the client's expression of psychological distress, conceptions of healing, and the therapeutic alliance. This requires not only knowledge of the literature examining the role of culture in mental health (e.g., culture-bound syndromes) but also cultural humility and commitment to integrate a contextual perspective when performing case conceptualization. This goes beyond, what at times is a trivial reporting of demographic features, to an earnest attempt to understand the client within the framework of his or her worldview and culture.

Practice Considerations

A useful starting point is to make a conscious, deliberate effort to bring "context" into the process of understanding and to be curious about the ways in which worldview and culture shape experience—the experience of your client and your own experience as a clinician. Also, rather than attempting to figure all of this out on your own, engage the client in a collaborative process, considering together the multiple sources of meaning and the cultural loyalties that influence interpretations of events and relationships. Be mindful of assumptions and biases, particularly when you might find yourself drawing conclusions rather than asking the client to clarify or discuss their experience. Also, it is important to remember that consideration of multicultural factors is not just relevant to assessment but should also inform all aspects of ongoing treatment.

Illustration

Lisa felt an immediate empathic connection with Johnna, when reflecting on her early experiences as an undergraduate. The more she learned about Johnna's ambition, her academic accomplishments and potential, her close knit and supportive family—who expected Johnna to be successful and tended to minimize her insecurities—Lisa felt almost as if they could be cousins, if not sisters. Since they were of the same race, roughly from the same socioeconomic class, and held a seemingly similar worldview, Lisa mistakenly thought issues of culture would not impact their therapeutic relationship. Her supervisor gently questioned this notion and Lisa began to reflect that the cultural borderlines (Falicov, 1995), which she shared with her client and led to a sense of connectedness, led her to make assumptions and to move through exploration of Johnna's distress too quickly. Lisa began to recognize that she and her client actually viewed the incident with the boy differently based in the nuances in their differing religious perspectives on sexuality. Lisa had missed that Johnna felt terribly guilty about having drank alcohol and disobeyed her religion's moral teachings about sexual behavior. Lisa began to be more curious and became even more committed to understanding her client's experience and the specific factors that influenced Johnna's distress, which led to a strengthening in the alliance.

Client Strengths and Protective Factors

To develop a comprehensive understanding of the client, it is essential to include consideration of strengths and protective factors of the client, which contribute to the client's wellbeing and serve as resources in coping with life's difficulties. Taking note of these features not only ensures that the clinician constructs a well-rounded picture of the client, but also counterbalances the emphasis on psychopathology and vulnerability found in psychiatric diagnosis. Strengths and protective factors include personal features such as resilience, intelligence, psychological mindedness, well-integrated beliefs and values, and physical health, as well as contextual and cultural factors, such as supportive families, friends, and religious faith community.

Practice Considerations

The process of identifying strengths and protective factors with the client can be therapeutic in itself. Such exploration may bring to light personal qualities and resources that were out of the client's awareness, due to his or her psychologically impaired state, and may contribute to reestablishing a sense of hope. However, when noting the client's strengths or history of coping, you should be careful to not minimize the current distress or feelings of hopelessness.

Illustration

Lisa noted that Johnna possessed a number of strengths, including her psychological-mindedness, concern for others, motivation, and contextual factors, such as her loving and supportive family and well-integrated religious belief system. While these had served as resources through Johnna's life, Lisa also understood that her psychological conflicts were impeding her use of these resources. For example, Johnna would need to resolve some of the conflict and shame, which she felt about the incident with the boy, to be able to open up to her family and reach out for their support.

Clinical Formulation

Clinical formulation is the centerpiece of case conceptualization. You will find that case conceptualization and formulation are often used interchangeably by supervisors and in the literature. We use *clinical formulation* to refer to the understanding that is developed regarding the nature of the client's difficulties (e.g., etiology, psychological dynamics, and maintaining factors). It provides a comprehensive understanding of the client, incorporating clinical data and findings from the theoretical and empirical literature. The therapist applies theory (e.g., cognitive theory, psychodynamic theory, systems theory, existential theory) to the formulation to facilitate coherence. The formulation consists of an integration of descriptive data and clinical hypotheses. The therapist's theoretical orientation plays a significant role in clinical formulation as he or she selects data to address his or her theory-driven hypotheses and inferences. Case conceptualization, on the other hand, involves the comprehensive understanding of the case and includes the clinical formulation, client motivation, the context in which the treatment is offered—in sum, all of the factors that influence the therapeutic process and outcome.

Practice Considerations

The clinical formulation should provide an internally consistent understanding of the client and explanation for his or her problems that is based on client data and informed by theory and empirical research. Instead of fitting the client's data into a theory, or dismissing data that contradict a preferred theoretical claim, the theory applied should make meaningful the data at hand. Best practices also incorporate *collaborative empiricism* (drawn from cognitive behavior therapy and consistent with theory regarding the therapeutic alliance) in which the client actively participates by providing self-reports, observations, and history; considers possible causes of his or her difficulties (provides confirming or disconfirming data); and works with the therapist to construct a viable and useful formulation (Kuyken et al., 2009).

Illustration

A number of theories might usefully be applied to Johnna's case. With respect to one aspect, a therapist approaching the case from the standpoint of cognitive behavioral theory would hypothesize that Johnna's coping behavior, which primarily consists of avoidance, has been reinforcing negative cognitions regarding poor self-efficacy and increasing her depressive symptoms.

Therapy Goals

Therapy goals include the explicit goals that have been mutually identified and agreed on by the client and therapist; these may be different from goals that the therapist initially identified on the basis of the clinical assessment and from taking into consideration the theoretical and empirical literature. The therapist's theoretical orientation plays an important role because it informs clinical observation and understanding and influences the identification of therapy goals.

Practice Considerations

Realistic and attainable therapy goals are identified through a collaborative effort between therapist and client.

Illustration

Being mindful of the need to form a therapeutic alliance, Lisa plans to focus on the goals she and Johnna have mutually identified; these concern reducing Johnna's anxiety and depression and helping her become more involved in dorm life, make friends, and do well academically. Although Lisa believes that the sexual assault (which is how she views it, because according to Johnna she was too inebriated to provide consent) played a major role in Johnna's anxiety, depression, and poor adjustment to college life, she recognizes that is related to her goal and not yet Johnna's. Lisa trusted that if her clinical hunch were correct, it would be borne out during the course of treatment.

Treatment Plan

The *treatment plan* is the means by which the therapy goals will be achieved. In practice, the treatment plan consists of immediate, intermediate, and long-term objectives and presents the overarching therapeutic approach and specific intervention strategies targeted to address the objectives.

Practice Considerations

Through active collaboration with the client, the therapist develops the treatment plan with the intent of targeting the treatment objectives by applying the principles of evidence-based practice. The therapist tailors the plan to the client's motivation, strengths, and psychological capacities, taking into consideration cultural and contextual factors.

Illustration

An immediate objective in Johnna's treatment is to interrupt the self-reinforcing cycle in which Johnna's isolation and depressive behaviors perpetuate negative cognitions. Lisa and Johnna plan to work collaboratively on developing a behavioral plan with self-monitoring and reinforcement components. They also agree that there are a number of unresolved conflicts related to the incident with the boy that they would need to explore.

Markers of Progress

Markers of progress are indicators of therapy progress and are used to evaluate the effectiveness of clinical interventions.

Practice Considerations

Supervisees and supervisors work collaboratively to evaluate the effectiveness of clinical interventions and client progress in achieving the treatment objectives. In addition to client reports, markers of progress can be identified at the beginning of treatment and provide a set of criteria to track progress. The use of markers aids in the continuous evaluation of the therapeutic process; supervisees can also use these data to monitor their fidelity to the treatment plan and use of interventions.

Illustration

We would expect that Johnna's use of a behavioral plan, which includes physical exercise and other activities aimed at increasing personal and academic efficacy, would be reflected in markers such as the BDI–II or self-reports of improved mood and motivation.

Although these tasks are conceptually sequential, in practice experienced clinicians often go back and forth through them as new information becomes available or hypotheses are disproven. Clinical navigation between different tasks (e.g., probing for information to test out hypotheses, connecting one piece of data with another, thus leading to a new understanding) may appear to be a seamless process; however, such expertise comes through years of practice and appears to require a form of clinical intuition that comes with experience. In the field of medicine, researchers have recognized the potential value of coupling intuition with evidence in supervision (Gawande, 2009); however, such intuition is not a God-given gift but instead reflects the outcome of countless clinical experiences in which the rules one learned in clinical training, and specifically during supervision, have been internalized and become an element of fully integrated clinical competence.

This practicing, over and over, of sets of skills—in this instance, skills in case conceptualization—is part of the supervisee's learning process. This learning begins by adopting a set of tasks (like the ones in the list we just presented) and practicing them in a somewhat rote fashion. The advanced beginner clinician has an accumulation of significant client contact and supervision, an enlarged repertoire of responses, and some knowledge of several theoretical orientations. After sufficient practice, the rules become more and more internalized and more automatically or intuitively performed. Barnett and Barber (2005), similar to H. L. Dreyfus and Dreyfus (1986), noted that novices are fairly rule bound and less attuned to context; however, with experience, supervisees develop higher level and more sophisticated rules that can be more readily recalled in a systematic manner and applied. As your pattern recognition in relation to client presentations grows, so too do your experience and your ability to generalize from one case to another as you apply to new client presentations what you have already learned. This is how you develop clinical competence.

For novice trainees, the aforementioned list of tasks may seem difficult to perform; however, collaboration with the supervisor will give you the means to gradually learn them. In doing so, as you develop the skills to meet the challenge, case conceptualization will seem less demanding over time. With that context in mind, we turn to the next section, which supplies a number of clinical tools to guide your practice.

Reflection Activity. Reflect on a current case and the set of tasks discussed earlier: data gathering, problem definition, individual diversity and multicultural context, client strengths and protective factors, clinical formulation, therapy goals, treatment plan, and markers of progress. In which of these tasks do you feel most proficient? Were there any tasks that, in retrospect, would be valuable to revisit?

PERFORMING CASE CONCEPTUALIZATION

Data gathering initiates the process of case conceptualization, as it provides a wealth of information about the client and his or her life that leads to clinical understanding and provides direction for the treatment. Although data are available in each moment throughout treatment, you should intentionally focus on gathering information in the early sessions. Conducting a clinical interview as well as facilitating exploration in psychotherapy involves the use of a number of interviewing or verbal techniques, each of which is intended to help you understand the client in different ways and shapes the nature of the therapist–client interaction. Each of us has developed certain verbal and interpersonal styles and has preferences in how we relate to people (and carry on conversations). Part of clinical training is expanding one's repertoire of verbal behavior and becoming more intentional in the selection of interventions. In Exhibit 7.1, we present a list of verbal interventions that are used in the contexts of nondirective and directive data gathering, exploration and hypothesis gathering, and summarizing and confirming. As with the tasks listed earlier, these interventions are presented in a linear fashion, but as you gain experience you will learn to adapt them to the unique dynamics unfolding in any particular session.

Novice trainees often feel stressed by a perceived demand to accomplish many tasks in a given session. Although it is important to not lose sight of the tasks and to prioritize appropriately, you also need to stay emotionally and empathically engaged with your clients and provide them an opportunity to tell their story, in their words and at their pace. This balancing of multiple tasks requires particular skill, which you will develop over time. A comprehensive understanding of the client's problems plays a central role in case conceptualization and the development of a viable treatment plan. Having a model to address the various aspects of a problem is helpful; in Exhibit 7.2, we present a framework to explore a client's presenting problem (Ingram, 2006).

> **Reflection Activity.** Before we discuss the role of theory in case conceptualization, reflect on your preferred theoretical orientation. How did you come to favor this orientation? What do you imagine are its strengths and limitations? To what extent do you believe theoretical orientation influences data gathering? Consider examples.

Role of Theory in Clinical Formulation and Case Conceptualization

During the process of gathering data, one develops hypotheses to explain the factors that contributed to and maintain the client's difficulties and result

EXHIBIT 7.1
Interviewing Approaches: Data Gathering, Reporting, and Supervision

Nondirective Data Gathering

In the initial phase of intake interviewing, open-ended questions and prompts are used to encourage clients to discuss their reasons for seeking counseling, describing what they see as their difficulties, and identifying their goals for treatment. Throughout the interviews, you should pay close attention to tracking the client's emotional reactions and behaviors.

Open-ended question:	"Perhaps we could begin with my asking, what brings you to seek counseling?"
Prompt:	"Uh huh"; or "Anything else come to mind?"; or active reflection (e.g., "You were feeling . . . ").
Reporting:	It is important that the data obtained are presented in supervision without interpretation or inference; you should report, as accurately as possible, the client's words and perspective, as well as any nonverbal behavior you observed.
Supervision:	By reviewing session audio or video recordings you can, with the help of your supervisor, become better aware of your personal tendencies in your interviewing style and expand your repertoire of interventions.

Directive Data Gathering

Later in the initial interview and in subsequent sessions, data gathering is done in a more directive style, although not exclusively so. The interventions range from clarifying questions, which serve to follow up what the client has said and encouraging further description, to specific questions aimed at obtaining information used in, for example, making a differential diagnosis. As you begin to form diagnostic hypotheses, you should seek information to confirm or disconfirm them and to lead the interaction so that so that you can get a more complete understanding of the client's history and the client's responses to the difficulties he or she has been experiencing.

Clarifying:	"You say that you have been having frequent headaches. Could you describe the last time you had a headache—a migraine headache, as you characterized it?"
Specific questions:	"How long did the experience of anxiety last? When was the first time in you can recall feeling such severe feelings of anxiety?" or "Did you experience anxiety as a child?"
Reporting:	It is important to report the data as accurately as possible, including a description of what informed your interview decision-making processes.

(*continues*)

Supervision: In addition to reviewing client data, your supervisor will likely facilitate a discussion regarding the knowledge and theory that informed your decision making and interventions. Your supervisor also can help you become skilled in asking clarifying questions and directing the inquiry with care to not turn the interview into an interrogation.

Exploration and Hypothesis Development

After obtaining a clear sense of the presenting problems and symptoms, including their history and progression, you may broaden the focus of your inquiry to obtain an understanding of the client's perspective regarding the meaning of his or her symptoms. You may start to develop clinical hypotheses for which you will want to seek further information. This may include asking open-ended questions, speculative questions eliciting clarification, or more confrontational questions to examine contradictions in the client's thinking or to assess the client's level of insight.

Open-ended question: "Well, you've reported that you've been experiencing a lot of headaches and other physical symptoms. What comes to mind about those symptoms?"

Speculative questions: "You mentioned that your job responsibilities were changed at work about the time when you began having headaches. Have you considered whether there might be a connection between the two events?"

Confronting contradictions: "You had said that you love your job, yet you also described how you were feeling bored and not appreciated by your supervisor. Could you help me to understand those different reactions?"

Theory-driven questions: "Sometimes when people are upset or angry, they develop physical reactions. You mentioned feeling upset at your boyfriend. Could there be a connection between those reactions and the headaches? Had you ever considered that possibility?"

Reporting: Again, accurate reporting is important. Your report must integrate not just verbal content but also direct observations as well as an assessment of the client's responsiveness to confrontations. How thoughtful, self-reflective, and psychologically minded does the client seem to be?

Supervision: The development of an initial case conceptualization occurs over a number of sessions. The supervision will focus not only on developing an understanding of the case on the basis of the data gathering you have done but also on integrating the various processes required in the conduct of evidence-based practice. This includes considering both your own expertise and your supervisor's competence in supervising certain treatment protocols while keeping in mind the client's values.

Summarizing and Confirmation

Summarizing and eliciting the perspectives of the client are valuable throughout the therapeutic process. In the initial intake session, it is important at times to paraphrase and summarize the information that the client is disclosing and to elicit his or her response. At the end of the first session it is important that you explicitly summarize the presenting problems and focus of the therapy (i.e., identify initial therapy goals) to be certain that you and the client have arrived at an initial consensus in respect to the goals and state in some way that therapy can be helpful. The aim is to consolidate the initial development of a therapeutic alliance. It is important to be very open to the client's perspective and comments and to encourage and reinforce that, by seeking treatment, the client has taken an important first step toward addressing his or her difficulties.

Summarizing: An example of a summary offered at the end of an initial session might sound like this:

There are a number of acute stressors that certainly are creating strain and difficulties for you: the conflicts in your job, financial worries, and dissatisfaction in your relationship with your boyfriend. Each of these is understandably affecting how you are feeling. We explored whether these stressors could be affecting how you are feeling, especially the symptoms of headaches. We both agreed that you were wise to seek help during this difficult time and that therapy can give us a chance to work together, so that you can begin to address certain areas of conflict and to feel better.

Reporting: Particular emphasis is placed on the building of a consensus and indicators of a therapeutic alliance. Your supervisor will want to be certain that you covered legal and ethical issues, including informed consent; that you performed risk assessment as appropriate; and that you addressed the practical details of the agency's policies and procedures (e.g., arranging appointments, payment, dealing with emergencies).

Supervision: The focus will be on factors related to development of a therapeutic alliance and formulating an initial case conceptualization. Your supervisor can help you with managing time; tailoring intervention approaches to clients; and the challenges of integrating the processes of data gathering, maintaining emotional engagement, and fostering the development of the therapeutic alliance.

EXHIBIT 7.2
Four Frames for Exploring a Specific Problem

Problem What's wrong? Since when? Why now?	Description of the problem: What are the complaints, symptoms, signs of distress? What is the "operational definition" of the problem behavior? When and how was the onset? Are there specific precipitating events? External stressors? Positive changes that tax an individual's coping abilities? What was time and cause of onset (of acute)? A specific event that triggered the presenting problem? A turning point when the problems began? What has been the course of the development of the problem? If the problem seems to be chronic, look for some point in time when things started to become worse. Specific details of progressive deterioration: Look for evidence of downward spirals. Do poor efforts to solve problems create new problems? Does increased stress lead to greater cognitive distortions followed by increased disorganization of behavior? What is the history? Are there prior episodes and early relevant experiences? When has the problem not occurred? Are there examples of successful coping? What has the client already done to try to solve this? What has been helpful? What has made things worse? Are there examples of independent use of resources?
Outcome What do you want?	How would things be different if the problem were resolved? What do you desire for the future? What is your vision of how it would be different if it were solved? What are the outcome goals? If you woke up tomorrow morning and the problem was gone, how would your life be different? Describe what the day would be like.
Obstacles Barriers to getting what you want	What prevents the achievement of your desired goals? What stops you? How do you stop yourself? Are there internal barriers in the form of thoughts or feelings? Are there external, environmental obstacles and barriers? Are there family members who are creating obstacles? Are there social or cultural barriers?
Resources What would help you get what you want?	What coping skills do you already have that can be applied to solving the problem and achieving the desired outcome? What strengths and assets have you demonstrated in the past that will help you with this problem? Have you been successful before in a similar situation? What social supports are available? Are there environmental changes or material tools that would help? What knowledge do you need? What community resources could help? What new skills are needed?

Note. From *Clinical Case Formulations* (p. 35), by B. L. Ingram, 2006, New York, NY: John Wiley & Sons. Copyright 2006 by John Wiley & Sons. Reprinted with permission.

in symptoms. Clinical theories offer a means of integrating a great deal of data into a comprehensive understanding of the client. We turn now to a discussion of the use of theory in clinical formulation, and as broadly applied in case conceptualization.

As Kurt Lewin (1951) observed, "There is nothing so practical as a good theory" (p. 169). Theories provide the conceptual glue that links observations, self-reports, and other clinical data into a meaningful whole and guides the therapeutic process. They provide the organizing principles that, in a very practical way, face the clinician in the right direction. Your theoretical stance, as well as that of your supervisor, not only influences how you interpret data but also shapes your data collection process, because different theories place importance on different factors. For example, a therapist working from a cognitive behavioral theoretical orientation is apt to pay close attention to a client's cognitions and carefully track the automatic thoughts that are triggered in the client in situations that are associated with the presenting problems. Clinicians working from a psychodynamic orientation, on the other hand, tend to focus on a client's capacity to experience and appropriately respond to emotional states. Of course, there is much more to both theories than these quick, general descriptions; the point is that theories will direct your attention and delimit the data you obtain and how you interpret them. Data are always theory laden. You might recall the often-told story of the blind men and the elephant: Each man touched a different part, (i.e., tail, trunk, tusk, ear, etc.) and came up with completely different descriptions of the mammal. In much the same way, in case conceptualization theories determine what part of the client's experience therapists focus on and consequently influences their clinical formulation. One of the challenges is to recognize how your observations are colored by the theories you prefer and to maintain an openness to other data and alternative viewpoints. An associated problem is that clinicians unwittingly ascribe factualism to ideas derived from clinical theory. Theories can be understood as "useful fictions" that have clinical utility, in contrast to empirically derived facts (Barbour, 1974). For example, it is impossible to actually *observe* a defense; instead, one observes behaviors, which one infers or believes are serving defensive purposes. For example, a therapist observes that a client changes the subject whenever it appears that the client begins to experience sadness; the therapist infers that changing the subject has the purpose of moving the discussion away from content that evokes sadness. This claim cannot be definitively proven; instead, it is offered as an interpretation based on clinical theory. Theories guide therapists' ways of understanding behavior in the moment, and they are indispensible in the task of case conceptualization. We turn now to a brief illustration.

Applying Theory: An Illustration

The reasons for a client's psychological difficulties can be understood in many different ways. Different theories might at first glance seem incompatible; in reality, however, many can be seen as complementary. This understanding has fostered efforts toward theoretical and technical integration. *Theoretical integration* involves the integrative use of multiple theories to arrive at a comprehensive understanding of the client, whereas technical integration concerns the application of clinical interventions originating in different forms of therapy. Individual theories provide a lens through which a therapist can examine specific psychological dimensions, and various theories combined together may contribute to a more comprehensive understanding of a particular client's case. Although a complete, multifaceted understanding might appear to be the therapist's aim in each case, it is in fact not, because such a goal may not be in keeping with the client's goals and motivation and, practically speaking, may not be necessary to initiate effective treatment. Also, the proposition that multiple perspectives can offer clinical utility does not suggest that every theoretical position has equal standing or relevance (let alone yield a reasonable correspondence to reality). The application of general theoretical models rests on a critical analysis of the theoretical and empirical literature.

Cognitive behavior therapy and psychodynamic psychotherapy are two widely practiced forms of treatment; both have received empirical support, and both are often approaches (in particular, cognitive behavior therapy) to which you will be exposed during clinical training and in which you will be expected to develop a foundational level of proficiency. In the paragraphs that follow, we highlight selected (and distinctively different) characteristics to illustrate how one could apply theory to obtain clinical understanding in the case of Johnna.

Psychological difficulties, including both emotional and behavioral reactions, when viewed from a cognitive behavioral perspective, are understood in terms of clients' perceptions of situations, which are based on their fundamental understanding of themselves, others, and the world in general (Beck, 2011). Beyond general theory, in practice, clinicians use a technique called *collaborative empiricism* (Kuyken et al., 2009), in which the client actively participates in identifying cognitions that function as automatic thoughts that directly (and predictably) influence emotions and behaviors and result in a cycle of dysfunctional thinking, negative emotions, and maladaptive behavior. From this theoretical perspective, clinical interviewing would generally focus on present cognitions, tracking automatic thoughts and their consequences on emotions and behavior. Through Socratic questioning, thought records, and perhaps use of the BDI–II, a great deal of evidence would likely be found to support the understanding that dysfunctional thoughts (e.g., "No one likes me," "No one finds me attractive," "Guys are jerks," "I make poor decisions," "I'm stuck here and I'm to blame"), and the client's response to such thoughts (e.g., withdrawal and avoidance) are producing the symptoms. In the example of Johnna, although her high school sexual encounter would be considered a potential contributing factor to her present symptoms, the initial focus would be on Johnna's present cognitions and how to interrupt the dysfunctional pattern.

In contrast to cognitive behavior theory, perspectives that are common to the various schools of psychodynamic psychotherapy (e.g., ego psychology, object relations, self psychology; Gabbard, 2000; Shafranske, 2009; see also Kassaw & Gabbard, 2002) view psychological problems as manifestations of unconscious conflict, influenced by early life experience, that affect an individual's ability to fully experience and express emotions and to engage in purposeful action to fulfill his or her needs. Particular attention is paid to the client's ability to experience emotion and to balance his or her expression of and desire for needs through the use of defenses. A therapist approaching Johnna's case from this perspective would focus the clinical interviewing on Johnna's affect states, her use of defenses to manage difficult emotional states and impulses, and the psychological impact of the incident with the boy within the context of previous and current relationships. Instead of attempting to directly modify Johnna's thoughts or behavior, the therapist would emphasize exploring and bolstering her ability to better tolerate affect, which would lead to improvements in her psychological functioning.

Although these depictions of the use of cognitive behavior and psychodynamic theory in the case of Johnna were not intended to, and in fact do not, capture the richness and utility of the models, the examples illustrate how theory critically influences the data that would be the focus of the therapist's inquiry. Also, these theoretical orientations would direct the therapist's attention to very different psychological processes hypothesized to play a role in Johnna's difficulties. Supervision can provide an important vehicle by which to examine the theoretical perspectives you bring to the process of case conceptualization. This issue is particularly relevant when one considers the importance of collaborating with the client to develop an understanding that will in part influence the nature of the means by which achieving the client's goals will be based.

EXPANDING THE SCOPE OF CASE CONCEPTUALIZATION

Case conceptualization has traditionally focused exclusively on developing an understanding of the client as one draws on clinical theory. We find it useful to incorporate additional perspectives to case formulation because the intent is to gain an understanding of the case as a whole instead of focusing the inquiry solely on the client. Our intent is not to deemphasize the importance of obtaining a comprehensive understanding of the client and of his or her difficulties and life situation; the client, of course, is the centerpiece of case conceptualization. Instead, this approach enlarges the reflective and conceptual process so that you can consider the client within the context of the treatment as a whole.

The Therapeutic Alliance

In light of its role in treatment outcome, it is important to continuously monitor the quality of the therapeutic alliance (see Chapter 5, this volume). You can accomplish this by reflecting on the following questions:

- Have you and the client collaboratively identified realistic, attainable goals for the treatment?
- Have you and the client collaboratively identified the means of achieving those goals, and are you working together to achieve the goals?
- Have there been any signs of strain in the alliance, or a lessened commitment or effort on the client's part to achieve the goals?

Assessment of the therapeutic alliance is crucial to the overall conceptualization of the case, because without a working partnership the goals of therapy cannot be attained. A client's inability or reluctance to identify or commit to consistent and realistic goals may also provide useful information about the nature of that client's challenges in deriving satisfaction from life. Similarly, difficulties in entering into the therapeutic relationship or idiosyncratic ways of relating to the therapist also provide insight into the client's difficulties.

Readiness for Change

Another factor to consider is the client's readiness to work constructively on the therapeutic goals. A client's motivation, as well as his or her position within the stages of change (see Chapter 5, this volume), will affect your conceptualization of the case. In the example of Johnna, the assessment of risk, prognosis, and the selection of interventions would be markedly different if Johnna were in the Precontemplation stage versus the Preparation stage. If Johnna were in the Precontemplation stage, she would be apt to externalize the reasons for her dissatisfaction; blame her misery on the lousy school, lousy students, and lousy professors; and possibly see Lisa's suggestion to be more active as off the mark and a sign that even the therapists at this university are lousy. On the other hand, if Johnna were entering the Preparation stage (e.g., she did accept the recommendation of the resident adviser and made an appointment to see a counselor), she may be ready to consider what she could do to improve her situation. These differences in readiness and motivation play a pivotal role in both in the case conceptualization and the immediate treatment goals and therapist interventions.

DEVELOPING COMPETENCE IN CASE CONCEPTUALIZATION

Clinical supervision provides a context in which you can develop competence in case conceptualization. It gives you the opportunity to see clients, and it helps you hone your skills in the following areas: client interviewing and case conceptualization; making distinctions between data and inferences; and identifying and challenging assumptions to guide the development of case formulation, while integrating into this process the principles of evidence-based practice. Your supervisor will help you by modeling these skills. Consideration of the following issues and *inherent tensions* (i.e., competing goals; Eells, 2007, p. 19) will strengthen your understanding of and enhance your sophistication in developing case conceptualizations:

- *Immediacy versus comprehensiveness.* You must balance these incompatible approaches by "identifying what is needed to help the patient and avoid areas that may be . . . interesting but have little to do with directly helping the patient" (Eells, 2007, p. 20).
- *Complexity versus simplicity.* You should achieve a balance that provides clear direction to the treatment and is consistent with the mutually agreed-on goals of the therapy.
- *Clinician bias versus objectivity.* As you strive to obtain an accurate understanding of the client, biases, distortions, and errors in logic naturally will occur (Eells, 2007). Therefore, any claims of objectivity you make should be tempered by a recognition of such factors, and you can usefully apply self-reflectivity to identify possible sources of bias.
- *Observation versus inference.* Case conceptualization involves both observations and inferences that usually are based on theoretical propositions. You must develop skill in distinguishing between the two and finding a balance when considering the accuracy of the case formulation.
- *Individual versus general formulations.* A balance must be struck between the application of a general formulation and a highly idiosyncratic understanding of the client (Eells, 2007). You have

to be careful to not overgeneralize or to uncritically apply clinical theory.

- *Acceptance of disconfirming data and application of the scientific literature.* Like licensed professionals, you as a supervisee need to be accepting of data that disconfirm your assumptions and theories; likewise, you need to apply to your case conceptualizations information gleaned from psychology as a discipline and science. Practicing exclusively on the basis of one's preferred theories or clinical hunches is not in keeping with evidence-based practice.
- *Internal consistency.* There should be consistency in the case conceptualization among the assembled data, theory, literature, client goals, and the treatment.

You can enhance your developing proficiency in case conceptualization by presenting de-identified client and treatment information to peers and taking opportunities in case conferences and in graduate courses to present material. The feedback you receive can open up new perspectives as well as identify areas where the coherence between data and theory and the conclusions might be in question. Exhibit 7.3 provides a useful tool to perform self-assessment and can serve as a helpful reference when you are working on case formulations.

EXHIBIT 7.3
Case Formulation Scoring Template

Score	Case formulation scoring criteria
Problem list	
5	All relevant problems noted; clearly distinguishing between primary and secondary issues.
4	
3	Most relevant problems noted; but no evidence of distinguishing between primary and secondary issues.
2	
1	Some relevant problems noted; but also some irrelevant issues noted AND at least one primary problem missed.
0	N/A
Predisposing factors	
5	Predisposing variables noted; and clearly linked to specific problems in problem list.
4	
3	Predisposing variables noted; but these are not clearly linked to specific problems in the problem list.
2	
1	No evidence of considering predisposing variables.
0	N/A

EXHIBIT 7.3
Case Formulation Scoring Template   *(Continued)*

Score	Case formulation scoring criteria

Precipitating factors

5 Precipitating event(s) noted; and clearly linked to specific problems in the problem list.

4

3 Precipitating event(s) noted; but not clearly linked to specific problems in the problem list.

2

1 No evidence of considering precipitating factors. (If no precipitating event is evident—adjust final score by 5)

0 N/A

Perpetuating factors

5 Perpetuating factors noted (e.g., core beliefs, contingencies of reinforcement etc.); and clearly linked to specific problems in problem list.

4

3 Perpetuating factors noted; but these are not clearly linked to specific problems in the problem.

2

1 No evidence of considering perpetuating factors.

0 N/A

Provisional conceptualization

5 Well-integrated hypothesis that links the relevant problems with predisposing, precipitating, and perpetuating factors, and provides a good explanation of the patient's presenting problem(s).

4

3 A hypothesis that provides a plausible but incomplete explanation of the patient's presenting problem(s).

2

1 A poorly integrated explanation of the patient's presenting problem(s).

0 N/A

Problems potentially hindering treatment and strengths and assets

5 Potential problem(s) and strength(s) or asset(s) noted; and clearly linked to specific problems in problem list OR specific aspects of treatment plan.

4

3 Potential problems and strength(s) or asset(s) noted; but not clearly linked to specific problems in problem list OR specific aspects of treatment plan.

2

1 No evidence of considering potential problems and strength(s) or asset(s).

0 N/A

Note. N/A = not applicable. From "Toward Science-Informed Supervision of Clinical Case Formulation: A Training Model and Supervision Method," by A. C. Page, W. G. K. Stritzke, and N. J. McLean, 2008, *Australian Psychologist, 43*, p. 94–95. Copyright 2008 by Taylor & Francis Ltd. Adapted with permission.

Reflection Activity. Evaluate a case conceptualization that you have completed (or are in the process of completing) using the Case Formulation Scoring Template presented in Exhibit 7.3.

CONCLUSION

Competence in case conceptualization is important not only because it helps guide you in the conduct of specific cases but also because through it you hone your thinking and help bring to light assumptions about the foundations of psychological difficulty and the means of achieving therapeutic change.

8

PRACTICING ETHICALLY

When you think of the term *ethics*, what comes to mind? Although ethics is a core competency of clinical practice, the topic is typically relegated to a single course focused on high-risk circumstances; however, ethical and legal considerations permeate every aspect of practice. Most likely you have taken one graduate course in ethics, and likely little or no attention was paid to identifying ethical issues in practice or the ethics of supervision. This chapter is devoted to providing you with a frame for ethical practice and ethics in supervision.

As a supervisee, your challenge is to learn to think ethically, to identify and work through clinical ethical dilemmas bearing in mind your own emotional and personal response, and bring these to supervision. For example, consider a supervisee who is seeing a child and family in the evening at an outpatient clinic, and one night the parents ask that the session be extended because they are getting so much out of it. The supervisee weighs the rules about session time limits, his supervisor's likely disapproval that he would be staying past the clinic's closing time, and his own fatigue, balanced against the excitement that he feels from this evidence that he is working effectively with the clients (a personally gratifying aspect). How easy will it be for the supervisee to bring the issue to his or her supervisor?

Infusing ethics and ethical decision making into both clinical practice and supervision to even the most seemingly mundane of presentations is a challenge. In this chapter, we frame ethical and legal considerations both from aspirational and risk-avoidant perspectives. We include an overview of ethics in practice and supervision, supervisors' and supervisees' perceptions of ethical dilemmas and infractions, specific ethical dimensions relevant to supervision, strategies for ethical decision making during supervision, and consideration of legal issues.

Resources are available to help you identify ethical issues and apply the American Psychological Association's (APA's) Ethical Principles of Psychologists and Code of Conduct (APA, 2010a; hereafter the APA *Ethics Code*; see http://www.apa.org/ethics/code/index.aspx) to clinical situations (Anderson & Handelsman, 2010; Knapp & VandeCreek, 2006; Koocher & Keith-Spiegel, 2008; Nagy, 2005; Pope & Vasquez, 2007) and address aspects of consultation, supervision, and mandated supervision (Thomas, 2010). However, none exclusively address the ethics of supervision from the perspective of the supervisee or address everyday supervision dilemmas. Ethics of supervision are generally extrapolated from the APA Ethics Code.[1]

ETHICAL CHALLENGES AND DISCIPLINARY ACTION: SUPERVISOR AND SUPERVISEE PERSPECTIVES

Much of your previous ethics training may have had a remedial focus, addressing rule infractions and/or avoiding legal consequences (Knapp & VandeCreek, 2006). Much of supervision ethics has had this focus as well. Beginning with an understanding of perceived ethical challenges sets the stage for plain talk about ethics. When Pope and Vetter (1992, cited in Pope & Vasquez, 2007) asked licensed psychologists about situations they found ethically challenging, they ranked the following incidents in descending order of frequency: confidentiality; dual or conflictual relationships; payment sources; teaching dilemmas and concerns about training; forensics; research; conduct of colleagues; sexual issues; questionable assessment or harmful interventions; and competence.

In contrast, although low in occurrence generally, reasons for disciplinary action for psychologists in the United States were for sexual/dual relationships with the patient; unprofessional/unethical/negligent practice, conviction of crimes, fraudulent acts, improper/inadequate record keeping, failure to comply

---

[1]The exception is the groundbreaking *Ethical Guidelines for Supervision in Psychology: Teaching, Research, Practice, and Administration*, adopted by the Canadian Psychological Association (2009) and the accompanying *Resource Guide for Psychologists: Ethical Supervision in Teaching, Research, Practice, and Administration* (Canadian Psychological Association, 2010).

with continuing education requirements, breach of confidentiality, and inadequate or improper supervision (Association for State and Provincial Psychology Boards [ASPPB], 2005, cited in Pope & Vasquez, 2007).

Psychologists believe that confidentiality is the most prevalent ethical issue facing their profession, but actual disciplinary data show that sexual/dual relationships with a client is the violation with the highest frequency of occurrence: Of cases opened by the APA Ethics Committee in 2007, 28% centered on sexual and nonsexual dual relationships (APA, 2008). The ASPPB reported that supervision represented the seventh-highest category of complaints against psychologists (ASPPB, personal communication, July 25, 2010).

Supervisees also have reported different ethical challenges—including what they perceive as unethical behavior by their supervisors; for example, Ladany, Lehrman-Waterman, Molinaro, and Wolgast's (1999) survey of a group of practicum students and interns revealed that 51% of their supervisors had engaged in practices the students viewed as unethical. The average number of ethical practice concerns with their current supervisor was 1.52 ($SD = 2.35$). The three most frequently cited practices were (a) failure to adhere to ethical guidelines regarding performance evaluation and general monitoring of student activities, (b) violating areas of confidentiality with respect to supervision, and (c) working with alternative theoretical perspectives. Supervisees described their supervisors as adherent with respect to sexual issues, the boundary between psychotherapy and supervision, termination, and follow-up issues. Once they had identified unethical practice, only 35% of the supervisees discussed their concerns with their supervisor; 84% discussed them with a peer or friend in the field, 33% with a significant other, 21% with another supervisor, and 18% with a personal therapist. Supervisees reported a mild to moderate (negative) impact of ethical infractions on their quality of clinical care. Greater frequency of unethical behavior by supervisors was associated with lower supervisee satisfaction; conversely, supervisors with fewer reported unethical behaviors were associated with more satisfied supervisees.

Ten years later, Wall's (2009) replication of Ladany, Lehrman-Waterman, et al.'s (1999) study surveyed the perceptions of 180 psychology interns about their supervisors' unethical practices. The interns reported the following unethical practices: failure to observe trainee performance and professional activity, failure to administer supervisory contracts (which we describe in detail later in this chapter), confidentiality breaches in supervision, and use of intervention methods by trainees for which the supervisor him- or herself had not received training. The respondents also reported that ethical nonadherence by their supervisors affected the supervisory alliance, their trust in their supervisor, their willingness to disclose information, their motivation to remain in the field, and their overall emotional well-being.

Ironically, the second highest perceived ethical violation in Ladany, Lerhman-Waterman, et al. (1999) study and third highest in Wall's (2009) study—violation of confidentiality in supervision—was not actually an ethical violation but a result of supervisees misunderstanding the limits of confidentiality in supervision. There are limits to such confidentiality because supervisors are directing and coordinating your clinical and professional development with a team of colleagues; reporting to graduate programs and licensing boards; and upholding ethical, legal, and institutional standards. Clarifying the limits of confidentiality is a supervisor's responsibility. If such limits are not addressed, ask your supervisor about them.

When Worthington, Tan, and Poulin (2002) questioned supervisees and supervisors about ethically questionable practices, substantial agreement was revealed on perceptions of what constituted "unethical" behavior. Many supervisees reported they had at least once had negative feelings about the supervisor and did not disclose them, did not complete timely documentation of client records, gossiped about a supervisory conflict did but not bring it to the supervisor, avoided talking about problems or mistakes in clinical work, did not discuss negative feelings toward a client, and did not address a strong personal (countertransference) reaction. Supervisee satisfaction with supervision was associated with greater disclosure (Yourman & Farber, 1996).

What do supervisees not disclose? Over one third of the supervisees in Worthington et al.'s (2002) sample said they fairly frequently omitted discussions of clinical errors by telling supervisors what they wanted to hear, and nearly 60% reported feeling uncomfortable disclosing negative feelings toward their supervisor.

What do supervisors not disclose? In Ladany and Melincoff's (1999) survey, 97% of supervisors said they had withheld some information from supervisees. The five highest ranked categories of supervisor nondisclosure were (a) negative reactions to a supervisee's counseling and professional performance; (b) supervisor personal issues; (c) negative reactions to a supervisee's supervision performance; (d) a supervisee's personal issues, including receptivity to feedback; and (e) negative supervisor self-efficacy or concerns about the effectiveness of their supervision. More than 10% of supervisors did not disclose positive reactions to supervisees' professional performance. Some of the nondisclosures by supervisors and supervisees are potential ethical infractions because they either run counter to the aspirational General Principles that inform the APA Ethics Code or they violate the enforceable numbered Standards of the Code. These Principles include Principle A: Beneficence and Nonmaleficence, and Principle C: Integrity. The relevant standards would be Standard 3.04: Avoiding Harm; Standard 3.10: Informed Consent (given that the purpose of practicum or internship is to enhance clinical skills and protect the client); and Standard 7.06: Assessing Student and Supervisee Performance (APA, 2010a).

Remember that a strong supervisory alliance is a requisite quality of successful supervision and predicts supervisee disclosure, satisfaction, multicultural competence, and engagement in difficult discussions of issues regarding clinical or supervision. Supervisor self-disclosure is also a part of good supervisory relationships and useful as a teaching tool to normalize developmental issues and focus on emotional reactions to clients (Knox, Burkard, Edwards, Smith, & Schlosser, 2008).

An important aspect of communicating seriousness is one's tone of voice and nonverbal behavior. Supervisors use a wide range of affect and communication, from warm positive, to neutral interactive, to firm or stern directive. A supervisor who does not use a range of affect and tone may confuse the supervisee. Supervisees have reported to us that they did not understand the seriousness of the directive if the supervisor stated it in an informal, "chatty" style, for example, "It would be great if you were to assess for child abuse." The absence of a more formal tone, of specific steps—either defined by the supervisor or elicited from the supervisee—might also be interpreted as a lack of seriousness. You will find it important to distinguish between directives that are imperatives and those that are suggestions. If there is a lack of clarity, ask your supervisor. If you do not believe you have the knowledge, skills, or attitudes to complete the action that is being required, communicate that directly to your supervisor and ask for guidance.

THE AMERICAN PSYCHOLOGICAL ASSOCIATION ETHICAL STANDARDS: PLAIN TALK

Practicum and internship are times for the integration of the APA Ethics Code into one's work (Handelsman, Knapp, & Gottlieb, 2009). Although prominently placed at the beginning of the code, the aspirational General Principles of promoting human welfare (which address the domains of, e.g., doing no harm, being faithful and responsible, maintaining one's own integrity, promoting justice and fairness, and respecting the dignity of others), have received lesser and inadequate attention (Handelsman et al., 2009); as a result, you may not have thought about how they relate to professional ethics.

As you develop as a professional, you will find that your perspective widens, from strict rule adherence to a broader consideration the General Principles of the APA Ethics Code. Your emphasis will be on doing the greatest good, aspiring to your highest ethical ideals, and maintaining a personal ethical sensitivity to the work being done as well as to personal well-being and happiness (Norcross & Guy, 2005). At the same time, Koocher and Keith-Spiegel (1998) cautioned that "holding ethical standards requires acting with benevolence and courage rather than donning protective armor and running for a safe place to hide" (p. 4).

Ethical values–based practice is a superordinate value in clinical supervision, just as it is in clinical practice. One of your goals should be to increase your reflection on the intersection of your own personal values and the values of the profession of psychology. This awareness includes moral, ethical, and personal frameworks that influence your judgments and intuition. Self-appraisal of ethical knowledge and skills, facility with the APA Ethics Code, ethical problem-solving frames, and understanding the role of one's worldview in ethical decision making all facilitate skilled and ethical practice.

However, knowing the APA Ethics Code does not guarantee that one actually implements it. In two different studies, psychologists (Pope & Bajt, 1988) and psychology graduate students (J. L. Bernard & Jara, 2008) were presented with ethical violation vignettes. A large disparity existed between what each group reported they thought *should* be done and what they *would* actually do: Knowledge of ethical codes did not directly translate into practice. Ironically, psychologists find it easier to question the ethics of others than to look closely at their own decisions and behavior. They also find it easier to question themselves in areas of uncertainty, whereas a wiser course of action would be to do so in areas of which one is most sure. Both of these strategies will enhance ethical thinking (Pope & Keith-Spiegel, 2008).

> *Reflection Activity.* Consider an incident in your experience in which an ethical issue arose. It could be anything from an issue with a client to a life situation. How did you address it? Reflect on the professional and personal principles that guided you.

The personal acculturation of ethics is an essential component of one's practice. Handelsman, Gottlieb, and Knapp (2005) adapted Berry's (2003) model of cultural acculturation to address the development of ethical acculturation. How does one mesh or integrate (or not) one's personal ethics, traditions, and values—those held *before* one completes psychology graduate work—with the adoption of the psychology professional ethics culture? Handelsman et al. (2005) identified four levels of ethical acculturation: (a) Integration, (b) Assimilation, (c) Separation, and (d) Marginalization. A supervisee is at the Integration level if he or she has high levels of personal ethics of origin—personal ethics developed prior to entering graduate training—and is high in his or her identification with psychology ethics. At the Integration level, one retains important values of his or her heritage while adopting the psychology ethics codes (e.g., the APA Ethics Code) and integrates the two. *Assimilation* refers to maintaining only a low level of personal ethics of origin, while adopting a high identification with psychology ethics. Divorce from one's personal values may prove to be problematic and may result in supervisees going through the motions of following professional ethics codes without the desirable degree of depth and integration; an example would be a supervisee refusing a gift from a child in response to perceived rules and ethical restrictions about gift giving without considering the family's culture or the child's developmental status or the ethical perspective of doing no harm. The high maintenance of the ethics and values of one's culture of origin and low adoption of the ethics of psychology characterize the Separation level, which manifests in imposing one's personal values on clients without regard for professional ethical standards. An example would be a person who is guided by his own religious or personal values when a client discusses getting a divorce and instructs the client accordingly (e.g., to stay with the spouse no matter what). *Marginalization*, the most problematic acculturation pattern, involves low identification with both one's personal values and ethics and with professional ethics. Individuals at this level are at the highest risk for ethical violations because they view ethical standards as capricious, arbitrary, and even oppressive (Handelsman et al., 2005).

How do you enhance your acculturation to ethics? Integration is associated with maintaining your personal ideals while integrating your professional status. A first step is your belief that ethics are not simply formulaic but complex, positive, and always evolving (Gottlieb, Handelsman, & Knapp, 2008). Adherence to the APA Ethics Code out of a fear of consequences harkens back to Kohlberg's stages of moral development, whereby individuals simply follow rules because they fear dire punitive consequences. Instead, through formal education and ethical exploration, you gain insight into the nuances of ethics and personal integration. Gottlieb et al. (2008) suggested that you may need to shed contextual or previously learned standards. If an individual who has just entered graduate school had previously been employed as a child protective services worker for several years, the ethical and legal frame of that individual's previous workplace, in which one views clients primarily through the lens of assessing cases of suspected child abuse and legal remedies, would need to be shed or reconstructed to accommodate the broader perspective of the psychologist. If the supervisee had been a substance abuse counselor before graduate school, that person would have to rid him- or herself of the practice of normatively disclosing personal substance abuse experience. A supervisee who had been a volunteer in homeless shelters would shed the practice of bringing food, gift cards, and clothing to clients in the practicum setting.

Although these examples may seem dramatic, or even obvious, supervisees' attentiveness to personal values leads to consideration of more subtle inferences and beliefs that influence the identification and practice of ethics. Gottlieb and Younggren (2009) further suggested that supervisees who both integrate aspirational ethics and balance their personal and professional values are at a substantially lower risk for ethical violations than those who do not. At high risk for ethical violations are those few who engage in marginalization or low identification with both personal values and professional ethics, potentially going down a slippery slope to an ethical violation because of lack of recognition of risk.

Reflection Activity. Consider some area of your personal experience or background that provides you with a particular lens or frame for your clinical work. Is it a strength? Is it something you may need to shed?

Separating figure from ground in ethics in the midst of the myriad clinical responsibilities is challenging. You have the responsibility of identifying subtle, embedded ethical issues in your clinical work. Instead of having ethical dilemmas highlighted by your supervisor or teachers, you are learning to apply ethics proactively across clinical and supervisory work and identify ethical dilemmas from the vast complex of client behavior. This transition will be greatly facilitated by supervision, peer discussion, and problem-solving frames.

Reflection Activity. Self-assess using the "Ethical Legal Standards and Policy" section of the Competency Benchmarks (see Appendix B). Consider your areas of strength and those that are in development. Make a list of each.

COMPETENCE: A KEY ETHICAL STANDARD

Ensuring proper assignment of cases, with close attention to your preparation, and providing a reasonable level of supervision, are ethical prerequisites for practice and supervision. How does a supervisor determine your level of competence, and how does that affect case assignments? The supervisor will factor in the Competency Benchmarks (Appendix A) or Practicum Competencies (Appendix B) self-assessment as well as other site-specific self-assessments. The results of these assessments will be combined with the knowledge of any previous training or experience you have had.

Competence is addressed in many parts of the APA Ethics Code, specifically in Standard 2, including Standard 2.01 (a), Boundaries of Competence and Standard 2.05, Delegation of Work to Others (APA, 2010a). Together, these ethical principles frame competent supervision practice. Their essential components are as follows:

- *Competency* is defined in terms of "education, training, supervised experience, consultation, study, or professional experience" (APA, 2010a) and is applicable to all therapy and to supervision.
- If you have had limited to no experience with respect to a particular client (e.g., diagnosis, culture, developmental level), then consider Standard 2.05, Delegation of Work to Others:

  [Supervisors] authorize only those responsibilities that such persons can be expected to perform on the basis of their education, training, or experience, either independently or with the level of supervision being provided.

Supervisor Competence

Many supervisors will provide a general outline of areas of their own personal competence (e.g., a specialty in child therapy and assessment with a subspecialty in structural and strategic family therapy) that generally encompasses the spectrum of what you would like to know about competency with regard to multiple diversity factors, theoretical orientations, and diagnoses and interventions for various clients. For areas in which your supervisor is less competent, he or she may identify auxiliary resources, including consultants, training, or referrals available. A discussion of competence is a central part of the development of the supervisory goals and objectives.

Considering Your Own Competence

How do you assess your own competence to treat particular clients and diagnoses with the level of supervision being provided? Performing a self-assessment with the Competency Benchmarks (Appendix A) or the Practicum Competencies (Appendix B) will help you evaluate your current and developing competencies, including your clinical experience. Your supervisor (with your help) will determine your level of "entrustability" (ten Cate, 2006) for a range of functions; that is, the supervisor will evaluate his or her confidence that you have the requisite knowledge and skills to perform therapy and services with a particular client or a range of clients. Supervisors have options to increase the level of supervision through more frequent meetings;

telephone check-ins; being available while you are seeing a particular client; spending more time on one particular client in supervision; reviewing audio or video tapes; conducting live supervision (i.e. observing the session through a one-way window); joining the client session; or, in most extreme instances, transferring the client to another, more senior staff member.

Your confidence may be increased by the knowledge that a therapist's number of years of experience does not predict positive client outcomes (Leon, Martinovich, Lutz, & Lions (2003); instead, they are related to other variables, such as the therapeutic alliance, empathy, or other personal factors. Although trusting your supervisor's judgment is important, sharing about particular clients who seem too difficult, and trying to articulate aspects of your training that seem overwhelming or difficult with as much specificity as possible, is essential. To clarify aspects of your discomfort, identify your knowledge, skills, and values with respect to therapy and your assessment of the particular client. If you have a strong knowledge base combined with few specific skills, then address with your supervisor your strengths and areas of lesser experience. If you feel a personal value or attitude is impeding therapy, then discussing this with the supervisor is urgent. The supervisor must factor in the wide range of your related previous experience. Sometimes it is difficult for the supervisor to know whether a super-visee is being too self-critical or self-effacing and thus underestimating his or her own competence, which happens with many supervisees! In other cases, the supervisor may determine that the assigned case is beyond the supervisee's pres-ent level of competence and may require additional supervisor support.

Mental health treatments develop and change so quickly that supervisors are challenged to keep up with the most current research and treatments. Evi-dence-based practices and practice parameters increasingly set standards of practice, but you may find that your graduate training was more intensive or specific to an emerging evidence-supported treatment program than the train-ing your supervisor has received. This competence issue must be addressed to ensure you do not feel that the treatment is ethically incompatible with standards of practice.

ETHICAL DILEMMAS

Ironically, the same ethical dilemmas that should be rich grist for the mill of supervision are the ones not discussed in supervision or graduate training at all! Pope, Sonne, and Greene (2006) addressed many of these in their book, *What Therapists Don't Talk About and Why: Understanding Taboos That Hurt Us and Our Clients*. Some of these topics include sexual arousal and attrac-tion, a wide range of personal responses to clients, and the process of therapy when it goes adrift or awry.

In the following sections, we discuss pivotal aspects of ethical practice and give examples to highlight ethical dilemmas and possible steps to resolution.

> *Reflection Activity.* Think of an ethical dilemma you have encountered in your clinical, supervision, or other work. Consider how you went about solving it. Then use the ethical problem-solving frames as they are introduced in the sections that follow.

Confidentiality

Confidentiality issues arise in relationships with clients, in supervision, and in dissemination of information about the supervisee to various constituencies. What are acceptable standards regarding confidentiality? Client confidentiality is governed by regulation, law, and ethical codes, with limits elaborately articulated. What about your own confidentiality? You may believe that everything you tell a supervisor about yourself is strictly confidential, whereas some of your peers may believe nothing is confidential. The reality is somewhere in between and is governed by the supervisor's formal responsibility to various entities, including the client, training site, licensing board, graduate institution, profession, legal standards, and respectful practice. If a supervisee described her recent turbulent separation from her significant other and asked the supervisor not to share that information with anyone, the supervisor most likely would inform the supervisee that he might need to share this information if he believed it to be relevant to her clinical work. Other examples are if a supervisee were to tell his supervisor about his insomnia, his mother's chronic illness, or his disinclination to work with a particular group. What is the expectation regarding whether this information would, or should, be shared? If there were behavioral indications of lapses in expected competence, or if the supervisory training group addressed the supervisee's fatigue, sadness, or other behavior, then information about these topics most likely would be disclosed for purposes of the supervisee's development. The issue of supervisee confidentiality comes up most often when the supervisee is not meeting performance criteria. The supervisor is legally and ethically required to act on a broad spectrum of categories, for example, a supervisee's intent to harm a client or violate a client's rights; ethical code infractions; posing a danger to self or others; using substances and coming to work under the influence; clinic or setting policy violations; and, more generally, performance issues or failure to meet competency criteria. Consider the examples given in the following two sections.

Example 1: Supervisee Confidentiality

The supervisee begins conducting therapy with a college student her own age whom she describes as very handsome. The client is tormented by his relationship with his mother and his failure to sustain relationships with women. The supervisee feels attracted to him and believes she could be better for him than the women he has been seeing. She is reluctant to bring her feelings to supervision.

This instance highlights the supervisee's competence in identifying sexual attraction and discussing this phenomenon in supervision. Supervisors will view disclosure of such feelings, which are normal in clinical work, as a strength and an informer of the clinical process. Disclosure is critical to ensure that the supervisee does not inadvertently respond to the predictable, normative emotional triggers elicited by the situation and does not violate ethical standards relating to multiple relationships, a topic we discuss later in this chapter.

Example 2: Client Confidentiality

A client arrives for her first session and seems very concerned about the limits of confidentiality statements. She questions the supervisee–therapist extensively about what would and would not be disclosed to third parties. After asking these elaborate questions, the client inquires whether just lightly slapping her son on the bottom now and then would need to be reported and whether that could result in her child being removed from the home by a social services agency. The supervisee–therapist reassures her that that is typical parenting and not of concern.

Think about your reactions to this vignette. How could you proceed once the question of confidentiality has been asked? Questions often have many layers. In this particular example, you would need to be thoughtful about the ethical principles that guide practice. Recall Principle C of the APA Ethics Code, Integrity:

> Psychologists seek to promote accuracy, honesty, and truthfulness in the science, teaching, and practice of psychology. In these activities psychologists do not steal, cheat, or engage in fraud, subterfuge, or intentional misrepresentation of fact. Psychologists strive to keep their promises and to avoid unwise or unclear commitments. In situations in which deception may be ethically justifiable to maximize benefits and minimize harm, psychologists have a serious obligation to consider the need for, the possible consequences of, and their responsibility to correct any resulting mistrust or other harmful effects that arise from the use of such techniques. (APA, 2010a)

Consider this principle in light of the client's question. It would be essential to follow up with a fuller exploration of her practices of spanking and child discipline that might reveal information raising suspicion of child abuse. A report may be mandated for the protection of both the child and client/parent. How could this supervisee best answer the question the parent raised while maintaining her professional integrity and addressing the relevant concerns?

The supervisee might say,

> It sounds like you have some concerns about your discipline with Malcolm. That is certainly an area we will be talking about a lot, given his significant behavior problems. I cannot promise you that we will never need to make a child abuse report, but part of the treatment will be helping you to find ways to discipline that do not involve spanking.

After this, she could conduct a more thorough exploration of this client's disciplinary practices. Also, the supervisee would be well advised to explore why the client raised this specific issue: Perhaps a child abuse report had been made previously.

Through this discussion, the limits of confidentiality are reinforced, with an emphasis on the client's needs and the treatment goals. Directly addressing client worries and informing them of the limits of confidentiality are practices that your supervisor will model, support, and help you to build. In this example, seeking supervisor guidance would be helpful, even while the client is still at the appointment. Disclosure of therapist–client interaction is a most important part of clinical supervision. Client confidentiality is a very complex topic, and a thorough understanding of it requires knowledge of current laws and regulations, including the Family Educational Rights and Privacy Act (Wise, King, Miller, & Pearce, 2011) and the Health Insurance Portability and Accountability Act of 1996 (Pub. L. 104-191).

Informed Consent

The term *informed consent* refers to the range of information, expectations, procedures, and consequences that are important to know so you can effectively structure your behavior and practice (see Standard 3.10, Informed Consent in the APA [2010a] Ethics Code). Falvey (2002) described five levels of informed consent for supervision:

1. Client consent for treatment by the supervisee
2. Client consent for supervision of his or her case
3. Supervisor consent to assume supervisory responsibility for the supervisee
4. Supervisee consent to supervision with a given supervisor
5. Institutional consent to comply with clinical, ethical, and legal parameters of supervision for the discipline involved

Clients have to knowingly consent to enter treatment with you, and they must be made aware that your supervisor is privy to all information, may observe sessions live or via video, and has the ultimate decision-making responsibility in each client's case. Many states have regulations regarding informing the client that the therapist is in training under the supervision of a licensed individual, with informed consent obtained from the client verbally or in writing.

For you as a supervisee, understanding your supervisor's expectations fulfills one aspect of informed consent. Supervisors may have many expectations, including that case notes be completed ahead of time and brought to the supervision session as well as that audio or video review of a session will occur before or during the supervision session. The supervisor may also expect you to propose diagnostic rule-outs (i.e., diagnoses that you think are pertinent to a client's case) you have considered, with provisional diagnoses identified; formulate case conceptualizations in the theoretical frame or frames specified, and/or propose a tentative treatment plan that takes into account diversity and cultural factors at all levels of assessment and treatment. Your supervisor will expect you to discuss relationship and how you will demonstrate respect for the client. In addition, your supervisor may expect you to identify and address any pertinent legal and ethical issues. You also may be expected to propose appropriate evidence-supported models of intervention for the client's diagnosis, culture, and developmental status or to explain why the client does not meet criteria for proposed models. Many of these expectations may be outlined in a supervision contract, which we describe in the next section.

At the outset of your practicum or internship, your supervisor will explain his or her expectations regarding your explorations and disclosure of personal information or personal responses to both client presentation/material and to the supervision process (refer to APA Standard 7.04, Student Disclosure of Personal Information; APA 2010a). Supervisors in most settings will describe to you the expectations regarding exploration of personal factors, countertransference, and strains and ruptures in the supervisory relationship, as well as client or supervision triggers to emotional response, that will be a part of clinical supervision.

The Supervision Contract

The supervision contract, which outlines the purpose, goals, and objectives of supervision, as well as more specific goals for you, is an excellent way to increase *transparency*—whereby the supervisor provides ongoing feedback in a competency frame that helps you understand and calibrate your learning so you can reach clearly defined performance criteria—and clarity of expectations for both you and your supervisor. The supervisor typically initiates this agreement, and your involvement strengthens the shared sense of responsibility for learning (Osborn & Kelly, 2010). The supervision contract is constructed to identify the following:

- the multiple site, contextual, legal, and supervisory expectations;
- agreed-on length of training;
- frequency and duration of supervision;
- location of training and supervision;
- supervision modality and type of monitoring to be used (e.g., theoretical orientation and whether there is video or audio recording expected);
- evaluation format (both formative and summative);
- contingency planning, including emergencies;
- individuals whom you can contact if your supervisor is not available;
- how canceled supervision sessions are handled and rescheduled;
- record-keeping policies; and
- expectations that personal factors (including emotional reactions), countertransference, conflict or disagreement, and supervisory strains and ruptures will all be handled during the supervision process.

Also included is the expectation that you may be referred for personal therapy or other forms of support if issues arise that cross the boundary between supervision and psychotherapy. Thomas (2007) provided an excellent resource for more information on supervision contracts.

An additional aspect of informed consent is supervisory evaluation. Although governed by APA Ethical Standard 7.06, Assessing Student and Supervisee Performance (APA, 2010a) the evaluative function and the supervisory power differential that underlies this are often the unacknowledged elephant in the room. Lack of supervisee monitoring and assessment of performance are among the major reported ethical infractions of supervisors (Ladany, Lehrman-Waterman, et al., 1999).

All evaluation and tracking tools are introduced at the onset of supervision, including definition of the methods of formative and summative evaluation. *Formative evaluation* refers to ongoing feedback and comparison against a particular standard, such as the Competency Benchmarks (Appendix A) or competency frames specific to the setting, whereas *summative evaluation* is the final assessment of whether the supervisee's performance meets criteria for success and may include an oral examination or observation of particular clinical tasks. Kaslow et al. (2009) described innovative techniques for assessing both. Transparency is a key component of evaluation. That is, the supervisor provides ongoing feedback in a competency frame that assists you to understand and calibrate learning, to reach clearly defined performance criteria.

Multiple Relationships

According to Standard 3.05 of the APA Ethics Code,

[A] multiple relationship occurs when a psychologist is in a professional role with a person and (1) at the same time is in another role with the same person, (2) at the same time is in a relationship with a person closely associated with or related to the person with whom the psychologist has the professional relationship, or (3) promises to enter into another relationship in the future with the person or a person closely associated with or related to the person. (APA, 2010a)

Because you and your supervisor will often participate in a wide range of activities together, some multiple relationships may be normative to the setting; however, it may be difficult at times to understand which boundaries are appropriate. Examples might be if a supervisor asked you to co-lead a group, coauthor a paper, work on an administrative task, babysit his or her child, or go out to dinner. How do you determine what is appropriate? Supervisors often use a form of informed consent to acquaint new supervisees with the range of multiple relationships and roles and jointly problem-solve potential rough spots or emergent circumstances. In the sections that follow, we discuss various issues that can arise between supervisee–therapists and clients and between supervisors and supervisees.

Boundary Crossings

A *boundary crossing* is a nonpejorative term referring to departures from commonly accepted clinical practice that may or may not benefit the client (Smith & Fitzpatrick, 1995) or, in this instance, you the supervisee. A boundary crossing is distinguished from a *boundary violation*, which is a departure from accepted practice that places the client or the therapeutic process at serious risk (Gutheil & Gabbard, 1993), for example, exploitation or sexual behavior. We discuss boundary violations in the next section. Boundary crossings include such behaviors as touch (e.g., hugs), gift giving (and receiving), and attendance at social events where the client or supervisor is present. A number of boundary crossings may occur in your therapy and in supervision. The complexity of supervisory boundary crossings is heightened by the power differential between you and your client and between you and your supervisor. How difficult is it for you to say no to a supervisor request when the supervisor is the one evaluating you, sending feedback to your school, and generally signing off on the work you do?

Kadushin (1968) wrote extensively about the "games" in which supervisors and supervisees sometimes engage during the supervision process. In one situation, the supervisee praises the supervisor's extensive knowledge and skill, discloses the reverence with which she regards the supervisor, and as a result has elevated the supervisor to a position in which he is infallible (i.e., is idealizing the supervisor). In another situation, the supervisee tells the supervisor that he views the supervisor as a wise parent and would like to get some parental advice on a pressing issue he is facing. In another, the supervisee or supervisor tells the other that he is hungry, because the supervision session is so close to lunchtime, and wouldn't it be great to walk down to the coffee shop to get a snack? Of course, discussing cases on the sidewalk or at the café is impossible, so the supervisor and supervisee discuss personal issues, and the hour is over by the time they return. This is an instance of negligent supervision, because there has been no discussion of cases. Numerous combinations of these games/dances exist, some supervisee initiated and some supervisor initiated, albeit not intentionally. Each represents a boundary issue and should be addressed.

Pope and Keith-Spiegel (2008) suggested a particular frame to use as a tool for reflecting on ethical issues applicable to boundary crossings: "What if I'm wrong about this? Is there something I'm overlooking? Could there be another way of understanding this situation? Could there be a more creative, more effective way of responding?" (p. 641).

Moving into supervisee–therapist–client examples, some boundary instances are more clear cut, as when a client asks the supervisee–therapist out on a dinner date, but there are many less distinct instances. You may wonder about your own self-disclosures to clients and how to deal with personal questions clients ask that catch you by surprise and raise the specter of crossing a line or boundary by, for example, disclosing your religion or sexual orientation. As with many boundary issues, remember to process the therapeutic relationship, client perspective, and take a reflective stance—and bring it to supervision!

Other boundary instances include the client loaning a supervisee–therapist a book; asking to hug the supervisee–therapist; inviting the supervisee–therapist to go next door for coffee; consistently bringing food or soft drinks to the supervisee–therapist; inviting the supervisee–therapist to attend the client's party; and/or bringing something to show the supervisee–therapist and then refusing to take the item back, and then doing that every week, commenting on how much the shared interest means to him (e.g., book, movie, or music). However, your intent in such interchanges is less important than what the boundary crossing means to the client. Even if you accept an item from a client in the interest of increasing rapport and making a connection, the client may have a distinctly different construction of the meaning. Bringing you gifts or tokens of remembrance may be construed by the client as an overture to transform the relationship from therapist–client to a social or romantic one. Cultural and contextual factors must be factored into the decision as well. As Vasquez (2007) stated, "Sometimes a taco is just a taco," reflecting that in the interest of cultural respect a therapist can accept a small gift, food, or token in the spirit in which it is given.

Another group of boundary crossings occur often in small communities, for example, when the client attends the same church or synagogue as the supervisee, or joins a self-help or 12-step group that the supervisee attends, or has a child on the same baseball team or in the same choir as the supervisee's child.

Schank and Skovholt (2006) addressed issues specific to small communities and proposed a set of strategies to minimize risk:

- Recognize that ethics codes or standards are necessary but not sufficient.
- Know relevant codes, regulations, and laws.
- Obtain informed consent (to set tone of professional relationship).
- Involve prospective clients in decision-making (regarding implications of overlapping social/business relationships).
- Talk directly with clients about the likelihood of out-of-therapy contact.
- Consider the type and severity of the client's presenting problem.
- Set clear expectations (for overlapping roles in community).
- Set clear boundaries, both within yourself and with clients.
- Be scrupulous about documentation.
- Be especially aware of issues of confidentiality.
- Be aware of broader community standards.
- Maintain a hierarchy of values.
- Know yourself.
- Participate in ongoing consultation [supervision] and discussions with your supervisor.
- Continue to educate yourself.
- Know when to stop (i.e., terminate therapy or arrange a referral). (pp. 179–188)

Because many mental health systems are adopting recovery models (as discussed in Chapter 2) for treatment, and some are urging greater latitude in multiple relationships (Zur, 2007), the standards of practice relating to many of these issues are shifting. Most important is that you understand the context and setting and draw on your supervisor's knowledge and skills to be prepared when boundary crossings occur, as they inevitably do. A warning signal is if the multiple relationship constitutes a behavior that is a deviation from normal practice. Such a deviation triggers the need for supervision so you can address the proposed multiple relationship, bearing in mind your duty to act in the client's best interest. Conducting therapy in community settings or clients' homes provides a different framework of behaviors that are culturally sensitive and acceptable in the clinical setting. If you feel strongly about not accepting food from clients, and refuse tea or foods served by clients when doing in-home services, the result may be a strain to or rupture of the relationship with the client. Cultural competence—and humility—is essential to prevent doing harm to the client when confronted with gifts, hugs, or other boundary issues. Boundaries are much less rigid with children; for example, clinicians routinely accept handmade gifts or purchase candy bars being sold for school fund raisers. Supervisors will be proactive in preparing you for boundary crossings, and you should feel comfortable raising questions when you are unsure. Some of the problem-solving frames we present later in this chapter also are useful tools.

> **Reflection Activity.** Consider the following scenarios and identify (a) feelings evoked by them and (b) how you might proceed should your supervisor do the following:
> - Asks you if you would like to buy her daughter's Girl Scout cookies
> - Requires you to write all supervision notes reflecting supervision session
> - Requires you to take all notes for a group co-led with the supervisor
> - Asks if you could babysit children in the clinic waiting room
> - Conducts supervision (in the car) during the supervisor's carpool
> - Requests your help in writing a grant proposal
> - Asks you to grade exams for a class the supervisor teaches
> - Asks if you would be willing to walk his or her dog
> - Requests that you pick up the supervisor's lunch weekly before supervision
> - Arranges supervisory sessions to occur in the cafeteria
> - Gives you a gift

How would you determine your response to each of these instances? Is it best to follow a set of rules, a template, or to base your response on personal feelings? Gottlieb, Robinson, and Younggren (2007) developed a very useful problem-solving frame for supervision. Consider the following sequence of probes for any of the dilemmas just listed.

- Is entering into a relationship in addition to the supervisory one necessary, or should the supervisor (or supervisee) avoid it?

- Can the additional relationship potentially cause harm to the supervisee?
- If harm seems unlikely or avoidable, would the additional relationship prove beneficial?
- Is there a risk the additional relationship could disrupt the supervisory relationship?
- Can the supervisor (or, in this instance, the supervisee) evaluate the matter objectively?

Imagine being invited to attend a play with your supervisor. A good first step is to consider your initial emotional response when first invited. Next, consider the pros and cons. Perhaps you both have learned of a mutual interest in a particular playwright, and the supervisor discovered that her favorite play by that person was being put on locally and so spontaneously purchased a pair of tickets so you and she could attend together. The supervisor presented the tickets to you at the next supervision hour (very early in the training year) and described how excited she was to learn of the play. After noting a brief hesitation by you, the supervisor begins to reflect: Perhaps she should have discussed the possibility of attending the play with you before buying the tickets. You might be thinking about what the other supervisees will think when they learn about the special outing, or you may be moved by her thoughtfulness. In the current setting, such invitations may be normative and the supervisor might systematically invite supervisees to special events. On the other hand, you might feel uncomfortable because there is no way to repay her for the tickets, and other supervisees may see it as favoritism. Both of you may feel the relationship between you has changed ever so slightly.

Now you can systematically apply Gottlieb et al.'s (2007) problem-solving frame. Is entering into this relationship (i.e., a social or recreational one) with the supervisor necessary, or should it be avoided? You are in a more vulnerable position because of the power differential between you and your supervisor. You may prefer to avoid going to the play but may feel powerless as to whether you have a choice, or voice, in the matter. If the supervisory relationship is a strong one, you may feel comfortable suggesting to the supervisor that she use this problem-solving framework as well!

Next, consider whether the additional relationship can potentially cause harm to you. It is most desirable to discuss this with your supervisor, but if you do not feel comfortable doing this, you can consider the worst-case scenario that could occur if you did attend the play together. Consider the best-case scenario as well.

Then, if harm seems unlikely or avoidable, consider whether the additional relationship could prove beneficial. Is there a risk that the additional relationship could disrupt the supervisor–supervisee relationship? Last, can you evaluate the matter objectively? You could consult a more experienced peer, or a faculty member.

Burian and Slimp (2000) added that it is helpful to consider the potential impact of the additional relationship on other staff members, interns, or trainees. Also, what is your ability to leave the additional relationship?

Another multiple relationship involves gifts. How do you feel about receiving gifts? What if a child client gives you a gift? What factors would you consider when deciding whether to accept it? What if it were handmade or clearly less than the particular dollar amount that the setting deems acceptable? What if you could not assess how expensive it is? This sort of dilemma is important to discuss in supervision before it happens so you can be prepared.

Consider the following hypothetical example: A supervisor had transferred one of his clients to his new supervisee. Right after Thanksgiving, he advised the supervisee that this particular family had always given him lavish Christmas gifts to thank him for all his efforts during the year and to commemorate the holiday season. He explained that this was culturally syntonic for them and that to refuse a gift from this family would be an insult. He described his gift the previous year: a very special motorcycle helmet ordered from Switzerland and custom sized to fit him because the family knew he loved motorcycles. The supervisor began speculating about what they might decide to give the supervisee.

The supervisee was taken aback, because this public agency had a rule against any gift that cost over $10, and such an expensive present sounded inappropriate, even exploitative. However, he was also mindful of doing no harm and not insulting the customs or traditions of his client family. The supervisee quietly stated, "Wow, that must have put you in a very difficult spot, given the clinic rule, our ethical code, and cultural considerations. I am so glad you warned me so we have time to think about it!" The supervisor responded, "I deserved it. I worked hard with that family and you are too. Just accept it gracefully! If you don't, you will hurt their feelings. That would negatively impact the therapy."

Several weeks later, the client family brought the supervisee a rare first edition of a Dickens novel because they had consulted with the supervisor, who had told them the supervisee loved Dickens. The supervisee has numerous choices. What should he do?

Here are some possible options:

- Accept the gift graciously, as the supervisor had urged.
- Politely thank the client family for the incredibly generous gift, discuss his appreciation for the care, thought, and planning that had clearly gone into the gift selection, and then explain why he could not accept it but would welcome it as a gift to the

public agency. He could express his appreciation of their desire to give back to someone who had been so giving of his time but explain that his recompense is that they were making such good progress.

- Discuss the cultural significance of the gift and how appreciative he is that they were so thoughtful and then collaboratively problem-solve with them how to be sure that they understood the depth of his appreciation as well as the depth of his commitment to the rules and regulations that govern the setting and the profession. The process could even be a metaphor for some of the issues in therapy.

How can you as a supervisee discuss such a potentially difficult issue with your supervisor? Possible openings, might be phrased thus:

> It was so helpful that you forewarned me about the gift possibility. It gave me so much time to think about it. I considered my notes and documents from my academic classes and used a problem-solving framework. I would love to go through it with you!

Or you could say, "This is an incredible opportunity for learning; I would love the chance to think about this whole process with you."

We now provide another case example, also of a gift. It is the last week of the supervisee's internship, and she has her last session with an 11-year-old Native American girl and her mother. About 10 minutes after the session begins, the girl presents the supervisee with a gift: a beautiful turquoise carved stone in a metal setting. After several efforts to deal with not accepting the gift, but expressing appreciation, she decides to call the supervisor for an urgent consult:

> I don't know exactly what to do . . . Noa gave me a present—here it is—she says she and her mom shopped for it for months and saved their money to get it. It is a piece of turquoise in a setting—and she says it reminds her of how beautiful our time together was, and how perfect their relationship is now after our work together, and this ensures I will always remember her! At first I was just going to accept it and thank her, because I think culturally, that would be the right thing. But then I started thinking about the value and the financial sacrifice . . . and what it would mean to them if I take it and what it would mean if I *don't* take it! I suggested taking a picture of it that I would always keep, but they insist I take the actual gift. I suggested giving it to the clinic, but they said the clinic is not me. So I don't know what to do! They will be very upset if I don't accept it, but I am feeling very uncomfortable accepting because it feels like it changes our relationship—and it is doing harm to them—it looks so expensive!

Together, the supervisor and supervisee briefly problem-solved, applying several approaches to the dilemma. One option would be to have the client donate the turquoise piece to the agency, but the supervisee explains they already refused this because they feel this is an undesirable outcome. The supervisee's cultural understanding helps her recognize that, from the client's perspective, valued aspects of treatment are therapist trustworthiness and the values of sharing and cooperation (LaFromboise & Dizon, 2003). The supervisor then helps the supervisee balance the positive outcome of the therapy that the family had made, including such a meaningful therapeutic interaction, with the ethics of multiple relationships and exploitation (Herlihy & Watson, 2003). At issues are the acceptance of and respect for the client by the therapist as well as the greater power of the therapist in the therapeutic relationship. A rupture in the therapeutic relationship could have severe consequences for the outcome of the therapy because the underlying platform of client–therapist trust could potentially be tarnished. What are other alternatives, and how would one achieve them?

Boundary Violations

In contrast to boundary crossings, boundary violations—which can include sex with a client and any form of exploitation (e.g., buying or selling real estate to or from a client or supervisor) —are ethically and legally prohibited. How can supervisees be proactive in identifying high-risk situations for potential boundary violations in clinical work? A first warning signal is whether the behavior is a deviation from normal practice. Supervisees should be vigilant for the following behaviors and feelings in their work (Hamilton & Spruill, 1999; Walker & Clark, 1999):

- strong emotional reaction(s) to a client that the supervisee does not address (or avoids addressing) in supervision;
- extending sessions or arranging them at the end of the day for a particular client;
- telephone calls that are frequent, undocumented, or take place outside business hours;
- inappropriate communication while transporting clients or performing in-home or community services;
- inappropriate gift giving between clinician and client;
- boundary problems in in-home therapy and home visits (e.g., staying after the session to watch TV, babysit, go to a movie, or other activities);
- overprotecting or overidentifying with a client;
- belief that a client, an aspect of the client, or the client's circumstance is unique;

- loans, barter, or sales of goods;
- touch—comforting and sexual contact; and
- therapist self-disclosures (are they thoughtful, planful, and guided by the proviso that they be in the best interests of the client's therapy?).

Once you have identified red flags, consider whether they constitute a pattern and whether they represent a deviation from regular practice. Regardless of your theoretical orientation, it is normative to have feelings toward clients (Kimerling, Zeiss, & Zeiss, 2000; Shafranske & Falender, 2008). Feelings and their triggers inform clinical practice and enhance supervision. The first step is to recognize the behavior or evoked emotion; the second step is to reflect on it; and the third is to bring it to supervision so your supervisor can assist in exploration, using the feeling state that has been induced in you to direct the therapy and supervision process.

What should you do when you identify red flags that represent a deviation from your regular practice? In situations where there is a strong supervisory relationship of trust and mutuality (always bearing in mind the power differential between the supervisor and supervisee), you may feel empowered to note the incident in supervision, perhaps by reflecting aloud on it:

> I was thinking about what we discussed last week and was wondering about your asking me to loan the client money for bus fare. It felt uncomfortable, and I would like if we could discuss it again. A colleague at another setting told me the agency purchases bus tokens that are available for emergencies.

Or "Remember how we discussed terminating my client Bob with no warning? I was wondering if we could talk about that again, as I had some thoughts about the ethics and practical issues." If these kinds of reflective statements do not seem possible, an excellent idea is to consult a faculty member at school—not to complain, but to learn how you can best proceed to highlight the dilemma in such a way that it can be processed fully. Another possible approach is this:

> I remembered my professor who always encouraged us to think of the worst thing that could happen if we were to resolve an ethical dilemma a particular way. Well, in this instance, if I attend Amanda's wedding, there are any number of worst things. For example, maybe she will begin to think of our relationship differently—more as a friendship than therapeutic—or maybe someone will ask me how I know Amanda, and I will either have to lie or betray confidentiality. It would be great if we could discuss this and maybe use an ethical problem-solving frame.

Another example is a supervisee working in a prison setting. One of the inmates, the supervisee's client, is a talented artist. On the last day of the supervisee's rotation, the client gives the supervisee a painting. The supervisor advises the supervisee that she may not keep the artwork because it is strictly against regulations and potentially exploitative. The supervisee is surprised because she had thought that anything that is handmade would be an acceptable gift. What are various ways to consider this?

A good strategy when confronted with an ethically ambiguous situation is to consider the worst-case scenario that could arise from a particular action. For example, if you were to bump into a client at a coffee shop after the session and have a quick cup of coffee together, what is the worst thing that could happen? What is the best thing that could happen? What process of thinking will help you decide? Consider all the problem-solving frames we have presented thus far and the multiple possibilities. In general, therapists discuss with clients the possibility of chance encounters and how they will respond, with the therapist often not acknowledging the client unless the client initiates contact and deferring to the wishes of the client regarding contact.

Discussion of countertransference in supervision is a legal standard. Several legal decisions (e.g., Simmons v. U.S., 1986; Marston and Williams v. Minneapolis Clinic of Psychiatry and Neurology, 1982) have determined that sexual attraction is a predictable part of psychotherapy, and that it is a standard of practice to discuss and manage it during the supervision process (Recupero & Rainey, 2007). Transference and boundary violations are foreseeable risks of treatment and must be addressed. Supervisors are responsible for educating supervisees about countertransferences as well as monitoring and addressing instances of it. Failure to do so constitutes negligent supervision (Recupero & Rainey, 2007). Over 80% of practicing psychologists, and corresponding numbers of practitioners in other mental health disciplines, report they have felt sexual attraction to a client at least once in their career (Pope et al., 2006); however, the vast majority of them did not bring it up in their supervision. Why did they not bring it up? Some of the reasons suggested by Pope, Keith-Spiegel, and Tabachnick (1986) and associated studies discussed in Pope et al. (2006) are that they were concerned that their supervisors would view them as less than mentally healthy, that they were concerned about evaluation, or that they were simply embarrassed. Very few supervisors provided adequate information to ensure that supervisees understood that such feelings are a predictable part of psychotherapy and grist for the mill of supervision (Pope et al., 2006).

In general, peers are the first to know if a fellow supervisee is demonstrating problematic behavior due to intensity of client contact, proximity, and/or intimacy (Rosenberg, Getzelman, Arcinue, & Oren, 2005). Supervisors typically are not aware of the impact of a supervisee's problematic behavior on the other supervisees and on learning (Rosenberg et al., 2005). How important are the actions of supervisees while in training, and how predictive are problematic behaviors of future difficulties? One answer comes from the medical profession. Papadakis et al. (2005) identified 235 physicians who had graduated from three major medical schools and who had been disciplined by a state medical board and matched them carefully with a control group of similar graduates who had not been disciplined. They conducted a retrospective analysis of school records and reported that there were significant relationships between problematic behavior in medical school and future disciplinary actions. These included severe irresponsibility (e.g., unreliable class attendance and failure to follow through with patient care) and severely diminished capacity for self-improvement (e.g., failure to accept constructive criticism, argumentativeness, and displaying a poor attitude). A subsequent analysis revealed that both behavioral and cognitive performance measures also were predictive of subsequent disciplinary actions (Papadakis, Arnold, Blank, Holmboe, & Lipner, 2008). It is possible that the disciplined individuals were marginalized in their ethical development, with neither personal values nor professional ethics as anchors (Gottlieb & Younggren, 2009). This study helps us understand how important it is in training to integrate constructive criticism and accountability. Supervisors bear a significant responsibility to clients, supervisees, and to the profession as a whole to ensure that supervisees' performance meets developmental criteria in all areas. They also bear the responsibility of ensuring that supervisees are open to feedback and criticism and that they use it responsibly to inform and improve performance.

DIRECT AND VICARIOUS LIABILITY

Supervisors are liable not only for their supervision but also for their supervisees' performance and behaviors. The actual rate of lawsuits regarding supervisee behavior is low (Slovenko, 1980). Supervisors are responsible for providing supervision that meets the standard of practice, that is, what reasonable psychologists would agree on and as articulated by the profession. Not providing supervision at the level of the standard of practice is deemed *negligent supervision*, and it comprises not knowing what the supervisee is doing, instructing the supervisee to do something in a client's case that is contraindicated, knowing of a supervisee's error but failing to take corrective action, or carelessness in monitoring a supervisee's work. Negligent supervision also involves *not* supervising by virtue of missing sessions or dozing through them. In general, it relates to the supervisor's own negligence.

Vicarious liability, or *respondeat superior*, is the liability of the supervisor as a result of the supervisee's actions. Disney and Stephens (1994) outlined three conditions that must be met for vicarious liability:

1. Supervisees voluntarily agree to work under the direction and control of supervisor and act in ways that benefit the supervisor.
2. Supervisees must be acting within the defined scope of tasks permitted by the supervisor.
3. The supervisor must have the power to control and direct the supervisees' work.

Multiple factors result in malpractice liability. For such liability to arise, according to Disney and Stephens (1994), several elements must be proven:

- A fiduciary relationship with therapist or supervisor, which means the supervisor is working in the best interests of the supervisee and clients.
- The supervisor's (or therapist's) conduct was improper or negligent and fell below the standard of care.
- The supervisee (or client) suffered demonstrable harm or injury.
- A causal relationship is demonstrated between the injury and negligence or improper conduct.

Understanding supervisor liability will help you better understand your own supervisor's responsibility and, as you advance in your professional development and begin to take on supervisory responsibilities yourself, liability will become a significant personal concern as well.

LEGAL CONSIDERATIONS: THE DUTY TO WARN AND PROTECT

Understanding legal statutes, case law, and standards will be an important part of your practice as a supervisee. Whether you are moving from another part of the country and/or entering a new practicum setting, be sure to learn about the legal reporting and confidentiality standards that exist in the state or province where you'll be practicing (Pabian, Welfel, & Beebe, 2009).

The phrase *duty to protect* refers to a mental health professional's legal obligation to breach client confidentiality to protect a third party (or parties) from the client's threatened violence. *Duty to warn* refers to the legal obligation to take action to inform or warn a third party who might be at risk of harm from a client by contacting the identified potential victim of the client's serious threats of harm and/or to notify law enforcement. Thirty-two states mandate a duty to protect regarding the professional's responsibility in regard to dangerous clients (Welfel, Werth, & Benjamin, 2009). Eighteen states and Canadian provinces permit but do not mandate action, and 14 jurisdictions do not discuss this at all (Welfel et al., 2009). Some jurisdictions have laws that include clients who are a danger to themselves. Many of these laws and standards are fast evolving, so clinicians must make a deliberate effort to apprise themselves of the most recent standards. An example is in California, where the case *Ewing v. Goldstein* (2004) resulted in an expansion of clinicians' reporting responsibilities, including if a parent or other individual were to inform the clinician of a client's dangerousness to another. Different standards exist across states for duty to warn versus duty to protect (Benjamin, Kent, & Sirikantraporn, 2009).

You as a supervisee should know several things before starting to practice:

- the relevant case law, statutes, and rules;
- the standards of informed consent covering limits of confidentiality;
- the procedures at the setting should a client present as indicating danger to the self or others;
- relevant assessment and documentation; and
- how to contact your supervisor.

It is important that if you have not had prior experience with the duty to warn and protect, and with potentially dangerous clients, to let your supervisor know and to request special supervision and guidance. Even seasoned practitioners find high-risk circumstances very challenging and need support. Consider the following example:

> Nan's previous supervisor had instructed her to make child abuse reports for many of her cases at a community clinic. Nan reported 11 cases out of the 17 clients she saw, in comparison to her peers with different supervisors, who reported zero to two during the year. Now beginning a new practicum, Nan is unsure what the reporting statutes for her locale actually are and wonders how to proceed with her present supervisor. Steps Nan could take include reviewing the child abuse reporting laws for the state in which she is practicing (they are readily available on state websites), consulting faculty at her school to learn standards of practice regarding reporting, and requesting information on this and other relevant subjects from her new supervisor with emphasis on specificity of what constitutes "suspicion" of child abuse or the standard of reporting for that state and what specific steps the supervisee should take.

EMERGING PRACTICES

If you are conducting therapy via telehealth or telepsychology (e.g., using telecommunication devices to deliver treatment), clarity regarding multiple factors is essential. One issue is the geographic location of the client in relation to the therapist and supervisor. States and provincial governments vary in regulations, but many states require that the therapist and supervisor be licensed in the state where the client resides.

The Internet, Online Social Networks, and Psychology Practice

Social networking is primarily used by young career psychologists and supervisees. The generational differential is notable: Supervisors may have different comfort levels or competence with technology and especially with social networking. Psychologists are increasingly confronting ethical issues raised when clients reach out to supervisees (or supervisors) by inviting them to be "friends" or "friended" on a social networking website. Also, an increasing number of psychologists have personal and professional websites. The use of online social networking for marketing purposes is becoming a valued tool. Zur, Williams, Lehavot, and Knapp (2009) and others have developed guidelines for psychologists regarding social networking that include clarity in informed consent in regard to practices (e.g., whether the psychologist will accept e-mail, accept—or not—a "friend" invitation on social networks as a matter of standard practice). You need to check with your training site about standards or policies regarding use of email and texting with clients and policies regarding "friending". Zur et al. cautioned that if therapists do agree to engage in online interaction with clients it is important that clients understand the risks of interacting online, the associated risk of lack of confidentiality and security, and a lack of privacy for private communications. It is essential that clients understand that e-mails or posts to websites are not communications that will receive immediate attention from the therapist. For example, the client should understand that he or she should not communicate suicidal intent via e-mail because the therapist does not consistently monitor e-mails or social networks.

You would be well served to discuss with your supervisor both of your expectations for communication, including e-mail with clients and with the supervisor. Should the setting encourage the supervisee to use e-mail with clients, know that those e-mails will become part of the client's record. All communications should meet criteria for professionalism.

Distance Supervision

If you are planning to receive distance supervision, it is essential that you consult the relevant state licensing boards as well as the ASPPB Handbook on Licensing and Certification Requirements (http://www.asppb.org/handbookpublic/before.aspx) to ensure that the hours you accrue will count toward licensure or whether face-to-face supervision is required. For an internship, such exploration is essential; for a practicum, it may be important if the practicum hours will later be counted toward licensure, as is possible in certain states. Distance supervision has been noted to be more strictly formatted, organized, and formal, with less specific attention to supervisee emotional reactions to the client and less attention to process of supervision. Nonverbal communication may be lost or diminished in distance supervision, requiring both supervisee and supervisor to be more direct, to summarize expectations, and to ensure that both parties are clear about conclusions and plans of action.

Ideally, you will have an opportunity to meet face to face with your supervisor before beginning distance supervision so you can begin to establish a supervisory relationship (McIlwraith, Dyck, Holms, Carlson, & Prober, 2005). Informed-consent aspects of supervision include notifying the client that your supervision is being conducted from a distance, likely via electronic telecommunication, and discussing with the client issues of confidentiality, encryption, and emergency contacts and backup. The Ohio Psychological Association's (2009) *Telepsychology Guidelines* is an important document to consult.

CONCLUSION

Supervision is the ideal time to refine and solidify your ethical problem-solving skills. The process of identifying and exploring ethical dilemmas provides fertile ground for inquiry and development. Supervisors value supervisees who ask questions and identify ethical issues. Other excellent developmental activities include becoming a student representative to the local or state psychological association ethics committee, or writing an article with your supervisor regarding an ethical issue that has arisen in your practice for the newsletter of one of those organizations.

III

ADVANCING REFLECTIVE PRACTICE IN SUPERVISION

9

TRANSFORMING SUPERVISION TO BE MORE SUCCESSFUL

In most, if not all, human relationships, misunderstanding, frustration, and disappointment can occur. Likewise, supervisory relationships have their own share of misattunement and strain. That isn't necessarily a bad thing; in many cases, resolving difficulties can strengthen relationships. However, just as in one's personal life, problems in supervision that are not addressed can fester and begin to negatively affect the relationship, compromise the supervisory alliance, and limit its effectiveness. In this chapter, we take up the issue of how to address strains that occur in clinical training and supervision.

Over the years, we have consulted with countless students and interns (affiliated with many different academic and training institutions, both locally and nationally) about conflicts, strains, problems, and outright unethical behavior they have encountered in clinical training. What has struck us, beyond reports of poor supervision and at times egregious conduct, is that most supervisees feel quite uncertain about how to address shortcomings in supervision. Many appear to believe that they are powerless to effect change and are willing to just finish out a poor training experience with the hope of receiving a positive evaluation. If you or a colleague are facing such a situation, we encourage you to take a different course—one in which you use your developing capacities to influence the behavior of others and to transform poor supervision into adequate or even possibly excellent supervision. We suggest this approach not only because we have observed that changes can indeed occur but also because we believe that one of the many competencies that a psychologist must learn is the ability to take appropriate responsibility and to engage constructively to improve relationships. Therefore, we see difficulties in supervision not only as problems to be solved but also as opportunities to build skills and confidence so one can effectively address challenges in professional relationships. These are important skills to have throughout your career. In addition to encouragement, we offer throughout this chapter various perspectives and provide practical recommendations to address difficulties in clinical training. You can also draw on these approaches to enhance supervision relationships that are going well.

IS A PROBLEM IN SUPERVISION ACTUALLY A PROBLEM?

The simple answer to this question is "Yes," although this response requires a bit of clarification. In many instances, problems in supervision occur because adequate attention has not been paid to clarifying expectations or providing timely feedback. Also, difficulties can arise when a supervisor either does something the supervisee does not want (e.g., give direct advice, when the supervisee wanted to explore, in a more collaborative manner, different clinical options), does not do something the supervisee wants (e.g., fails to give direction after a direct request for guidance), or offers feedback in manner that is vague and not particularly helpful (e.g., "You're doing just fine"). These examples illustrate shortcomings that commonly occur in supervision. Although it has been our experience that most supervisees take such experiences in stride and do not characterize these events as major problems, they nevertheless reflect poor supervision practice, even if they occur only occasionally. Also, if not addressed, these shortcomings may pose difficulties in the relationship, strain the supervisory alliance, and limit the effectiveness of supervision. At the time you notice a shortcoming, or when given the opportunity, you should clearly state the kind of feedback and assistance you are seeking while acknowledging the efforts your supervisor has made to be helpful. We have found that most supervisors strive to meet supervisees' training needs; however, they need honest, respectful feedback to correct any shortcomings. Furthermore, supervisors and supervisees need to actively collaborate to better understand the kinds of experiences in supervision that will provide support and facilitate learning.

Sometimes, supervisors pay minimal attention to how supervision itself is structured, leading to ineffective and poorly focused interactions in which little learning occurs, or perhaps the supervisor is using an approach that has been highly effective and appreciated by supervisees in the past yet is not in sync with a particular supervisee's needs or learning style. By not paying careful attention to the supervision process and each supervisee's needs, supervisors can unwittingly set into motion a pattern that weakens collaboration and threatens the supervisory alliance, leading to problems. Supervision can be arranged in a highly structured fashion, or it can be more loosely structured, with the aim of each session to address the unique training needs the supervisee presents at the time. Emphasis may be placed on skills in diagnosis and conceptualization, building and maintaining the therapeutic alliance, intervention techniques, professionalism, or on process dimensions, such as the supervisee's reactions and parallel process. With so much at hand to potentially address, and so many ways to go about it, feedback and collaboration are required to ensure that the supervisor's approach effectively facilitates learning. We hesitate to simply characterize missteps in the learning process as "problems"; instead, we wish to focus on the need for ongoing reflective practice, metacommunication about the supervision process, and openness to making adjustments throughout the course of supervision. In our opinion, supervisors and supervisees should regularly check in with each other about the learning activities that structure the supervision. Because supervisors develop over time their own unique styles (which have been reinforced by positive outcomes and feedback), they may initially fail to recognize their contributions to ineffective practice. They need feedback to be able to assess what is working and what is not (as well as to be able to appraise the supervisee's contributions to ineffective practice) in order to refocus the process and address overt problems. It is sound supervisory practice to identify one's own shortcomings as a supervisor and, through collaboration with the supervisee, identify areas in need of improvement and make necessary adjustments throughout the course of supervision. In the following sections, we discuss some of the ways in which adjustments to supervision can be accomplished.

NEED FOR INCREASED STRUCTURE

There may be times when it is useful to introduce more structure into supervision. This is usually done to ensure that particular aspects of treatment are addressed, to achieve specific learning objectives, or to provide better continuity between supervision sessions to enhance your skill development so you can continue to build competence. You or your supervisor may suggest a particular format. One option is *cognitive therapy organization* (Beck, Sarnat, & Barenstein, 2008; Liese & Beck, 1997), in which supervision parallels the format of a cognitive therapy clinical session. The following steps structure each supervision session in this format:

- Check-in to identify any particular pressing issues or feelings
- Agenda setting, assisted by the supervisor who has viewed the supervisee's therapy tapes, to determine what to work on; difficulties the supervisee is experiencing; and generally developmentally appropriate conceptualization, treatment, interpersonal strategies
- Bridging from the previous therapy session: relating what was learned in previous therapy sessions to present cases
- Inquiry about previously supervised therapy cases; review of progress and difficulties
- Review of collaboratively set homework (readings, conceptualizing in writing, or experimenting) since previous supervision session or exploring obstacles to homework completion
- Prioritizing and discussing agenda items; this includes identification and modification of maladaptive thought processes that contribute to negative supervisee–therapist–client interactions and perhaps the use of role play to practice clinical interventions or responses
- Assigning new homework that is related to the discussion of agenda items, or encouraging the supervisee–therapist to use cognitive therapy techniques, such as daily thought record or weekly activity scheduling, him- or herself
- Supervisor's capsule summaries in which the supervisor reflects on and synthesizes material discussed in the current session
- Elicitation of feedback from the supervisee–therapist, with targeted questions about responses to a particular technique, its utility, and questions such as "What have you gotten out of today's session?"

This model can be adapted and provides an excellent starting point to address structure in supervision. Another structure that would be appropriate for therapists who do not work from a cognitive orientation might include the following elements: check-in; identification of pressing issues; selected case discussion (assuming all cases are addressed regularly); review of video recordings, and supervisor–supervisee discussion of content and process of the client sessions, including therapeutic alliance development, countertransference, and assessment of intervention effectiveness, as well as articulation of plans for follow-up for the next clinical and supervision sessions.

Also, supervisors should think about the ways supervision has been structured, the effectiveness of such an approach, and consider how strategies that were beneficial in previous training might be introduced in the present supervision. For example, you may have found it helpful to begin a session with case discussion followed by processing and analysis of what occurred in the session or what was omitted or could be changed (e.g., discussion of your emotional responses, theory, or interventions). Alternatively, you could initiate formal introduction of outcome measures collected weekly from each client and use them as a frame for discussion and intervention planning.

The discussion that ensues from a request that a supervisor introduce structure or change the format of supervision may be pivotal in changing the focus and process of supervision as well as in enhancing the supervisory working alliance.

Receiving and responding to evaluative information is a competence in itself, as is skill in assessing performance and giving feedback. We discussed this particular competency in Chapter 3, paying special attention to the potential difficulty you may encounter when receiving corrective or evaluative feedback. Encouraging supervisor feedback will reduce or eliminate the possibility of surprises (i.e., evaluations for which you had no advance warning). Ideally, feedback should be a part of every supervisory session to enhance your competence and to identify areas of future growth.

ENHANCING REFLECTIVE PRACTICE

At times, a supervisor may need to step back from activities that primarily involve giving advice and case management to focus on supervisees' subjective experience, personal reactions, and clinical decision making. Although all supervision contributes to the development of reflective practice, some approaches and supervisory procedures direct particular attention to the supervisee's subjective experiences and dynamics that influence the therapeutic process. Psychodynamic-oriented supervision is an example of one approach that emphasizes these features, in particular in its use of free association and attention to countertransference and parallel process (Beck et al., 2008, pp. 69–79; Frawley-O'Dea & Sarnat, 2000). Interpersonal process recall (IPR; H. Kagan & Kagan, 1997) illustrates another method to enhance reflective practice, and it can be applied to any theoretical orientation.

IPR provides a structure to help examine the various factors that influence a clinician's decision making and behavior. Although the technique was established for supervisor–supervisee inquiry, you could use the question frames yourself during supervision to explore emotional responses and possible alternative actions in your clinical work. IPR also could be used in informal peer consultation or group supervision. The process begins with a review of the session video: Begin playing the video and stop it at any juncture, pose and answer questions, reflect on your answers, and then advance the tape slightly. The following are some possible questions (H. Kagan & Kagan, 1997; N. Kagan, 1980):

- What do you wish you had said to the client?
- How do you think the client would have reacted if you had said that?
- What would have been the risk in saying what you wanted to say?
- If you had the chance now, how might you tell the client what you are thinking and feeling?
- Were there any other thoughts going through your mind?
- How did you want the client to perceive you?
- Were those feelings located physically in some part of your body?
- Were you aware of any feelings? Does that feeling have any special meaning for you?
- What did you want the client to tell you?
- What do you think the client wanted from you?
- Did he or she remind you of anyone in your life?

As you can imagine, such a process (whether used in supervision or for self-reflection) requires awareness and, in supervision, disclosure of both the personal and professional influences that shape the clinician's experience and influence behavior. Therefore, we offer the following cautionary note: IPR should be used in supervision only after a strong, trusting supervisory alliance has been established because of the level of inquiry, introspection, and disclosure required.

EXPERIENTIAL LEARNING

The main purpose of clinical supervision (in addition to overseeing client welfare) is to develop your clinical competence; hence it is a fundamentally an individualized learning process. Instead of characterizing supervision as a top-down teaching or training process, we choose to emphasize learning. Teaching and training focus on *input* (i.e., what is provided to the you, the supervisee); we prefer the term *learning* because what matters in supervision concerns *output* (i.e., what you have learned or, better yet, how your competence has been enhanced). Evidence and logic suggest that experiential learning—observing and practicing—is vital to the learning process (Falender & Shafranske, 2004; Milne, 2009); however, surveys and our casual observation indicate that the use of experiential activities in supervision is limited. Experiential learning in supervision includes live supervision, cotherapy in which the supervisor conducts treatment with the supervisee (this often occurs in group modalities), observing the supervisor conduct treatment, and role plays of clinical interaction. We (as both supervisors and former supervisees) have found such experiences to be very instructive. In addition to the more commonly used activities, such as reflection, discussion, and didactic instruction, supervisees can recommend the use of more experiential learning. For example, after discussing a particular intervention, you might ask your supervisor to demonstrate it, to review a session tape, or to perform the intervention in a role play with you and then reverse the roles so that you can practice. These are simple ways to enhance learning and develop competence in supervision.

In addition, we suggest that you recall how you have learned best in other education and training experiences and discuss with your supervisor how those learning processes might be incorporated into supervision. We encourage you to reflect on your learning style and actively consider ways to enhance the effectiveness of supervision through better attention to how you learn best.

REFLECTIVE PRACTICE: BETTER UNDERSTANDING AND EXPRESSING YOUR NEEDS IN SUPERVISION

Because supervision is a two-way process, your supervisor has expectations for appropriate supervisee performance, and you have similar expectations for his or her performance. With your progressing development as a supervisee comes a corresponding increasing responsibility for the supervision process. Even as a novice, however, it is perfectly fine to tell your supervisor when you do not understand or are unclear about what he or she said, even if this seems difficult. It is also acceptable to tell him or her when you are worried about a client; aspects of treatment; or your inexperience with a particular situation, diagnosis, or critical incident. In addition, it is important to reflect and to discuss with your supervisor about the ways in which his or her interventions in supervision are helpful as well as areas in which you need more assistance. Be mindful that an important aspect of the discussion is the attitude you convey: A respectful, nonconfrontational reflection on your level of training and experience will most likely be successful. If you need training in a specific area, identifying and describing that need is a strength, and if further training is not available at the setting, explore with the supervisor ways you can pursue it.

Remedies vary dramatically depending on what you have identified as pertinent issues and what you would like to achieve—and what is not happening. A common critique by supervisees is that supervision is not directed to the needs of the supervisee and his or her clients and so the supervisees leave supervision without clarity or, as one supervisee said to us, "I still don't know what I'm doing or what I should be doing." Think about whether it is your supervisor's knowledge, skills, or attitudes, in the context of your own, that is at issue. Is your supervisor instructing you to do something you are unsure about? Is your supervisor inattentive to your affective responses? Does he or she disagree with you about an aspect of client therapy? Sometimes the mere process of identifying what you would like to address or improve will open avenues of thought and discussion, leading to progress.

If you are concerned about your supervisory relationship, think: Was there a time when it was better? Do you have any recollection of when that was, and events, cases, and discussions that occurred during that time? Think about clients you were treating, supervisory interactions, and treatment interventions, and whether there were any critical incidents: memorable things that may have changed supervision for the worse. In our experience, many psychologists, when thinking back on their own supervision, recall some turning point that was never addressed and negatively influenced future supervision. If you do remember events or incidents that affected your supervision, it is still possible to repair the relationship. Refer back to the steps for repair we offered in Chapter 5.

When addressing points of conflict in the supervisory relationship, you could begin by reflecting with your supervisor about aspects of supervision you have benefited from—reminding him or her of specific interventions, conceptualizations, or reflections that were helpful. The supervisor may spontaneously address the change—or not—but, either way, you can begin to support effective interactions. You may find particular chapters of this book useful to refer to with your supervisor to identify aspects or practices of supervision that are effective (e.g., Chapter 3).

If the supervisory relationship has been unsatisfactory from the outset, then you could try to problem-solve or propose adding some structure to the supervision sessions. Some supervisees have reported to us that they simply change their expectations to focus on what the supervisor can provide—whether it be more skills based, more conceptual, or research oriented. Developing an affirmative relationship with the supervisor, in which you express appreciation of his or her areas of strength, may be transformative in and of itself.

Implicit in this discussion is our view of the collaborative nature of the supervisory relationship and the shared responsibility of supervisee and supervisor to critically evaluate the effectiveness of processes used in supervision and to commit to continuous improvement by engaging in reflective practice, sharing feedback, and experimenting with novel ways of learning. The aim is to transform good supervision to excellent supervision.

DEALING WITH PROBLEMATIC AND INADEQUATE SUPERVISION

Up to this point in our discussion, we have considered ways to make improvements in supervisory relationships that are functioning fairly effectively. We turn now to those relatively infrequent and difficult situations in which the supervision is inadequate and someone must give feedback to the super-visor in an effort to get the process back on track to ensure both client welfare and the development of supervisee competency. These are situations in which shortcomings have become significant problems. In such unfortunate circum-stances it is likely that the supervisory alliance has broken down: Supervisees have little trust in the supervisor and consequently disclose little of the clinical challenges they are facing, and client welfare is being jeopardized by the lack of supervisor oversight. In common language, we are referring to lousy or bad supervision, which cannot be ignored and in regard to which some action must be taken. You might be wondering: What constitutes inadequate supervision? This question is similar to the earlier one: When is a problem in supervision actually a problem? To help you to answer that question, we provide the following discussion of problematic, inadequate supervision.

The Range of Lousy Supervision: From Inadequate to Harmful

The term *inadequate supervision* refers to supervision that simply does not meet the supervisee's needs and/or the standards of supervision practice. Sometimes supervision, when it is below the accepted standard of practice, might be legally negligent. Should a catastrophic event (e.g., a suicide) of a client occur, the supervisor would bear direct liability for negligent super-vision, and the client's family might press charges. An example of *negligent supervision* would be one in which the prescribed frequency of supervision hours per supervised cases was not met or oversight of all cases was not performed. *Inadequate supervision*, on the other hand, might be lacking in focus, mis-directed, or one in which the supervisory relationship never adequately formed. Even with positive commitment and attempts on the supervisee's part to provide feedback, the supervisory experience may remain poor and ineffective: To say it clearly, supervision may be lousy. We think it will be useful to identify some supervisor behaviors that contribute to a poor super-visory experience to help you understand how one can subjectively experience supervision as poor. Consider the following categories to identify aspects of supervision that are present or lacking. Factors associated with lousy supervision include supervision that has one or more of the following char-acteristics (Magnuson, Wilcoxen, & Norem, 2000):

- *Unbalanced*—focused on one aspect while neglecting other, more relevant ones, even after having been provided feedback about this, for example, if the supervisor focuses his or her attention exclusively on administrative responsibilities, such as productivity or charting, or on clinical theory or research, or on relational-affective components to the exclusion of other dimensions (e.g., cognitions or behavior), such that the supervisor does not see the entire picture or adequately cover all of the training responsibilities.

- *Developmentally inappropriate for the supervisee*—focused on clinical or supervisory issues not related to the supervisee's competencies or stage in competency development, for example, training a supervisee to conduct prolonged exposure therapy when that supervisee has a very limited understanding of trauma and virtually no clinical experience.
- *Intolerant of differences in the supervisee (or even the client) with an inflexible approach to address the supervisee's learning objectives*—for example, the supervisor refuses to offer any clinical recommendations even when the supervisee admits that she doesn't know what she is doing and needs direct guidance, or dismissing perspectives offered by the supervisee from an alternative theoretical model or empirically supported approach.
- *Poorly models professional/personal attributes, and possibly engages in unethical conduct*—for example, engaging in gossip, failing to fulfill commitments, directing supervisee behavior contrary to legal obligations (e.g., mandated reporting).
- *Untrained and professionally apathetic*—For example, minimal commitment to professional obligations, misapplication of techniques, or misunderstanding of theory or empirically supported treatments.

In addition to explicit behaviors that produce inadequate or poor supervision, there are a number of factors, including values and capacities, that we suggest contribute to the supervisory alliance. Reflection on these features can often help you identify areas of core difficulty that are contributing to a lack of trust, an unsatisfactory alliance, and inadequate supervision. Review the items in Exhibit 9.1 and assess areas of strength and possible sources of conflict in your own supervisory relationship.

In addition to failing to meet the basic requirements of training, inadequate supervision directly affects client care. Failure to perform adequate oversight and lack of attention to supervisee competence may result in significant harm to the client. The impact of lousy supervision on supervisees may also be profound in that it places them in situations in which they are not prepared to adequately meet standards of client care, increasing their anxiety and eliciting feelings of disappointment, anger, and sadness. As a supervisee you will need to adjust, to some extent, to the unique personalities, talents, and perspectives of your supervisor; however, you should not passively accept inadequate supervision, because this compromises not only client welfare but

EXHIBIT 9.1
Factors That Influence the Supervisory Alliance

Factors with a positive influence	Factors with a negative influence
Mutual respect	Disrespect
Honesty	Dishonesty
Comfort	Discomfort
Confidence	Worry
Insight	Lack of insight
Understanding	Lack of understanding
Accurate communication	Communication difficulties
Clarity	Confusion
Collaborative goal definition	Unclear goals
Tasks defined and carried out	Undefined tasks
Concern by supervisor for welfare of supervisee	Perceived lack of concern for supervisee welfare
Concern by supervisor for welfare of client	Perceived lack of concern for client welfare
Confidence in supervisor's competence	Lack of confidence in supervisor's competence

also your own training. This is even more true when supervision is personally and professionally harmful.

Harmful supervision, which is the most extreme in impact, has been defined as resulting in psychological, emotional, and/or physical harm or trauma to the supervisee (Ellis, Siembor, Swords, Morere, & Blanco, 2008). The supervisor inflicts harm by acting inappropriately, engaging in negligent supervision, or violating ethical standards. It is differentiated from bad supervision by the significant emotional, psychological, or physical impact on the supervisee (Ellis et al., 2008). It may involve a single incident, several incidents, or ongoing behavior. Ellis and Swords (2009) reported that, among the supervisees they sampled, two thirds reported they had experienced some type of harmful supervision. If you have experienced harmful supervision, please bring it to the attention of your clinical graduate program faculty so they can assist you in mitigating its effects and planning what to do. It is important to address these experiences with professionals whom you respect and trust, because the consequences of inadequate and harmful supervision can affect your well-being and compromise your ability to effectively engage in future supervision and training.

Returning to the "lousy" and "inadequate" categories, we believe a single lousy supervision event may have the potential to be a prelude to a stronger supervisory alliance if the supervisee can initiate a process with the supervisor to acknowledge the incident and engage in a nonreactive process of repair. The supervisee can demonstrate both commitment and character in seeking the advice of faculty and, as appropriate, the director of training or the academic director of clinical training to implement steps to correct the supervision problems through respectful engagement of the supervisor and communication of feedback to him or her. It means not giving up on the process (just as one doesn't give up on clients) but instead working constructively and collaboratively to improve supervision. We turn now to general principles and recommendations for addressing inadequate or harmful supervision.

How to Address Inadequate, Lousy, or Harmful Supervision

It is usually helpful, when faced with inadequate, lousy, or harmful supervision, to seek advice from a trusted faculty member or the academic director of clinical training so that he or she can help you consider the most appropriate ways to address the problems and to provide feedback about how to work to improve the supervision. The first step is to identify the specific inadequacies in the supervisory process—that is, what is missing that is required to ensure client welfare and clinical training—as well as what is interfering with effective supervision practice. We find that it is particularly important to focus on specific behaviors or processes that are occurring or are not being provided, instead of focusing entirely on attitudinal aspects. Such a focus will usefully orient the discussion and subsequent intervention toward behaviors that can be changed in supervision. When reflecting on the inadequacies in the supervision, it is essential that your first step is to consider your contributions as well as identify shortcomings in the supervisor's management of the supervisory process. The second step, as we have mentioned, is to discuss the situation with one or more trusted faculty advisors and perhaps with the academic director of clinical training to obtain their perspectives and some advice to map out the next steps. After receiving this input, reflect carefully on what you are seeking to gain by discussing these issues with your supervisor. Reestablishing or revising the learning objectives and the means to achieve the goals can be an important way to frame the discussion and to initiate the process. When offering constructive criticism and discussing what you perceive as shortcomings in supervision you should include ideas about possible solutions; these solutions should be framed in behavioral terms and include ways in which you yourself will contribute to improving the supervisory process. Next, you should consider any concerns or emotional reactions you may have when you discuss these issues with your supervisor. In our experience, the power differential between the supervisor and supervisee is always an area of concern. Although the differences in status and power always influence the process, they have even more of an effect when supervisees are in the position of needing to address inadequacies and problems in supervision. Developmental competence level also can play an important role in that more advanced supervisees will be more skilled at identifying problems and not personalizing problematic or indifferent supervisor behaviors (Muratori, 2001).

In our experience, most supervisees have concerns about potential fall-out from discussing the shortcomings in supervision and fear receiving a poor evaluation as well as anxiety about how clinical training will proceed after they bring problems into the open. This is quite understandable. We suggested earlier that supervisees working with a problematic supervisor carry a much greater burden than a supervisor working with a problematic supervisee because of lack of established procedures or guidelines and because of the power differential (Falender & Shafranske, 2004). Additional support is generally useful as one prepares to address the issues with a supervisor. Again, the supervisee should reflect on his or her own contributions to the supervisory process and formulate concrete recommendations to improve supervision. It is not unusual for supervisees to have "cold feet," to begin to minimize the problems, and to want to "give it more time" before acting.

We understand the hesitancy to address such matters directly and the inclination to minimize difficulties, to resort to simply complaining to colleagues, and the desire to just survive the rotation. However, failure to address inadequate supervision not only compromises your training but also jeopardizes the welfare of your clients. Keeping significant supervision problems to oneself and not informing appropriate others is a disservice to clients (who rely on competent supervision to protect their welfare) as well to the supervisee and in itself constitutes an ethical concern. Although addressing supervision problems is difficult for supervisees, these are situations in which professionalism and ethical conduct are essential, and supervisees likely will find significant support from many professionals when they act in the best interest of clients, even when such action may exacerbate strains in supervision. Fortunately, such a step rarely needs to be taken; however, it is important that supervisees are aware of and understand appropriate courses of action.

Remember that directors of clinical training, both in training settings and in academic institutions, are aware of the difficulties that supervisees face, are invested in their students or interns receiving high-quality training, are mindful of client welfare, and usually have expertise in addressing training problems. Discuss any supervision problems with them early in the process, and often, before the supervisory relationship is at a breaking point. They can help you to clearly identify the areas of inadequacy in behavioral terms; work with you to consider intervention strategies to get the supervision on track; provide support; offer advice; and, if need be, to arrange for you to be reassigned to another supervisor or rotation. One advantage that academic directors of training have is that they are less affected by the power differential and may at times be in the most superior position (i.e., over the supervisor). Also, although they may be motivated to maintain a professional and cordial relationship with the individuals involved in training their students, their primary obligation is to their students—and, by extension, their students' clients—and they will be as motivated as you to ensure that you receive the best quality training available.

INADEQUATE SUPERVISION AND APPROACHES TO TRANSFORMATION

In this chapter, we have presented an overview of the kinds of challenges that supervisees face in supervision, from isolated lapses in good supervisory practice to problematic, inadequate, and even harmful supervision. Although this last category is the rare exception, we thought it important to cover the full gamut of supervision experiences. Also, although we have emphasized supervisor conduct and lapses, our view is that both parties (i.e., supervisee and supervisor) bear the responsibility of working collaboratively to address challenges and to ensure effective supervision. We now continue our discussion, shifting the focus somewhat to challenge you to consider what you would do if faced with particular supervisor shortcomings. Again, our point is not to overstate the case of problematic supervisor behavior but to have you consider what responsible course of action you would take in various situations to get supervision back on track. As you read the following examples, reflect on your level of comfort in addressing the difficulties and which situations would you be more likely to minimize or ignore.

We start with some brief examples. Consider whether these are shortcomings or examples of inadequate supervision and, if the latter, what action you might take to address the problems:

- Dr. Smythe is often 30 minutes late for your 50-minute supervision session; he rarely reviews your chart notes, and although he has promised to do so, he has never reviewed videos of your sessions.
- Dr. Gramm corrects the punctuation, grammar, and spelling in your written reports but seems disinterested in the client or your work. In fact, she often confuses clients and issues advice about one case that is intended for another. She often comments that working in the public sector can be very discouraging.
- Dr. Claire gives explicit directions, directives, and advice on interventions, rarely if ever asking for your input. His position is that you should learn from him, because he has the legal responsibility for the clients you are treating.

- Dr. Seymour is distracted, and generally seems to be thinking of other things during supervision. At one point in supervision, he interrupts your presentation of a case to tell a story about how he became interested in psychology.
- Dr. Crumb interrupts frequently, and suggests interventions that seem culturally insensitive. You inquire about how to adapt a treatment to a particular client, and he responds that all people are fundamentally alike. He appears to be confused about your question.

How would you characterize these examples of inappropriate supervisor behavior? How might such behavior affect you? What might you do? Is there a way to act proactively? How might you set into motion a process resulting in improvement?

In the next section, we present examples of problematic supervision that are not uncommon and that illustrate how a supervisee might respond in a way that contributes to a transformation in the supervision.

Unclear Expectations

Inattention to expectations and structural aspects of supervision may lead to confusion and dissatisfaction and strain the supervisory alliance. When supervisees use their skills to address these situations they can create more optimal outcomes.

Example 1

Nicole's previous supervisor had always praised everything she did, even when Nicole was certain what she had done with a client was not great. Her supervisor had been exuberant and lavish in her praise. Nicole's new supervisor seemed remote and even critical, and did not praise her at all, yet she was very even handed in her supervision, reflecting on Nicole's work and offering alternative interpretations and formulations, but sometimes in a mechanical way. Nicole missed the praise and was concerned that the new supervisor was displeased with her performance, even though she felt she was learning from her. Nicole realized she may have simply gotten used to all the praise, but she misses it. What could Nicole do? It would appear that these two supervisors were approaching the task with very different expectations of the process of supervision and feedback. It is likely that clarification of the role of the supervisor, expectations for feedback, and the anchoring of supervision in competencies would be very helpful. For example, Nicole could ask her new supervisor how she likes to proceed, how she tracks supervision process, and what constitutes successful practice. These questions might initiate a discussion of the process of supervision, mutual expectations, and what works best for both parties in giving feedback on perceived performance, as well as introduce tools to assist in the process. Rather than constructing a specter of disinterested supervision, this discussion can strengthen the supervisory alliance.

Example 2

Alan expressed grave concern to a faculty advisor that his supervisor was always telling him what to do and not giving him any chance to reflect, formulate, or engage in more psychodynamic thinking, in line with what he was learning. The faculty member asked if Alan and his supervisor had ever discussed the structure of supervision, including the theoretical orientation of the therapy done with the client and of the supervision. Alan realized that he and the supervisor had simply begun with the first case with no preliminary discussions, so he really was unsure about the ground rules. In fact, he was happy to report the next week that when he had asked the supervisor for some background and structure, the supervisor told him he always began with behavioral interventions for novice supervisees because he felt that they would be most comfortable with those. The supervisor was surprised but very interested to learn that this particular supervisee had significant developing knowledge of psychodynamic theory and psychotherapy. The discussion led to clarity with the introduction of supervisee-specific practice that reflected Alan's pattern of competencies.

Example 3

Colleen's supervisor seemed playful and more like a friend than a supervisor. She spent the first session joking and telling stories. Colleen hoped that in subsequent sessions they would establish a more professional rapport; however, two more weeks passed with informal chatting such as inquiries about dates, restaurants, and vacations. Colleen became increasingly uncomfortable and expressed concern that she needed supervision because the cases she had been assigned were complex and involved areas in which she had had minimal experience. Although the supervisor listened carefully, there was no change in the supervisor's behavior. In the next session, Colleen told the supervisor that she was enjoying their time together and felt it was helpful getting to know the supervisor, but that she would find it very exciting to transition to a more structured case discussion, perhaps with a format she had found useful in the past: a check-in on pressing issues and then presentation of each case on a rotating basis with specific questions for the supervisor. After several weeks in the new format with collaborative feedback, the supervisor expressed how useful she was finding the structure and told Colleen she was adopting it in her other supervisory sessions.

Example 4

Monica was seeing her first adult client after several years of experience in child therapy. The adult she was assigned had co-occurring diagnoses (psychiatric diagnosis and substance abuse diagnosis) and was not eager for treatment but had been suggested by a court to attend for several sessions. At intake, the client had been adamant that she was no longer using any substances. Monica saw the client two times and felt she was establishing excellent rapport. During the third session, the client disclosed that she was drinking five to six shots nightly after putting her very young children to bed. Once the supervisor was informed of this, he told Monica the case had to be closed and the client referred to a substance abuse program. Monica was very confused about the supervisor's reasoning because she thought this disclosure might constitute a case of suspected child abuse or neglect in light of the client's alcohol use, which could impair her ability to take care of her child. What if the child woke up in the night and the mother was too inebriated to take care of him? She thought that not doing so would be a legal and ethical infraction and that simply transferring the woman after she began to disclose the reality of her situation would constitute client abandonment, another ethical infraction. After conferring with a faculty member at her school, Monica approached her supervisor to discuss the case further, including ethical and clinical aspects. The supervisor explained that he had taken a shortcut, that his thinking was that this case was too serious for Monica in light of her lack of training in adult therapy and that the setting was ill equipped to deal with the client's difficulties, and then he asked for her perspective. Monica explained her concerns about the ethics of client abandonment, legal mandates for child abuse reporting, and her perspectives on interventions that would be sensitive to what she had learned about the parent and child, and she expressed concern that simply closing the case was not the best solution. The supervisor praised Monica for raising the issues and agreed that together they would meet with the site treatment team to review the case, address the child abuse reporting issue, and either consider a more smooth transition or retain involvement with this client.

Think about what would empower a supervisee to initiate these types of discussions. Have difficult issues come up for you in supervision? What could be learned from the example experiences we have just presented?

Inadequate Guidance

Another area of potential problems or inadequacy is when you do not receive adequate guidance to address clinical challenges or perform case management. Consider the example of a supervisee, Mark, who is treating a child client who often becomes out of control in session. Mark has presented this to his supervisor and asked for help and has been confused by the supervisor's advice to simply repeat the rules to the child (to not destroy any toys, and to obey the clinic rules). Mark has tried these interventions, but when the child throws herself on the floor, throwing doll parts, screaming, kicking, and biting, it is apparent that repeating the rules is not an effective intervention. Furthermore, Mark is concerned that the child is so out of control she could hurt herself, and in fact she has done so at the school setting, which was the reason that she was referred to therapy in the first place. Also, this past week, Mark's arm was severely twisted when he tried to keep the child from hitting her head on a bookcase. When the supervisor asks what precipitates the child's intense responses, Mark described how it could be anything—in the past three sessions, the tantrums were provoked by entering the therapy room, by a question about what she would like to play with, and by silence. Mark is unsure how to proceed. What can he do to achieve a more effective and safe session?

First, it would be helpful if Mark explains to the supervisor his level of concern about the child and her safety. Second, it would be important for the supervisor to consider the child's behavior in light of Mark's level of experience and competence. In this case, although Mark has worked in child settings, he has never encountered a child this out of control, and he has had no training in physical restraint. Third, Mark likely should ask what the supervisor would do to manage the situation as well as inquire about available resources and supports. Disclosing this information would appropriately alert the supervisor to the level of challenge Mark is facing. Also, Mark's clear description of what he knows and does not know, as well as his awareness of the limits of his experience, demonstrates metacompetence and provides the supervisor with useful information to assess the needs in the case and what level of supervisor intervention may be necessary to ensure the client's welfare and to adequately support Mark's professional development. Some possibilities might be for the supervisor to join a session, to observe a session, or to bring this management issue to a case conference to obtain multiple perspectives on ways to proceed and to determine whether the setting is capable of providing the most appropriate level of care for this child. In the best of circumstances, a supervisor with solid experience and a high level of competence will effectively intervene.

There are times, however, when a supervisor may not have the requisite experience or competence to effectively manage the clinical demands of a particular case and provide adequate training and supervision. Unfortunately, it is not unusual for clinical staff to be stretched to the limits of their competencies. In such circumstances, both supervisor and supervisee may be practicing beyond the limits of their capabilities, and strain is likely to occur because each is functioning outside of her or his comfort zone. Also, the supervisor is facing an unenviable ethical dilemma: having responsibility for a case in which he or she does not have the requisite expertise. This might explain the supervisor's inability to provide adequate guidance. In the meantime, the supervisee would be feeling anxious and confused about how to proceed both in the case and in supervision. In respect to clarifying the nature of the difficulties in supervision, it would be useful for the supervisee to initially check with peers to identify whether others are having similar training difficulties with that particular supervisor. If the supervisee finds that others are experiencing positive supervision, then it is possible that there is something idiosyncratic in the interaction of supervisor and supervisee. Further reflection, self-assessment, and conferring with others would be necessary to begin to identify the source of the difficulties in obtaining appropriate guidance. If, on the other hand, peers report similar shortcomings in supervision, the supervisee may need to take responsibility to obtain additional input and adopt a more problem-solving, collaborative approach with the supervisor, instead of primarily asking for advice.

CONCLUSION: MAKING A COMMITMENT TO ENHANCE AND TRANSFORM SUPERVISION

Our decision to dedicate a chapter to problems in supervision was based in part on our experience of consulting with graduate students and interns and recognizing that many trainees are uncertain of how to understand or respond to training relationships that are not reaching their full potential. It is our hope that by better understanding the nature of the problems that can occur in supervision, you will proactively engage in or initiate processes that transform supervision to meet your training needs.

Although we have focused most of our attention in this chapter on supervisor conduct, we do not believe that supervisors bear the full responsibility for the quality of the relationship or the effectiveness of supervision. As supervisors ourselves, we know that this is simply not the case. We believe that supervision is dynamically coconstructed, and effective supervision is the responsibility of both the supervisor and supervisee.

10

BECOMING A REFLECTIVE CLINICIAN

As you read this closing chapter, it is time for you to think about your journey as a supervisee—and your process moving forward. It is now, during your training as a graduate student in practicum or as an intern, that you are in the best position to begin instituting specific practices that will lead to superior professional performance, now and in the future. In this chapter, we discuss steps you can take as you move ahead as a supervisee and, eventually, become a supervisor.

S. Miller, Hubble, and Duncan (2007) sought to identify the characteristics of exceptionally effective and talented therapists, or "supershrinks," as they called them. Discouraged when they found that it was neither the attributes of the person as a therapist nor the technical prowess each possessed that distinguished an exceptional clinician from a run-of-the-mill one, they looked further. Ericsson, Charness, Hoffman, and Feltovich (2006, cited in S. Miller et al., 2007), who had studied experts in multiple fields, provided the clue: "The best of the best simply work harder at improving their performance than others do" (p. 30). Furthermore, as Ericsson et al. pointed out, the key element was in *deliberate practice*, the amount of time "specifically devoted to reaching for objectives just beyond one's level of proficiency" (p. 30).

Ironically, a barrier to attaining superiority is achieving proficiency. As clinicians move into a phase of competence, they are not motivated to expend time and resources to make further adjustments (S. Miller et al., 2007). They unwittingly become complacent. What is required to excel is the commitment to deliberate practice in which one continuously *thinks, acts,* and *reflects.*

The centerpiece of these practices is reflection. S. Miller et al. (2007) found that supershrinks consistently sought client feedback, both regarding client feelings toward them and the process of the work, and, even more important, the best clinicians engaged in *forethought:* setting set specific goals and identifying particular ways to reach goals.

What does this mean for you as a supervisee? If you aspire to superior performance, you should proactively seek *feedback,* thoughtfully reflect and use other tools to establish a *baseline* of clinical performance, engage in *forethought* about the *next step* in development, and *reflect on the means* to improve in the next session. Then you should follow up with the same deliberative, reflective process to become a reflective and effective clinician. These very same steps will be a foundation for you as you progress toward independent practice and become a supervisor yourself.

REFLECTIVE PRACTICE

Self-reflection and self-assessment have been identified as essential components of the assessment and development of competence (Belar et al., 2001; Falender & Shafranske, 2007, Kaslow et al., 2007). Similarly, *metacompetence*—the ability to assess what one knows and what one does not know—plays a pivotal role throughout professional development (Falender & Shafranske, 2007; Hatcher & Lassiter, 2007). Reflective practice, self-assessment, and self-care were identified as benchmarks in the Competency Benchmarks (see Appendix A) and include the following Foundational Competencies at the practicum stage of training: reflection on action, knowledge of core competencies and self-assessment, attention to self-care, demonstrates readiness for internship by use of resources to enhance reflectivity, consistent monitoring and evaluation of practice activities, and understands the central role of self-care to effective practice. Self-reflection, which serves as the central principle, "has been described by learning theorists as the cyclical process whereby individuals engage in a critical evaluation of their affective, cognitive, and behavioral experiences, and through dialogue and generalization, produce insight and fundamental shifts in their assumptions and beliefs" (Orchowski, Evangelista, & Probst, 2010, p. 51).

Kolb (1984) proposed an experiential learning cycle in which the learner acts or performs, then shifts from an actor to an observer and, after reflection, abstracts a conclusion, which informs future action. This model fits well with what happens during clinical training: You engage in clinical practice, then reflect on the concrete experiences of the session (both individually and in collaboration with the supervisor), then reach a tentative assessment about the interventions and effectiveness in the session and use this reflection to consider future action. Such a process reflects what Schön (1983, 1987) has referred to as *reflection-on-action*. Supervisees progress in a developmental sequence from reflection-on-action to internalizing the reflection process (Hatcher & Lassiter, 2007).

Schön (1983) suggested that, with experience, professionals engage in *reflection-in-action*: When they confront something that is unexpected, when something novel emerges, they think on their feet; that is, they reflect on the data as those data are emerging. When events transpire quickly in a clinical session, you have to make quick sense of what is going on; capture the essential components of what has transpired to bring to supervision; and, then independently and in supervision, engage in reflection and self-assessment. The ability to engage in self-reflection as a deliberate practice is an essential feature in the development of competence and is a required part of becoming a supershrink or at least a professional who is highly self-reflective on his or her own competence. We emphasize deliberate practice because we believe there is an important distinction between supervisees who casually reflect (or reflect just before or during supervision) and those who really make a commitment and make an *intentional* decision to consistently perform such reflection and self-assessment. As you progress in your training, you will find that reflection is a critical part of practice in general.

There are many ways to understand what is involved in reflective practice. Moon (2008) provided a useful summary:

- *Reflective practice as set of abilities or skills*. This focuses on specific competencies or behaviors, such as the ability for self-awareness or an activity such as journaling about an event. This approach emphasizes performance of reflective activities.
- *Reflective practice and criticality*. This refers to looking back in a critical way at what has happened and using the resulting knowledge to tackle new situations. This is akin to Kolb's (1984) experiential learning cycle, in which reflection leads one to analyze on the effects of an intervention.
- *Reflective practice as a state of mind*. This could be characterized as a gentle process of noticing and being concerned, similar to applications of mindfulness. Safran, Muran, Stevens, and Rothman (2008) described a mindfulness induction exercise they use in which participants "carefully [attend] to the experience

of eating a raisin . . . focusing on their bodies for a few moments" (p. 145) that they have used to open group supervision sessions: "Over time, this kind of mindfulness work helps trainees increase their awareness of subtle feelings, thoughts, and fantasies that emerge when working with their client, which provide important information about what is occurring in the work" (p. 145). Such an approach emphasizes adopting an attitude of receptivity to reflective experience.

- *Reflective practice as an orientation to problem solving.* Similar to criticality, such a conscious process aims to identify problematic issues and consider solutions.
- *Reflective practice, intuition, and emotion.* In this approach, outcomes of reflection are turned into *tacit competence:* knowledge or skills that one uses in a given therapeutic moment with little conscious deliberation. This form of action typifies expert clinicians (or violists, or skiers, etc.), who seemingly understand and perform complex actions without the level of deliberateness that one observes in a beginner.

> **Reflection Activity.** After reviewing the different forms of reflection, consider the form of reflective practice in which you typically engage and the form of reflection that is primarily used in supervision.

ENHANCING REFLECTIVE PRACTICE

Reflective practice begins through the activities that are facilitated in clinical supervision. These practices are important not only because they ensure quality client care but also because they help supervisees develop skill in self-assessment and self-reflection. Understanding the function of these techniques can enhance the effectiveness of supervision. Also, these processes can begin a lifelong habit of self-reflection.

SELF-REFLECTIVE PRACTICE, SELF-CARE, AND VICARIOUS TRAUMATIZATION

An important aspect of reflective practice and self-assessment is self-care as included in the Competency Benchmarks (Appendix A). A significant risk on the road to becoming a psychologist is the risk that one's self-care has been sacrificed in the process. Psychology graduate students put self-care activities very low on their list of priorities in the interest of completing all the degree requirements, leaving them too overwhelmed and busy (Kaslow & Rice, 1985). Norcross (2002) urged a career-long approach to assessing wellness and sources of self-care—and the reality of its actual occurrence. Self-care is an ethical imperative. According to Standard 2.06 (b) of the American Psychological Association's *Ethical Principles of Psychologist and Code of Conduct*, the psychologist is responsible for self-monitoring and acting proactively:

> When psychologists become aware of personal problems that may interfere with their performing work-related duties adequately, they take appropriate measures, such as obtaining professional consultation or assistance, and determine whether they should limit, suspend, or terminate their work-related duties. (American Psychological Association, 2010a)

Coster and Schwebel (1997) found that engaging in social, emotional, physical, and spiritual self-care activities promote resiliency among mental health professionals faced with challenging circumstances. Such self-care strategies included social support, personal therapy, exercise, stretching, healthy eating, self-reflection, spiritual activities, and relaxation exercises (Coster & Schwebel, 1997; Jennings & Skovholt, 1999). Self-care also can include mindfulness meditation classes, Tai Chi, massage, exercise classes, and even group walks. Your supervisors are often encouraged to model healthy dietary patterns and ensure that students have access to healthy foods nearby. Unfortunately, in a study of the prevalence of self-care in graduate programs (Munsey, 2006, cited in Barnett & Cooper, 2009), 85% of graduate students surveyed reported that their programs did not disseminate educational materials about self-care, 63% reported self-care activities were not sponsored, and 59% reported that self-care was not encouraged or promoted (Barnett & Cooper, 2009; Schwebel & Coster, 1998). Although mentoring may provide a model or support of self-care modeling, you must initiate your own self-care if your supervisor does not model it. Initiating half-hour yoga sessions or mindfulness during the lunch hour, brown bag social lunch, and other creative activities will enhance your relationships and serve essential self-care functions.

Supervisees' most effective coping strategies include obtaining social support from family and friends, seeking pleasurable experiences, clarity about the hazards of a full caseload of therapy, self-awareness to identify signs that one is becoming stressed, avoiding self-blame, and various personal and professional activities emphasizing human relationships (Turner et al., 2005). To reflect on and to self-assess your self-care status, consider these additional coping factors (from Turner et al., 2005):

- Adopting a solution-focused approach to problems
- Utilizing supervision (e.g., discussing issues and feelings that arise in supervision)
- Peer support
- Recalling positive, life-transforming events that occurred in therapy
- Cognitive reframing of errors

To assess your general self-care status, consider not only sleep, eating, exercise, worry, and vacations but also protective factors, such as spirituality, religion, and commitment to social justice (Norcross & Guy, 2007). Norcross and Guy (2007) provided a comprehensive self-care checklist intended for individuals after licensure.

Self-care is particularly important in light of the strains that psychotherapists face. Clinicans may face *vicarious traumatization*—harmful changes that occur in professionals' views of themselves, others, and the world as a result of exposure to the graphic and/or traumatic materials clients present (McCann & Pearlman, 1990)—is an occupational hazard of psychotherapy, and it may be more intense and acute for beginning therapists. Vicarious traumatization is a normal response, but it can result in decreased motivation, efficacy, and empathy, or even symptoms of posttraumatic stress disorder. Exposure to graphic abuse or trauma, reenactments in psychotherapy, or multiple sessions with trauma survivors all increase therapist risk. Therapists in general have more extensive trauma histories than the nontherapist population, including physical abuse, sexual molestation, parental alcoholism, psychiatric hospitalization of a parent, death of family member, and family dysfunction (Elliott & Guy, 1993). The risk of vicarious traumatization is higher for an individual with primary trauma exposure. Spiritual beliefs may be a significant protective factor or even a protective outcome of trauma work (Brady, Guy, Poelstra, & Brokaw, 1999).

ON THE ROAD TO EXPERTISE

The development of expertise is a lifelong process of discovery and innovation, founded on reflection and building on your own strengths and developing competencies. As you embark on further professional training and licensure, the reflective experience of clinical work and supervision will be internalized and ultimately transformed as you find yourself beginning to supervise your own trainees. All of the processes and hard lessons of training will crystallize into strategies that will help you continue to grow and to effectively lead other students to develop and enhance their clinical skills. Clinical supervision is but one step in your development. Your present experiences will prepare you for a lifetime of personal and professional transformation.

APPENDIX A: COMPETENCY BENCHMARKS

Foundational Competencies

Professionalism—Professional values and ethics as evidenced in behavior and comportment that reflects the values and ethics of psychology, integrity, and responsibility

Developmental Level

Readiness for Practicum	Readiness for Internship	Readiness for Entry to Practice
A. Integrity—Honesty, Personal Responsibility and Adherence to Professional Values		
Essential Component: **Understanding of professional values; honesty, personal responsibility**	Essential Component: **Work as psychologist-in-training infused with adherence to professional values. Recognizes situations that challenge adherence to professional values**	Essential Component: **Continually monitors and independently resolves situations that challenge professional values and integrity**
Behavioral Anchor: ■ Demonstrates honesty, even in difficult situations ■ Takes responsibility for own actions ■ Displays basic understanding of core professional values ■ Demonstrates ethical behavior & basic knowledge of APA (2010a) Ethical Principles & Code of Conduct (see below, Ethical Legal Standards and Policy)	Behavioral Anchor: ■ Demonstrates knowledge of professional values ■ Demonstrates adherence to professional values ■ Identifies situations that challenge professional values, and seeks faculty/supervisor guidance as needed ■ Demonstrates ability to share, discuss and address failures and lapses in adherence to professional values with supervisors/faculty as appropriate	Behavioral Anchor: ■ Articulates professional values ■ Takes independent action to correct situations that are in conflict with professional values

(*continues*)

Readiness for Practicum	Readiness for Internship	Readiness for Entry to Practice
	B. Deportment	
Essential Component: **Understands how to conduct oneself in a professional manner**	Essential Component: **Professionally appropriate communication and physical conduct, including attire, across different settings**	Essential Component: **Consistently conducts self in a professional manner across and settings and situations**
Behavioral Anchor: ■ Demonstrates appropriate personal hygiene and attire ■ Distinguishes between appropriate and inappropriate language and demeanor in professional contexts	Behavioral Anchor: ■ Demonstrates awareness of the impact behavior has on client, public and profession ■ Utilizes appropriate language and demeanor in professional communications ■ Demonstrates appropriate physical conduct, including attire, consistent with context	Behavioral Anchor: ■ Verbal and nonverbal communications are appropriate to the professional context including in challenging interactions
	C. Accountability	
Essential Component: **Accountable and reliable**	Essential Component: **Consistently reliable; consistently accepts responsibility for own actions**	Essential Component: **Independently accepts personal responsibility across settings and contexts**
Behavioral Anchor: ■ Turns in assignments in accordance with established deadlines ■ Demonstrates personal organization skills ■ Plans and organizes own workload ■ Aware of and follows policies and procedures of institution	Behavioral Anchor: ■ Completes required case documentation promptly and accurately ■ Accepts responsibility for meeting deadlines ■ Available when "on-call" ■ Acknowledges errors ■ Utilizes supervision to strengthen effectiveness of practice	Behavioral Anchor ■ Works to fulfill client–provider contract ■ Enhances productivity ■ Holds self accountable for and submits to external review of quality service provision

Readiness for Practicum	Readiness for Internship	Readiness for Entry to Practice

D. Concern for the Welfare of Others

Readiness for Practicum	Readiness for Internship	Readiness for Entry to Practice
Essential Component: Awareness of the need to uphold and protect the welfare of others	**Essential Component: Consistently acts to understand and safeguard the welfare of others**	**Essential Component: Independently acts to safeguard the welfare of others**
Behavioral Anchor ■ Displays initiative to help others ■ Articulates importance of concepts of confidentiality, privacy, informed consent ■ Demonstrates compassion	Behavioral Anchor: ■ Regularly demonstrates compassion ■ Displays respect in interpersonal interactions with others including those from divergent perspectives or backgrounds ■ Determines when response to client needs takes precedence over personal needs	Behavioral Anchor ■ Communications and actions convey sensitivity to individual experience and needs while retaining professional demeanor and deportment ■ Respectful of the beliefs and values of colleagues even when inconsistent with personal beliefs and values ■ Acts to benefit the welfare of others, especially those in need

E. Professional Identity

Readiness for Practicum	Readiness for Internship	Readiness for Entry to Practice
Essential Component: Beginning understanding of self as professional, "thinking like a psychologist"	**Essential Component: Emerging professional identity as psychologist; uses resources (e.g., supervision, literature) for professional development**	**Essential Component: Consolidation of professional identity as a psychologist; knowledgeable about issues central to the field; evidence of integration of science and practice**
Behavioral Anchor: ■ Has membership in professional organizations ■ Demonstrates knowledge of the program and profession (training model, core competencies) ■ Demonstrates knowledge about practicing within one's competence ■ Understands that knowledge goes beyond formal training	Behavioral Anchor: ■ Attends colloquia, workshops, conferences ■ Consults literature relevant to client care	Behavioral Anchor ■ Keeps up with advances in profession ■ Contributes to the development & advancement of the profession and colleagues ■ Demonstrates integration of science in professional practice

Reflective practice/self-assessment/self-care—Practice conducted with personal and professional self-awareness and reflection; with awareness of competencies; with appropriate self-care

	Developmental Level	
Readiness for Practicum	**Readiness for Internship**	**Readiness for Entry to Practice**
	A. Reflective Practice	
Essential Component: **Basic mindfulness and self-awareness; basic reflectivity regarding professional practice (reflection-on-action)**	Essential Component: **Broadened self-awareness; self-monitoring; reflectivity regarding professional practice (reflection-on-action); use of resources to enhance reflectivity; elements of reflection-in-action**	Essential Component: **Reflectivity in context of professional practice (reflection-in-action), reflection acted upon, self used as a therapeutic tool**
Behavioral Anchor: Displays: ■ problem solving skills ■ critical thinking ■ organized reasoning ■ intellectual curiosity and flexibility Demonstrates openness to: ■ considering own personal concerns & issues ■ recognizing impact of self on others ■ articulating attitudes, values, and beliefs toward diverse others ■ self-identifying multiple individual and cultural identities ■ systematically reviewing own professional performance with supervisors/teachers	Behavioral Anchor: ■ Articulates attitudes, values, and beliefs toward diverse others ■ Recognizes impact of self on others ■ Self-identifies multiple individual and cultural identities ■ Describes how others experience him/her and identifies roles one might play within a group ■ Responsively utilizes supervision to enhance reflectivity ■ Systematically and effectively reviews own professional performance via videotape or other technology with supervisors ■ Initial indicators of monitoring and adjusting professional performance in action as situation requires	Behavioral Anchor: ■ Demonstrates frequent congruence between own and others' assessment and seeks to resolve incongruities ■ Models self-care ■ Monitors and evaluates attitudes, values and beliefs towards diverse others ■ Systematically and effectively monitors and adjusts professional performance in action as situation requires ■ Consistently recognizes and addresses own problems, minimizing interference with competent professional functioning

Readiness for Practicum	Readiness for Internship	Readiness for Entry to Practice
	B. Self-Assessment	
Essential Component: **Knowledge of core competencies; emerging self-assessment re: competencies**	Essential Component: **Broadly accurate self-assessment of competence; consistent monitoring and evaluation of practice activities**	Essential Component: **Accurate self-assessment of competence in all competency domains; integration of self-assessment in practice**
Behavioral Anchor: ■ Demonstrates awareness of clinical competencies for professional training ■ Develops initial competency goals for early training (with input from faculty)	Behavioral Anchor: ■ Self-assessment comes close to congruence with assessment by peers and supervisors ■ Identifies areas requiring further professional growth ■ Writes a personal statement of professional goals ■ Identifies learning objectives for overall training plan ■ Systemically and effectively reviews own professional performance via videotape or other technology	Behavioral Anchor: ■ Accurately identifies level of competence across all competency domains ■ Accurately assesses own strengths and weaknesses and seeks to prevent or ameliorate impact on professional functioning ■ Recognizes when new/improved competencies are required for effective practice

C. Self-Care (Attention to Personal Health and Well-Being to Assure Effective Professional Functioning)

Readiness for Practicum	Readiness for Internship	Readiness for Entry to Practice
Essential Component **Understanding of the importance of self-care in effective practice; knowledge of self-care methods; attention to self-care**	Essential Component **Monitoring of issues related to self-care with supervisor; understanding of the central role of self-care to effective practice**	Essential Component **Self-monitoring of issues related to self-care and prompt interventions when disruptions occur**
Behavioral Anchor: ■ Demonstrates basic awareness and attention to self-care	Behavioral Anchor: ■ Works with supervisor to monitor issues related to self-care ■ Takes action recommended by supervisor for self-care to ensure effective training	Behavioral Anchor: ■ Anticipates and self-identifies disruptions in functioning and intervenes at an early stage/with minimal support from supervisors ■ Models self-care

Scientific Knowledge and Methods—Understanding of research, research methodology, techniques of data collection and analysis, biological bases of behavior, cognitive–affective bases of behavior, and development across the lifespan. Respect for scientifically derived knowledge

	Developmental Level	
Readiness for Practicum	**Readiness for Internship**	**Readiness for Entry to Practice**

A. Scientific Mindedness

Essential Component: **Critical scientific thinking**	Essential Component: **Values and applies scientific methods to professional practice**	Essential Component: **Independently applies scientific methods to practice**
Behavioral Anchor: ■ Aware of need for evidence to support assertions ■ Questions assumptions of knowledge ■ Evaluates study methodology and scientific basis of findings ■ Presents own work for the scrutiny of others	Behavioral Anchor: ■ Articulates, in supervision and case conference, support for issues derived from the literature ■ Formulates appropriate questions regarding case conceptualization ■ Generates hypotheses regarding own contribution to therapeutic process and outcome ■ Performs scientific critique of literature	Behavioral Anchor: ■ Independently accesses and applies scientific knowledge & skills appropriately and habitually to the solution of problems ■ Readily presents own work for the scrutiny of others

B. Scientific Foundation of Psychology

Essential Component: **Understanding of psychology as a science**	Essential Component: **Knowledge of core science**	Essential Component: **Knowledge of core science**
Behavioral Anchor: ■ Demonstrates understanding of core scientific conceptualizations of human behavior ■ Demonstrates understanding of psychology as a science, including basic knowledge of the breadth of scientific psychology. For example: able to cite scientific literature to support an argument ■ Evaluates scholarly literature on a topic	Behavioral Anchor: ■ Displays intermediate level knowledge of and respect for scientific bases of behavior	Behavioral Anchor: ■ Demonstrates advanced level of knowledge of and respect for scientific knowledge of the bases for behaviors

Readiness for Practicum	Readiness for Internship	Readiness for Entry to Practice
C. Scientific Foundation of Professional Practice		
Essential Component: **Understanding the scientific foundation of professional practice**	Essential Component: **Knowledge, understanding, and application of the concept of EBP**	Essential Component: **Knowledge and understanding of scientific foundations independently applied to practice**
Behavioral Anchor: <ul><li>Understands the development of evidence based practice in psychology (EBP) as defined by APA</li><li>Displays understanding of the scientific foundations of the functional competencies</li><li>Cites scientific literature to support an argument</li><li>Evaluates scholarly literature on a practice-related topic</li></ul>	Behavioral Anchor: <ul><li>Applies EBP concepts in case conceptualization, treatment planning, and interventions</li><li>Compares and contrasts EBP approaches with other theoretical perspectives and interventions in the context of case conceptualization and treatment planning</li></ul>	Behavioral Anchor: <ul><li>Reviews scholarly literature related to clinical work and applies knowledge to case conceptualization</li><li>Applies EBP concepts in practice</li><li>Compares and contrasts EBP approaches with other theoretical perspectives and interventions in the context of case conceptualization and treatment planning</li></ul>

Relationships—Relate effectively and meaningfully with individuals, groups, and/or communities

Developmental Level		
Readiness for Practicum	Readiness for Internship	Readiness for Entry to Practice
A. Interpersonal Relationships		
Essential Component: **Interpersonal skills**	Essential Component: **Forms and maintains productive and respectful relationships with clients, peers/colleagues, supervisors and professionals from other disciplines**	Essential Component: **Develops and maintains effective relationships with a wide range of clients, colleagues, organizations and communities**

(*continues*)

Readiness for Practicum	Readiness for Internship	Readiness for Entry to Practice
Behavioral Anchor: ■ Listens and is empathic with others ■ Respects and shows interest in others' cultures, experiences, values, points of view, goals and desires, fears, etc. ■ Demonstrates skills verbally and non-verbally ■ Receives feedback	Behavioral Anchor: ■ Forms effective working alliance with clients ■ Engages with supervisors to work effectively ■ Works cooperatively with peers ■ Involved in departmental, institutional, or professional activities or governance ■ Demonstrates respectful and collegial interactions with those who have different professional models or perspectives	Behavioral Anchor: ■ Effectively negotiates conflictual, difficult and complex relationships including those with individuals and groups that differ significantly from oneself ■ Maintains satisfactory interpersonal relationships with clients, peers, faculty, allied professionals, and the public

B. Affective Skills

Readiness for Practicum	Readiness for Internship	Readiness for Entry to Practice
Essential Component: **Affective skills**	Essential Component: **Negotiates differences and handles conflict satisfactorily; provides effective feedback to others and receives feedback nondefensively**	Essential Component: **Manages difficult communication; possesses advanced interpersonal skills**
Behavioral Anchor: ■ Demonstrates affect tolerance ■ Tolerates and understands interpersonal conflict ■ Tolerates ambiguity and uncertainty ■ Demonstrates awareness of inner emotional experience ■ Demonstrates emotional maturity ■ Listens to and acknowledges feedback from others	Behavioral Anchor: ■ Works collaboratively ■ Demonstrates active problem-solving ■ Makes appropriate disclosures regarding problematic interpersonal situations ■ Acknowledges own role in difficult interactions ■ Provides feedback to supervisor regarding supervisory process ■ Provides feedback to peers regarding peers' clinical work in context of group supervision or case conference ■ Accepts and implements supervisory feedback nondefensively	Behavioral Anchor: ■ Seeks clarification in challenging interpersonal communications ■ Demonstrates understanding of diverse viewpoints in challenging interactions ■ Accepts, evaluates and implements feedback from others

Readiness for Practicum	Readiness for Internship	Readiness for Entry to Practice
C. Expressive Skills		
Essential Component: **Expressive skills**	Essential Component: **Clear and articulate expression**	Essential Component: **Effective command of language and ideas**
Behavioral Anchor: ■ Communicates ideas, feelings, and information verbally and non-verbally	Behavioral Anchor: ■ Communicates clearly using verbal, nonverbal, and written skills ■ Demonstrates understanding of professional language	Behavioral Anchor: ■ Demonstrates descriptive, understandable command of language, both written and verbal ■ Communicates clearly and effectively with clients

Individual and Cultural Diversity—Awareness, sensitivity and skills in working professionally with diverse individuals, groups and communities who represent various cultural and personal background and characteristics defined broadly and consistent with APA policy

Developmental Level		
Readiness for Practicum	Readiness for Internship	Readiness for Entry to Practice

A. Self as Shaped by Individual and Cultural Diversity (e.g., cultural, individual, and role differences, including those based on age, gender, gender identity, race, ethnicity, culture, national origin, religion, sexual orientation, disability, language, and socioeconomic status) **and Context**

Readiness for Practicum	Readiness for Internship	Readiness for Entry to Practice
Essential Component: **Knowledge, awareness, and understanding of one's own dimensions of diversity and attitudes towards divers others**	Essential Component: **Monitors and applies knowledge of self as a cultural being in assessment, treatment, and consultation**	Essential Component: **Independently monitors and applies knowledge of self as a cultural being in assessment, treatment, and consultation**
Behavioral Anchor: ■ Demonstrates this self knowledge, awareness, and understanding. For example: articulates how ethnic group values influence who one is and how one relates to other people	Behavioral Anchor: ■ Understands and monitors own cultural identities in relation to work with others ■ Uses knowledge of self to monitor effectiveness as a professional ■ Critically evaluates feedback and initiates supervision regularly about diversity issues	Behavioral Anchor: ■ Independently articulates, understands, and monitors own cultural identity in relation to work with others ■ Regularly uses knowledge of self to monitor and improve effectiveness as a professional ■ Critically evaluates feedback and initiates consultation or supervision when uncertain about diversity issues

(continues)

Readiness for Practicum	Readiness for Internship	Readiness for Entry to Practice

B. Others as Shaped by Individual and Cultural Diversity (e.g., cultural, individual, and role differences, including those based on age, gender, gender identity, race, ethnicity, culture, national origin, religion, sexual orientation, disability, language, and socioeconomic status) **and Context**

Readiness for Practicum	Readiness for Internship	Readiness for Entry to Practice
Essential Component: **Knowledge, awareness, and understanding of others individuals as cultural beings**	Essential Component: **Applies knowledge of others as cultural beings in assessment, treatment, and consultation of others**	Essential Component: **Independently monitors and applies knowledge of others as cultural beings in assessment, treatment, and consultation**
Behavioral Anchor: ■ Demonstrates knowledge, awareness and understanding of the way culture and context shape the behavior of other individuals	Behavioral Anchor: ■ Understands multiple cultural identities in work with others ■ Uses knowledge of others' cultural identity in work as a professional ■ Critically evaluates feedback and initiates supervision regularly about diversity issues with others	Behavioral Anchor: ■ Independently articulates, understands, and monitors cultural identity in work with others ■ Regularly uses knowledge of others to monitor and improve effectiveness as a professional ■ Critically evaluates feedback and initiates consultation or supervision when uncertain about diversity issues with others

C. Interaction of Self and Others as Shaped by Individual and Cultural Diversity (e.g., cultural, individual, and role differences, including those based on age, gender, gender identity, race, ethnicity, culture, national origin, religion, sexual orientation, disability, language, and socioeconomic status) **and Context**

Readiness for Practicum	Readiness for Internship	Readiness for Entry to Practice
Essential Component: **Knowledge, awareness, and understanding of interactions between self and diverse others**	Essential Component: **Applies knowledge of the role of culture in interactions in assessment, treatment, and consultation of diverse others**	Essential Component: **Independently monitors and applies knowledge of diversity in others as cultural beings in assessment, treatment, and consultation**

Readiness for Practicum	Readiness for Internship	Readiness for Entry to Practice
Behavioral Anchor: ■ Demonstrates knowledge, awareness, and understanding of the way culture and context shape interactions between and among individuals	Behavioral Anchor: ■ Understands the role of multiple cultural identities in interactions among individuals ■ Uses knowledge of the role of culture in interactions in work as a professional ■ Critically evaluates feedback and initiates supervision regularly about diversity issues with others	Behavioral Anchor: ■ Independently articulates, understands, and monitors multiple cultural identities in interactions with others ■ Regularly uses knowledge the role of culture in interactions to monitor and improve effectiveness as a professional ■ Critically evaluates feedback and initiates consultation or supervision when uncertain about diversity issues with others

D. Applications Based on Individual and Cultural Context

Essential Component: **Basic knowledge of and sensitivity to the scientific, theoretical, and contextual issues related to ICD (as defined by APA policy) as they apply to professional psychology. Understanding of the need to consider ICD issues in all aspects of professional psychology work (e.g., assessment, treatment, research, relationships with colleagues)**	Essential Component: **Applies knowledge, sensitivity, and understanding regarding ICD issues to work effectively with diverse others in assessment, treatment, and consultation**	Essential Component: **Applies knowledge, skills, and attitudes regarding intersecting and complex dimensions of diversity, for example, the relationship between one's own dimensions of diversity and one's own attitudes towards diverse others to professional work**

(*continues*)

Readiness for Practicum	Readiness for Internship	Readiness for Entry to Practice
Behavioral Anchor: ■ Demonstrates basic knowledge of literatures on individual and cultural differences and engages in respectful interactions that reflects this knowledge ■ Demonstrates understanding of the need to consider ICD issues in all aspects of professional psychology work through respectful interactions	Behavioral Anchor: ■ Demonstrates knowledge of ICD literature and APA policies including guidelines for practice with diverse individuals, groups and communities ■ Demonstrates ability to address ICD issues across professional settings and activities ■ Works effectively with diverse others in professional activities ■ Demonstrates awareness of effects of oppression and privilege on self and others	Behavioral Anchor: ■ Articulates an integrative conceptualization of diversity as it impacts clients, self and others (e.g., organizations, colleagues, systems of care) ■ Habitually adapts one's professional behavior in a culturally sensitive manner, as appropriate to the needs of the client, that improves client outcomes and avoids harm ■ Articulates and uses alternative and culturally appropriate repertoire of skills and techniques and behaviors ■ Seeks consultation regarding addressing individual and cultural diversity as needed ■ Uses culturally relevant best practices

Ethical Legal Standards and Policy—Application of ethical concepts and awareness of legal issues regarding professional activities with individuals, groups, and organizations

Developmental Level		
Readiness for Practicum	Readiness for Internship	Readiness for Entry to Practice

A. Knowledge of Ethical, Legal and Professional Standards and Guidelines

Readiness for Practicum	Readiness for Internship	Readiness for Entry to Practice
Essential Component: **Basic knowledge of the principles of the APA [2010a] Ethical Principles [of Psychologists] and Code of Conduct [ethical practice and basic skills in ethical decision making]; beginning knowledge of legal and regulatory issues in the practice of psychology that apply to practice while placed at practicum setting**	Essential Component: **Intermediate level knowledge and understanding of the APA [2010a] Ethical Principles [of Psychologists] and Code of Conduct and other relevant ethical/professional codes, standards and guidelines; laws, statutes, rules, regulations**	Essential Component: **Routine command and application of the APA [2010a] Ethical Principles [of Psychologists] and Code of Conduct and other relevant and other ethical, legal and professional standards and guidelines of the profession**

Readiness for Practicum	Readiness for Internship	Readiness for Entry to Practice
Behavioral Anchor: ■ Displays a basic understanding of this knowledge (e.g., APA [2010a] Ethics Code and principles, ethical decision making models) ■ Demonstrates knowledge of typical legal issues (e.g., child and elder abuse reporting, HIPAA, confidentiality, informed consent)	Behavioral Anchor: ■ Identifies ethical dilemmas effectively ■ Actively consults with supervisor to act upon ethical and legal aspects of practice ■ Addresses ethical and legal aspects within the case conceptualization ■ Discusses ethical implications of professional work ■ Recognizes and discusses limits of own ethical and legal knowledge	Behavioral Anchor: ■ Spontaneously and reliably identifies complex ethical & legal issues, analyzes them accurately and proactively addresses them ■ Aware of potential conflicts in complex ethical and legal issues and seeks to prevent problems and unprofessional conduct ■ Aware of the obligation to confront peers and or organizations regarding ethical problems or issues and to deal proactively with conflict when addressing professional behavior with others

B. Awareness and Application of Ethical Decision Making

Readiness for Practicum	Readiness for Internship	Readiness for Entry to Practice
Essential Component: **Demonstrates the importance of an ethical decision model applied to practice**	Essential Component: **Knows and applies an ethical decision-making model and is able to apply relevant elements of ethical decision making to a dilemma**	Essential Component: **Commitment to integration of ethics knowledge into professional work**
Behavioral Anchor: ■ Recognizes the importance of basic ethical concepts applicable in initial practice (e.g., child abuse reporting, informed consent, confidentiality, multiple relationships, and competence) ■ Identifies potential conflicts between personal belief systems, APA (2010a) Ethics Code and legal issues in practice	Behavioral Anchor: ■ Uses an ethical decision-making model when discussing cases in supervision ■ Readily identifies ethical implications in cases and to understand the ethical elements in any present ethical dilemma or question ■ Discusses ethical dilemmas and decision making in supervision, staffings, presentations, practicum settings	Behavioral Anchor: ■ Applies applicable ethical principles and standards in professional writings and presentations ■ Applies applicable ethics concepts in research design and subject treatment ■ Applied ethics and professional concepts in teaching and training activities ■ Develops strategies to seek consultation regarding complex ethical and legal dilemmas *(continues)*

Readiness for Practicum	Readiness for Internship	Readiness for Entry to Practice

C. Ethical Conduct

Readiness for Practicum	Readiness for Internship	Readiness for Entry to Practice
Essential Component: **Ethical attitudes and values evident in conduct**	Essential Component: **Knowledge of own moral principles/ethical values integrated in professional conduct**	Essential Component: **Independently and consistently integrates ethical and legal standards with all foundational and functional competencies**
Behavioral Anchor: ■ Evidences desire to help others ■ Demonstrates openness to new ideas ■ Shows honesty/integrity/values ethical behavior ■ Demonstrates personal courage consistent with ethical values of psychologists ■ Displays a capacity for appropriate boundary management ■ Implements ethical concepts into professional behavior	Behavioral Anchor: ■ Articulates knowledge of own moral principles and ethical values in discussions with supervisors and peers about ethical issues ■ Spontaneously discusses intersection of personal and professional ethical and moral issues	Behavioral Anchor: ■ Integrates an understanding of ethical–legal standards policy when performing all functional competencies ■ Demonstrates awareness that ethical legal standards and policy competence inform and are informed by all foundational competencies ■ Takes responsibility for continuing professional development

Interdisciplinary Systems—Knowledge of key issues and concepts in related disciplines. Identify and interact with professionals in multiple disciplines

Developmental Level		
Readiness for Practicum	Readiness for Internship	Readiness for Entry to Practice

A. Knowledge of the Shared and Distinctive Contributions of Other Professions

Readiness for Practicum	Readiness for Internship	Readiness for Entry to Practice
Essential Component: **Beginning, basic knowledge of the viewpoints and contributions of other professions/professionals**	Essential Component: **Awareness of multiple and differing worldviews, roles, professional standards, and contributions across contexts and systems, intermediate level knowledge of common and distinctive roles of other professionals**	Essential Component: **Working knowledge of multiple and differing worldviews, professional standards, and contributions across contexts and systems, intermediate level knowledge of common and distinctive roles of other professionals**

Readiness for Practicum	Readiness for Internship	Readiness for Entry to Practice
Behavioral Anchor: ■ Demonstrates knowledge, respect, and valuing of roles, functions and service delivery systems of other professions	Behavioral Anchor: ■ Reports observations of commonality and differences among professional roles, values, and standards	Behavioral Anchor: ■ Demonstrates ability to articulate the role that others provide in service to clients ■ Displays ability to work successfully on interdisciplinary team

B. Functioning in Multidisciplinary and Interdisciplinary Contexts

Essential Component: **Cooperation**	Essential Component: **Beginning knowledge of strategies that promote interdisciplinary collaboration vs. multidisciplinary functioning**	Essential Component: **Beginning, basic knowledge of and ability to display the skills that support effective interdisciplinary team functioning, such as communicating without jargon, dealing effectively with disagreements about diagnosis or treatment goals, supporting and utilizing the perspectives of other team members**
Behavioral Anchor: ■ Demonstrates ability to cooperate with others in task completion	Behavioral Anchor: ■ Demonstrates knowledge of the nature of interdisciplinary vs. multidisciplinary function and the skills that support interdisciplinary process	Behavioral Anchor: ■ Demonstrates skill in interdisciplinary clinical settings in working with other professionals to incorporate psychological information into overall team planning and implementation

C. Understands How Participation in Interdisciplinary Collaboration/Consultation Enhances Outcomes

Essential Component: **Knowledge of how participating in interdisciplinary collaboration/ consultation can be directed toward shared goals**	Essential Component: **Participates in and initiates interdisciplinary collaboration/ consultation directed toward shared goals**	Essential Component: **Recognizes and engages in opportunities for effective collaboration with other professionals toward shared goals at an intermediate level of ability**

(*continues*)

Readiness for Practicum	Readiness for Internship	Readiness for Entry to Practice
Behavioral Anchor: ■ Demonstrates understanding of concept	Behavioral Anchor: ■ Consults with and cooperates with other disciplines in service of clients	Behavioral Anchor: ■ Systematically collaborates successfully with other relevant partners

D. Respectful and Productive Relationships With Individuals From Other Professions

Readiness for Practicum	Readiness for Internship	Readiness for Entry to Practice
Essential Component: **Awareness of the benefits of forming collaborative relationships with other professionals**	Essential Component: **Develops and maintains collaborative relationships and respect for other professionals**	Essential Component: **Develops and maintains collaborative relationships over time despite differences**
Behavioral Anchor: ■ Expresses interest in developing collaborative relationships and respect for other professionals	Behavioral Anchor: ■ Communicates effectively with individuals from other profession	Behavioral Anchor: ■ Communicates effectively with individuals from other professions ■ Appreciates and integrates perspectives from multiple professions

---

Functional Competencies

Assessment—Assessment and diagnosis of problems, capabilities and issues associated with individuals, groups, and/or organizations

Developmental Level

Readiness for Practicum	Readiness for Internship	Readiness for Entry to Practice

A. Measurement and Psychometrics

Readiness for Practicum	Readiness for Internship	Readiness for Entry to Practice
Essential Component: **Basic knowledge of the scientific, theoretical, and contextual basis of test construction and interviewing**	Essential Component: **Selects assessment measures with attention to issues of reliability and validity**	Essential Component: **Independently selects and implements multiple methods and means of evaluation in ways that are responsive to and respectful of diverse individuals, couples, families and groups and context**

Readiness for Practicum	Readiness for Internship	Readiness for Entry to Practice
Behavioral Anchor: ■ Demonstrates awareness of the benefits of standardized assessment ■ Demonstrates knowledge of the construct(s) being assessed ■ Evidences understanding of basic psychometric constructs such as validity, reliability, and test construction	Behavioral Anchor: ■ Identifies appropriate assessment measures for cases seen at practice site ■ Routinely consults with supervisor regarding selection of assessment measures	Behavioral Anchor: ■ Demonstrates awareness and competent use of culturally sensitive instruments, norms ■ Seeks consultation as needed to guide assessment ■ Demonstrates limitations of assessment data clearly reflected in assessment reports

B. Evaluation Methods

Readiness for Practicum	Readiness for Internship	Readiness for Entry to Practice
Essential Component: **Basic knowledge of administration and scoring of traditional assessment measures, models and techniques, including clinical interviewing and mental status exam**	Essential Component: **Awareness of the strengths and limitations of administration, scoring and interpretation of traditional assessment measures as well as related technological advances**	Essential Component: **Independently understands the strengths and limitations of diagnostic approaches and interpretation of results from multiple measures for diagnosis and treatment planning**
Behavioral Anchor: ■ Accurately and consistently administers and scores various assessment tools in nonclinical (e.g., course) contexts ■ Demonstrates knowledge of initial interviewing (both structured and semi-structured interviews, mini-mental status exam)	Behavioral Anchor: ■ Demonstrates intermediate level ability to accurately and consistently select, administer, score and interpret assessment tools with client populations ■ Collects accurate and relevant data from structured and semi-structured interviews and mini-mental status exams	Behavioral Anchor: ■ Accurately and consistently selects, administers, and scores and interprets assessment tools with clinical populations ■ Selection of assessment tools reflects a flexible approach to answering the diagnostic questions ■ Comprehensive reports include discussion of strengths and limitations of assessment measures as appropriate ■ Interview and report leads to formulation of a diagnosis and the development of appropriate treatment plan

(*continues*)

Readiness for Practicum	Readiness for Internship	Readiness for Entry to Practice
	C. Application of Methods	
Essential Component: **Knowledge of measurement across domains of functioning and practice settings**	Essential Component: **Selects appropriate assessment measures to answer diagnostic question**	Essential Component: **Independently selects and administers a variety of assessment tools and integrates results to accurately evaluate presenting questions appropriate to the practice site and broad area of practice**
Behavioral Anchor: ■ Demonstrates awareness of need to base diagnosis and assessment on multiple sources of information ■ Demonstrates awareness of need for selection of assessment measures appropriate to population/problem	Behavioral Anchor: ■ Selects assessment tools that reflect awareness of patient population served at a given practice site ■ Regularly selects and uses appropriate methods of evaluation ■ Demonstrates ability to adapt environment and materials according to client needs (e.g., lighting, privacy, ambient noise)	Behavioral Anchor: ■ Independently selects assessment tools that reflect awareness of client population served at practice site ■ Interprets assessment results accurately taking into account limitations of the evaluation method ■ Provides meaningful, understandable and useful feedback that is responsive to client need
	D. Diagnosis	
Essential Component: **Basic knowledge regarding the range of normal and abnormal behavior in the context of stages of human development and diversity**	Essential Component: **Applies concepts of normal/abnormal behavior to case formulation and diagnosis in the context of stages of human development and diversity**	Essential Component: **Utilizes case formulation and diagnosis for intervention planning in the context of stages of human development and diversity**

Readiness for Practicum	Readiness for Internship	Readiness for Entry to Practice
Behavioral Anchor: ■ Identifies *DSM* criteria ■ Describes normal development consistent with broad area of training	Behavioral Anchor: ■ Articulates relevant developmental features and clinical symptoms as applied to presenting question ■ Demonstrates ability to identify problem areas and to use concepts of differential diagnosis	Behavioral Anchor: ■ Treatment plans incorporate relevant developmental features and clinical symptoms as applied to presenting problem ■ Demonstrates awareness of *DSM* and relation to *International Classification of Diseases* (World Health Organization, 2007) codes ■ Regularly and independently identifies problem areas and makes a diagnosis

E. Conceptualization and Recommendations

Essential Component: **Basic knowledge of formulating diagnosis and case conceptualization**	Essential Component: **Utilizes systematic approaches of gathering data to inform clinical decision-making**	Essential Component: **Independently and accurately conceptualizes the multiple dimensions of the case based on the results of assessment**
Behavioral Anchor: ■ Demonstrates the ability to discuss diagnostic formulation and case conceptualization ■ Prepares basic reports which articulate theoretical material	Behavioral Anchor: ■ Presents cases and reports demonstrating how diagnosis is based on case material	Behavioral Anchor: ■ Independently prepares reports ■ Administers, scores and interprets test results ■ Formulates case conceptualizations incorporating theory and case material

F. Communication of Findings

Essential Component: **Awareness of models of report writing and progress notes**	Essential Component: **Writes assessment reports and progress notes**	Essential Component: **Communication of results in written and verbal form clearly, constructively, and accurately in a conceptually appropriate manner**
Behavioral Anchor: ■ Demonstrates this knowledge including content and organization of test reports, mental status examinations, interviews	Behavioral Anchor: ■ Writes a basic psychological report ■ Demonstrates ability to communicate basic findings verbally ■ Reports reflect data that has been collected via interview	Behavioral Anchor ■ Writes an effective comprehensive report ■ Effectively communicates results verbally ■ Reports reflect data that has been collected via interview and its limitations

Intervention—Interventions designed to alleviate suffering and to promote health and well-being of individuals, groups, and/or organizations

Developmental Level		
Readiness for Practicum	**Readiness for Internship**	**Readiness for Entry to Practice**

A. Knowledge of Interventions

Essential Component: **Basic knowledge of scientific, theoretical, and contextual bases of intervention and basic knowledge of the value of EBP and its role in scientific psychology**	Essential Component: **Knowledge of scientific, theoretical, empirical and contextual bases of intervention, including theory, research, and practice**	Essential Component: **Applies knowledge of EBP, including empirical bases of intervention strategies, clinical expertise, and client preferences**
Behavioral anchor: ■ Articulates the relationship of EBP to the science of psychology ■ Identifies basic strengths and weaknesses of intervention approaches for different problems and populations	Behavioral Anchor: ■ Demonstrates knowledge of interventions and explanations for their use based on EBP ■ Demonstrates the ability to select interventions for different problems and populations related to the practice setting ■ Investigates existing literature related to problems and client issues ■ Writes a statement of one's own theoretical perspective regarding intervention strategies	Behavioral Anchor: ■ Writes a case summary incorporating elements of EBP ■ Presents rationale for intervention strategy that includes empirical support

B. Intervention Planning

Essential Component: **Basic understanding of the relationship between assessment and intervention**	Essential Component: **Formulates and conceptualizes cases and plan interventions utilizing at least one consistent theoretical orientation**	Essential Component: **Independent intervention planning, including conceptualization and intervention planning specific to case and context**

Readiness for Practicum	Readiness for Internship	Readiness for Entry to Practice
Behavioral Anchor: ■ Articulates a basic understanding of how intervention choices are informed by assessment	Behavioral Anchor: ■ Articulates a theory of change and identifies interventions to implement change; as consistent with the AAPI ■ Writes understandable case conceptualization reports and collaborative treatment plans incorporating EBPs	Behavioral Anchor: ■ Accurately assesses presenting issues taking in to account the larger life context, including diversity issues ■ Conceptualizes case independently and accurately ■ Independently selects an intervention or range of interventions appropriate for the presenting issue(s)

C. Skills

Readiness for Practicum	Readiness for Internship	Readiness for Entry to Practice
Essential Component: **Basic helping skills**	Essential Component: **Clinical skills**	Essential Component: **Clinical skills and judgment**
Behavioral Anchor: ■ Demonstrates helping skills, such as empathic listening, framing problems	Behavioral Anchor: ■ Develops rapport with most clients ■ Develops therapeutic relationships ■ Demonstrates appropriate judgment about when to consult supervisor	Behavioral Anchor: ■ Develops rapport and relationships with wide variety of clients ■ Uses good judgment about unexpected issues, such as crises, use of supervision, confrontation ■ Effectively delivers intervention

D. Intervention Implementation

Readiness for Practicum	Readiness for Internship	Readiness for Entry to Practice
Essential Component: **Basic knowledge of intervention strategies**	Essential Component: **Implements evidence-based interventions that take into account empirical support, clinical judgment, and client diversity (e.g., client characteristics, values, and context)**	Essential Component: **Implements interventions with fidelity to empirical models and flexibility to adapt where appropriate**
Behavioral Anchor: ■ Articulates awareness of theoretical basis of intervention and some general strategies	Behavioral Anchor: ■ Applies specific evidence-based interventions ■ Presents case that documents application of EBP	Behavioral Anchor: ■ Independently and effectively implements a typical range of intervention strategies appropriate to practice setting ■ Independently recognizes and manages special circumstances ■ Terminates treatment successfully ■ Collaborates effectively with other providers or systems of care

(*continues*)

Readiness for Practicum	Readiness for Internship	Readiness for Entry to Practice
E. Progress Evaluation		
Essential Component: **Basic knowledge of the assessment of intervention progress and outcome**	Essential Component: **Evaluate treatment progress and modify treatment planning as indicated, utilizing established outcome measures**	Essential Component: **Evaluate treatment progress and modify planning as indicated, even in the absence of established outcome measures**
Behavioral Anchor: ■ Demonstrates basic knowledge of methods to examine intervention outcomes	Behavioral Anchor: ■ Assesses and documents treatment progress and outcomes ■ Alters treatment plan accordingly ■ Describes instances of lack progress and actions taken in response	Behavioral Anchor: ■ Independently assesses treatment effectiveness and efficiency ■ Critically evaluates own performance in the treatment role ■ Seeks consultation when necessary

Consultation—The ability to provide expert guidance or professional assistance in response to a client's needs or goals

	Developmental Level	
Readiness for Practicum	Readiness for Internship	Readiness for Entry to Practice
A. Role of Consultant		
Essential Component: **No expectation for pre-practicum level**	Essential Component: **Knowledge of the consultant's role and its unique features as distinguished from other professional roles (such as therapist, supervisor, teacher)**	Essential Component: **Determines situations that require different role functions and shift roles accordingly**
	Behavioral Anchor: ■ Articulates common and distinctive roles of consultant ■ Compares and contrast consultation, clinical and supervision roles	Behavioral Anchor: ■ Recognizes situations in which consultation is appropriate ■ Demonstrates capability to shift functions and behavior to meet referral needs

Readiness for Practicum	Readiness for Internship	Readiness for Entry to Practice

B. Addressing Referral Question

Readiness for Practicum	Readiness for Internship	Readiness for Entry to Practice
Essential Component: **No expectation for pre-practicum level**	**Essential Component:** **Knowledge of and ability to select appropriate means of assessment to answer referral questions**	**Essential Component:** **Knowledge of and ability to select appropriate and contextually sensitive means of assessment/data gathering that answers consultation referral question**
	Behavioral Anchor: ■ Implements systematic approach to data collection in a consultative role ■ Identifies sources and types of assessment tools	Behavioral Anchor: ■ Demonstrates ability to gather information necessary to answer referral question ■ Clarifies and refines referral question based on analysis/assessment of question

C. Communication of Findings

Readiness for Practicum	Readiness for Internship	Readiness for Entry to Practice
Essential Component: **No expectation for pre-practicum level**	**Essential Component:** **Identifies literature and knowledge about process of informing consultee of assessment findings**	**Essential Component:** **Applies knowledge to provide effective assessment feedback and to articulate appropriate recommendations**
	Behavioral Anchor: ■ Identifies appropriate approaches and processes for providing written and verbal feedback and recommendation to consultee	Behavioral Anchor: ■ Prepares clear, useful consultation reports and recommendations to all appropriate parties ■ Provides verbal feedback to consultee of results and offers appropriate recommendations

D. Application of Methods

Readiness for Practicum	Readiness for Internship	Readiness for Entry to Practice
Essential Component: **No expectation for pre-practicum level**	**Essential Component:** **Identifies and acquires literature relevant to unique consultation methods (assessment and intervention) within systems, clients or settings**	**Essential Component:** **Applies literature to provide effective consultative services (assessment and intervention) in most routine and some complex cases**
	Behavioral Anchor: ■ Identifies appropriate interventions based on consultation assessment findings	Behavioral Anchor: ■ Identifies and implements consultation interventions based on assessment findings ■ Identifies and implements consultation interventions that meet consultee goals

Research/Evaluation—Generating research that contributes to the professional knowledge base and/or evaluates the effectiveness of various professional activities

	Developmental Level	
Readiness for Practicum	**Readiness for Internship**	**Readiness for Entry to Practice**

A. Scientific Approach to Knowledge Generation

Essential Component: **Basic scientific minded-ness, critical thinking**	Essential Component: **Development of skills and habits in seeking, applying, and evaluat-ing theoretical and research knowledge relevant to the prac-tice of psychology**	Essential Component: **Generation of knowledge**
Behavioral Anchor: ■ Demonstrates under-standing that psycholo-gists evaluate the effectiveness of their professional activities ■ Open to scrutiny of one's work by peers and faculty	Behavioral Anchor: ■ Demonstrates under-standing of research methods and tech-niques of data analysis ■ Demonstrates research and scholarly activity, which may include pre-sentations at confer-ences; participation in research teams; sub-mission of manuscripts for publication ■ Demonstrates being a critical consumer of research	Behavioral Anchor ■ Engages in systematic efforts to increase the knowledge base of psy-chology through imple-menting and reviewing research ■ Uses methods appro-priate to the research question, setting and/or community ■ Consults and partners with community stake-holders when conduct-ing research in diverse communities

B. Application of Scientific Method to Practice

Essential Component: **No expectation at this level**	Essential Component: **Apply scientific methods to evaluat-ing own practice**	Essential Component: **Evaluation of outcomes**
	Behavioral Anchor: ■ Discusses EBPs ■ Compiles and analyzes data on own clients (out-come measurement) ■ Participates in program evaluation	Behavioral Anchor: ■ Evaluates the progress of own activities and uses this information to improve own effectiveness ■ Describes how out-comes are measured in each practice activity

Supervision—Supervision and training in the professional knowledge base and of evaluation of the effectiveness of various professional activities

	Developmental Level	
Readiness for Practicum	**Readiness for Internship**	**Readiness for Entry to Practice**

A. Expectations and Roles

Readiness for Practicum	Readiness for Internship	Readiness for Entry to Practice
Essential Component: **Basic knowledge of expectations for supervision**	Essential Component: **Knowledge of purpose for and roles in supervision**	Essential Component: **Understands complexity of the supervisor role including ethical, legal, and contextual issues**
Behavioral Anchor: ■ Demonstrates knowledge of the process of supervision	Behavioral Anchor: ■ Identifies roles and responsibilities of the supervisor and supervisee in the supervision process	Behavioral Anchor: ■ Articulates a philosophy or model of supervision and reflects on how this model is applied in practice, including integrated contextual, legal, and ethical perspectives

B. Processes and Procedures

Readiness for Practicum	Readiness for Internship	Readiness for Entry to Practice
Essential Component: **No pre-practicum expectation**	Essential Component: **Knowledge of procedures and processes of supervision** Behavioral Anchor: ■ Identifies goals and tasks of supervision related to developmental progression ■ Tracks progress achieving goals and setting new goals	Essential Component: **Knowledge of procedures and practices of supervision** Behavioral Anchor: ■ Prepares supervision contract ■ Demonstrates knowledge of limits of competency to supervise (assesses metacompetency) ■ Constructs plans to deal with areas of limited competency

C. Skills Development

Readiness for Practicum	Readiness for Internship	Readiness for Entry to Practice
Essential Components **Interpersonal skills of communication and openness to feedback**	Essential Component: **Knowledge of the supervision literature and how clinicians develop to be skilled professionals**	Essential Component: **Engages in professional reflection about one's clinical relationships with supervisees, as well as supervisees' relationships with their clients**

(continues)

Readiness for Practicum	Readiness for Internship	Readiness for Entry to Practice
Behavioral Anchor ■ Completes self-assessment (e.g., Appendix B, this volume) ■ Integrates faculty/supervisor feedback into self-assessment	Behavioral Anchor: ■ Successfully completes coursework on supervision ■ Demonstrates formation of supervisory relationship integrating theory and skills including knowledge of development, educational praxis	Behavioral Anchor: ■ Clearly articulates how to use supervisory relationships to leverage development of supervisees and their clients

D. Awareness of Factors Affecting Quality

Essential Component: **Basic knowledge of and sensitivity to issues related to individual and cultural differences (i.e., the APA definition) as they apply to the supervision process and relationships**	Essential Component: **Knowledge about the impact of diversity on all professional settings and supervision participants including self as defined by APA policy; beginning knowledge of personal contribution to therapy and to supervision**	Essential component: **Understanding of other individuals and groups and intersection dimensions of diversity in the context of supervision practice, able to engage in reflection on the role of one's self on therapy and in supervision**
Behavioral Anchor: ■ Demonstrates basic knowledge of literature on individual and cultural differences and engages in respectful interactions that reflect that knowledge	Behavioral Anchor: ■ Demonstrates knowledge of ICD literature and APA guidelines in supervision practice ■ Demonstrates awareness of role of oppression and privilege on supervision process	Behavioral Anchor: ■ Demonstrates integration of diversity and multiple identity aspects in conceptualization of supervision process with all participants (client[s], supervisee, supervisor) ■ Demonstrates adaptation of own professional behavior in a culturally sensitive manner as appropriate to the needs of the supervision context and all parties in it ■ Articulates and uses diversity-appropriate repertoire of skills and techniques in supervisory process ■ Identifies impact of aspects of self in therapy and supervision

Readiness for Practicum	Readiness for Internship	Readiness for Entry to Practice

E. Participation in Supervision Process

Essential Component: **Awareness of need for straightforward, truthful, and respectful communication in supervisory relationship**	Essential Component: **Observation of and participation in supervisory process (e.g., peer supervision)**	Essential Component: **Provides supervision independently to others in routine cases**
Behavioral Anchor: ■ Demonstrates willingness to admit errors, accept feedback	Behavioral Anchor: ■ Reflects on supervision process, areas of strength and those needing improvement ■ Seeks supervision to improve performance, presenting work for feedback, and integrating feedback into performance	Behavioral Anchor: ■ Provides supervision to less advanced trainees, peers or other service providers in typical cases appropriate to the service setting.

F. Ethical and Legal Issues

Essential Component: **Knowledge of principles of ethical practice and basic skills in supervisory ethical decision making, knowledge of legal and regulatory issues in supervision**	Essential Component: **Knowledge of and compliance with ethical/ professional codes, standards and guidelines; institutional policies; laws, statutes, rules, regulations, and case law relevant to the practice of psychology and its supervision**	Essential Component: **Command of and application of relevant ethical, legal, and professional standards and guidelines**
Behavioral Anchor: ■ Demonstrates understanding of this knowledge (e.g., APA [2010a] Ethical Principles of Psychologists and Code of Conduct)	Behavioral Anchor: ■ Behaves ethically ■ Recognizes ethical and legal issues in clinical practice and supervision	Behavioral Anchor: ■ Spontaneously and reliably identifies complex ethical and legal issues in supervision, and analyzes and proactively addresses them ■ Demonstrates awareness of potential conflicts in complex ethical and legal issues in supervision

Teaching—Providing instruction, disseminating knowledge, and evaluating acquisition of knowledge and skill in professional psychology

Developmental Level		
Readiness for Practicum	**Readiness for Internship**	**Readiness for Entry to Practice**
A. Knowledge		
Essential Component: **Awareness of theories of learning and how they impact teaching**	Essential Component: **Knowledge of didactic learning strategies and how to accommodate developmental and individual differences**	Essential Component: **Knowledge of outcome assessment of teaching effectiveness**
Behavioral Anchor ■ Observes differences in teaching styles and need for response to different learning skills	Behavioral Anchor: ■ Demonstrates knowledge of one learning strategy ■ Demonstrates clear communication skills	Behavioral Anchor: ■ Demonstrates knowledge of one technique of outcome assessment ■ Demonstrates knowledge of methodological considerations in assessment of teaching effectiveness
B. Skills		
Essential Component: **Knowledge of application of teaching methods**	Essential Component: **Application of teaching methods in multiple settings**	Essential Component: **Evaluation of effectiveness of learning/teaching strategies addressing key skill sets**
Behavioral Anchor: ■ Demonstrates example of application of teaching method ■ Demonstrates ability to organize and present information related to a topic	Behavioral Anchor: ■ Identifies and differentiates factors for implementing particular teaching methods ■ Demonstrates accommodation to diverse others (e.g., cultural, individual, and role differences, including those based on age, gender, gender identity, race, ethnicity, culture, national origin, religion, sexual orientation, disability, language, and socioeconomic status) and context ■ Introduces innovation/creativity into application of teaching method	Behavioral Anchor: ■ Demonstrates strategy to evaluate teaching effectiveness of targeted skill sets ■ Articulates concepts to be taught and research/empirical support ■ Utilizes evaluation strategy to assess learning objectives met ■ Integrates feedback to modify future teaching strategies

Management–administration—Manage the direct delivery of services (DDS) and/or the administration of organizations, programs, or agencies (OPA)

Developmental Level		
Readiness for Practicum	Readiness for Internship	Readiness for Entry to Practice
A. Management		
Essential Component: **Awareness of roles of management in organizations**	Essential Component: **Participates in management of direct delivery of professional services; responds appropriately in management hierarchy**	Essential Component: **Manages direct delivery of professional services; awareness of basic principles of resource allocation and oversight**
Behavioral Anchor: ■ Articulates understanding of management role in own organization(s)	Behavioral Anchor: ■ Responds appropriately to managers and subordinates ■ Manages DDS under supervision (e.g., scheduling, billing, maintenance of records) ■ identifies responsibilities, challenges, and processes of management	Behavioral Anchor ■ Independently and regularly manages and evaluates own DDS, identifying opportunities for improvement ■ Recognizes role of and need for clerical and other staff, role of human resources
B. Administration		
Essential Component: **Awareness of the functions of policies and procedures, ability to comply with regulations**	Essential Component: **Knowledge of and ability to effectively function within professional settings and organizations, including compliance with policies and procedures**	Essential Component: **Awareness of principles of policy and procedures manual for OPA, awareness of basic business, financial and fiscal management issues**
Behavioral Anchor: ■ Completes assignments by due dates ■ Complies with relevant regulations ■ Responds appropriately to direction provided by managers	Behavioral Anchor: ■ Articulates approved organizational policies and procedures ■ Completes reports and other assignments promptly ■ Complies with record-keeping guidelines ■ Demonstrates understanding of quality improvement (QI) procedures in direct delivery of services basic management of direct services, QI procedures	Behavioral Anchor ■ Responds promptly to organizational demands ■ Participates in the development of policies ■ Functions within budget ■ Negotiates and collects fees, pays bills ■ Uses technological resources for information management ■ Identifies resources needed to develop a basic business plan

(continues)

Readiness for Practicum	Readiness for Internship	Readiness for Entry to Practice

C. Leadership

Essential Component: **No pre-practicum expectation**	Essential Component: **Recognition of own role in creating policy, participation in system change, and management structure**	Essential Component: **Development of mission, goal-setting, implementing systems to accomplish goals and objectives; team-building and motivational skills**
	Behavioral Anchor: ■ Articulates agency mission and purpose and its connection to goals & objectives ■ Implements procedures to accomplish goals and objectives	Behavioral Anchor: ■ Develops mission or purpose of DDS and/or OPA ■ Provides others with face to face and written direction ■ Demonstrates capacity to develop system for evaluating supervisees/ staff/employees ■ Communicates appropriately to parties at all levels in the system

D. Evaluation of Management and Leadership

Essential Component: **Autonomous judgment of organization's management and leadership**	Essential Component: **Able to develop and prepared to offer constructive criticism and suggestions regarding management and leadership of organization**	Essential Component: **Develops own plans for how best to manage and lead an organization**
Behavioral Anchor: ■ Applies theories of effective management and leadership to form an evaluation of organization	Behavioral Anchor: ■ Identifies strengths and weaknesses of management and leadership or organization ■ Provides input appropriately, participates in organizational assessment	Behavioral Anchor: ■ Articulates steps and actions to be effective manager or leader appropriate to the specifics of the organization

Advocacy—Actions targeting the impact of social, political, economic or cultural factors to promote change at the individual (client), institutional, and/or systems level

Developmental Level		
Readiness for Practicum	Readiness for Internship	Readiness for Entry to Practice
A. Empowerment		
Essential Component: **Awareness of social, political, economic and cultural factors that impact individuals, institutions and systems, in addition to other factors that may lead them to seek intervention**	Essential Component: **Uses awareness of the social, political, economic, or cultural factors that may impact human development in the context of service provision**	Essential Component: **Intervenes with client to promote action on factors impacting development and functioning**
Behavioral Anchor: ■ Articulates social, political, economic, or cultural factors that may impact on human development and functioning	Behavioral Anchor: ■ Identifies specific barriers to client improvement (e.g., lack of access to resources) ■ Assists client in development of self-advocacy plans	Behavioral Anchor: ■ Promotes client self-advocacy ■ Assesses implementation and outcome of client's self-advocacy plans
B. Systems Change		
Essential Component: **Understanding the differences between individual and institutional level interventions and system's level change**	Essential Component: **Promotes change to enhance the functioning of individuals**	Essential Component: **Promotes change at the level of institutions, community, or society**
Behavioral Anchor: ■ Articulates role of therapist as change agent outside of direct patient contact	Behavioral Anchor: ■ Identifies target issues/agencies most relevant to specific issue ■ Formulates and engages in plan for action ■ Demonstrates understanding of appropriate boundaries and times to advocate on behalf of client	Behavioral Anchor: ■ Develops alliances with relevant individuals and groups ■ Engages with groups with differing viewpoints around issue to promote change

Note. APA = American Psychological Association; ICD = individual and cultural differences; HIPAA = Health Insurance Portability and Accountability Act; DSM = *Diagnostic and Statistical Manual of Mental Disorders* (e.g., American Psychiatric Association, 2000); AAPIC = Association of Psychology Postdoctoral and Internship Centers.

APPENDIX B: THE PRACTICUM COMPETENCIES OUTLINE: REPORT ON PRACTICUM COMPETENCIES

AIMS AND USES OF THIS REPORT

The Association of Directors of Psychology Training Clinics (ADPTC) has practicum training as its main focus. The ADPTC recognizes the importance of defining, training for, and assessing core competencies in psychology. The motivation for preparing this document arises from these values.

Aims of This Document

1. To assemble and organize descriptions of currently identified core competencies for the professional psychologist.
2. To characterize the levels of competence in these core domains that are expected at the beginning of practicum training and at the end of practicum training, prior to beginning internship.

Potential Uses for This Document

1. Assist in developing practicum training programs by defining competency goals.
2. Assist in communication between practicum sites and graduate programs regarding training goals.
3. Develop competency assessments for practicum trainees.
4. Provide a basis for evaluating outcomes for practicum training programs.
5. Stimulate thinking concerning competency goals for more advanced training.

Scope and Applicability of This Document

1. This document covers an extensive set of competencies, most of which have been endorsed more or less strongly by various groups

Adapted from "Initial Training in Professional Psychology: The Practicum Competencies Outline," by R. L. Hatcher and K. D. Lassiter, 2007, *Training and Education in Professional Psychology, 1*, 49–63. Copyright 2007 by the American Psychological Association.

in professional psychology as required for a fully competent psychologist.

2. We recognize that professional psychology as a whole has not endorsed a list of competencies regarded as essential for the fully competent professional psychologist.

3. We recognize that individual psychology programs, depending on their educational goals, will likely select a subset of the competencies listed below that reflect the thrust of their program's goals. This point should be stressed, lest readers conclude that every practicum program should teach all of the competencies described below. The aim of this document is to provide a comprehensive account of relevant competencies, which can inform a program's effort to develop and implement its own training model. In its *Guidelines and Principles for Accreditation of Programs in Professional Psychology*, the American Psychological Association (APA; 2005) notes that "The accreditation process involves judging the degree to which a program has achieved the goals and objectives of its stated training model. That is, an accreditation body should not explicitly prescribe a program's educational goals or the processes by which they should be reached . . . " (Section II.a).

Sources for This Document

This document is based on the work of the ADPTC Competencies Workgroup, with input from the CCTC Competencies Workgroup and the CCTC itself. It draws on many sources. Key are reports from two conferences held by psychology educators: The 2001 APA Education Leadership Conference (ELC), with its Workgroup on Practicum Competencies, whose report may be found at http://www.apa.org/ed/elc/home.html; and the Association of Professional Psychology Internship Centers Competencies Conference: Future Directions in Education and Credentialing in Professional Psychology, held in November 2002 in Scottsdale, Arizona, whose report may be found at http://www.appic.org/news/3_1_news_Competencies.htm. An explicit decision was made not to seek consensus of the total Competencies Conference group on the specification of competencies for psychologists. Although the present document assembles specifications for competencies into one document, we are not claiming consensus on which of these competencies are "core," or essential competencies for the field (see point #3 under "Scope and Applicability of This Document" above).

DESCRIBING LEVELS OF COMPETENCE

A guiding principle for this competencies document was that practicum training should prepare the psychology student to make effective use of the internship. We worked to specify the level of competence in the various skill domains that would characterize a well-prepared beginning psychology intern. This approach is based on a doctoral level training model (vs. terminal masters) and assumes that clinical work will begin only after the student has had a period of classroom- based preparation. We recognize that not all programs endorse or adhere to this model. A second guiding principle for the document was that psychology students should be adequately prepared to *begin* practicum. We describe the various qualities and skills that we believe should be present in students who begin practicum training.

We have found that it is important to recognize that competencies are acquired at different rates. Some competencies, such as administrative or supervisory skills, may come slowly and later in professional development. Other more basic competencies, such as timeliness, ability to utilize supervision, etc., may be expected and/or required to be substantially attained very early in training. These differences in the rate of development are reflected in the level of competence expected at the conclusion of practicum training.

One of the most widely used schemes for describing the development of competence is that of Dreyfus and Dreyfus (1986), who define five stages, from Novice to Advanced Beginner to Competent to Proficient to Expert. The Dreyfuses' overall idea (in common with many other skill development and competency models) is that as the learner becomes more and more familiar with the analytic and action tasks of the field, performance becomes more integrated, flexible, efficient, and skilled. Patterns and actions that have to be carefully thought about and/or taught by supervisors become internalized and increasingly automatic.

When discussing competence, keeping the terms straight is a challenge, since similar-sounding terms refer to different concepts. In particular, note that "competency" refers to a skill domain (e.g., assessment), "competence" or "level of competence" refers to the level of skill an individual has acquired (e.g., intermediate level of competence in assessment), and "competent" is a description of a particular level of skill (e.g., this psychologist is competent in neuropsychological assessment). There is also the forensic definition of competent and competence, which one encounters when doing a web search on these terms, but these meanings are irrelevant to the current discussion. The attached document utilizes the following categories in describing the level of competence expected at the conclusion of the practicum. Again please note that in some areas, substantial competence is expected, while in others, just the beginning of understanding is expected—a student, or any psychologist for that matter, may be expert in some areas and a novice in others. The definitions (based on Dreyfus & Dreyfus, 1986) are modified versions of definitions offered by Benner (1984), with further input from Alexander (2004). Some of the category labels and descriptive contents have been changed to fit the particular circumstances of psychology training.

1. *Novice (N)*: Novices have limited knowledge and understanding of (a) how to analyze problems and of (b) intervention skills and the processes and techniques of implementing them. Novices do not yet recognize patterns, and do not differentiate well between important and unimportant details; they do not have filled-in cognitive maps of how, for example, a given client may move from where he/she is to a place of better functioning.

2. *Intermediate (I)*: Psychology students at the intermediate level of competence have gained enough experience through practice, supervision, and instruction to be able to recognize some important recurring domain features and to select appropriate strategies to address the issue at hand. Surface level analyses of the Novice stage are less prominent, but generalization of diagnostic and intervention skills to new situations and clients is limited, and support is needed to guide performance.

3. *Advanced (A)*: At this level, the student has gained deeper, more integrated knowledge of the competency domain in question, including appropriate knowledge of scholarly/research literature as needed. The student is considerably more fluent in his/her ability to recognize important recurring domain features and to select appropriate strategies to address the issue at hand. In relation to clinical work, recognition of overall patterns, of a set of possible diagnoses and/or treatment processes and outcomes for a given case, are taking shape. Overall plans, based on the more integrated knowledge base and identification of domain features are clearer and more influential in guiding action. At this level, the student is less flexible in these areas than the proficient psychologist (the next level of competence) but does have a feeling of mastery and the ability to cope with and manage many contingencies of clinical work.

4. *Proficient:* The proficient psychologist perceives situations as wholes rather than in terms of chopped up parts or aspects. Proficient psychologists understand a situation as a whole because they perceive its meaning in terms of longer-term goals. The proficient psychologist learns from experience what typical events to expect in a given situation and how plans need to be modified

in response to these events. The proficient psychologist can recognize when the expected normal picture does not materialize and takes steps to address these situations (including seeking supervision, reviewing research literature). This holistic understanding improves the proficient psychologist's decision making; it becomes less labored because the psychologist now has a perspective on which of the many existing attributes and aspects in the present situation are the important ones—the psychologist has developed a nuanced understanding of the clinical situation.

5. *Expert:* The expert no longer relies on an analytic principle (rule, guideline, or maxim) to connect her or his understanding of the situation to an appropriate action. The expert psychologist, with an enormous background of experience, now has an intuitive grasp of each situation and zeroes in on the accurate region of the problem without wasteful consideration of a large range of unfruitful, alternative diagnoses and solutions. The expert operates from a deep understanding of the total situation. This is not to say that the expert never uses analytic tools. Highly skilled analytic ability is necessary for those situations with which the psychologist has had no previous experience. Analytic tools are also necessary for those times when the expert gets a wrong grasp of the situation and then finds that events and behaviors are not occurring as expected. When alternative perspectives are not available to the clinician, the only way out of a wrong grasp of the problem is by using analytic problem solving.

Trajectory of Acquiring Competence

As noted above, it is important to recognize that competencies are acquired at different rates. Some competencies, such as administrative or supervisory skills, may come slowly and later in professional development. Other more basic competencies, such as timeliness, ability to utilize supervision, etc., may be expected and/or required to be achieved at a fully professional level very early in training. These differences in trajectory are reflected in the level of competence expected at the conclusion of practicum training. For example, in Section B.1.a.i below, "Ability to take a respectful, helpful professional approach to patients/clients/families" is expected to be at the Advanced, or "A" level by the end of the practicum, since these skills are basic or foundational clinical skills; in Section B.2.a below, "Development of skills and habits in seeking and applying theoretical and research knowledge relevant to practice of psychology in the clinical setting, including accessing and applying scientific knowledge bases" is expected to be at the Intermediate or

"I" level at the end of practicum, since these skills will be a focus of considerable work in the internship year.

Individual and Cultural Difference

A core principle behind all competencies listed in this document is awareness of, respect for, and appropriate action related to individual and cultural difference (ICD). Issues of ICD are relevant to each of the competencies described, but take a particularly large role in some. In these instances, we have made an effort to mention ICD specifically.

Required/Expected Number of Practicum Hours

The CCTC and the ADPTC Competencies Workgroups do not take a stand on how many hours of practicum are needed to acquire the levels of competence described in this document. We believe that the expected domains and levels of competence should be defined first, and the question of how much training is needed to achieve these levels should be determined empirically.

Given that programs vary widely in how much practicum experience is required, the ADPTC Workgroup experimented with estimating the level a student should achieve in all the areas at each step of practicum training, based on 500 hour units, corresponding to 1 year of ¼ time practicum. We looked at three years, totaling 1500 hours of practicum training (the amount recommended by the ELC Practicum Workgroup report). However, a recent survey regarding practicum training conducted with the help of ADPTC members indicates that, because there is large variability in the duration and intensity of practicum training, dividing practicum training into three sets 500 hour units was not reasonable. Therefore the accompanying document simply indicates an estimate of the competence level we believe should be reached by the end of practicum training, without specifying how many hours would be needed to achieve these levels.

PRACTICUM COMPETENCIES OUTLINE

A. Baseline Competencies: Skills, Attitudes, and Knowledge that students should possess prior to their practicum training experience:

Before beginning practicum the student should possess and demonstrate a set of basic personal and intellectual skills, attitudes and values, and a core of professional knowledge. This core knowledge and these skills, attitudes, and values are baseline competencies of the professional psychologist. We argue that it is inappropriate to undertake formal clinical professional training with students who have not acquired these skills. The work of subsequent clinical training is to shape and refine these baseline skills into professional skills.

1. Personality Characteristics, Intellectual and Personal Skills

a) Interpersonal skills: ability to listen and be empathic with others; respect for/interest in others' cultures, experiences, values, points of view, goals and desires, fears, etc. These skills include verbal as well as non-verbal domains. An interpersonal skill of special relevance is the ability to be open to feedback.

b) Cognitive skills: problem-solving ability, critical thinking, organized reasoning, intellectual curiosity, and flexibility.

c) Affective skills: affect tolerance; tolerance/understanding of interpersonal conflict; tolerance of ambiguity and uncertainty.

d) Personality/Attitudes: desire to help others; openness to new ideas; honesty/integrity/valuing of ethical behavior; personal courage.

e) Expressive skills: ability to communicate one's ideas, feelings and information in verbal, non-verbal, and written forms.

f) Reflective skills: ability to examine and consider one's own motives, attitudes, and behaviors and one's effect on others.

g) Personal skills: personal organization, personal hygiene, appropriate dress.

2. Knowledge From Classroom Experience:

The practicum experience will engage and develop skills and knowledge that have been the focus of pre-practicum coursework:

General: Prior to practicum training, students should have acquired basic theoretical and research knowledge related to diagnosis, assessment, and intervention; diversity; ethics; skills in seeking out and applying research knowledge in the clinical setting. Practicum students should possess sufficient mastery of basic information and skills to prepare them to make good use of the practicum experience. Some coursework may occur concurrently with practicum, but care must be taken to be sure that the practicum does not demand knowledge that the student does not yet possess. This may be a matter for negotiation between practicum sites and the graduate program. Early coursework should provide sufficient training in the following specific areas:

a) Assessment & Clinical Interviewing
   i) Knowledge regarding psychopathology related to the population(s) served by the practicum sites.
   ii) Knowledge of scientific, theoretical, empirical, and contextual bases of psychological assessment.
   iii) Knowledge of test construction, validity, score reliability, and related assessment psychometrics.
   iv) Training in principles and practice of systematic administration, data-gathering, and interpretation for assessment, including identifying problems, formulating diagnoses, goals and case conceptualizations; understanding the relationship between assessment and intervention, assessment of treatment progress, and outcome.
   v) Training in the models and techniques of clinical interviewing.

b) Intervention*
   i) Knowledge of scientific, theoretical, empirical, and contextual bases of intervention.
   ii) Training in basic clinical skills, such as empathic listening, framing problems, etc.
   iii) Training in assessment of treatment progress and outcome.
   * Specific features of "Intervention" are more fully described in Section B.4 below.

c) Ethical & Legal
   i) Principles of ethical practice and decision making (APA, 2010a)
   ii) Legal knowledge related to the practice of psychology (federal [e.g., Health Insurance Portability and Accountability Act [HIPAA], state law)

(continues)

d) Individual and Cultural Difference (ICD)
   i) Knowledge and understanding of the principles and findings related to ICD as they apply to professional psychology.
   ii) Understanding of one's own situation (e.g., one's ethnic/racial, socioeconomic, gender, sexual orientation; one's attitudes towards diverse others) relative to the dimensions of ICD (e.g., class, race, physical disability, etc.).
   iii) Understanding of the need to consider ICD issues in all aspects of professional psychology work (e.g., assessment, treatment, research, relationships with colleagues, etc.).

B. Description of Skills Leading to Competencies That Are Developed During the Practicum Experience

Competence Level expected by the completion of practicum is indicated in the column on the right. N = Novice; I = Intermediate; A = Advanced. See introduction for definition of these levels.

These competencies are built upon fundamental personality characteristics, intellectual and personal skills (see Section A1).

Completed Practicum

1. Relationship/Interpersonal Skills

The ability to form and maintain productive relationships with others is a cornerstone of professional psychology. Productive relationships are respectful, supportive, professional, and ethical. Professional psychologists should possess these basic competencies when they first begin their clinical training. Although the ability to form such relationships is grounded in basic skills that most students will have developed over the course of their lives to date, helping the student hone and refine these abilities into professional competencies in the clinical setting is a key aim of the practicum.

In particular, the practicum seeks to enhance students' skills in forming relationships:

a) With patients/clients/families:
   i) Ability to take a respectful, helpful professional approach to patients/clients/families.   A
   ii) Ability to form a working alliance.   I
   iii) Ability to deal with conflict, negotiate differences.   I
   iv) Ability to understand and maintain appropriate professional boundaries.   I
b) With colleagues:
   i) Ability to work collegially with fellow professionals.   A
   ii) Ability to support others and their work and to gain support for one's own work.   I
   iii) Ability to provide helpful feedback to peers and receive such feedback nondefensively from peers.   I
c) With supervisors, the ability to make effective use of supervision, including:
   i) Ability to work collaboratively with the supervisor.   A
   Collaboration means understanding, sharing, and working by a set of common goals for supervision. Many of these goals will change as the student gains professional competence, although a core goal, of working cooperatively to enhance the student's skills as a clinician, will remain constant. It is this aspect of collaboration that is expected to be at the "A" level by

the end of practicum training. Competencies ii & iii below may be considered aspects of collaboration with the supervisor.

ii) Ability to prepare for supervision.	A
iii) Ability/willingness to accept supervisory input, including direction; ability to follow through on recommendations; ability to negotiate needs for autonomy from and dependency on supervisors.	A
iv) Ability to self-reflect and self-evaluate regarding clinical skills and use of supervision, including using good judgment as to when supervisory input is necessary.	I

d) With support staff:
i) Ability to be respectful of support staff roles and persons.	A

e) With teams at clinic:
i) Ability to participate fully in team's work.	A
ii) Ability to understand and observe team's operating procedures.	I

f) With community professionals:
i) Ability to communicate professionally and work collaboratively with community professionals.	I

g) For the practicum site itself:
i) Ability to understand and observe agency's operating procedures.	A
ii) Ability to participate in furthering the work and mission of the practicum site.	A
iii) Ability to contribute in ways that will enrich the site as a practicum experience for future students.	A

2. Skills in Application of Research

Clinical practice in all health-care fields (e.g., medicine, nursing, dentistry) is based on accumulating research results, knowledge derived from practice, and the good judgment of the clinician (for psychology, see the APA Presidential Task Force on Evidence-Based Practice, 2006). A core research knowledge base and training in accessing and applying research knowledge to clinical practice form a core competency for psychologists.

a) Development of skills and habits in seeking and applying theoretical and research knowledge relevant to practice of psychology in the clinical setting, including accessing and applying scientific knowledge bases.	I
b) Understanding and application of theoretical and research knowledge related to diagnosis/assessment and intervention, diversity, supervision, ethics, etc.	I

3. Psychological Assessment Skills

Psychological assessment is a fundamental competency for psychologists, and it includes comprehensive and integrated assessment from the initial interview, psychological testing, intervention, and the evaluation of the outcome of psychological service. A foundation of knowledge and skill is needed for psychological assessment.

a) Ability to select and implement multiple methods and means of evaluation in ways that are responsive to and respectful of diverse individuals, couples, families, and groups.	I

(continues)

	Completed Practicum

b) Ability to utilize systematic approaches to gathering data to inform clinical decision making. — I

c) Knowledge of psychometric issues and bases of assessment methods. — A

d) Knowledge of issues related to integration of different data sources. — A

e) Ability to integrate assessment data from different sources for diagnostic purposes. — I

f) Ability to formulate and apply diagnoses; to understand the strengths and limitations of current diagnostic approaches. — I

g) Capacity for effective use of supervision to implement and enhance skills. — A

4. Intervention Skills

Intervention includes preventive, developmental, and remedial interventions. Intervention and Psychological Assessment are the two fundamental operational competencies for psychologists, and they are typically the major focus of practicum training. The mention below of competencies in empirically supported practice is not intended to restrict the range of training to a particular domain of interventions; competencies in treatment approaches based on other traditions, including "empirically supported relationships", are highly valued by many, and are intended to be included in sections "a–c" and "g–i" below.

a) Ability to formulate and conceptualize cases. — I

b) Ability to plan treatments. — I

c) Ability to implement intervention skills, covering a wide range of developmental, preventive, and "remedial" interventions, including psychotherapy, psychoeducational interventions, crisis management, and psychological/psychiatric emergency situations, depending on the focus and scope of the practicum site. — I

d) Knowledge regarding psychotherapy theory, research, and practice. — I

e) Knowledge regarding the concept of empirically supported practice methods and relationships. — A

f) Knowledge regarding specific empirically supported treatment methods and activities. — I

g) Ability to apply specific empirically supported treatment methods (e.g. cognitive behavior therapy, empirically supported relationships). — I

h) Assessment of treatment progress and outcome. — I

i) Linking concepts of therapeutic process and change to intervention strategies and tactics. — I

j) Effective use of supervision to implement and enhance skills. — A

5. Consultation Skills/Interprofessional Collaborations:

The workgroup at the 2002 Competencies Conference viewed consultation as a key competency for psychologists in the 21st century, citing the importance of psychologists being able to "serve as competent and engaged consultants who bring value to a broad range of settings, contexts, and systems that can benefit from skillful application [of] psychological knowledge" (Arredondo, Shealy, Neale, & Winfrey,

2004). Exposure to consultation practice has increased in many practicum sites. Competencies in this domain include:

a) Knowledge of the unique patient care roles of other professionals.
b) Ability to effectively relate to other professionals in accordance with their unique patient care roles.
c) Understanding of the consultant's role as an information provider to another professional who will ultimately be the patient care decision maker.
d) Capacity for dialoguing with other professionals which avoids use of psychological jargon.
e) Ability to choose an appropriate means of assessment to answer referral questions.
f) Ability to implement a systematic approach to data collection in a consultative role.
g) Consultative reports are well organized and succinct and provide useful and relevant recommendations to other professionals.

6. Diversity—Individual and Cultural Differences:

The APA Multicultural Guidelines (APA, 2003) noted that "All individuals exist in social, political, historical, and economic contexts, and psychologists are increasingly called upon to understand the influence of these contexts on individuals' behavior" (p. 377). Thus every competency listed in this document is thoroughly linked to matters of individual and cultural difference (ICD), including knowledge related to ICD, as well as awareness of, respect for, and appropriate action related to ICD. It is critical that practicum students begin to learn that culture influences the way that clients are perceived, the way that clients perceive the counselor, and that culture-centered practices may be more effective than practices developed for use with only one cultural group (e.g., European Americans). Practicum students need to know how individual and cultural differences influence clients' recognition of a problem and appropriate solutions for that problem.

Specific competency areas related to ICD are important to identify and train for include:

a) Knowledge of self in the context of diversity (one's own beliefs, values, attitudes, stimulus value, and related strengths/limitations) as one operates in the clinical setting with diverse others (i.e., knowledge of self in the diverse world).
b) Knowledge about the nature and impact of diversity in different clinical situations (e.g., clinical work with specific racial/ethnic populations).
c) Ability to work effectively with diverse others in assessment, treatment, and consultation.

7. Ethics:

During the practicum, the student will build on coursework in ethical practice, developing individual, practical knowledge of ethical practice, including linkage of the APA ethics code (APA, 2010a) to behavior and decision making in actual clinical settings. In addition, students should increase and apply their understanding of legal standards

(continues)

(state and federal, e.g., HIPAA) and APA practice guidelines. Note that each of the domains described in this document is expected as a matter of course to be grounded in ethical practice.

More specifically, during practicum training the student will work to develop the following ethical competencies:

a)	Knowledge of ethical/professional codes, standards, and guidelines; knowledge of statutes, rules, regulations, and case law relevant to the practice of psychology.	I
b)	Recognize and analyze ethical and legal issues across the range of professional activities in the practicum setting.	I
c)	Recognize and understand the ethical dimensions/features of his/her own attitudes and practice in the clinical setting.	I
d)	Seek appropriate information and consultation when faced with ethical issues.	A
e)	Practice appropriate professional assertiveness related to ethical issues (e.g., by raising issues when they become apparent to the student).	I
f)	Evidence commitment to ethical practice.	A

8. Development of Leadership Skills:

The 2001 ELC Practicum Competencies Workgroup identified beginning training in management and leadership skills as important. Presumably management and leadership skills are in evidence in any organized training setting; some deliberate effort to engage students in considering and practicing these skills in the practicum setting could foster their development. In particular, practicum students may gain beginning understanding and practice in leadership through leading research teams, mentoring newer students in vertical team settings, acting as Assistant Directors in clinics, participating in clinic discussions of organizational goals and policies regarding clinical, training, and management activities. Note that beginning familiarity with these issues is expected at the end of the practicum, as indicated by the "N" or Novice level of competence in the right-hand column:

a)	Recognition of one's role in creating policy, participation in system change, and management.	N
b)	Understand the relationship between roles of supervisor, manager, and executive.	N
c)	Understand the role of leadership in management success.	N
d)	Ability to identify leadership, business, and management skills.	N
e)	Understand the purpose and process of strategic planning.	N
f)	Understand the basics of financial management as it pertains to clinical service delivery.	N
g)	Understand the purpose and structure of meetings and how to run them well.	N
h)	Ability to self-evaluate one's skills as manager and leader.	N

9. Supervisory Skills:

Supervision is widely considered to be a core competency in professional psychology (e.g., Falender et al., 2004) during the practicum, even though the core requirements for competent supervisory practice await the mastery of the other competencies listed in this document.

Practicum programs are encouraged to consider how best to introduce students to this critical role. The basic groundwork that is specific to developing supervisory competency may be addressed to
some extent in the practicum experience, including some exposure to
the following areas. Note that beginning familiarity only with these
issues is expected at the end of the practicum, as indicated by the
"N" or Novice level of competence in the right-hand column:

a) Knowledge of literature on supervision (e.g., models, theories & research).   N

b) Knowledge concerning how clinicians develop to be skilled professionals.   N

c) Knowledge of methods and issues related to evaluating professional work, including delivering formative and summative feedback.   N

d) Knowledge of limits of one's supervisory skills.   N

e) Knowledge of how supervision responds appropriately to individual and cultural differences.   N

10. Professional Development:

Practicum training is a key experience in professional development
for the novice psychologist. Certain central features that characterize professional development in later professional life are a particular focus during the practicum, and serve as a foundation for
continuing professional development. These can be gathered
under the heading of:

a) Practical Skills to Maintain Effective Clinical Practice

The student will develop practical professional skills such as

     i) Timeliness: completing professional tasks in allotted/ appropriate time (e.g., evaluations, notes, reports); arriving promptly at meetings and appointments.   A

     ii) Developing an organized, disciplined approach to writing and maintaining notes and records.   A

     iii) Negotiating/managing fees and payments.   I

     iv) Organizing and presenting case material; preparing professional reports for health care providers, agencies, etc.   I

     v) How to self-identify personal distress, particularly as it relates to clinical work.   I

     vi) How to seek and use resources that support healthy functioning when experiencing personal distress.   I

     vii) Organizing one's day, including time for notes and records, rest and recovery, etc.   I

These features may be considered to be a focal subset of a broader
group of skills related to the clinician's professional development that
will continue throughout the career. This broader group includes:

b) Professional Development Competencies

     i) Critical thinking and analysis.   I

     ii) Using resources to promote effective practice (e.g., published information, input from colleagues, technological resources).   A

(continues)

	Completed Practicum
iii) Responsibility and accountability relative to one's level of training, and seeking consultation when needed.	A
iv) Time management.	I
v) Self-awareness, understanding, and reflection.	I
vi) Self-care.	I
vii) Awareness of personal identity (e.g., relative to individual and cultural differences).	I
viii) Awareness of one's own beliefs and values as they relate to and impact professional practice and activity.	A
ix) Social intelligence; ability to interact collaboratively and respectfully with other colleagues.	A
x) Willingness to acknowledge and correct errors.	A
xi) Ability to create and conduct an effective presentation.	I

11. Metaknowledge/Metacompetencies—Skilled Learning

The training program should help students begin on the path of reflective understanding and knowledge about their own knowledge and competencies.

A broadly drawn definition characterizes metaknowledge as *knowledge about knowledge—knowing what you know and what you don't know.* Metaknowledge includes being aware of the range and limits of what you know; knowing your own intellectual strengths and weaknesses, how to use available skills and knowledge to solve a variety of tasks, how to acquire new or missing skills, or being able to judge that a task can't be done with current knowledge. Metacompetencies similarly refer to the ability to judge the availability, use, and learnability of personal competencies. The development of metaknowledge and metacompetencies depends on self-awareness, self-reflection, and self-assessment (Weinert, 2001).

For psychologists, this would include:

	Completed Practicum
a) Knowing the extent and the limits of one's own skills; learning the habit of and skills for self-evaluation of clinical skills.	I
b) The ability to use supervision, consultation, and other resources to improve and extend skills (note the related relationship competence—to work collegially and responsively with supervisors).	A
c) Knowledge of the process for extending current skills into new areas.	I
d) Knowledge of the epistemologies underlying various aspects of clinical practice (e.g., assessment, diagnosis, treatment).	I
e) Commitment to life-long learning and quality improvement.	A
f) Awareness of one's identity as a psychologist (Belar, Nelson, & Wasik, 2003): an aspect and reflection of metaknowledge that is role specific, knowing what one knows and can do (and should do) as a psychologist.	I

APPENDIX C: PRACTICES AND BELIEFS QUESTIONNAIRE

Directions: Below you will find a list of 52 possible psychotherapist behaviors. Across your career, please consider each behavior *in the context of doing psychotherapy with clients who are racially or ethnically different from you.*

In the first column, rate how often you engage in each behavior when clinically appropriate. If you do not have the opportunity to engage in each behavior, rate it NA for "not applicable." If a particular multicultural situation rarely occurs but, on those occasions, you often or very often respond with the behavior listed, then you should check "4" or "5" even though you seldom engage in this behavior because the opportunity to do so is limited.

In the second column, rate the importance of each behavior to competent professional practice. Please rate all behaviors in both columns.

Behavior	How Often Do You Do This?						Importance to Competent Practice				
	Never	Rarely	Sometimes	Often	Very Often	Not Applicable	Never Important	Rarely Important	Sometimes Important	Often Important	Always Important
1. Consider the impact of race/ethnicity on psychological disorders	1	2	3	4	5	NA	1	2	3	4	5
2. Evaluate the Effects of therapist–client language differences	1	2	3	4	5	NA	1	2	3	4	5
3. Actively seek feedback on one's multicultural competence	1	2	3	4	5	NA	1	2	3	4	5
4. Refer a client to a more culturally qualified provider	1	2	3	4	5	NA	1	2	3	4	5

(continues)

Adapted from "Do We Practice What We Preach? An Exploratory Survey of Multicultural Psychotherapy Competencies," by N. D. Hansen, K. V. Randazzo, A. Schwartz, M. Marshall, D. Kalis, R. Frazier, . . . G. Norvig, 2006, *Professional Psychology: Research and Practice, 37,* pp. 70–71. Copyright 2006 by the American Psychological Association.

| Behavior | How Often Do You Do This? | | | | | | Importance to Competent Practice | | | | |
	Never	Rarely	Sometimes	Often	Very Often	Not Applicable	Never Important	Rarely Important	Sometimes Important	Often Important	Always Important
5. Modify interventions to take into account the sociopolitical events affecting clients	1	2	3	4	5	NA	1	2	3	4	5
6. Integrate relevant multi-cultural literature into treatment planning	1	2	3	4	5	NA	1	2	3	4	5
7. Evaluate when one's assumptions, values, and biases are negatively impacting treatment	1	2	3	4	5	NA	1	2	3	4	5
8. Make *DSM–IV–TR* (American Psychiatric Association, 2000) culture-specific diagnoses	1	2	3	4	5	NA	1	2	3	4	5
9. Assess clients' level of acculturation	1	2	3	4	5	NA	1	2	3	4	5
10. Ask sensitive racial/ethnic questions	1	2	3	4	5	NA	1	2	3	4	5
11. Help clients develop skills to interface with different cultures	1	2	3	4	5	NA	1	2	3	4	5
12. Recognize stereotyping, prejudice, and discrimination on institutional and societal levels	1	2	3	4	5	NA	1	2	3	4	5
13. Recognize one's own racial/ethnic identity	1	2	3	4	5	NA	1	2	3	4	5
14. Identify family dynamics common to different racial/ethnic groups	1	2	3	4	5	NA	1	2	3	4	5
15. Strive to repair racially/ethnically-based mistakes in treatment	1	2	3	4	5	NA	1	2	3	4	5
16. Integrate indigenous resources into treatment	1	2	3	4	5	NA	1	2	3	4	5
17. Differentiate within- from between-group behavioral influences when conceptualizing clients	1	2	3	4	5	NA	1	2	3	4	5
18. Advocate for clients against systemic barriers	1	2	3	4	5	NA	1	2	3	4	5

Behavior	How Often Do You Do This?						Importance to Competent Practice				
	Never	Rarely	Sometimes	Often	Very Often	Not Applicable	Never Important	Rarely Important	Sometimes Important	Often Important	Always Important
19. Modify interventions to take into account clients' non-verbal communication style	1	2	3	4	5	NA	1	2	3	4	5
20. Consider the impact of race/ethnicity on personality development	1	2	3	4	5	NA	1	2	3	4	5
21. Show respect for client's worldview	1	2	3	4	5	NA	1	2	3	4	5
22. Help clients discern how cultural prejudices affect clinical problems	1	2	3	4	5	NA	1	2	3	4	5
23. Seek culture-specific case consultation	1	2	3	4	5	NA	1	2	3	4	5
24. Modify intervention to take into account the history, manifestations, and psychological effects of oppression, prejudice, and discrimination	1	2	3	4	5	NA	1	2	3	4	5
25. Negotiate appropriate language(s) for treatment	1	2	3	4	5	NA	1	2	3	4	5
26. Assess client's level of acculturative stress	1	2	3	4	5	NA	1	2	3	4	5
27. Initiate and explore issues of racial/ethnic differences between the therapist and client	1	2	3	4	5	NA	1	2	3	4	5
28. Evaluate when one's lack of requisite skills negatively impacts treatment	1	2	3	4	5	NA	1	2	3	4	5
29. Modify interventions to take into account client's help-seeking style	1	2	3	4	5	NA	1	2	3	4	5
30. Develop culturally relevant case conceptualizations	1	2	3	4	5	NA	1	2	3	4	5
31. Use translators when linguistically-appropriate clinician not available	1	2	3	4	5	NA	1	2	3	4	5

(continues)

Behavior	How Often Do You Do This?						Importance to Competent Practice				
	Never	Rarely	Sometimes	Often	Very Often	Not Applicable	Never Important	Rarely Important	Sometimes Important	Often Important	Always Important
32. Prepare a cultural formulation (per *DSM–IV–TR*, Appendix I [American Psychiatric Association, 2000])	1	2	3	4	5	NA	1	2	3	4	5
33. Take responsibility for transcending one's own negative racial/ethnic cultural conditioning	1	2	3	4	5	NA	1	2	3	4	5
34. Use racially/ethnically sensitive data gathering techniques	1	2	3	4	5	NA	1	2	3	4	5
35. Demonstrate appreciation for within-group differences	1	2	3	4	5	NA	1	2	3	4	5
36. Regularly evaluate one's own multicultural competence	1	2	3	4	5	NA	1	2	3	4	5
37. Establish rapport and convey empathy in racially/ethnically sensitive ways	1	2	3	4	5	NA	1	2	3	4	5
38. Help clients develop awareness of their own racial/ethnic assumptions and biases	1	2	3	4	5	NA	1	2	3	4	5
39. Consider the impact of race/ethnicity on coping behaviors	1	2	3	4	5	NA	1	2	3	4	5
40. Integrate racially/ethnically-based community resources into treatment	1	2	3	4	5	NA	1	2	3	4	5
41. Evaluate client's language proficiency	1	2	3	4	5	NA	1	2	3	4	5
42. Help clients further develop their own socio-cultural identification	1	2	3	4	5	NA	1	2	3	4	5
43. Actively seek client feedback about services provided	1	2	3	4	5	NA	1	2	3	4	5

Behavior	How Often Do You Do This?						Importance to Competent Practice				
	Never	Rarely	Sometimes	Often	Very Often	Not Applicable	Never Important	Rarely Important	Sometimes Important	Often Important	Always Important
44. Avoid idealizing racial/ethnic groups	1	2	3	4	5	NA	1	2	3	4	5
45. Modify interventions to take into account client's beliefs about illness	1	2	3	4	5	NA	1	2	3	4	5
46. Identify gender roles common to different racial/ethnic groups	1	2	3	4	5	NA	1	2	3	4	5
47. Integrate racially/ ethnically derived religious/spiritual beliefs and practices into treatment	1	2	3	4	5	NA	1	2	3	4	5
48. Help clients identify and develop effective responses to institutional barriers	1	2	3	4	5	NA	1	2	3	4	5
49. Evaluate clients' generational and immigration history	1	2	3	4	5	NA	1	2	3	4	5
50. Implement a personal professional development plan to improve one's multicultural competence	1	2	3	4	5	NA	1	2	3	4	5
51. Present cogent and logical rebuttals to objections raised to multiculturalism	1	2	3	4	5	NA	1	2	3	4	5
52. Outside of treatment, build relationships with persons racially/ ethnically different from yourself	1	2	3	4	5	NA	1	2	3	4	5

REFERENCES

Adams, S. A. & Riggs, S. A. (2008). An exploratory study of vicarious trauma among therapist trainees. *Training and Education in Professional Psychology, 2*, 26–34. doi:10.1037/1931-3918.2.1.26

Alexander, P. A. (2004). A model of domain learning: Reinterpreting expertise as a multidimensional, multistage process. In D. Y. Dai & R. J. Sternberg (Eds.), *Motivation, emotion and cognition: Integrative perspectives on intellectual functioning and development* (pp. 273–298). Mahwah, NJ: Erlbaum.

American Psychiatric Association. (2000). *Diagnostic and statistical manual of mental health* (4th ed., Text Revision). Washington, DC: Author.

American Psychological Association. (2003a). *Guidelines for psychological practice with older adults*. Retrieved from http://www.apa.org/practice/guidelines/older-adults.pdf

American Psychological Association. (2003b). Guidelines on multicultural education, training, research, practice, and organizational change for psychologists. *American Psychologist, 58*, 377–402. doi:10.1037/0003-066X.58.5.377

American Psychological Association. (2005). *Guidelines and principles for accreditation of programs in professional psychology*. Washington, DC: American Psychological Association. Retrieved from http://www.apa.org/ed/accreditation/about/policies/guiding-principles.pdf

American Psychological Association. (2007). *Guidelines for psychological practice with girls and women*. Retrieved from http://www.apa.org/about/division/girlsand women.pdf

American Psychological Association. (2008). *Report of the APA Task Force on the Implementation of the Multicultural Guidelines*. Retrieved from http://www.apa.org/about/governance/council/policy/multicultural-report.pdf

American Psychological Association. (2009). *Guidelines and principles for accreditation of programs in professional psychology*. Retrieved from http://www.apa.org/ed/accreditation/about/policies/guiding-principles.pdf

American Psychological Association. (2010a). *Ethical principles of psychologists and code of conduct* (2002, Amended June 1, 2010). Retrieved from http://www.apa.org/ethics/code/index.aspx

American Psychological Association. (2010b). *Model Act for State Licensure of Psychologists*. Retrieved from http://www.apa.org/about/governance/council/policy/model-act-2010.pdf

American Psychological Association. (2011). *Practice guidelines for LGB clients*. Retrieved from http://www.apa.org/pi/lgbt/resources/guidelines.aspx

American Psychological Association, Division 44/Committee on Lesbian, Gay, & Bisexual Concerns Task Force. (2000). Guidelines for psychotherapy with lesbian, gay, and bisexual clients. *American Psychologist, 55*, 1440–1451. doi:10.1037/0003-066X.55.12.1440

American Psychological Association Ethics Committee. (2008). Report of the Ethics Committee, 2007. *American Psychologist, 63*, 452–459. doi:10.1037/0003-066X. 63.5.452

American Psychological Association, Presidential Task Force on Evidence-Based Practice. (2006). Evidence-based practice in psychology. *American Psychologist, 61*, 271–285. doi:10.1037/0003-066X.61.4.271

Amering, M., Schmolke, M., & Stastey, P. (2009). *Recovery in mental health: Reshaping scientific and clinical responsibilities*. New York, NY: Wiley-Blackwell.

Ancis, J. R., & Ladany, N. (2001). A multicultural framework for counselor supervision. In L. J. Bradley & N. Ladany (Eds.), *Counselor supervision: Principles, process, and practice* (3rd ed., pp. 63–90). New York, NY: Brunner-Routledge.

Anderson, S. K., & Handelsman, M. M. (2010). *Ethics for psychotherapists and counselors: A proactive approach*. West Sussex, England: Wiley-Blackwell.

Arnold, L. (2002). Assessing professional behavior: Yesterday, today, and tomorrow. *Academic Medicine, 77*, 502–515. Retrieved from http://journals.lww.com/academicmedicine/pages/default.aspx doi:10.1097/00001888-200206000-00006

Arredondo, P., Shealy, C., Neale, M. C., & Winfrey, L. L. (2004). Consultation and interprofessional collaboration: Modeling for the future. *Journal of Clinical Psychology, 80*, 787–800. doi:10.1002/jclp.20015

Aspland, H., Llewelyn, S., Hardy, G. E., Barkham, M., & Stiles, W. (2008). Alliance ruptures and rupture resolution in cognitive behavior therapy: A preliminary task analysis. *Psychotherapy Research, 18*, 699–710. doi:10.1080/10503300802291463

Association of Directors of Psychology Training Clinics Practicum Competencies Workgroup. (2006). *The practicum competencies outline: Report on practicum competencies*. Retrieved from http://www.aptc.org/public_files/Practicum%20Competencies%20FINAL%20(Oct%20'06%20Version).pdf

Association of Psychology Postdoctoral and Internship Centers. (2002). *Future directions in education and credentialing in professional psychology*. Retrieved from http://www.appic.org/news/3_1_news_Competencies.htm

Association of State and Provincial Psychology Boards Task Force on Practicum Guidelines for Licensure. (2009). *Guidelines on practicum experience for licensure*. Retrieved from http://www.asppb.net/files/public/Final_Prac_Guidelines_1_31_09.pdf

Aten, J. D., Strain, J. D., & Gillespie, R. E. (2008). A transtheoretical model of clinical supervision. *Training and Education in Professional Psychology, 2*, 1–9. doi:10.1037/1931-3918.2.1.1

Baker, T. B., McFall, R. M., & Shoham, V. (2008). Current status and future prospects of clinical psychology: Toward a scientifically principled approach to mental and behavioral health care. *Psychological Science in the Public Interest, 9*, 68–103. Retrieved from http://www.psychologicalscience.org/journals/pspi/pspi_9-2.pdf

Baker, T., McFall, R., & Shoham, V. (2009, November 15). Is your therapist a little behind the times? *The Washington Post*. Retrieved from http://www.washingtonpost.com/wp-dyn/content/article/2009/11/13/AR2009111302221.html

Balas, E. A., & Boren, S. A. (2000). Managing clinical knowledge for health care improvement. In J. van Bemmel & A. T. McCray (Eds.), *Yearbook of medical informatics* (pp. 65–70). Stuttgart, Germany: Schattauer Publishing.

Bandura, A., Lipsher, D. H., & Miller, P. E. (1960). Psychotherapists approach–avoidance reactions to paitents' expressions of hostility. *Journal of Consulting Psychology, 24,* 1–8. doi:10.1037/h0043403

Barbour, I. G. (1974). *Myths, models, and paradigms.* New York, NY: Harper & Row.

Barnett, J. E., & Cooper, N. (2009). Creating a culture of self-care. *Clinical Psychology: Science and Practice, 16,* 16–20. doi:10.1111/j.1468-2850.2009.01138.x

Barnett, J. E., & Johnson, W. B. (2011). Integrating spirituality and religion into psychotherapy: Persistent dilemmas, ethical issues, and a proposed decision-making process. *Ethics & Behavior, 21,* 147–164. doi:10.1080/10508422.2011.551471

Barrett, M. S, & Barber, J. P. (2005). A developmental approach to the supervision of therapists in training. *Journal of Contemporary Psychotherapy, 35,* 169–183. doi:10.1007/s10879-005-2698-8

Beck, J. S. (2011). *Cognitive behavior therapy: Basics and beyond* (2nd ed.). New York, NY: Guilford.

Beck, J. S., Sarnat, J. E., & Barenstein, V. (2008). Psychotherapy-based approaches to supervision. In C. A. Falender, & E. P. Shafranske (Eds.). *Casebook for clinical supervision: A competency-based approach.* (pp. 57–96). Washington, DC: American Psychological Association.

Belar, C. D., Brown, R. A., Hersch, L. E., Hornyak, L. M., Rozensky, R. H., Sheridan, E. P., . . . Reed, G. W. (2001). Self-assessment in clinical health psychology: A model for ethical expansion of practice. *Professional Psychology: Research and Practice, 32,* 135–141. doi:10.1037/0735-7028.32.2.135

Belar, C. D., Nelson, P. D., & Wasik, B. H. Rethinking education in psychology and psychology in education. *American Psychologist, 58,* 678–684. doi:10.1037/0003-066X.58.8.678

Benjamin, G. A. H., Kent, L., & Sirikantraporn, S. (2009). A review of duty-to-protect statutes, cases, and procedures for positive practice. In J. L. Werth, E. R. Welfel, & G. A. H. Benjamin (Eds.), *The duty to protect: Ethical, legal, and professional considerations for mental health professionals* (pp. 9–28). Washington, DC: American Psychological Association. doi:10.1037/11866-002

Benner, P. (1984). *From novice to expert: Excellence and power in clinical nursing practice.* Menlo Park, CA: Addison-Wesley.

Berk, M. S. & Anderson, S. M. (2000). The impact of past relationships in interpersonal behavior: Confirmation in the social-cognitive process of transference. *Journal of Personality and Social Psychology, 79,* 546–562. doi:10.1037/0022-3514.79.4.546

Bernard, J. L., & Jara, C. S. (2008). The failure of clinical psychology graduate students to apply understood ethical principles. In D. N. Bersoff (Ed.), *Ethical conflicts in psychology* (4th ed., pp. 60–73). Washington, DC: American Psychological Association.

Bernard, J. M. (1997). The discrimination model. In C. E. Watkins (Ed.), *Handbook of psychotherapy supervision* (pp. 310–327). New York, NY: Wiley.

Bernard, J. M., & Goodyear, R. K. (2009). *Fundamentals of clinical supervision* (4th ed.). Upper Saddle River, NJ: Pearson.

Berry, J. W. (2003). Conceptual approaches to acculturation. In K. M. Chun, P. B. Organista, & G. Marin (Eds.), *Acculturation: Advances in theory, measurement, and applied research* (pp. 17–37). Washington, DC: American Psychological Association.

Betan, E., Heim, A., Conkin, C. Z., & Western, D. (2005). Countertransference phenomena and personality pathology in clinical practice: An empirical investigation. *The American Journal of Psychiatry, 162,* 890–898. doi: 10.1176/appi.ajp.162.5.890

Bhat, C. S., & Davis, T. E. (2007). Counseling supervisors' assessment of race, racial identity, and working alliance in supervisory dyads. *Journal of Multicultural Counseling and Development, 35,* 80–91. Retrieved from http://www.counseling.org/Publications/Journals.aspx

Bordin, E. S. (1979). The generalizability of the psychoanalytic concept of the working alliance. *Psychotherapy: Theory, Research & Practice, 16,* 252–260. doi:10.1037/h0085885

Bordin, E. S. (1994). Theory and research in the therapeutic working alliance: New directions. In A. O. Horvath and L. S. Greenberg (eds.), *The working alliance: Theory, research, and practice* (pp. 13–37). New York, NY: Wiley.

Bouchard, M.-A., Normandin, L., & Séguin, M.-H. (1995). Countertransference as instrument and obstacle: A comprehensive and descriptive framework. *The Psychoanalytic Quarterly, 64,* 717–745.

Bowers, A. M. V., & Bieschke, K. J. (2005). Psychologists' clinical evaluations and attitudes: An examination of the influence of gender and sexual orientation. *Professional Psychology: Research and Practice, 36,* 97–103. doi:10.1037/0735-7028.36.1.97

Brabeck, M., & Brown, L. (1997). Feminist theory and psychological practice. In J. Worell & N. G. Johnson (Eds.), *Shaping the future of feminist psychology* (pp. 15–35). Washington, DC: American Psychological Association. doi:10.1037/10245-001

Brady, J. L., Guy, J. D., Poelstra, P. L., & Brokaw, B. F. (1999). Vicarious traumatization, spirituality, and the treatment of sexual abuse survivors: A national survey of women psychotherapists. *Professional Psychology: Research and Practice, 30,* 386–393. doi:10.1037/0735-7028.30.4.386

Burckell, L. A., & Goldfried, M. R. (2006). Therapist qualities preferred by sexual-minority individuals. *Psychotherapy: Theory, Research, Practice, Training, 43,* 32–49. doi:10.1037/0033-3204.43.1.32

Burian, B. K., & Slimp, A. O. (2000). Social dual-role relationships during internship: A decision-making model. *Professional Psychology: Research and Practice, 31,* 332–338. doi:10.1037/0735-7028.31.3.332

Burkard, A. W., Johnson, A. J., Madson, M. B., Pruitt, N. T., Contreras-Tadych, D. A., Kozlowski, J. M., . . . Knox, S. (2006). Supervisor cultural responsiveness and unresponsiveness in cross-cultural supervision. *Journal of Counseling Psychology, 53*, 288–301. doi:10.1037/0022-0167.53.3.288

Campbell, L., Vasquez, M., Behnke, S., & Kinscherff, R. (2010). Competence. In L. Campbell, M. Vasquez, S. Behnke, & R. Kinscherff (Eds.), *APA Ethics Code commentary and case illustrations* (pp. 45–74). Washington, DC: American Psychological Association.

Canadian Psychological Association. (2009). *Ethical guidelines for supervision in psychology: Teaching, research, practice, and administration.* Ottawa, Canada: Author. Retrieved from http://www.cpa.ca/cpasite/userfiles/Documents/COESupGuide RevApproved7Feb09revisedfinal.pdf

Canadian Psychological Association. (2010). *Resource guide for psychologists: Ethical supervision in teaching, research, practice, and administration.* Ottawa, Canada: Author. Retrieved from http://www.cpa.ca/docs/file/Ethics/CPAcoeEthical SuperGuideApprovedNovember2010.pdf

Carter, J. W., Enyedy, K. C., Goodyear, R. K., Arcinue, F., & Puri, N. N. (2009). Concept mapping of the events supervisees find helpful in group supervision. *Training and Education in Professional Psychology, 3*, 1–9. doi:10.1037/a0013656

Castonguay, L. G., Constantino, M. J., McAleavey, A. A., & Goldfried, M. R. (2010). The therapeutic alliance in cognitive-behavioral therapy. In J. C. Muran & J. P. Barber (Eds.), *The therapeutic alliance* (pp. 150–171). New York, NY: Guilford.

Chang, V. N., Scott, S. T., & Decker, C. L. (2006). *A care-based approach to practice.* New York, NY: Thompson.

Chen, S., Fitzsimons, G. M., & Andersen, S. M. (2007). Automaticity in close relationships. In J. A. Bargh (Ed.), *Social psychology and the unconscious* (pp. 133–172). New York, NY: Psychology Press.

Constantine, M. G., Warren, A. K., & Miville, M. L. (2005). White racial identity dyadic interactions in supervision: Implications for supervisees' multicultural counseling competence. *Journal of Counseling Psychology, 52*, 490–496. doi:10.1037/0022-0167.52.4.490

Coster, J. S., & Schwebel, M. (1997). Well-functioning in professional psychologists. *Professional Psychology: Research and Practice, 28*, 5–13. doi:10.1037/0735-7028.28.1.5

Council of Chairs of Training Councils Practicum Workgroup. (2007). *Defining the practicum.* Retrieved from http://www.psychtrainingcouncils.org/pubs/CCTC%20 Practicum%20Definition%203-22-07.pdf

Crits-Cristoph, P., Crits-Cristoph, K., & Gibbons, M. B. C. (2010). Training in alliance-fostering techniques. In J. C. Muran & J. P. Barber (Eds.), *The therapeutic alliance* (pp. 304–319). New York, NY: Guilford Press.

Daniel, C. H. (2008). *The relationship between the supervisory alliance and countertransference disclosure among psychology interns* (Doctoral dissertation). Retrieved from ProQuest Dissertations and Theses database. (AAT 3324654)

Davidson, L., Rakfeldt, J., & Strauss, J. S. (2010). *The roots of the recovery movement in psychiatry: Lessons learned.* Hoboken, NJ: Wiley. doi:10.1002/9780470682999

Davis, D. A., Mazmanian, P. E., Fordis, M., Van Harrison, R., Thorpe, K. E., & Perrier, L. (2006). Accuracy of physician self-assessment compared with observed measures of competence: A systematic review. *JAMA, 296,* 1094–1102. doi:10.1001/jama.296.9.1094

DeMers, S. T., Van Horne, B. A., & Rodolfa, E. R. (2008). Changes in training and practice of psychologists: Current challenges for licensing boards. *Professional Psychology: Research and Practice, 39,* 473–479. doi:10.1037/0735-7028.39.5.473

Disney, M. J., & Stephens, A. M. (1994). *Legal issues in clinical supervision.* Alexandria, VA: American Counseling Association.

Dovidio, J. F. (2001). On the nature of contemporary prejudice: The third wave. *Journal of Social Issues, 57,* 829–849. doi:10.1111/0022-4537.00244

Dressel, J. L., Consoli, A. J., Kim, B. S. K., & Atkinson, D. R. (2007). Successful and unsuccessful multicultural supervisory behaviors: A Delphi poll. *Journal of Multicultural Counseling and Development, 35,* 51–64. Retrieved from http://www.counseling.org/Publications/Journals.aspx

Dreyfus, H. L., & Dreyfus, S. E. (1986). *Mind over machine: The power of human intuition and expertise in the era of the computer.* New York, NY: Free Press.

Drieschner, K. H., Lammers, S. M. M., & van der Staak, C. P. F. (2004). Treatment motivation: An attempt for clarification of an ambiguous concept. *Clinical Psychology Review, 23,* 1115–1137. doi:10.1016/j.cpr.2003.09.003

Duncan, B. L., Miller, S. D., Wampold, B. E., & Hubble, M. A. (Eds.). (2010). *The heart and soul of change: Delivering what works in therapy* (2nd ed.). Washington, DC: American Psychological Association. doi:10.1037/12075-000

Dunning, D., Heath, C., & Suls, J. M. (2004). Flawed self-assessment: Implications for health, education, and the workplace. *Psychological Science in the Public Interest, 5,* 69–106. doi:10.1111/j.1529-1006.2004.00018.x

Eells, T. D. (Ed.). (2007). *Handbook of psychotherapy case conceptualization.* New York, NY: Guilford Press.

Elliott, D. M., & Guy, J. D. (1993). Mental health professionals versus non-mental health professionals: Childhood trauma and adult functioning. *Professional Psychology: Research and Practice, 24,* 83–90. doi:10.1037/0735-7028.24.1.83

Ellis, M. (2009, June). *Bridging the science and practice of clinical supervision: Some discoveries, some misconceptions.* Plenary address delivered at the 5th International Interdisciplinary Conference on Clinical Supervision, Buffalo, NY.

Ellis, M. V., & Ladany, N. (1997). Inferences concerning supervisees and clients in clinical supervision: An integrative review. In C. E. Watkins Jr. (Ed.), *Handbook of psychotherapy supervision* (pp. 447–507). New York, NY: Wiley.

Ellis, M. V., Siembor, M. J., Swords, B. A., Morere, L., & Blanco, S. (2008, June). *Prevalence and characteristics of harmful and inadequate clinical supervision.* Paper presented at the 4th annual International Interdisciplinary Clinical Supervision Conference, Buffalo, NY.

Ellis, M. V., & Swords, B. A. (2009, June). *What can we do about both inadequate and harmful clinical supervision?* Roundtable discussion conducted at the 5th annual International Interdisciplinary Conference on Clinical Supervision, Buffalo, NY.

Elman, N. S., & Forrest, L. (2007). From trainee impairment to professional competence problems: Seeking new terminology that facilitates effective action. *Professional Psychology: Research and Practice, 38*, 501–509. doi:10.1037/0735-7028.38.5.501

Elman, N. S., Forrest, L. M., Gizara, S., & Vacha-Haase, T. (1999). A systems perspective on trainee impairment: Continuing the dialogue. *The Counseling Psychologist, 27*, 712–721. doi:10.1177/0011000099275005

Elman, N. S., Illfelder-Kaye, J., & Robiner, W. N. (2005). Professional development: Training for professionalism as a foundation for competent practice in psychology. *Professional Psychology: Research and Practice, 36*, 367–375. doi:10.1037/0735-7028.36.4.367

Enyedy, K. C., Arcinue, F., Puri, N. N., Carter, J. W., Goodyear, R., K., & Getzelman, M. A. (2003). Hindering phenomena in group supervision: Implications for practice. *Professional Psychology: Research and Practice, 34*, 312–317. doi:10.1037/0735-7028.34.3.312

Epstein, R. M. (1999). Mindful practice. *JAMA, 282*, 833–839. doi:10.1001/jama.282.9.833

Epstein, L., & Feiner, A. H. (1979). Countertransference: the therapist's contribution to treatment. *Contemporary Psychoanalysis, 15*, 489–513.

Epstein, R. M., & Hundert, E. M. (2002). Defining and assessing professional competence. *JAMA, 287*, 226–235. doi:10.1001/jama.287.2.226

Ericsson, K. A., Charness, N., Hoffman, R. R., & Feltovich, P. J. (2006). *The Cambridge handbook of expertise and expert performance*. New York, NY: Cambridge University Press.

Eva, K. W., & Regehr, G. (2008). "I'll never play professional football" and other fallacies of self-assessment. *Journal of Continuing Education in the Health Professions, 28*, 14–19. doi: 10.10020chp.150

Ewing v. Goldstein, 120 Cal. App. 4th 807 (2004).

Falender, C. A. (2010). Relationship and accountability: Tensions in feminist supervision. *Women & Therapy, 33*, 22–41. doi:10.1080/02703140903404697

Falender, C. A., Cornish, J. A. E., Goodyear, R., Hatcher, R., Kaslow, N. J., Leventhal, G., . . . Sigmon, S. T. (2004). Defining competencies in psychology supervision: A consensus statement. *Journal of Clinical Psychology, 60*, 771–785. doi:10.1002/jclp.20013

Falender, C. A., & Shafranske, E. P. (2004). *Clinical supervision: A competency-based approach*. Washington, DC: American Psychological Association. doi:10.1037/10806-000

Falender, C. A., & Shafranske, E. P. (2007). Competence in competency-based supervision practice: Construct and application. *Professional Psychology: Research and Practice, 38*, 232–240. doi:10.1037/0735-7028.38.3.232

Falender, C. A., & Shafranske, E. P. (Eds.). (2008). *Casebook for clinical supervision: A competency-based approach*. Washington, DC: American Psychological Association. doi:10.1037/11792-000

Falender, C. A., & Shafranske, E. P. (2010). Psychotherapy-based supervision models in an emerging competency-based era: A commentary. *Psychotherapy: Theory, Research, Practice, Training, 47*, 45–50. doi:10.1037/a0018873

Falicov, C. J. (1995). Training to think culturally: A multidimensional comparative framework. *Family Process, 34*, 373–388. Retrieved from http://www.family process.org/ doi:10.1111/j.1545-5300.1995.00373.x

Falicov, C. J. (1998). *Latino families in therapy: A guide to multicultural practice*. New York, NY: Guilford Press.

Falvey, J. (2002). *Managing clinical supervision: Ethical practice and legal risk management*. Pacific Grove, CA: Brooks/Cole.

Field, L. D., Chavez-Korell, S., & Rodriguez, M. M. D. (2010). No hay rosas sin espinas: Conceptualizing Latina–Latina supervision from a multicultural developmental supervisory model. *Training and Education in Professional Psychology, 4*, 47–54. doi:10.1037/a0018521

Fitzpatrick, M. R., Janzen, J., Chamodraka, M., & Park, J. (2006). Client critical incidents in the process of early alliance development: A positive emotion-exploration spiral. *Psychotherapy Research, 16*, 486–498. doi:10.1080/10503300500485391

Forrest, L., Miller, D. S. S., & Elman, N. S. (2008). Psychology trainees with competence problems: From individual to ecological conceptualizations. *Training and Education in Professional Psychology, 2*, 183–192. doi:10.1037/1931-3918.2.4.183

Fouad, N. A., Grus, C. L., Hatcher, R. L., Kaslow, N. J., Hutchings, P. S., Madson, M. B., . . . Crossman, R. E. (2009). Competency benchmarks: A model for understanding and measuring competence in professional psychology across training levels. *Training and Education in Professional Psychology, 3*(4, Suppl.), S5–S26. doi:10.1037/a0015832

Frank, J. D. H., & Frank, J. B. (1991). *Persuasion and healing* (3rd ed.). Baltimore, MD: Johns Hopkins University Press.

Frawley-O'Dea, M. G., & Sarnat, J. E. (2001). *The supervisory relationship: A contemporary psychodynamic approach*. New York, NY: Guilford Press.

Frazier, R. E., & Hansen, N. D. (2009). Religious/spiritual psychotherapy behaviors: Do we do what we believe to be important? *Professional Psychology: Research and Practice, 40*, 81–87. doi:10.1037/a0011671

Fuertes, J. N., Stracuzzi, T. I., Bennett, J., Scheinholtz, J., Mislowack, A., Hersh, M., & Chen, D. (2006). Therapist multicultural competency: A study of therapy dyads. *Psychotherapy: Theory, Research, Practice, Training, 43*, 480–490. doi:10.1037/0033-3204.43.4.480

Gabbard, G. O. (2000). *Psychodynamic psychiatry in clinical practice* (3rd ed.). Washington, DC: American Psychiatric Press.

Gabbard, G. O. (2001). A contemporary psychoanalytic model of countertransference. *Journal of Clinical Psychology, 57,* 983–991. doi:10.1002/jclp.1065

Gallardo, M. E., Yeh, C. J., Trimble, J.E., & Parham, T. A. (Eds). (2012). *Culturally adaptive counseling skills: Demonstrations of evidence-based practices.* Los Angeles, CA: Sage.

Gawande, A. (2009). *The checklist manifesto: How to get things right.* New York, NY: Metropolitan Books.

Gelso, C. J., & Hayes, J. A. (2002). The management of countertransference. In J. C. Norcross (Ed.), *Psychotherapy relationships that work: Therapist contributions and responsiveness to patients* (pp. 267–283). New York, NY: Oxford University Press.

Gelso, C. J., & Hayes, J. A. (2007). *Countertransference and the therapist's inner experience: Perils and possibilities.* Mahwah, NJ: Erlbaum.

Goodyear, R. K., & Nelson, M. L. (1997). The major formats of psychotherapy supervision. In C. E. Watkins Jr. (Ed.), *Handbook of psychotherapy supervision* (pp. 328–344). New York, NY: Wiley.

Gottlieb, M. C., Handelsman, M. M., & Knapp, S. (2008). Some principles for ethics education: Implementing the acculturation model. *Training and Education in Professional Psychology, 2,* 123–128. doi:10.1037/1931-3918.2.3.123

Gottlieb, M. C., Robinson, K., & Younggren, J. N. (2007). Multiple relations in supervision: Guidance for administrators, supervisors, and students. *Professional Psychology: Research and Practice, 38,* 241–247. doi:10.1037/0735-7028.38.3.241

Gottlieb, M. C., & Younggren, J. N. (2009). Is there a slippery slope? Considerations regarding multiple relationships and risk management. *Professional Psychology: Research and Practice, 40,* 564–571. doi:10.1037/a0017231

Granello, D. H., Kindsvatter, A., Granello, P. F., Underfer-Babalis, J., & Moorhead, H. J. H. (2008). Multiple perspectives in supervision: Using a peer consultation model to enhance supervisor development. *Counselor Education and Supervision, 48,* 32–47. Retrieved from http://www.unco.edu/ces/

Green, D., Callands, T. A., Radcliffe, A. M., Luebbe, A. M., & Klonoff, E. A. (2009). Clinical psychology students' perceptions of diversity training: A study of exposure and satisfaction. *Journal of Clinical Psychology, 65,* 1056–1070. doi:10.1002/jclp.20605

Gutheil, T. G., & Gabbard, G. O. (1993). The concept of boundaries in clinical practice: Theoretical and risk-management dimensions. *The American Journal of Psychiatry, 150,* 188–196. Retrieved from http://ajp.psychiatryonline.org/index.dtl

Hage, S. M. (2005). Future considerations for fostering multicultural competence in mental health and educational settings: Social justice implications. In M. G. Constantine & D. Wing (Eds.), *Strategies for building multicultural competence in mental health and educational settings* (pp. 285–302). Hoboken, NJ: Wiley.

Halpert, S. C., Reinhardt, B., & Toohey, M. J. (2007). Affirmative clinical supervision. In K. J. Bieschke, R. M. Perez, & K. A. DeBord (Eds.), *Handbook of counseling and psychotherapy with lesbian, gay, bisexual, and transgender clients* (2nd ed., pp. 341–358). Washington, DC: American Psychological Association. doi:10.1037/11482-014

Hamilton, J. C., & Spruill, J. (1999). Identifying and reducing risk factors related to trainee–client sexual misconduct. *Professional Psychology: Research and Practice, 30,* 318–327. Retrieved from http://www.advocateweb.org/hamilton_and_spurill_risk_factors_sexual_misconduct%20(2).pdf doi:10.1037/0735-7028.30.3.318

Handelsman, M. M., Gottlieb, M. C., & Knapp, S. (2005). Training ethical psychologists: An acculturation model. *Professional Psychology: Research and Practice, 36,* 59–65. doi:10.1037/0735-7028.36.1.59

Handelsman, M. M., Knapp, S., & Gottlieb, M. C. (2009). Positive ethics. In C. R. Snyder & S. J. Lopez (Eds.), *Handbook of positive psychology* (pp. 731–744). New York, NY: Oxford University Press.

Hansen, N. D., Randazzo, K. V., Schwartz, A., Marshall, M., Kalis, D., Frazier, R., . . . Norvig, G. (2006). Do we practice what we preach? An exploratory survey of multicultural psychotherapy competencies. *Professional Psychology: Research and Practice, 37,* 66–74. doi:10.1037/0735-7028.37.1.66

Hatcher, R. L., & Barends, A. W. (2006). How a return to theory could help alliance research. *Psychotherapy: Theory, Research, Practice, Training, 43,* 292–299. doi:10.1037/0033-3204.43.3.292

Hatcher, R. L., & Lassiter, K. D. (2007). Initial training in professional psychology: The practicum competencies outline. *Training and Education in Professional Psychology, 1,* 49–63. doi:10.1037/1931-3918.1.1.49

Hayes, J. A., & Gelso, C. J. (2001). Clinical implications of research on countertransference: Science informing practice. *Journal of Clinical Psychology, 57,* 1041–1051. doi:10.1002/jclp.1072

Heimann, P. (1950). On countertransference. *International Journal of Psycho-Analysis, 31,* 81–84.

Helms, J. E. (1995). An update of Helms' White and people of color racial identity models. In J. G. Ponterotto, J. M. Casas, L. A. Suzuki, & C. M. Alexander (Eds.), *Handbook of multicultural counseling* (pp. 181–198). Thousand Oaks, CA: Sage.

Henretty, J. R., & Levitt, H. M. (2010). The role of therapist self-disclosure in psychotherapy: A qualitative review. *Clinical Psychology Review, 30,* 63–77. doi:10.1016/j.cpr.2009.09.004

Herlihy, B., & Watson, Z. E. (2003). Ethical issues and multicultural competence in counseling. In F. D. Harper & J. McFadden (Eds.), *Culture and counseling: New approaches* (pp. 363–378). Needham Heights, MA: Allyn & Bacon.

Hernández, P., & McDowell, T. (2010). Intersectionality, power, and relational safety in context: Key concepts in clinical supervision. *Training and Education in Professional Psychology, 4,* 29–35. doi:10.1037/a0017064

Hill, C. E. (2009). *Helping skills: Facilitating, exploration, insight, and action* (3rd ed.). Washington, DC: American Psychological Association.

Hill, C. E. (2010). Qualitative studies of negative experiences in psychotherapy. In J. C. Muran & J. P. Barber (Eds.), *The therapeutic alliance* (pp. 63–73). New York, NY: Guilford Press.

Hill, C. E., & Knox, S. (2009). Processing the therapeutic relationship. *Psychotherapy Research, 19,* 13–29. doi:10.1080/10503300802621206

Hoffman, I. Z. (1992). Some practical implications of a social-constructivist view of the psychoanalytic situation. *Psychoanalytic Dialogues, 2,* 87–304.

Hoffman, M. A., Hill, C. E., Holmes, S. E., & Freitas, G. F. (2005). Supervisor perspective on the process and outcome of giving easy, difficult, or no feedback to supervisees. *Journal of Counseling Psychology, 52,* 3–13. doi:10.1037/0022-0167.52.1.3

Holloway, E. L. (1995). *Clinical supervision: A systems approach.* Thousand Oaks, CA: Sage.

Horvath, A. O. (1994). Empirical validation of Bordin's pantheoretical model of alliance: The Working Alliance Inventory perspective. In A. O. Horvath and L. S. Greenberg (Eds.), *The working alliance: Theory, research and practice* (pp. 13–37). New York, NY: Wiley.

Horvath, A. O. (2001). The alliance. *Psychotherapy: Theory, Research, Practice, Training, 38,* 365–372. doi:10.1037/0033-3204.38.4.365

Horvath, A. O., & Bedi, R. P. (2002). The alliance. In J. C. Norcross (Ed.), *Psychotherapy relationships that work: Therapist contributions and responsiveness to patients* (pp. 37–69). New York, NY: Oxford University Press.

Horvath, A. O., & Symonds, B. D. (1991). Relation between working alliance and outcome in psychotherapy: A meta-analysis. *Journal of Counseling Psychology, 38,* 139–149. doi:10.1037/0022-0167.38.2.139

Hubble, M. A., Duncan, B. L., Miller, S. D., & Wampold, B. E. (2010). Introduction. In B. L. Duncan, S. D. Miller, B. E. Wampold, & M. A. Hubble (Eds.), *The heart and soul of change* (2nd ed., pp. 23–46). Washington, DC: American Psychological Association. doi:10.1037/12075-001

Ibrahim, F. A., & Kahn, H. (1987). Assessment of world views. *Psychological Reports, 60,* 163–176. Retrieved from http://www.ammonsscientific.com/AmSci/

Ingram, B. L. (2006). *Clinical case formulations.* New York, NY: Wiley.

Inman, A. G., & Ladany, N. (2008). Research: The state of the field. In A. K. Hess, K. D. Hess, & T. H. Hess (Eds.), *Psychotherapy supervision: Theory, research, and practice* (2nd ed., pp. 500–517). Hoboken, NJ: Wiley.

Jennings, L., & Skovholt, T. M. (1999). The cognitive, emotional, and relational characteristics of master therapists. *Journal of Counseling Psychology, 46,* 3–11. doi:10.1037/0022-0167.46.1.3

Jernigan, M. M., Green, C. E., Helms, J. E., Perez-Gualdron, L., & Henze, K. (2010). An examination of people of color supervision dyads: Racial identity matters as much as race. *Training and Education in Professional Psychology, 4,* 62–73. doi:10.1037/a0018110

Kadushin, A. (1968). Games people play in supervision. *Social Work, 13*(3), 23–32.

Kaduvettoor, A., O'Shaughnessy, T., Mori, Y., Beverly, C., Weatherford, R. D., & Ladany, N. (2009). Helpful and hindering multicultural events in group supervision: Climate and multicultural competence. *The Counseling Psychologist, 37,* 786–820. doi:10.1177/0011000009333984

Kagan, H., & Kagan, N. I. (1997). Interpersonal process recall: Influencing human interaction. In C. E. Watkins (Ed.), *Handbook of psychotherapy supervision* (pp. 296–309). New York, NY: Wiley.

Kagan, N. (1980). Influencing human interaction—Eighteen years with IPR. In A. K. Hess (Ed.), *Psychotherapy supervision: Theory, research, and practice* (pp. 262–283). New York, NY: Wiley.

Kamen, C., Veilleux, J. C., Bangen, K. J., VanderVeen, J. W., & Klonoff, E. A. (2010). Climbing the stairway to competency: Trainee perspectives on competency development. *Training and Education in Professional Psychology, 4,* 227–234. doi: 10:1037/a0021092

Kaslow, N. J. (2004). Competencies in professional psychology. *American Psychologist, 59,* 774–781. doi:10.1037/0003-066X.59.8.774

Kaslow, N. J., Borden, K. A., Collins, F. L., Forrest, L., Illfelder-Kaye, J., Nelson, P. D., . . . Willmuth, M. E. (2004). Competencies Conference: Future directions in education and credentialing in professional psychology. *Journal of Clinical Psychology, 60,* 699–712. doi:10.1002/jclp.20016

Kaslow, N. J., & Deering, C. G. (1994). A developmental approach to psychotherapy supervision of interns and postdoctoral fellows. *Psychotherapy Bulletin, 24,* 20–23. Retrieved from http://www.divisionofpsychotherapy.org/publications/psychotherapy-bulletin/

Kaslow, N. J., Grus, C. L., Campbell, L. F., Fouad, N. A., Hatcher, R. L., & Rodolfa, E. R. (2009). Competency assessment toolkit for professional psychology. *Training and Education in Professional Psychology, 3*(4, Suppl.), S27–S45. doi:10.1037/a0015833

Kaslow, N. J., Pate, W. E., & Thorn, B. (2005). Academic and internship directors' perspectives on practicum experiences: Implications. *Professional Psychology: Research and Practice, 36,* 307–317. doi:10.1037/0735-7028.36.3.307

Kaslow, N. J., & Rice, D. G. (1985). Developmental stresses of psychology internship training: What training staff can do to help. *Professional Psychology: Research and Practice, 16,* 253–261. doi:10.1037/0735-7028.16.2.253

Kaslow, N. J., Rubin, N. J., Bebeau, M. J., Leigh, I. W., Lichtenberg, J. W., Nelson, P. D., . . . Smith, I. L. (2007). Guiding principles and recommendations for the assessment of competence. *Professional Psychology: Research and Practice, 38,* 441–451. doi:10.1037/0735-7028.38.5.441

Kassaw, K., & Gabbard, G. O. (2002). Creating a psychodynamic formulation from a clinical evaluation. *The American Journal of Psychiatry, 159,* 721–726. doi:10.1176/appi.ajp.159.5.721

Katzow, A. W., & Safran, J. D. (2007). Recognizing and resolving ruptures in the therapeutic alliance. In P. Gilbert & R. L. Leahy (Eds.), *The therapeutic rela-*

tionship in the cognitive behavioral psychotherapies (pp. 90–105). New York, NY: Routledge.

Kavanagh, D. J., Spence, S., Sturk, H., Strong, J., Wilson, J., Worrall, L., . . . Skerrett, R. (2008). Outcomes of training in supervision: Randomised controlled trial. *Australian Psychologist, 43,* 96–104. doi:10.1080/00050060802056534

Kendjelic, E. M., & Eells, T. D. (2007). Generic psychotherapy case formulation training improves formulation quality. *Psychotherapy: Theory, Research, Practice, Training, 44,* 66–77. doi:10.1037/0033-3204.44.1.66

Kiesler, D. J. (2001). Therapist countertransference: In search of common themes and empirical referents. *Journal of Clinical Psychology, 57,* 1053–1063. doi:10.1002/jclp.1073

Kimerling, R. E., Zeiss, A. M., & Zeiss, R. A. (2000). Therapist emotional responses to patients: Building a learning-based language. *Cognitive and Behavioral Practice, 7,* 312–321. doi:10.1016/S1077-7229(00)80089-9

Klein, M. (1946). Notes on some schizoid mechanisms. *International Journal of Psychoanalysis, 27,* 99–110.

Knapp, S. J., & VandeCreek, L. D. (2006). *Practical ethics for psychologists: A positive approach.* Washington, DC: American Psychological Association. doi:10.1037/11331-000

Knox, S., Burkard, A. W., Edwards, L. M., Smith, J. J., & Schlosser, L. Z. (2008). Supervisors' reports of the effects of supervisor self-disclosure on supervisees. *Psychotherapy Research, 18,* 543–559. doi:10.1080/10503300801982781

Kolb, D. A. (1984). *Experiential learning.* Upper Saddle River, NJ: Prentice-Hall.

Koocher, G. P. (2009). Ethics and the invisible psychologist. *Psychological Services, 6,* 97–107. doi:10.1037/a0013925

Koocher, G. P., & Keith-Spiegel, P. (1998). *Ethics in psychology: Professional standards and cases* (2nd ed.). New York, NY: Oxford University Press.

Koocher, G. P., & Keith-Spiegel, P. (2008). *Ethics in psychology and the mental health professions: Standards and cases* (3rd ed.). New York, NY: Oxford University Press.

Kuyken, W., Padesky, C. A., & Dudley, R. (2009). *Collaborative case conceptualization: Working effectively with clients in cognitive-behavioral therapy.* New York, NY: Guilford Press.

Ladany, N., Ellis, M. V., & Friedlander, M. L. (1999). The supervisory working alliance, trainee self-efficacy, and satisfaction. *Journal of Counseling & Development, 77,* 447–455. Retrieved from http://www.counseling.org/publications

Ladany, N., Friedlander, M. L., & Nelson, M. L. (2005). *Critical events in psychotherapy supervision.* Washington, DC: American Psychological Association.

Ladany, N., Hill, C. E., Corbett, M. M., & Nutt, E. A. (1996). Nature, extent and importance of what psychotherapy trainees do not disclose to their supervisors. *Journal of Counseling Psychology, 43,* 10–24. doi:10.1037/0022-0167.43.1.10

Ladany, N., Inman, A. G., Constantine, M. G., & Hofheinz, E. W. (1997). Supervisee multicultural case conceptualization ability and self-reported multicultural competence as functions of supervisee racial identity and supervisor focus. *Journal of Counseling Psychology, 44*, 284–293. doi:10.1037/0022-0167.44.3.284

Ladany, N., Lehrman-Waterman, D., Molinaro, M., & Wolgast, B. (1999). Psychotherapy supervisor ethical practices: Adherence to guidelines, the supervisory working alliance, and supervisee satisfaction. *The Counseling Psychologist, 27*, 443–475. doi:10.1177/0011000099273008

Ladany, N., & Melincoff, D. S. (1999). The nature of counselor supervisor nondisclosure. *Counselor Education and Supervision, 38*, 161–176. Retrieved from http://www.unco.edu/ces/

Ladany, N., Walker, J. A., Pate-Carolan, L. M., & Evans, L. G. (2008). *Practicing counseling and psychotherapy: Insights from trainees, supervisors, and clients.* New York, NY: Routledge.

LaFromboise, T., & Dizon, M. R. (2003). American Indian children and adolescents. In J. T. Gibbs & L. N. Huang (Eds.), *Children of color: Psychological interventions with culturally diverse youth* (pp. 45–90). San Francisco, CA: Jossey-Bass.

Lambert, M. J. (2010). Yes, it is time for clinicians to routinely monitor treatment outcome. In B. L. Duncan, S. D. Miller, B. E. Wampold, & M. A. Hubble (Eds.), *The heart and soul of change* (2nd ed., pp. 239–266). Washington, DC: American Psychological Association.

Lambert, M. J., & Barley, D. G. (2001). Research summary on the therapeutic relationship and psychotherapy outcome. *Psychotherapy: Theory, Research, Practice, Training, 38*, 357–361. doi:10.1037/0033-3204.38.4.357

Lambert, M. J., Morton, J. J., Hatfield, D., Harmon, C., Hamilton, S., Reid, R. C., . . . Burlingame, G. M. (2004). *Administration and scoring manual for the Outcome Questionnaire, 45.* Salt Lake City, UT: OQ Measures.

Lambert, M J., & Shimokawa, K. (2011). Collecting client feedback. *Psychotherapy: Theory, Research & Practice, 48*, 72–79. doi:10.1037/a0022238

Leon, S. C., Martinovich, C., Lutz, W., & Lyons, J. S. (2003). The effect of therapist experience on psychotherapy outcomes. *Clinical Psychology and Psychotherapy, 12*, 417–426. doi:10.1002/cpp.473

Leong, F. T. L., & Wagner, N. S. (1994). Cross-cultural counseling supervision: What do we know? What do you need to know? *Counselor Education and Supervision, 34*, 117–131. Retrieved from http://www.unco.edu/ces/

Lewin, K. (1951). *Field theory in social science: Selected theoretical papers* (D. Cartwright, Ed.). New York, NY: Harper & Row.

Lewis, B. L. (2010). Social justice in practicum training: Competencies and developmental implications. *Training and Education in Professional Psychology, 4*, 145–152. doi: 10:1037/a0017383

Lewis, B. L., Hatcher, R. L., & Pate, W. E. (2005). The practicum experience: A survey of practicum site coordinators. *Professional Psychology: Research and Practice, 36*, 291–298. doi:10.1037/0735-7028.36.3.291

Liese, B. S., & Beck, J. S. (1997). Cognitive therapy supervision. In C. E. Watkins Jr. (Ed.), *Handbook of psychotherapy supervision* (pp. 114–133). Hoboken, NJ: Wiley.

Lyon, R. C., Heppler, A., Leavitt, L., & Fisher, L. (2008). Supervisory training experiences and overall supervisory development in predoctoral interns. *The Clinical Supervisor, 27,* 268–284. doi:10.1080/07325220802490877

Magnuson, S., Wilcoxon, S. A., & Norem, K. (2000). A profile of lousy supervision: Experienced counselors' perspectives. *Counselor Education and Supervision, 39,* 189–202. Retrieved from http://www.counseling.org/Publications/Journals.aspx

Marston v. Minneapolis Clinic of Psychiatry and Neurology, Ltd., 329 N.W.2d 306 (Minn. 1982) (en banc).

Martin, D. J., Garske, J. P., & Davis, K. M. (2000). Relation of the therapeutic alliance with outcome and other variables: A meta-analytic review. *Journal of Consulting and Clinical Psychology, 68,* 438–450. doi:10.1037/0022-006X.68.3.438

Matsumoto, D., Yoo, S. H., & Chung, J. (2010). The expression of anger across cultures. In M. Potegal, G. Stemmler, G., & C. Spielberger (Eds.), *International handbook of anger: Constituent and concomitant biological, psychological, and social processes* (pp. 125–137). New York, NY: Springer.

McCann, I. L., & Pearlman, L. A. (1990). *Psychological trauma and the adult survivor: Theory, therapy, and transformation.* Philadelphia, PA: Brunner/Mazel.

McIlwraith, R. D., Dyck, K. G., Holms, V. L., Carlson, T. E., & Prober, N. G. (2005). Manitoba's rural and northern community-based training program for psychology interns and residents. *Professional Psychology: Research and Practice, 36,* 164–172. doi:10.1037/0735-7028.36.2.164

Miller, D. S. S., Forrest, L., & Elman, N. S. (2009). Training directors' conceptualizations of the intersections of diversity and trainee competence problems: A preliminary analysis. *The Counseling Psychologist, 37,* 482–518. doi:10.1177/0011000008316656

Miller, S., Hubble, M., & Duncan, B. (2007, November–December) Supershrinks: What's the secret of their success? *Psychotherapy Networker.* Retrieved from http://www.scottdmiller.com/?q=node/4

Milne, D. (2009). *Evidence-based clinical supervision: Principles and practice.* Leicester, UK: Malden Blackwell.

Mintz, L. B., Jackson, A. P., Neville, H. A., Illfelder-Kaye, J., Winterowd, C. L., & Loewy, M. I. (2009). The need for a counseling psychology model training values statement addressing diversity. *The Counseling Psychologist, 37,* 644–675. doi:10.1177/0011000009331931

Miville, M. L., Duan, C., Nutt, R. L., Waehler, C. A., Suzuki, L., Pistole, M. C., . . . Corpus, M. (2009). Integrating practice guidelines into professional training: Implications for diversity competence. *The Counseling Psychologist, 37,* 519–563. doi:10.1177/0011000008323651

Moon, J. A. (2008). *Reflection in learning and professional development: Theory and practice*. New York, NY: RoutledgeFalmer.

Mori, Y., Inman, A. G., & Caskie, G. I. L. (2009). Supervising international students: Relationship between acculturation, supervisor multicultural competence, cultural discussions, and supervision satisfaction. *Training and Education in Professional Psychology, 3*, 10–18. doi:10.1037/a0013072

Morris, A. S., Silk, J. S., Steinberg, L., Myers, S. S., & Robinson, L. R. (2007). The role of the family context in the development of emotion regulation. *Social Development, 16*, 361–388. doi:10.1111/j.1467-9507.2007.00389.x

Munsey, C. (2006). Questions of balance: An APA survey finds a lack of attention to self-care among training programs. *GradPSYCH, 4*(4). Retrieved from http://www.apa.org/gradpsych/2006/11/cover-balance.aspx

Muran, J. C., Safran, J. D., & Eubanks-Carter, C. (2010). Developing therapist abilities to negotiate alliance ruptures. In J. C. Muran & J. P. Barber (Eds.), *The therapeutic alliance* (pp. 320–340). New York, NY: Guilford Press.

Muratori, M. C. (2001). Examining supervisor impairment from the counselor trainee's perspective. *Counselor Education and Supervision, 41*, 41–56.

Nagy, T. F. (2005). *Ethics in plain English: An illustrative casebook for psychologists* (2nd ed.). Washington, DC: American Psychological Association.

National Council of Schools and Programs of Professional Psychology. (2004). *Advocacy as a professional value and attitude*. Retrieved from http://www.ncspp.info/Advocacyres.pdf

National Council of Schools and Programs in Professional Psychology. (2009). *National Council of Schools and Programs in Professional Psychology Practicum guidelines: Draft document approved at the 2009 Midwinter Conference*. Retrieved from http://www.ncspp.info/pdfs/Practicum%20Guidelines%20Draft%20APPROVED%20at%20NCSPP%201-24-09.pdf

Neufeldt, S. A., Pinterits, E. J., Moleiro, C. M., Lee, T. E., Yang, P. H., Brodie, R. E., & Orliss, M. J. (2006). How do graduate student therapists incorporate diversity factors in case conceptualization? *Psychotherapy: Theory, Research, Practice, Training, 43*, 464–479. doi:10.1037/0033-3204.43.4.464

Newman, C. F. (2010). Competency in conducting cognitive-behavioral therapy: Foundational, functional, and supervisory aspects. *Psychotherapy: Theory, Research, Practice, Training, 47*, 12–19. doi:10.1037/a0018849

Norcross, J. C. (Ed.). (2002). *Psychotherapy relationships that work: Therapist contributions and responsiveness to patients*. New York, NY: Oxford University Press.

Norcross, J. C. (2010). The therapeutic relationship. In B. L. Duncan, S. D. Miller, B. E. Wampold, & M. A. Hubble (Eds.), *The heart and soul of change (2nd Ed.)* (pp. 113–141). Washington, DC: American Psychological Association.

Norcross, J. C., & Guy, J. D. (2005). Therapist self-care checklist. In G. P. Koocher, J. C. Norcross, & S. S. Hill III (Eds.), *Psychologists' desk reference* (2nd ed., pp. 677–682). New York, NY: Oxford University Press.

Norcross, J. C., & Guy, J. D., Jr. (2007). *Leaving it at the office: A guide to psycho-therapist self-care*. New York, NY: Guilford.

Orchowski, L., Evangelista, N. M., & Probst, D. R. (2010). Enhancing supervisee reflectivity in clinical supervision: A case study illustration. *Psychotherapy: Theory, Research, Practice, Training, 47*, 51–67. doi:10.1037/a0018844

Orlinsky, D. E. (2010). Foreword. In B. L. Duncan, S. D. Miller, B. E. Wampold, & M. A. Hubble (Eds.), *The heart and soul of change* (2nd Ed.) (pp. xix-xxv). Washington, DC: American Psychological Association.

Orlinsky, D. E., Botermans, J., & Rønnestad, M. H. (2001). Towards an empirically grounded model of psychotherapy training: Four thousand therapists rate influences on their development. *Australian Psychologist, 36*, 139–148. doi:10.1080/00050060108259646

Orlinsky, D. E., & Rønnestad, M. H. (2005). *How psychotherapists develop: A study of therapeutic work and professional growth*. Washington, DC: American Psychological Association.

Osborn, C. J., & Kelly, B. L. (2010). No surprises: Practices for conducting supervisee evaluations. In J. R. Culbreth & L. L. Brown (Eds.), *State of the art in clinical supervision* (pp. 19–44). New York, NY: Routledge.

Pabian, Y. L., Welfel, E., & Beebe, R. S. (2009). Psychologists' knowledge of their states' laws pertaining to Tarasoff-type situations. *Professional Psychology: Research and Practice, 40*, 8–14. doi:10.1037/a0014784

Page, A. C., Stritzke, W. G. K., & McLean, N. J. (2008). Toward science-informed supervision of clinical case formulation: A training model and supervision method. *Australian Psychologist, 43*, 88–95. doi:10.1080/00050060801994156

Papadakis, M. A., Arnold, G. K., Blank, L. L., Holmboe, E. S., & Lipner, R. S. (2008). Performance during internal medicine residency training and subsequent disciplinary action by state licensing boards. *Annals of Internal Medicine, 148*, 869–876. Retrieved from http://www.annals.org/

Papadakis, M. A., Teherani, A., Banach, M. A., Knettler, T. R., Rattner, S. L., Stern, D. T., . . . Hodgson, C. S. (2005). Disciplinary action by medical boards and prior behavior in medical schools. *New England Journal of Medicine, 353*, 2673–2682. doi: 10.1056/NEJMsa052596

Peterson, Z. D. (2002). More than a mirror: The ethics of therapist self-disclosure. *Psychotherapy: Theory, Research, Practice, Training, 39*, 21–31. doi:10.1037/0033-3204.39.1.21

Pope, K. S., & Bajt, T. R. (1988). When laws and values conflict: A dilemma for psychologists. *American Psychologist, 43*, 828–829. doi:10.1037/0003-066X.43.10.828

Pope, K. S., & Keith-Spiegel, P. (2008). A practical approach to boundaries in psychotherapy: Making decisions, bypassing blunders, and mending fences. *Journal of Clinical Psychology, 64*, 638–652. doi:10.1002/jclp.20477

Pope, K. S., Keith-Spiegel, P., & Tabachnick, B. G. (2006). Sexual attraction to clients: The human therapist and the (sometimes) inhuman training system. *Training and Education in Professional Psychology, S*(2), 96–111. doi:10.1037/1931-3918.S.2.96

Pope, K. S., Sonne, J. L., & Greene, B. (2006). *What therapists don't talk about and why: Understanding taboos that hurt us and our clients.* Washington, DC: American Psychological Association. doi:10.1037/11413-000

Pope, K. S., & Vasquez, M. J. (2007). *Ethics in psychotherapy and counseling: A practical guide* (3rd ed.). San Francisco, CA: Wiley.

President's New Freedom Commission on Mental Health. (2003). *Final report of the New Freedom Commission.* Retrieved from http://www.mentalhealthcommission. gov/reports/FinalReport/downloads/FinalReport.pdf

Prochaska, J. M., Levesque, D. A., Prochaska, J. O., Dewart, S. R., & Wing, G. R. (2001). Mastering change: A core competency for employees. *Brief Treatment and Crisis Intervention, 1,* 7–15. doi:10.1093/brief-treatment/1.1.7

Prochaska, J. O., & DiClemente, C. C. (1982). Transtheoretical therapy: Toward a more integrative model of change. *Psychotherapy: Theory, Research, Practice, Training, 19,* 276–288. doi:10.1037/h0088437

Prochaska, J. O., & DiClemente, C. C. (1984). *The transtheoretical approach: Crossing the traditional boundaries of therapy.* Homewood, IL: Dow Jones-Irwin.

Prochaska, J. O., & Norcross, J. C. (2010). *Systems of psychotherapy: A transtheoretical analysis* (7th ed.). Belmont, CA: Brooks/Cole.

Quarto, C. J. (2002). Supervisors' and supervisees' perceptions of control and conflict in counseling supervision. *The Clinical Supervisor, 21,* 21–37. doi:10.1300/ J001v21n02_02

Recupero, P. R., & Rainey, S. E. (2007). Liability and risk management in outpatient psychotherapy supervision. *Journal of the American Academy of Psychiatry and the Law, 35,* 188–195.

Reese, R. J., Usher, E. L., Bowman, D. C., Norsworthy, L. A., Halstead, J. L., Rowlands, S. R., & Chisolm, R. R. (2009). Using client feedback in psychotherapy training: An analysis of its influence on supervision and counselor self-efficacy. *Training and Education in Professional Psychology, 3,* 157–168. doi:10.1037/ a0015673

Riva, M. T., & Cornish, J. A. E. (2008). Group supervision practices at psychology predoctoral internship programs: 15 years later. *Training and Education in Professional Psychology, 2,* 18–25. doi:10.1037/1931-3918.2.1.18

Roberts, M. C., Borden, K. A., Christiansen, M. D., & Lopez, S. J. (2005). Fostering a culture shift: Assessment of competence in the education and careers of professional psychologists. *Professional Psychology: Research and Practice, 36,* 355–361. doi:10.1037/0735-7028.36.4.355

Robinson, B., Bradley, L. J., & Hendricks, C. G. (2000). Multicultural counseling supervision: A four-step model towards competency. *International Journal for the Advancement of Counselling, 22,* 131–141. doi:10.1023/A:1005567609258

Rodolfa, E., Bent, R., Eisman, E., Nelson, P., Rehm, L., & Ritchie, P. (2005). A cube model for competency development: Implications for psychology educators and regulators. *Professional Psychology: Research and Practice, 36,* 347–354. doi:10.1037/ 0735-7028.36.4.347

Roe, R. A. (2002). What makes a competent psychologist? *European Psychologist, 7*, 192–202. doi:10.1027/1016-9040.7.3.192

Rogers, C. R. (1957). The necessary and sufficient conditions of therapeutic personality change. *Journal of Consulting Psychology, 21*, 95–103. doi:10.1037/h0045357

Rosenberg, J. I., Getzelman, M. A., Arcinue, F., & Oren, C. Z. (2005). An exploratory look at students' experiences of problematic peers in academic professional psychology programs. *Professional Psychology: Research and Practice, 36*, 665–673. doi:10.1037/0735-7028.36.6.665

Rubin, N. J., Bebeau, M., Leigh, I. W., Lichtenberg, J. W., Nelson, P. D., Portnoy, S., & Kaslow, N. J. (2007). The competency movement within psychology: An historical perspective. *Professional Psychology: Research and Practice, 38*, 452–462. doi:10.1037/0735-7028.38.5.452

Rudd, M., & Joiner, T. (1997). Countertransference and the therapeutic relationship: A cognitive perspective. *Journal of Cognitive Psychotherapy, 11*, 231–250.

Russell, S. R., & Yarhouse, M. A. (2006). Training in religion/spirituality within APA-accredited psychology predoctoral internships. *Professional Psychology: Research and Practice, 37*, 430–436. doi:10.1037/0735-7028.37.4.430

Safran, J. D. (2009). Therapeutic alliance. In I. B. Weiner & W. E. Craighead (Eds.), *The Corsini encyclopedia of psychology* (pp. 1–3). New York, NY: Wiley. doi:10.1002/9780470479216.corpsy0992

Safran, J. D., & Muran, J. C. (1996). The resolution of therapeutic of ruptures in the therapeutic alliance. *Journal of Consulting and Clinical Psychology, 64*, 447–458. doi:10.1037/0022-006X.64.3.447

Safran, J. D., & Muran, J. C. (2000a). *Negotiating the therapeutic relationship*. New York, NY: Guilford Press.

Safran, J. D., & Muran, J. C. (2000b). Resolving therapeutic alliance ruptures: Diversity and integration. *Journal of Clinical Psychology, 56*, 233–234.

Safran, J. D., Muran, J. C., Samstag, L. W., & Stevens, C. (2001). Repairing alliance ruptures. *Psychotherapy: Theory, Research, Practice, Training, 38*, 406–412. doi:10.1037/0033-3204.38.4.406

Safran, J. D., Muran, J. C., Stevens, C., & Rothman, M. (2008). A relational approach to supervision: Addressing ruptures in the alliance. In C. A. Falender & E. P. Shafranske (Eds.), *Casebook for clinical supervision: A competency-based approach* (pp. 137–157). Washington, DC: American Psychological Association. doi:10.1037/11792-007

Sandler, J. (1976). Countertransference and role responsiveness. *International Review of Psychoanalysis, 3*, 43–47.

Sarnat, J. (2010). Key competencies of the psychodynamic psychotherapist and how to teach them in supervision. *Psychotherapy: Theory, Research, Practice, Training, 47*, 20–27. doi:10.1037/a0018846

Schank, J. A., & Skovholt, T. (2006). *Ethical practice in small communities: Challenges and rewards for psychologists*. Washington, DC: American Psychological Association. doi:10.1037/11379-000

Schön, D. A. (1983). *The reflective practitioner: How professionals think in action*. New York, NY: Basic Books.

Schön, D. A. (1987). *Educating the reflective practitioner*. San Francisco, CA: Jossey-Bass.

Schwebel, M., & Coster, J. (1998). Well-functioning in professional psychologists: As program heads see it. *Professional Psychology: Research and Practice, 29*, 284–292. doi:10.1037/0735-7028.29.3.284

Schweitzer, A. (1935, December 3). Visit of Albert Schweitzer. *The Silcoatian*. Retrieved from http://myhome.spu.edu/sperisho/SchweitzerInTheSilcoatian.pdf

Seligman, M. E. P. (2002). *Authentic happiness: Using the new positive psychology to realize your potential for lasting fulfillment*. New York, NY: Free Press.

Shafranske, E. P. (2005). The psychology of religion in clinical and counseling psychology. In R. F. Paloutzian & C. L. Park (Eds.), *Handbook of the psychology of religion and spirituality* (pp. 496–514). New York, NY: Guilford Press.

Shafranske, E. P. (2009). Spiritually oriented psychodynamic psychotherapy. *Journal of Clinical Psychology, 65*, 147–157. doi:10.1002/jclp.20565

Shafranske, E. P., & Falender, C. A. (2008). Supervision addressing personal factors and countertransference. In C. A. Falender & E. P. Shafranske (Eds.), *Casebook for clinical supervision: A competency-based approach* (pp. 97–120). Washington, DC: American Psychological Association. doi:10.1037/11792-005

Shafranske, E. P., & Malony, H. N. (1990). Clinical psychologists' religious and spiritual orientations and their practice of psychotherapy. *Psychotherapy: Theory, Research, Practice, Training, 27*, 72–78. doi:10.1037/0033-3204.27.1.72

Shedler, J. (2010). The efficacy of psychodynamic psychotherapy. *American Psychologist, 65*, 98–109. doi:10.1037/a0018378

Simmons v. United States, 805 F.2d 1363 (9th Cir. 1986).

Singh, A., & Chun, K. Y. S. (2010). "From the margins to the center": Moving towards a resilience-based model of supervision for queer people of color supervisors. *Training and Education in Professional Psychology, 4*, 36–46. doi:10.1037/a0017373

Slovenko, R. (1980). Legal issues in psychotherapy supervision. In A. K. Hess (Ed.), *Psychotherapy supervision: Theory, research, and practice* (pp. 453–473). New York, NY: Wiley.

Smith, D., & Fitzpatrick, M. (1995). Patient–therapist boundary issues: An integrative review of theory and research. *Professional Psychology: Research and Practice, 26*, 499–506. doi:10.1037/0735-7028.26.5.499

Stahl, J. V., Hill, C. E., Jacobs, T., Kleinman, S., Isenberg, D., & Stern, A. (2009). When the shoe is on the other foot: A qualitative study of intern-level trainees' perceived learning from clients. *Psychotherapy: Theory, Research, Practice, Training, 46*, 376–389. doi:10.1037/a0017000

Sterba, R. (1934). The fate of the ego in analytic therapy. *The International Journal of Psychoanalysis, 15*, 117–126.

Stoltenberg, C. D., & McNeill, B. W. (2009). *IDM supervision: An integrative developmental model for supervising counselors and therapists* (3rd ed.). New York, NY: Routledge.

Stoltenberg, C. D., McNeill, B. W., & Delworth, U. (1998). *IDM supervision: An integrated developmental model for supervising counselors and therapists*. San Francisco, CA: Jossey-Bass.

Sue, D. W., Arredondo, P., & McDavis, R. J. (1992). Multicultural counseling competencies and standards: A call to the profession. *Journal of Counseling & Development, 70*, 477–486. Retrieved from http://www.counseling.org/Publications/Journals.aspx

Sue, D. W., Capodilupo, C. M., Torino, G. C., Bucceri, J. M., Holder, A. M. B., Nadal, K. L., & Esquilin, M. (2007). Racial microaggressions in everyday life: Implications for clinical practice. *American Psychologist, 62*, 271–286. doi:10.1037/0003-066X.62.4.271

Sue, D. W., & Sue, D. (2007). *Counseling the culturally different*. New York, NY: Wiley.

Sue, D. W., Torino, G. C., Capodilupo, C. M., Rivera, D. P., & Lin, A. I. (2009). How White faculty perceive and react to difficult dialogues on race: Implications for education and training. *The Counseling Psychologist, 37*, 1090–1115. doi:10.1177/0011000009340443

ten Cate, O. (2006). Medical education: Trust, competence, and the supervisor's role in postgraduate training. *British Medical Journal, 333*, 748–751. doi:10.1136/bmj.38938.407569.94

Tervalon, M., & Murray-Garcia, J. (1998). Cultural humility versus cultural competence: A critical distinction in defining physician training outcomes in multicultural education. *Journal of Health Care for the Poor and Underserved, 9*, 117–125.

Thomas, J. T. (2007). Informed consent through contracting for supervision: Minimizing risks, enhancing benefits. *Professional Psychology: Research and Practice, 38*, 221–231. doi:10.1037/0735-7028.38.3.221

Thomas, J. T. (2010). *The ethics of supervision and consultation: Practical guidance for mental health professionals*. Washington, DC: American Psychological Association. doi:10.1037/12078-000

Thompson, C. E., & Jenal, S. T. (1994). Interracial and intraracial quasi-counseling interactions when counselors avoid discussing race. *Journal of Counseling Psychology, 41*, 484–491. doi:10.1037/0022-0167.41.4.484

Tracy, E. N., Bucchianeri, M. M., & Rodofa, E. R. (2011). Internship hours revisited: Further evidence for a national standard. *Training and Education in Professional Psychology, 5*, 97–101. doi:10.1037/a0023294

Tryon, G. S., & Winograd, G. (2011). Goal consensus and collaboration. *Psychotherapy: Theory, Research & Practice, 48*, 50–57. doi:10.1037/a0022061

Turner, J. A., Edwards, L. M., Eicken, I. M., Yokoyama, K., Castro, J. R., Tran, A. N., & Haggins, K. L. (2005). Intern self-care: An exploratory study into strategy use and effectiveness. *Professional Psychology: Research and Practice, 36*, 674–680. doi:10.1037/0735-7028.36.6.674

Utsey, S. O., Gernat, C. A., & Hammar, L. (2005). Examining White counselor trainees' reactions to racial issues in counseling and supervision. *The Counseling Psychologist, 33,* 449–478. doi:10.1177/0011000004269058

Van Kaam, A. L. (1966). *The art of existential counseling.* Denville, NJ: Dimension Books.

Vasquez, M. J. T. (2007). Sometimes a taco is just a taco. *Professional Psychology: Research and Practice, 38,* 406–408. doi:10.1037/0735-7028.38.4.401

Verdinelli, S., & Biever, J. L. (2009). Experiences of Spanish/English bilingual supervisees. *Psychotherapy: Theory, Research, Practice, Training, 46,* 158–170. doi:10.1037/a0016024

Vespia, K. M., Heckman-Stone, C., & Delworth, U. (2002). Describing and facilitating effective supervision behavior in counseling trainees. *Psychotherapy: Theory, Research, Practice, Training, 39,* 56–65. doi:10.1037/0033-3204.39.1.56

Walker, R., & Clark, J. J. (1999). Heading off boundary problems: Clinical supervision as risk management. *Psychiatric Services, 50,* 1435–1439. Retrieved from http://psychservices.psychiatryonline.org/cgi/reprint/50/11/1435

Wall, A. (2009). *Psychology interns' perceptions of supervisor ethical behavior* (Doctoral dissertation). Retrieved from ProQuest Dissertations and Theses database (AAT 3359934).

Wampold, B. E. (2007). Psychotherapy: The humanistic (and effective) treatment. *American Psychologist, 62,* 855–873. doi:10.1037/0003-066X.62.8.857

Wampold, B. E. (2010). *The basics of psychotherapy.* Washington, DC: American Psychological Association.

Wang, S., & Kim, B. S. K. (2010). Therapist multicultural competence, Asian American participants' cultural values, and counseling process. *Journal of Counseling Psychology, 57,* 394–401. doi:10.1037/a0020359

Warner, R. (2010). Does the scientific evidence support the recovery model? *The Psychiatrist, 34,* 3–5. doi:10.1192/pb.bp.109.025643

Weatherford, R., O'Shaughnessy, T., Mori, Y., & Kaduvettoor, A. (2008). The new supervisee: Order from chaos. In A. K. Hess, K. D. Hess, & T. H. Hess (Eds.), *Psychotherapy supervision: Theory, research, and practice* (2nd ed., pp. 40–54). Hoboken, NJ: Wiley.

Weinert, F. E. (2001). Concept of competence: A conceptual clarification. In D. S. Rychen & L. H. Salganik (Eds.), *Defining and selecting key competencies* (pp. 45–66). Seattle, WA: Hogrefe & Huber.

Welfel, E. R., Werth, J. L., & Benjamin, G. A. H. (2009). Introduction to the duty to protect. In J. L. Werth, E. R. Welfel, & G. A. H. Benjamin (Eds.), *The duty to protect: Ethical, legal, and professional considerations for mental health professionals* (pp. 3–8). Washington, DC: American Psychological Association. doi:10.1037/11866-001

Whaley, A. L., & Davis, K. E. (2007). Cultural competence and evidence-based practice in mental health services: A complementary perspective. *American Psychologist, 62,* 563–574. doi:10.1037/0003-066X.62.6.563

Wilcoxon, S. A., Norem, K., & Magnuson, S. (2005). Supervisees' contributions to lousy supervision outcomes. *Journal of Professional Counseling: Practice, Theory, & Research, 33,* 31–49. Retrieved from http://www.txca.org

Wilson J. P., & Lindy J. D. (1994). Empathic strain and countertransference. In J. P. Wilson & J. D. Lindy (Eds.), *Countertransference in the Treatment of PTSD* (pp. 5–30). New York, NY: Guilford.

Winnicott, D. W. (1949). Hate in the countertransference. *International Journal of Psychoanalysis, 30,* 69–75.

Wise, R. A., King, A. R., Miller, J. C., & Pearce, M. W. (2011). When HIPAA and FERPA apply to university training clinics. *Training and Education in Professional Psychology, 5,* 48–56. doi:10.1037/a0022857

World Health Organization. (2007). *International statistical classification of diseases and related health problems* (10th Revision). Geneva, Switzerland: Author.

Worthen, V. E., & Lambert, M. J. (2007). Outcome oriented supervision: Advantages of adding systematic client tracking to supportive consultations. *Counselling & Psychotherapy Research, 7*(1), 48–53. doi:10.1080/14733140601140873

Worthington, R. L., Tan, J. A., & Poulin, K. (2002). Ethically questionable behaviors among supervisees: An exploratory investigation. *Ethics & Behavior, 12,* 323–351. doi:10.1207/S15327019EB1204_02

Young, J. E. (1999). *Cognitive therapy for personality disorders: A schema-focused approach* (3rd ed.). Sarasota, FL: Professional Resource Press.

Yourman, D. B., & Farber, B. A. (1996). Nondisclosure and distortion in psychotherapy supervision. *Psychotherapy: Theory, Research, Practice, Training, 33,* 567–575. doi:10.1037/0033-3204.33.4.567

Zur, O. (2007). *Boundaries in psychotherapy: Ethical and clinical explorations.* Washington, DC: American Psychological Association. doi:10.1037/11563-000

Zur, O., Williams, M. H., Lehavot, K., & Knapp, S. (2009). Psychotherapist self-disclosure and transparency in the Internet age. *Professional Psychology: Research and Practice, 40,* 22–30. doi:10.1037/a0014745

INDEX

Acculturation, ethical, 164–166
Action stage, 31, 32, 89–90
Advocacy, 77–78
Affirmative clinical supervision, 65
American Psychological Association
     (APA), 11, 26, 116, 160
Anxiety
     in countertransference, 133
     in integrative development model,
          22–23
     supervisor response to, 41–42
APA. *See* American Psychological
     Association
APA Ethics Code. *See* "Ethical Princi-
     ples of Psychologists and Code of
     Conduct"
APA Ethical Standards. *See* "Ethical
     Principles of Psychologists and
     Code of Conduct"
Apathetic supervision, 200
Aspland, H., 99–100
ASPPB (Association for State and
     Provincial Psychology Boards), 7,
     161, 187
Assessment. *See also* Self-assessment
     APA Ethical Standards for, 173
     of clinical supervision training, 10
     manuals or protocols for, 27
     self-directed seeking of, 29–30
Assimilation, 165
Association for State and Provincial
     Psychology Boards (ASPPB), 7,
     161, 187
Assumptions, 59
Attitude
     in multicultural supervision
          competence, 59
     shifts in, for supervisee, 19–21,
          28–29
     in social justice, 78
     in stages of change model, 30–31
     on Supervisor Utilization Rating
          Form, 38, 39
     that impede therapy, 168
Aversive racism, 60–61
Awareness, 40, 130–132

Baker, T., 26
Bandura, A., 120
Barber, J. P., 145
Barnett, J. E., 76
Barrett, M. S., 145
BDI–II (Beck Depression Inventory—II),
     144–145
Beck Depression Inventory—II
     (BDI–II), 144–145
Beck, J. S., 193–195
Behaviors
     of boundary violations, 181–182
     client change in, 91–92
     dimensions of, for supervisees, 38, 39
     in harmful supervision, 201
     in inadequate supervision, 199–200
     in inappropriate supervision, 204–205
     in multicultural supervision, 66–69
     in quality supervisory relationship,
          43–45
     in stages of change model, 31
     in therapeutic alliance, 84–85
     of therapist, 93
Bernard, J. M., 6, 24, 62
Berry, J. W., 164
Biever, J. L., 76, 77
Bilingual supervisee, 76–77
Bonding, 82
Borderlines, cultural, 64–69
Bordin, E. S., 82, 103, 104
Boundary crossings, 174–181
Boundary violations, 174, 181–184
Burian, B. K., 179

Campbell, L., 77
Career building, 3–5
Case conceptualization, 135–158
     assessment of, 156–157
     competence in, 155–158
     functions of, 136–138
     process of, 145–153
     role of theory, 146–152
     scope of, 153–155
     structure of, 138–145
Case formulation, 156–157
Catalytic interventions, 23

Challenges, 124–133, 160–163
Chang, V. N., 41
Change. *See also* Stages of change model
   in client behaviors, 91–92
   culture of, in training process, 10
   readiness for, 87–91, 154–155
   as strain/rupture marker, 101
   supervisee willingness to, 30–32, 42
   and therapeutic alliance, 82, 83
   transtheoretical model of, 89–90
Charness, N., 211
Childhood experiences, 114
Clarity of expectations, 35–36
Classroom setting, 3, 5
Client outcomes
   collaboration on, 87
   expectancies about, 88
   management systems for, 92–93
   in Supervisor Utilization Rating
      Form, 39, 40, 41
   and therapeutic alliance, 81, 82
   and years of experience, 168
Clients
   case conceptualization benefits for,
      136–137
   confidentiality of, 170–171
   dangerous, 185–186
   inadequate supervision effects on,
      200–201
   as teachers, 19
   traumatic experiences of, 118,
      214–216
Clinical formulation, 142–143
Clinical supervision, 3–15
   as career foundation, 3–5
   components of process, 46
   definitions of, 5–6
   early sessions of, 41–45
   outcomes of, 40
   process of, 7–8
   training settings for, 8–15
Cognitive behavior therapy, 152–153
Cognitive therapy organization, 193–194
Collaboration
   on client outcomes, 87
   in clinical supervision, 6–7
   on reactivity identification and
      management, 126
   in resolution of strain, 92–93, 99
   in stages of change model, 91

   in therapeutic alliance, 83–86
   of therapist and client, 136–137
   on treatment application, 92
Collaborative empiricism, 142–143,
      152–153
Collaborative reflection, 131–132
Community settings, 176, 177
Competence. *See also* Multicultural
      competence
   in case conceptualization, 155–158
   in competency-based supervision, 30
   and confidentiality, 169–170
   in countertransference management,
      132–133
   cultural, 177, 179–181
   in dealing with differences, 62–63
   definitions of, 30
   early in supervision process, 30
   in ethical practice, 166–168
   in multicultural supervision, 56–57,
      63–64, 66–69
   in reactivity management, 132–133
   in reflective practice, 212–214
   self-assessment of, 167–168
   supervisees with problems in, 51–52
   of supervisor, 77, 167
Competencies Conference, 12–13
Competency-based supervision, 17–34
   attitudinal shifts in, 19–21, 28–29
   competence in, 30
   and evidence-based practices, 26–27
   multiple roles in, 29
   and practicum or internship readi-
      ness, 32–34
   professionalism in, 25
   and recovery model, 27–28
   self-directed assessment seeking in,
      29–30
   stages of change in, 30–32
   supervisee disclosure in, 20–21
   supervision theories for, 21–24
Competency Benchmarks, 13, 14,
      217–247
Competency Cube, 12–13
Conceptualization skills, 24, 133
Confidentiality
   in ethical practice, 72, 169–171
   supervisor breaches in, 161, 162
Confirmation, 149
Conflicts, 105, 191–192, 198

Consent, informed, 171–172
Consultant role, 24
Consumer perspective, 28
Consumers, 27
Contemplation stage, 31, 89
Context
    historical, 10, 121–123
    multicultural, 140–141
Context, multicultural, 140–141
Contextual standards, 165
Conversations, difficult, 69
Coping strategies, 215–216
Corrective feedback, 47, 50–51
Coster, J. S., 215
Council of Chairs of Training Councils
    Practicum Workgroup, 9
Counselor role, 24
Countertransference
    and boundary violations, 183
    competence in management of,
        132–133
    external, 109
    in historical context, 121–123
    management of, 124–129
    model for processing of, 129–132
    objective/subjective, 120
    and reactivity, 119–120
    and relationship schemas, 115
    subjective, 120
Criterion-referenced, 18
Crits-Cristoph, P., 84
Cultural borderlines, 64–69
Cultural competence, 177, 179–181
Cultural humility, 56
Cultural infusion, 64
Culturally responsive supervision, 65
Cultural neutrality, 63–64

Dangerous clients, 185–186
Data gathering
    in case conceptualization, 139
    in early sessions, 146
    interviewing approaches for,
        147–149
    and theoretical stance, 151
Decker, C. L., 41
Deliberate practice, 211
Delphi method, 66–67
Developmentally inappropriate
    supervision, 200

Developmental perspective, 21–24
Diagnosis, 139–140
Didactic format, 19–20
Differences, 62–63
Difficult conversations, 69
Difficult feedback, 50–51
Difficulties, 40
Directive data gathering, 147–148
Direct liability, 184
Disagreements, 49–50
Disciplinary action, 160–163, 184
Disclosure
    as boundary crossing, 175
    in competency-based supervision,
        20–21
    and informed consent, 172
    in supervision effectiveness, 46–47
    of therapist, 129
    withholding of, 162–163
Discrimination model, 24
Disney, M. J., 184–185
Distance supervision, 187–188
Diversity, 8, 55–79, 140–141. See also
    Multicultural competence
Dressell, J. L., 66–69
Dreyfus, H. L., 145
Dreyfus, S. E., 145
Driescher, K. H., 87–88
Dual relationships, 160, 161
Duncan, B., 211
Duty to protect, 185–186
Duty to warn, 185–186

Ecological niche, 57, 63
Educational praxis, 8
Eells, T. D., 135, 155–156
Effective supervision, 45–46
Ellis, M. V., 22, 201
Elman, N., 25, 51
E-mails, 187
Embeddedness, 103
Emerging practices, 186–188
Emotional bond, 82
Empathic understanding, 108–110
Empathy, 133
Empiricism, collaborative, 152–153
Empowerment, 27–28
Engagement, 84, 130
Ericsson, K. A., 211
Ethical acculturation, 164–165

Ethical practice, 159–188
  APA Ethical Standards for, 163–166
  boundary crossings in, 174–181
  boundary violations in, 181–184
  challenges in, 160–163
  competence in, 166–168
  confidentiality in, 169–171
  and disciplinary actions, 160–163
  in emerging practices, 186–188
  informed consent in, 171–172
  legal considerations, 185–186
  liabilities in, 184–185
  for multicultural supervision, 70–75
  multiple relationships in, 174
  and supervision contract, 172–174
"Ethical Principles of Psychologists and
    Code of Conduct," 116, 160,
    163–167, 171, 173, 174, 215
Ethical values-based practice, 8
Ethics, 159–188
Ethnic identity, 60–64
Evaluation
  attitudinal shift towards, 20–21
  power differential in, 50, 173–174
  receiving and responding to, 195
  summative, 48
  in supervision effectiveness, 47–51
Evidence-based professional practice
    (EBPP)
  case conceptualization in, 135
  and competency-based supervision,
    26–27
  transition to, 26–27
  for treatment approach, 86–87
Ewing v. Goldstein, 186
Expectations, 35–52
  clarity about, 35–36, 172–173
  expression of, 197–198
  in informed consent, 172
  for internship performance, 11
  and practice, 41–45
  for practicum performance, 10–11
  problems with, 192
  for self, 124–133
  and supervision effectiveness, 45–52
  in Supervisor Utilization Rating
      Form, 37–41
  unclear, 205–207
  understanding of, 197–198
Experience, 168

Experiential learning, 196–197,
    212–213
Exploration, 148–150
External countertransference, 109
External pressure, 88

Falender, C. A., 6, 111
Falicov, C., 57
Fallibility, 40
Falvey, J., 171
Feedback
  ability to absorb, 29–30
  from clients, 92–93
  disagreements about, 49–50
  lack of, 49
  negative, 48, 50–51
  openness to, 40, 42, 48
  proactive seeking of, 212
  problems with, 192
  in supervision effectiveness, 47–51
  to supervisor, 45–46, 48–49,
      198–199
  in supervisory relationship, 18–19
Feltovich, P. J., 211
Forethought, 212
Formative evaluation, 173–174
Formulation, clinical, 142–143
Forrest, L., 51
Fouad, N. 13, 79, 217
Foundational competencies, 12, 14, 212
Frank, J. D. H., 136
"Friending," 187
Functional competencies, 12–14

Gatekeeping, 3
Gelso, C. J., 107, 120, 131, 132, 133
Gifts, 175–176, 179–181
Goals of supervision, 77, 104
Goals of therapy
  in case conceptualization, 143
  collaboration on, 85–86
  consensus on, 136–137
  identification of, 84
  reestablishment of, 104
  with strain/rupture, 102–103
  and therapeutic alliance, 91–92
Gottlieb, M. C., 164–166, 177, 178
Greene, B., 168
Group supervision, 45, 69–75
Guidance, inadequate, 207–209

Guidelines on Multicultural Education, Training, Research, Practice, and Organizational Change for Psychologists, 64, 73–74
Guy, J. D., 216

Handelsman, M. M., 164, 165
Hansen, N., 59, 263
Harmful supervision, 201–204
Hatcher, R. L., 13, 32, 83, 212–213, 249
Hayes, J. A., 107, 120, 131, 132, 133
Hill, C. E., 41, 97, 102
Historical context, 10, 121–123
Hoffman, R. R., 211
Hubble, M., 211
Humility, 56, 177
Hypothesis development, 148–149

Identification
    of harmful supervision, 202–204
    of presenting problem and goals, 84
    projective, 120
    of reactivity, 126–133
    of relationship schemas, 128
    of strain/rupture marker, 101
    with values, 165, 166
Identity(-ies)
    ethnic, 60–64
    multiple diversity, 57
    professional, 3, 25
    racial, 60–64
    White, 61
IDM (integrative developmental model), 21–24
Inadequate guidance, 207–209
Inadequate supervision
    identification and management of, 202–204
    range of, 199–202
    and reflective practice, 198–199
    transformation of, 204–209
Indirect liability, 184–185
Induction, role, 37
Informed consent, 171–172
Infusion, cultural, 64
Inherent tensions, 155–156
Input, 10, 196
Inquiry, 7–8
Integration, 152, 164–165
Integrative developmental model (IDM), 21–24

Integrity, 8, 170–171
Internet practice, 187
Internships
    expectations for performance in, 11
    readiness for, 32–34
    specific competencies for, 32–34
    as training setting, 9–10
Interpersonal competencies, 108–110, 114
Interpersonal process recall (IPR), 195–196
Interpersonal skills, 107–108
Intersectional postcolonial model, 65
Intersubjectivity, 120
Interviewing, 147–149
Intolerance, 200
Intrapersonal competencies, 108–110, 114
IPR (interpersonal process recall), 195–196

Johnson, W. B., 6

Kaam, Adrian von, 134
Kadushin, A., 175
Kaslow, N. J., 10, 12, 21, 173
Keith-Spiegel, P., 175, 183
Kendjelic, E. M., 135
Kiesler, D. J., 119
Knapp, S., 164, 187
Knowledge
    as competency, 15
    from past relationships, 115
    practice vs., 164
    of self, 57–60
    in social justice, 78
Knox, S., 97
Kohlberg, Lawrence, 165
Kolb, D. A., 212–213
Koocher, G., 75, 164

Ladany, N., 41, 47, 56, 161, 162, 173
Lambert, M. J., 27, 92
Lammers, S. M. M., 87–88
Language, 76–77
Lassiter, K. D., 32, 249
Learning, 196
Legal considerations, 183, 184, 185–186
Lehavot, D., 187
Leahy, 128

Lehrman-Waterman, D., 161, 162
Level of suffering, 87–88
Lewin, K., 151
Lewis, B. L., 77, 78
Liability, 28, 184–185
Licensure, 11, 187–188
Lindy, J. D., 118
Lipsher, D. H., 120

Maintenance stage, 90
Majority identity development, 61
Marginalization, 165
Markers
    of countertransference, 131–132
    of progress, 144–145
    of strains and ruptures, 101
McNeill, B. W., 21, 23
Melincoff, D. S., 162
Metacommunication
    in resolution of strains/ruptures, 99,
        101–103
    in Supervisor Utilization Rating
        Form, 40
    in supervisory relationship, 105
Metacompetence, 5, 212
Microaggressions, 60
Miller, P. E., 120
Miller, S., 211, 212
Milne, D., 196
Miscommunication, 97
Molinaro, M., 161
Moon, J. A., 213–214
Moral development stages, 165
Motivation, 87–92
Multicultural competence, 55–79
    in bilingual supervisee experience,
        76–77
    cultural borderlines in, 64–69
    in group supervision, 69–75
    identity development in, 60–64
    religion and spirituality in, 75–76
    self and others in, 57–60
    and social justice, 77–78
Multicultural context, 140–141
Multicultural developmental supervi-
        sory model, 65
Multicultural Guidelines. See Guidelines
        on Multicultural Education, Train-
        ing, Research, Practice, and Orga-
        nizational Change for Psychologists

Multicultural supervision
    practices for, 63–64
    successful/unsuccessful, 66–69
    worldview in, 56–57, 63–64
Multiple diversity identities, 57
Multiple roles and relationships
    balancing of, 29
    and boundary crossing, 176–181
    in competency-based supervision, 29
    in ethical practice, 174
Multiple supervisors, 17–18
Muran, J. C., 96, 97, 99, 102
Mutual alliance, 18–19

Negative feedback, 48, 50–51
Negligent supervision, 199
Neutrality, cultural, 63–64
New experiences, 42
Nondirective data gathering, 147
Nonverbal behavior, 163
Norcross, J. C., 81, 89–90, 164, 215, 216

Objective countertransference, 120
Observations, 151
Ongoing feedback, 48
Online social networks, 187
Opportunities, 5, 124–133
Oppression, 58
Other(s), 57–60
Outcome Questionnaire–45, 92
Output, 10, 196

Papadakis, M. A., 184
Participation, 39–40
Personal factors
    in reactivity, 117–120
    in therapeutic alliance, 110–117
Personality disorders, 95
Personalization skills, 24
Perspective, 111–112
Peterson, Z. D., 129
Pillars, 7
Planning state, 132
Pope, K. S., 160, 161, 168, 175, 183
Postcolonial model, 65
Poulin, K., 162
Power differential
    advocacy balanced with, 18–19
    in boundary crossings, 174–175, 178
    in evaluation and feedback, 50,
        173–174

in multicultural competence, 62–64,
  67–68
in problematic supervision, 202–204
in supervisor relationship, 6–7
Practice, 41–45, 211
Practices and Beliefs Questionnaire,
  263–267
Practicum
  expectations for performance in,
    10–11
  readiness for, 32–34
  specific competencies for, 32–34
  as training setting, 8–9
Practicum Competencies Outline, 13,
  249–262
Praxis, educational, 8
Precontemplation stage, 31, 89, 154
Preparation
  in readiness for change, 154, 155
  as stage of change, 31–32, 89
  for supervision sessions, 42–43
Presenting problem
  client approach to, 91
  identification of, 84
  recognition of, 88
President's New Freedom Commission
  on Mental Health, 27
Pressure, 88, 94
Primary supervisors, 17–18
Privilege, 58
Problem definition, 139–140
Problem solving
  for ethically ambiguous situation, 183
  model for, 178–181
  and professionalism, 25
  in supervisory relationship, 191–192
Process-based supervision, 24
Process discussion, 69
Prochaska, J. O., 89–90
Professional development, 137–138,
  163–164
Professional factors, 110–117
Professional identity, 3, 25
Professionalism
  apathetic, 200
  defined, 25
  modeled by supervisor, 200
Proficiency, 211–212
Progress, markers of, 144–145
Projective identification, 120

Protect, duty to, 185–186
Protective factors, 141–142
Psychodynamic-oriented supervision, 195
Psychodynamic psychotherapy, 152, 153
Psychological contact, 108–110, 130

Queer people of color resilience
  model, 65

Racial identity, 60–64
Racism, aversive, 60–61
Rational model, 99, 100
Reactivity
  identification of, 126–133
  in integrative developmental model,
    22–23
  management of, 124–133
  personal factors in, 117–120
  to personality disorder in client,
    95–96
  and responsiveness, 117–120
  in strain, 99
  in therapeutic relationship, 108–110
Readiness for change, 30–32, 87–91,
  154–155
Recovery model, 27–28
Red flags, 181–182
Reflection
  collaborative, 131–132
  in deliberate practice, 212
  immediately after session, 126–127
  in self-assessment, 29–30
Reflection-on-action, 213
Reflective practice
  components of, 211–214
  self-care in, 214–216
  and supervisory relationship,
    195–198
Relational experiences, 81–82, 95
Relationships, sexual/dual, 160, 161
Relationship schemas
  and emotional responsiveness,
    113–115
  identification of, 128
  and reactivity, 119
Religion, 59–60, 75–76
Remedial focus, 160
Reporting, 147–149
Respect, 62–63
Respondeat superior, 28–29, 184–185

Responsiveness
  and engagement, 130
  reactivity vs., 129–130
  and relationship schemas, 113–115
  and self, 117–119
  in strain, 99
Rice, D. G., 21
Risk taking, 5
Robinson, K., 177
Rogers, C. R., 107–108
Role induction, 37
Rothman, M., 97, 213–214

Safran, J. D., 96, 97, 99, 101–103,
      213–214
Schank, J. A., 176
Schön, D. A., 213
Schwebel, M., 215
Science-informed practice, 8
Scott, S. T., 41
Self, 107–134
  challenges for, 124–133
  in countertransference, 119–133
  and empathic understanding,
      108–110
  expectations for, 124–133
  identifying and managing reactivity
      of, 126–133
  insight into, 40
  in multicultural competence,
      57–60
  opportunities for, 124–133
  personal and professional factors of,
      110–117
  in psychological contact, 108–110
  in responsiveness and reactivity,
      117–119
Self-appraisal, 29–30
Self-assessment
  of competence, 167–168
  early in supervision process, 29–30
  of initial competencies, 43
  in multicultural supervision, 60–61
Self-care, 214–216
Self-directed assessments, 29–30
Self-insight, 133
Self-integration, 133
Self-knowledge, 57–60
Seligman, M. E. P., 117
Settings, training, 8–15

Sexual/dual relationships, 160, 161
Shafranske, E. P., 6, 83–84, 98, 111
Signature strengths, 116–117
Silos, 78
Skills
  for alliance ruptures, 97
  expectations for, 15
  practicing of, 145
  in social justice, 78
Skovholt, T., 176
Slimp, A. O., 179
Small communities, 176
Socialization, 19–20, 114
Social justice, 77–78
Social networking, 187
Social role models, 24
Sociopolitical oppression, 58
Sonne, J. L., 168
Spirituality, 59–60, 75–76
Stages of change model
  client position in, 87–91, 154–155
  collaboration in, 91
  in competency-based supervision,
      30–32, 89–90
  and interventions, 90–91
  stages in, 89–90
Standards, 165
Stephens, A. M., 184–185
Stevens, C., 97, 213–214
Stoltenberg, C. D., 21–23
Strains and ruptures, 82–83, 93
  causes of, 103
  for client, 93–94
  markers of, 101
  resolution of, 92–93, 96–104
  for trainees/supervisees, 94–96
  in supervisory relationship, 104–105
Strengths, 116–117, 141–142
Structure
  of case conceptualization, 138–145
  of supervision, 192–193
  of supervisory relationship, 193–195
Subjective countertransference, 120
Sue, S., 61
Sue, D. W., 58, 60, 61
Suffering, 87–88
Summarizing, 149
Summative evaluation, 48
Superordinate values, 7, 8, 164
"Supershrinks," 211

Supervisee(s)
    attitudinal shifts in, 19–21, 28–29
    bilingual, 76–77
    case conceptualization benefits for,
        137–138
    with competence problems, 51–52
    confidentiality with, 170
    disclosure by, 20–21
    role of, 4–5
    strain causes for, 94–96
Supervision
    affirmative clinical, 65
    apathetic, 200
    contract for, 172–174
    culturally responsive/unresponsive,
        65, 66
    definitions of, 6
    distance, 187–188
    effectiveness of, 45–52
    group, 69–75
    level of, 167–168
    in strain resolution, 98–99
    theories of, 21–24
Supervisor(s)
    case conceptualization benefits
        for, 138
    competence of, 167
    feedback for, 45–46, 48–49, 198–199
    lack of feedback from, 49
    multiple roles of, 29
Supervisor Utilization Rating Form
        (SURF), 37–41
Supervisory alliance
    building of, 43–44
    disclosure in, 47, 163
    diversity in, 63–64
    factors influencing, 201
    initiation of, 41
    repair of, 201–202
Supervisory relationship, 191–209
    alliance and, 104–105
    and experiential learning, 196–197
    feedback in, 18–19
    initiation of, 41
    metacommunication in, 105
    as mutual alliance, 18–19
    past problematic incidents in, 36
    problematic, 192–193, 198–204
    problem solving model for, 178–181
    and reflective practice, 197–198

    reflective practice in, 195–196
    structure of, 193–195
    supervisee behaviors in, 44–45
    and therapeutic alliance, 104–105
    transformation of, 204–209
SURF (Supervisor Utilization Rating
        Form), 37–41
Swords, B. A., 201

Tabachnick, B. G., 183
Tan, J. A., 162
TCPP (trainee with competence per-
        formance problems), 51–52
Technical integration, 152
Telehealth, 186–187
Telepsychology, 186–187
Telepsychology Guidelines (Ohio Psycho-
        logical Association), 188
Tensions, inherent, 155–156
Termination stage, 90
Theoretical models
    application of, 152–153
    in case conceptualization, 146, 151
    in clinical formulation, 142–143,
        146, 151
    evidence-based support for, 26
    for process-based supervision, 24
Therapeutic alliance, 81–105
    and client outcome, 82
    fostering of, 84–85
    development of, 83–91
    monitoring of, 154
    in process of therapy, 91–93
    as relational experience, 81–82
    resolution of strains/ruptures in,
        99–104
    strains and ruptures in. See Strains
        and ruptures
    and supervisory relationship, 104–105
Therapeutic relationship
    competencies needed for, 108–110
    self in, 107–108
    in strain resolution, 97
Therapist disclosure, 129
Therapy goals. See Goals of therapy
Therapy tasks
    and client alliance strains, 93–94
    consensus on, 136–137
    readiness to engage in, 87–91
    reestablishment of, 104

Therapy tasks, *continued*
  and therapeutic alliance, 91–92,
    102–103
  and trainee alliance strains, 94–95
  in treatment process, 84–87
  in working alliance, 82
Thomas, J. T., 160, 173
Tone of voice, 163
Trainee with competence performance
    problems (TCPP), 51–52
Training process, 10
Training settings, 8–15
Transference, 183. *See also* Counter-
    transference
Transformation, 25, 204–209
Transparency, 39–40, 172–174
Transtheoretical model of change, 89–90
Traumatic experiences, 118, 214–216
Treatment
  approach to, 87
  costs of, 88
  current research and techniques for,
    168
  perceived suitability of, 88
  stages of change in, 90–91
  therapy tasks in, 84–87
  and trainee skill set, 86–87
Treatment plan, 143–144
Trust, 64, 168
Tryon, G. S., 87

Unbalanced supervision, 199–200
Understanding
  empathic, 108–110
  of expectations, 197–198
  as perspectival, 111–112
Unethical conduct
  most reported practices of, 160–161
  perceptions of, 162
  by supervisor, 200
Untrained supervisors, 200

Values
  in career development, 116–117
  as competency, 15
  in professional development,
    164–166
  social justice, 77–78
  in strain resolution, 98–99
  superordinate, 7, 8, 164
  in therapy process, 168
van der Staak, C. P. F., 87–88
Vasquez, M. J. T., 176
Verdinelli, S., 76, 77
Vetter, V., 160
Vicarious liability, 28, 184–185
Vicarious trauma, 118, 214–216
Vulnerability, 103

Wall, A., 161, 162
Wampold, B. E., 87
Warn, duty to, 185–186
Websites, 187
*What Therapists Don't Talk About and
    Why* (K. S. Pope, J. L. Sonne, &
    B. Greene), 168
White identity, 61
Williams, M. H., 187
Wilson, J. P., 118
Winograd, G., 87
Wise, E., 171
Withholding information, 162–163
Wolgast, B., 161
Worldview
  in multicultural supervision, 56–57,
    63–64
  as personal factor, 111
Worthington, R. L., 162

Young, J. E., 120
Younggren, J. N., 166, 177

Zur, O., 187

ABOUT THE AUTHORS

Carol A. Falender, PhD, has directed American Psychological Association (APA) accredited internship programs and supervised interns and practicum students for over two decades. Currently, she teaches doctoral students, supervises, and provides clinical supervision workshops. She has served as president of APA Division 37, Society for Child and Family Policy and Practice, co-chair of the Los Angeles County Psychological Association Ethics Committee, and as a member of the Association of State and Provincial Psychology Boards Supervision Guidelines Task Force and delegate to the Competencies Conference and to Benchmarks. She is an APA council representative, clinical professor in the Department of Psychology at the University of California, Los Angeles and adjunct professor at Pepperdine University. She is coauthor of *Clinical Supervision: A Competency-Based Approach,* co-editor of *Casebook for Clinical Supervision: A Competency-Based Approach,* both published by the American Psychological Association and she has also written numerous journal articles on supervision.

Edward P. Shafranske, PhD, ABPP, currently serves as a professor of psychology, Muriel Lipsey Endowed Chair for Counseling and Clinical Psychology, and director of the PsyD program in clinical psychology at Pepperdine

University. He also lectures in the Psychiatry Residency Program at the University of California, Los Angeles and has served as president of American Psychological Association (APA) Division 36: Psychology of Religion and Spirituality, and on the APA Council of Representatives. He currently teaches courses on psychotherapy, supervises first-year students through postgraduates, and advises students in research on clinical supervision. He is coauthor of *Clinical Supervision: A Competency-Based Approach*, coeditor of *Casebook for Clinical Supervision: A Competency-Based Approach*, editor of *Religion and the Clinical Practice of Psychology*, and coauthor of *Spiritually Oriented Psychotherapy*, each published by the American Psychological Association.